W9-DHV-690

The Female World from a Global Perspective

HQ
1154
.B42
1987

THE

FEMALE

WITHDRAWN

WORLD

from a
GLOBAL
PERSPECTIVE

JESSIE BERNARD

INDIANA UNIVERSITY PRESS   BLOOMINGTON & INDIANAPOLIS

GOSHEN COLLEGE LIBRARY
GOSHEN, INDIANA

© 1987 by Jessie Bernard
All rights reserved

No part of this book may be reproduced or utilized in any form or by any
means, electronic or mechanical, including photocopying and recording, or by
any information storage and retrieval system, without permission in writing
from the publisher. The Association of American University Presses' Resolution
on Permissions constitutes the only exception to this prohibition.

Manufactured in the United States of America
Library of Congress Cataloging-in-Publication Data

Bernard, Jessie Shirley, 1903–
    The female world from a global perspective.

    Bibliography: p.
    Includes index.
    1. Women—Social conditions. 2. Feminism. I. Title.
HQ1154.B42   1987   305.4   86-45475
ISBN 0-253-32167-0
1 2 3 4 5   91 90 89 88 87

CONTENTS

PROLEGOMENA

This book has not turned out to be the book I originally envisaged, a book my kindly disposed but critical friends called "visionary." The "vision" I had in mind was analogous to a Mercator projection of the female world without the distortions such a projection of a sphere imposes on a flat plane. It was, in brief, to be a view of the female world from a perch that could offer a global view unbiased by its location, an admittedly absurd "mission impossible." Among the countless obstacles in the way of such a "vision" were some that are semantic in nature and some intrinsically biasing.

First some semantic difficulties. Most of what we know about the female world is about women who live in ostensibly political entities—usually nations—of one kind or another. This leaves out a great many female infants, girls, and women who are not actually incorporated into these nations, including the females among the so-called tribals.[1] Any inclusive conceptualization of the female world in international terms would therefore be short of the mark. Elise Boulding's term *global* seemed more appropriate than international, in brief, because I felt it essential to pay them the courtesy of recognizing, at least in the title, our shared female humanhood.

A second semantic problem arises from the fact that the language used—"American" English—suffers a serious defect. It lacks an adjective for the United States. The common surrogate for this missing word is *American* and there is usually no misunderstanding of the referent, despite the fact that there are millions of other Americans from Canada to Patagonia who are thus arrogantly read out. I struggled for some time to avoid the use of *American* for *United States*. But my efforts were awkward and distracting. It was easy to rationalize the use of *American* on the grounds that it was residual. When one had characterized the other Americans as Argentineans or as Bolivians, there were some women still unaccounted for. They were Americans too, but Americans without a name of their own. The problem had long since been resolved by common usage which, if not wholly valid, was, admittedly, justified on grounds of expediency. But if only as a gesture of courtesy to the millions of American women who do not live in the United States I have, at the expense of cadence, used *United States* or *U.S.* as the adjective for those of us who do live "there." (I might add parenthetically that the use of *there* instead of *here* reflects another attempt to overcome the assumption that where I stand is "here," the center of the world.)

The term *Third World* is also semantically troublesome. It seems to imply a low rank in a hierarchical order. It implies that the world making such an assignment—presumably the white First, or capitalist, world—is in some absolute way superior. In many measurable ways it is—in longevity, in health, in educational opportunities, for example— but certainly not sub specie aeternitatis. A less invidious term would have been preferable. Further, in the feminist movement in the United States the term *Third World women* has come to refer to a wide gamut of women—Black, Hispanic, Chinese, Japanese, Vietnamese, Filipino, native American—who have in common only that they are not Caucasian. Still, in the absence of a more suitable word, the term *Third World* is retained.

One other related item. The terms *female world* and *women* are not synonymous. The first refers to a sociological entity, a de facto cultural structure—of laws, customs, mores, traditions, attitudes, beliefs—in which female infants are born and shaped. The term *women* refers to distributions of adult female human beings who vary widely over a relative range, wide or narrow, with respect to any given biological, psychological, or social quality or trait.

Another difficulty one must wrestle with when writing about the female world is grammatical rather than semantic—namely the generic male pronoun. As a simply grammatical difficulty, it is subject to a more or less acceptable, if awkward, solution. But the mind-set that undergirds it is harder to deal with, namely the male-oriented bias in practically all human knowledge, a bias which skews our perspective on the global female world.

> Those who are most anxious that the boundaries of knowledge should be enlarged, ought to be most eager that the influence of women should be increased in order that every resource of the human mind be at once and quickly brought into play. [Henry T. Buckle, 1858]

Lacking the "influence of women" that Buckle was calling for a century and a quarter ago, human knowledge has been an almost exclusively male creation, derived from male research directed toward problems and issues important in the male world. Thus, for example, the concepts and categories through which statistical data are gathered dealing, let us say, with "work" strain out a great deal of the unpaid work contributed by the female world (chapter 1). Female scholars have thus inherited a male-created and male-oriented body of knowledge and way of creating it. They have had to apply a conceptual tool kit devised by men.[2] Overcoming this bias is crucial for understanding the female world because it deals with the very way we think as well as the nature of the data on which our thinking rests, a defect which the Feminist Enlightenment has only recently begun to correct (chapter 6). We are just beginning to restore data that has been filtered out by the prism through which the male world has seen women. Furthermore, most of our knowledge is not only male-oriented but is also heavily skewed in the direction of modern, especially Western, societies. They are the most widely researched, so it is they which supply most of the data. We are thus showered with information about the United States, Sweden, Germany, Britain, France, Italy, even Eastern Europe. Other parts of the world remain less illuminated. The result is a limited view of the current global female world. Related to this bias is also an elitist one. The educated, the professional, the middle-class tend to receive more social-science attention than the outcasts, the losers. In the global female world the tendency is for only the elites to meet one another, to read one another's work, to address similar issues. These elites are the surrogates for millions of women who tend to be left out of even the most global view of the female world. It may not be possible to eliminate this bias entirely; this book has certainly not. But recognizing it seems to be a minimum essential.

Related to this elitist bias is another kind of status bias. There has been a growing realization among students of the sociology of knowledge that the relationship between the researcher and the researched reflects a kind of status discrepancy (Evans, 1982, 248–49). It is the researcher, not the researched, who is conceptualizing the situation, defining it, formulating the question, determining the perspective from which it is viewed. It is a kind of I-Them relationship in which "I" holds all the good cards. To recognize this situation is not the same as overcoming it. Some of the negative consequences of this asymmetry between the developed and developing countries have been commented on by students of international and transcultural associations (chapter 7). Just as women scholars have resented having women defined and researched by men as the "other," so now women in other cultures are coming to feel the same kind of resentment vis-à-vis Western researchers, female as well as male. They do not always relish being researched, even by women of the West, being in effect "used" by them (chapter 6). Even the descendants of the women who were researched a generation ago by Margaret Mead in Papua New Guinea have now gone to college themselves and want to do their own research. They resent her having seen them from a foreign point of view (Nova television program, 1 November 1983).[3] They wanted to read about their own culture in books written by themselves, not by outsiders, to see it with their own, not foreign, eyes.

Women in the West are, further, sometimes charged by women in the Third World with cultural imperialism, with applying Western paradigms, models, methodologies on their worlds where they are not appropriate (chapter 6). A reality does seem to exist which can be interpreted as validating these charges. The thinking, vocabulary, concepts, of Western academia do seem to find their way everywhere (chapter 7). At international professional conferences the papers by women— as well as by men—tend to converge in style, in general conceptualization, in questions posed, approaching what might be called "Western academic" style. Expertise in "Western academic" style among Third-World women varies; some succeed so well that their papers could have been prepared for colloquia on Western campuses.[4] Indeed, the author may well have been trained at such campuses. At the highest intellectual level there may, indeed, be such cultural imperialism, whether by design or not (chapter 6).[5] The resulting bias is a constant hazard in conceptualizing a global female world. As, analogously, the distortions of Mercator's projections on a flat plane hinder the conceptualizing of a spherical earth. It was only after the nth reordering of the materials available on the global female world that I reluctantly conceded that it was impossible to project the global female world from Mercator's point of view.

Finally, personal biases in perspective. I am well aware that I am not a blank page on which data fall, self-organized and already interpreted, ready for my typewriter. They come, rather, from a computer programmed by researchers who, like me, asked it certain questions and fed it appropriate variables. The data therefore may never have been touched by human hands, but human minds were guiding the process from start to finish, and these minds were no more virginal than my own. I am well aware, therefore, that what goes through my typewriter is not a mere mass of simple, immaculate "findings" tested and found not wanting; this input includes also the hearts as well as the minds of an indeterminate number of women and men with their own built-in computers which accepted and rejected according to idiosyncratic programs, including those that blotted out the female world entirely. I recognize therefore that what finds its way to my typewriter is the product of an endlessly complex process, that I am—to change the figure of speech—only one of a vast company of swimmers in a sea of "information" and data. That anything coherent emerges is extraordinary; it can do so only because a lot has had to be jettisoned. I have tried to winnow out what was least relevant for my purposes. I do not pretend to have hit upon the best way to conceptualize the global female world, but it seems to me that even an inadequate one may suggest a better one to others, one with both scientific and practical fallout, one that would not only add to our knowledge but also improve the self-knowledge of women and thereby their position everywhere.

I have sought to balance a macrosociological perspective with a microsociological one by use of numerous cases in point, despite the disturbing hitch in continuity their intrusion might sometimes introduce. Such dependence on microsociological cases in point may look like the nineteenth-century scholarly transgression when students—Herbert Spencer and W. G. Sumner among them—culled data from a variety of anthropological sources and combined them to arrive at universal stages of cultural evolution or universal laws and principles. As Janet M. Bujra notes, the validity of the comparative method is at issue here (1982, 17). She cites S. F. Nadel to the effect that it is "bound up with judgments on the identity and difference of social facts. The 'same' social fact in different social contexts could be seen either as 'the same thing varied,' or as something 'essentially' different" (1951, 224–25). In general, sociobiologists tend to see "the same thing varied," anthropologists, the uniqueness of what they observe. The cases in point here are used primarily for illustration, not as validating evidence for any special overarching paradigm. The objective is fairly straightforward: to look at the 2.5 billion females on the globe today as, in their unique or common way, they live out their lives (chapter 1) in their separate worlds (chapter 2) and how they work out their relations with the male world in an integrated or separatist way on several stages (chapters 3, 4, and 5). Whether separatist or integrationist relations are sought or achieved, a great deal depends on knowledge of the female world globally. How such knowledge of one another is being generated—by personal contacts (chapter 7) or by way of the media (chapters 8 and 9) is glanced at. Whether or not such knowledge will ever result in global female solidarity is still moot. The Feminist Enlightenment has, after all, only recently begun to illuminate the course (chapter 6).

Since the global female world even at the local level is only now in process of becoming visible, writing about it must of necessity be tentative. And since at a global level it is still more difficult to see, writing about it may be little more than "visionary." What it will look like even a generation from now is difficult to say. Greater longevity among women, especially in developing countries, will mean more time for them to learn, and reduced birth rates will mean more time and energy to apply this new knowledge. Their world will cease to be primarily a nursery for the human species. The technologies of communication increasingly available among women everywhere will have incalculable potential for expanding their world. The present picture is thus only one frame in a rapidly moving picture. It is tentative both because our knowledge is expanding and because the world itself is changing.

Writing about the global female world at present is, then, like writing on water. So much of what is happening is at the margin between history and news. History is taking place at such a breathless pace that what one learns from a scholarly research study may be valid for only a moment; within a day or two there has been a coup, a military takeover, a revolution, a different policy inaugurated. Whatever one learns from the scholarly research may become of merely historical interest almost before the ink on it is dry. So why bother? Because, for one thing, the impact of modern technologies means we can no longer remain inside our own provincial, parochial boundaries, whether they be geographic or racial or ethnic or religious or, even, intellectual. Extending the feminist horizon to include all parts of the global female world seems to me essential.

Still, not all changes are so fast. Some take a lot of time, seem discouragingly slow. They call for a different figure of speech. The enormous historical "shifts" now in process constitute a radical restructuring of human "continental plates." On the surface of the earth the movements of the great undergirding floating continental supports are scarcely noticeable except with the finest instruments. But over time they realign continents. The movements of the metaphorical "continental plates" which support the male and female worlds are more rapid than those undergirding the continents, though still not rapid enough to me immediately recognized by many inhabitants of the earth. It seems to me important that we learn to sense them and learn what they mean and how to make the best of them.

Where did you do your field work? was one of the first questions I was asked when I mentioned this book in process. My "field work" began in Buenos Aires some sixty years ago where I was working at the University library on a wholly unrelated research project but talking, mainly for practice in the language, to anyone who would listen—to the women who cleaned our rooms, to waitresses, sales girls—and visiting in the homes of members of the U.S. community, including those of missionaries. I did research also—this time in a private library—for several months, fifty years ago in Paris and lived in a pension where half a dozen young working women lived. They shared their lives with me in exchange for the delicacies I brought back from the neighborhood food shops which I was systematically exploring. And a month in girls' hostels in London and Edinburgh where, around a roaring fire we sat in the long winter evenings talking about the events of the day. There was also a year I spent in Graz with my children in the mansion home of the one-time university librarian—"retired" for anti-Nazism during World

War II—now a recluse protected in his great library by his busy wife and mother—who, at seventy-five, could hardly wait for a trip to the moon—trying hard to restore the pre-Nazi ambience of their home.

On a trans-Siberian trek I once took from Moscow to Japan, the two bustling babushkas kept the train clean and orderly even if they had to stop the train in the middle of the night to throw a drunken passenger off. Otherwise they were very much like concerned Parisian concierges. I just happened to be in Kabul the very day women first appeared on the street without the chador; they were airline attendants. I just happened also to be in Moscow the day the first fashion show was produced by French designers in Gum, the great department store. In Tashkent I once watched the buses arriving at the textile factory on schedule to take nursing mothers to the factory-run crèche where they fed their infants. The head of the Amerika Haus in Seoul introduced me to members of the faculty of the Women's University; he also arranged a trip throughout the country where I was entertained by women's groups in small towns and, in return, talked to them about my own world. Less fruitful was my visit to Saigon where my host, agricultural adviser to President Diem, was hesitant to arrange contacts with Vietnamese women but did introduce me to U.S. families on official diplomatic missions. From my hotel window in Calcutta I once watched a mother come with her children in the morning to bathe at a street hydrant. And on the streets of Beijing, I observed scores of mothers bicycling to work in the morning with babies on their backs, and, in a Hong Kong park, I watched mothers gracefully exercising together.

International meetings—which I have been attending for half a century—have provided a different stage for "field work." In the mid-thirties such scholarly meetings still retained the aura of a time when intellectuals were viewed, even by royalty, as an elite worthy of recognition. Men were still paying homage to women by kissing their hands. Elaborate and royally elegant entertainment for both participants and their wives was provided in the grand imperial tradition. On our own separate excursions, we wives managed to carry on social chitchat about our families, our children, our social lives. World War II, of course, changed all that. When international sociological meetings resumed in the 1950s they reflected a totally different world. They came to be like Oriental bazaars where thousands of scholars and researchers displayed their intellectual wares. I now participated in my own right, especially, in time, in the sessions organized by and about women—from which I have learned as much as from the wives of yore.

At one of the first such meetings the lesson was so mind-boggling that it took a long time for me to assimilate it. One young woman from North Africa was dazzlingly beautiful in her chic Parisian outfit, until she learned that her brother was arriving the next day to see her. Almost before our eyes this ravishingly beautiful woman shed her Parisian chic and was transformed by her chador into a shapeless figure. We saw the struggle between the inertia of an ancient past and the seduction of an onrushing future. At that same meeting a woman holding one of the highest-level positions in her Middle East country's civil service reminded Western women that one gained more with honey than with vinegar. She opposed the planned women's confrontation with the organization's male power hierarchy. She recommended instead a more appeasing approach. Three days later it was she who, as leader of the confrontation, seized the microphone from the speaker at the business meeting and presented the women's demands. Again we were witnessing one woman's epiphany as exposure to a view of the female world different from that of her culture's transformed her.

In addition to the lessons I learned from women at these meetings, under the personal, though unwitting, tutelage of women—from Norway to South Africa, from Switzerland and Italy to India, from England to Israel—I have had my mind extended and my feminist consciousness raised by way of correspondence.

Some of the "field work" was vicarious, done by a cadre of talented young social scientists who in the last decade and a half had been creating a body of research and writing that gave me at least a glimmering of the female world outside my own country and a starting point for exploring it. They helped me overcome the constant threat of parochialism that hovers over the researchers who become so absorbed in the immediate context of their own research that it is often difficult for them to look outside the limits of their particular disciplinary, let alone national, boundaries. As a result of their work we have at our disposal a truly astonishing body of recent and current work by anthropologists, sociologists, political scientists, economists, literary critics, activists, political leaders, as well as archives full of reports, records of meetings, and other documents. All this has been grist for my mill. So, far from viewing such dependence on "secondary" sources as something to apologize for—as reviewers sometimes imply—I view it as something to express appreciation for. I am grateful to all those who have spent months, perhaps even years, in the field patiently observing, interacting, interpreting, and appreciative of the end product of their efforts, the Feminist Enlightenment.

Not the kind of "field work" a bona fide researcher would dream of putting on her vita, not even designed as "field work," nor even recognized as such while it was in process, has been the busy round of activities always going on in Washington which is, in many ways, a capitol of the global female world. One can go every day for a week to a different seminar, luncheon, discussion group, dinner, congressional hearing, fund-raising event—all related to some aspect of the global female world. There are literally dozens of organizations active in global activities related in whole or in part to women. Conferences may include participants currently residing in the United States from Bangladesh, China, Egypt, India, Jordan, Lebanon, Malawi, Mexico, Nigeria, Pakistan, Turkey, and Uganda. Native U.S. women may report on their own work or research in Cyprus, Fiji, Guinea-Bissau, Hong Kong, Kenya, Korea, Malaysia, Nepal, Niger, South Africa, Tanzania, Burkina Faso. . . .

I have been especially rewarded at small meetings sponsored by the State Department or local universities, where, after the guests and I had lunched together and I had given my little talk, they undertook to set me right, not condescendingly or reprovingly or even purposively, but rather by their account of the way their world looked from their perspective. Especially the women of Africa! Joyous, exuberent, laughing, they let their hair down and confided to one another and to me all the problems they had with their husbands, brothers, sons, government representatives, employers. But it was no big deal. They could handle it.

Contacts with Soviet women changed over time. At first they reassured us that they had no need for a feminist movement; women already had all the rights, prerogatives, and privileges that U.S. women were struggling for, all guaranteed by the Constitution and by law. After a while, though, especially in off-the-record unofficial gatherings at hostesses' homes, they conceded that there still remained a lot that needed doing. By that time even Brezhnev was making that concession.

There was Jean Lipman-Blumen's Washington Salon, which entertained interested women in her home when there were distinguished women visitors from abroad, whether scholars, activists, political figures, or artists. Distinguished women from South Africa, Portugal, Scandinavia, Latin America, Israel, France, among other countries, talked to us informally as we sat on the floor listening and asking questions that some of the guests could handle and others could not. (Among those who could was Margo, engaged at the time in organizing prostitutes in U.S. cities.) There was also that wonderful time when Arlene Fraser headed the Women-in-Development office of the U.S. Agency for International Development and recruited a stream of extraordinarily talented young women to tell us about women in development when that was still an exciting new research frontier. And all those groups of women lobbyists who kept us informed on the international scene; and guests from the embassies who told us what was going on for women in their countries. And all the women running agencies, raising funds for projects in the Third World. . . . A heady place to be doing "field work" in.

A final word. My own feminist bias is, I think, clear. It emphasizes the positive. A social movement like feminism, it seems to me, needs hope as well as anger; so without denying the motivating force of anger, my view emphasizes the motor of hope. Several years ago I wrote, about marriage:

> . . . however one defines happiness, some men and women in the past under all kinds of regimes have experienced the best possible marriages . . . and some, . . . have experienced the worst. . . . What the future can do is to make it possible for more to have a chance at the best, to doom fewer to the worst. [1972, 1982, 282]

In the present context I might put it this way: there are some women living happy and fulfilled lives all over the global female world, developed and undeveloped, rich and poor, with high literacy and low; what I hope for is a world in which more are able to achieve such happy and fulfilled lives. This is surely not beyond human reach.

PART ONE

The Inhabitants of the Global Female World and the World They Inhabit

INTRODUCTION

The Jesuits, it has been said, won all their arguments because they were trained to know and be able to state their opponent's case better than he could himself. I do not claim that talent. But I do respect different, even opposing, points of view, including those of critics who reject the concept of a global female world because of the diversity among women and the cultures that shape them. I respect the point of view that challenges the arrogant assumption that generalizations about women based on research on Western history and experience are valid also for all women everywhere; the differences among women are so great as to invalidate any such sweeping generalizations. So great, in fact, as to seem to preclude even the concept of a global female world at all. I accept the emphasis on diversity but not the belief that it renders the concept of a global female world invalid.

Chapter 1 plunges in at once to clear the air by disclaiming the assumptions sometimes alleged that "females" are a homogeneous category of human beings, beginning with evidence of the rock-bottom demographic differences among the roughly 2.5 billion inhabitants of the female world[1] to serve, literally, as an introduction to the human beings—female infants, girls, women—the discussion is to be all about.

In the first book of the Old Testament, women were assigned the function of reproduction (Gen. 3:16), and men, hard—farm—labor (Gen. 3:19, 23). Actually, women both bore children and did agricultural work as well as, according to another part of that Book, a great deal more (Prov. 31:10–27). Both reproduction and production have universally been the lot of the female world from time immemorial. Chapter 1 glances at the part both reproduction and productivity play in the lives of women, the first being easier to trace than the second. For reproduction—conception, gestation, birthing, nurturing—has remained fairly

1

standard over the centuries, however much medical care has improved it, and however differently cultures have scheduled it. Demographers may have problems with records—underregistration, nonregistration, and the like—but not with biological sex definitions. A birth is a birth; a death, a death. But when the subject is work or productivity, a second theme of chapter 1, the referent is not universally the same.

Activities producing "sweat of the face" appear fairly early in the human record (Gen. 3:19). But the specific nature of productive activity has varied enormously over time and still does, over place. In attempting to catch a glimpse of such activity in the female world a host of technical difficulties must be overcome including, as most attempts make clear, differences in definitions, dates, samples, and the like. One of the main lessons one learns from the attempts to conceptualize the productive activities of the female world is that most of them, because they are unpaid, are invisible. Old as work is, then, many of the concepts dealing with it—"work force" for example—are of relatively recent origin, and much of the thinking about work has been by male researchers in industrialized, especially market, economies in the West. Their concepts have had definitive influence on statistical records the world over, with the result that an enormous part of the work of the world—especially the unpaid part performed in the female world—does not appear in the statistical records. Mao is quoted as having said that women did, indeed, hold up half the sky but that the part they held up was heavier. And, he might have added as noted above, less visible as well.

Chapter 2 changes the perspective on work and looks at it from the point of view of the sexual division of labor which—along with reproduction—is one of the factors giving rise to the distinctly separate male and female worlds. Here the data are more qualitative than quantitative in nature. Although we may not know the names of the women we are going to be looking at—women selling couscous on the streets of Mauritania, or women threshing beanstalks in Kenya who complain about their husbands far away in town—they are not faceless; they are very real people.

The concept of the female world accommodates not only diversity among women but also differences between it and the male world. The female life course traced in chapter 1 shows that almost everywhere women spend a considerable amount of their lives bearing and rearing children and that they also do a considerable amount of the work of feeding families and taking care of households. These are usually different from the kinds of work men do. Chapter 2 shows that, as a result, men and women live not only in separate psychological and social worlds but also in spatially separate worlds, and it raises questions about the resulting relationships between them.

Women hold up half the sky, says the old Chinese adage.
To which Mao added that their half weighed more.

Courtesy of the *United Nations State of the World's Women 1985*.
Illustrator, Wendy Hoile.

CHAPTER ONE

Faceless Females

Every child may be said, figuratively, to be born endowed with a "dowry"—a "gift," as the Oxford English Dictionary has it, "of nature or fortune"—in the form of a cache of years to be lived. It is large in some parts of the world, small in other parts and, in both, large in the case of some infants, small in the case of others. The size of this "endowment," whether of "nature" or of "fortune," makes a difference in the child's life course. An enormous difference, in fact, at every step of the way, short or long, especially in the lives of females.

Demographers have a less poetic way to look at all this.[1] They speak matter-of-factly of life expectancy, not in any individual determinist, astrological, or palm-reading sense but as "the number of years newborn children would live if subject to the morality risks prevailing for the cross section of population at the time of their birth" (World Bank, 1984, 275). Life expectancy reflects the kind of world these children live in and the kind of life it provides for those who are going to live in it. Female life expectancy is, then, a basic fact of life—and death—which sets limits to the pattern of women's lives. Childbearing, childrearing, homemaking, education, work—these are the strands that weave this female life pattern the world over. The patterns vary widely and the resulting lives differ accordingly. Basic in determining these patterns is the number of years available to the female infant for weaving them. Like thread wrapped around a spindle these strands will play themselves out sequentially and concomitantly in the course of her life. Since the thread is far longer for female infants in some parts of the globe than in others, they will have many more years in which to do this weaving than will female infants in other parts. They will have more time to do more things. The resulting pattern can be more complex, more varied, more innovative.

Thus, infant girls born in a country with low life expectancy may die at an age when female infants born at the same time in another part of the world will be just beginning to hit their stride, with perhaps as

4

many as forty years ahead of them. To take the most extreme case, a female infant born in Afghanistan has a probable average life expectancy of 37 years, whereas a female infant born in Switzerland has an average life span of 81 years (World Bank, 1984, 262–63).[2] If we begin with a little girl born in Afghanistan in 1949, she would die this year, 1986. The little girl born in Switzerland in 1949 would be only 37 years old, with a probable 44 years ahead of her. The disparities are not so spectacular in other cases.[3] But, on average, in nearly two-fifths of 126 countries female infants could anticipate as many as 70 years of life; in about a fifth, fewer than 50 years (Handbook, 1976).

Some of these differences in life expectancies are related to high infant mortality rates which "use up" some of the total number of years lived by any cohort, cutting down the total number of years left to be lived by the remaining cohort members as a whole. These rates also vary spectacularly. Because of the greater viability of females, the proportion of infant deaths that are female should be somewhat less than half. In 92 countries, fewer than half (43.68 percent) of infant deaths were, in fact, female (Handbook, 1976, 289). The Handbook, like the World Bank Report, offers caveats:

> The data must be interpreted in light of the fact that the female infant is considered less valuable than the male in many parts of the world and, consequently, the female births *may* be less likely to be registered in the first place (280).

And if a female birth is not worth registering, even less so would a female death be. So it is already clear that the female infant's "gift of fortune" may, in some places, be not of fortune but of misfortune. There are doubtless numerous other reasons for the differences among countries in life expectancy other than differential infant death rates. Three seem especially relevant: health care, nutrition, and geography.

In general, it does seem that the greater the proportion of national income that is dedicated to providing health services, the longer life expectancy appears to be (World Bank, table 24). Similarly, the more doctors and nurses there are available for a given population, the greater the life expectancy for that population is likely to be. The absolute amount of resources available for health services will, in turn, depend on the gross national product of a country. And, indeed, life expectancy is greater in the richer economies. Female infants born in low-income economies have life expectancies only two-thirds as long (52 years on average) as those of infant girls born in richer economies (78 years) (World Bank, table 23). Stated conversely, little girls born in a high-income industrial economy would live a life and a half as compared with only one life for little girls born in a poorer part of the world.[4]

Nutrition is also involved in life expectancy. The daily calorie supply per capita in 1981 ranged from 3,916 in Belgium—161 percent of requirements—to less than half that—1,621 calories—in Mali, less than three-fourths of requirements (World Bank, table 24).[5] These calorie data are not broken down separately for males and females, but it is probably safe to assume that the proportion consumed by women in any one country is less than that consumed by men[6] and that women everywhere share their food with children when resources are scarce. As with health care, calorie consumption also is, understandably, related to life expectancy (Handbook, 279).

The Handbook offers data which show that another aspect of nutrition, protein consumption, was also related to life expectancy. The range was from 32.7 grams in Zaire to more than three times that many, 108.4 in New Zealand (Handbook, 282).[7]

In countries where, for whatever reason, female life expectancy is low, the female population will be young. Thus, for example, there were almost twice as many 15–19 year olds in Korea (6.0 percent), where life expectancy was low, as in Sweden (3.2 percent), where it was high (Bachu, 1983, 7). Almost half (45 percent) of the population in Africa is younger than 15 (Zero Population Growth Reporter, March–April, 1984). The Western concept of teenager can hardly exist in a society where so many girls marry and give birth in their teen years. "Age" can mean quite different things. Thus, for example, in an interview with a woman leader in South Yemen, in answer to the question, "So most of your members are younger women?" the informant replied, "The majority are between 20 and 30. Hardly any are over 30. It's very difficult to change an old woman" (Molyneux, 1977, 3). The interviewer replied, was 30 old? There was no answer, but it might well have been an affirmative one.

The third variable related to longevity—geography—is highly derivative, for it is not the strictly geographic dimensions that are assumed to be relevant but rather the historical, cultural, economic, and political aspects in the several regions into which the countries are classified. In the Handbook they were: Europe–North America, Latin America, Asia, North Africa–Middle East, and Africa. The average female life expectancies were: 72.9, 59.8, 51.6, and 40.9, respectively (Handbook, 190). The world population report in 1983 by the U.S. Bureau of the Census listed Africa, with a median average life expectancy of 48; Asia, with 63; Latin America, with 66; North America, Europe, and the USSR, with 72; and Oceana, with 62. Other groupings give similar results.[8]

In addition to infant mortality, health services, nutrition, wealth, and geography as influences on longevity, female literacy has also been found to be relevant. Several years ago, in fact, the World Bank pointed out that one of the best ways to reduce infant mortality—hence to increase overall life expectancy—was to teach girls to read, because "the children of a literate mother have a strikingly better chance of survival than the children, living in the same place at the same level of income, of a mother who remains illiterate" (*Washington Post*, editorial, 25 December 1984). In fact, the rank correlation among seven regions of the world between female literacy and infant mortality was 0.72 (World Bank, tables 23, 25) and 1.0 among the five geographic areas (Handbook, 138, 215).

> With her delicate neck stretched stiff to hand-balance the heavy can, the young girls formed a common, sex-determined African tableau of female water fetcher. . . . If drawn further into the social traditions of her gender, the centuries-old route for the overwhelming majority of poor women throughout the Cape Verde Islands, she can expect to give birth to her first child in her first year of menstruation, give birth every year after that (except when nature protests with a natural abortion), raise a family without a husband, grow muscular working hard alongside of men for less pay, fetch water daily until her body gives out, and die in her early forties [Dash, 1981].

Within the demographic limits of their local worlds the lives of women in different countries show a great deal of variety in the way they spend the years, many or few, that they can expect to live. Behind the cold, formal, impersonal figures we may see the social fabric of mores, customs, traditions, beliefs—"the social traditions of her gender"—that shape their life course, that prescribe the way they are programmed to spend the years allotted to them, that trace the pattern they will weave. The proportion of the limited number of years invested in the several uses to which they can be put and the timing of these uses make a difference in the kinds of lives women live.

Almost everywhere in the female world there is great pressure to marry. A Jordan woman, member of the Fatah wing of the PLO, put it this way: "An Arab woman has to marry if she wants to live in society" (*Connexions*, no. 2, 1981, 24). And, at least until recently, a woman in the United States might well have echoed the same note. Thus, most females the world over will marry, and soon thereafter bear a child. Almost everywhere this event will be determinative of the course their lives will take, especially if it takes place when they are very young. The proportion of women married by ages 20 to 24 ranges widely, from 25 percent in Sweden to 97 percent in Bangladesh (Bachu, 1983, 12).[9]

Although at least a minimal amount of time in the life course of practically every married female in the world will be invested in childbearing, the actual amount of such time may be of relatively brief duration or, contrariwise, it may consume most of her cache of years. Since in many parts of the world—as, for example, in Somali—"the

prestige or status of an individual Somali woman is directly propor-
tional to the number of male children she bears" (*Connexions*, no. 2,
1981, 27), she is rewarded for this investment of time. There are few if
any alternative uses for it; so childbearing is, in effect, her "career."
Such dedication to childbearing is likely to be found where literacy and
labor-force participation rates—especially in white-collar occupations—are low (Bachu, 10).

However rewarded women may be for childbearing, the actual fertility differences among women in the global female world are consider-
ably greater than differences in the desired number of children. The
actual number of children women bear varies from less than two to as
many as six or seven (Bachu, 2); but the desired number varies from 2.5
to only 4.00. Thus, for example, women in Jordan complain at times that
"they are merely 'people factories made to have boys' " (*Connexions*, 24).
So at least some of the years devoted to childbearing are probably not
all that willingly given by many women. Still, if the "social traditions of
her gender" call for early and continuing childbearing there is little she
can do to violate them. Gaining control by women of their bodies is—
though for different reasons in different regions—one of the major
issues in the female world today.[10]

Equally interesting and relevant in the present context is the way
childbearing is distributed over the life course. The pattern in Europe–
North America is strikingly different from that in other areas. In this
part of the female world the proportion of all births to girls under 15
and to young women under 20 was the lowest among the five regions
distinguished in the Handbook (229–47). These women, as compared to
women elsewhere, were concentrating their childbearing in the years 20
to 34, leaving the years before 20 and after 35 free for other activities, for
education in the early or teenage years, for example, and expanded
nonfamily activities in the later or postchildbearing years, when there
were many uses for them. At the other extreme was the female world in
North Africa–Middle East, where the women not only began having
babies earlier, but also ranked highest among the geographic areas in
proportion of all births in a given year borne by women 35 and over.[11]
Such a demographic pattern leaves only a small number of years for
education before childbearing begins and few after age 45 for anything
else.[12]

Child care must also be considered in looking at the uses made of
expected years of life. The number of years devoted to such care may be
inferred from the child-woman ratio. Where there are many infants and
small children to be taken care of—a function almost universally assigned to females (chapter 2)—this ratio will be high, and where it is
high it means that a considerable amount of the time—and energy—of
women will be invested in such care. This ratio ranged from a high of

980 per thousand women in Kuwait to 150 in Monaco (Handbook, 203–4). For 120 countries, almost half (55) had ratios of seven or more children under five to be taken care of for every ten women to take care of them. The ratio was highest—800 per thousand—in North Africa–Middle East, where it was more than twice as high as in Europe–North America—397 per thousand. That is, the women in Europe–North America had fewer than half as many children to look after as did the women in North Africa–Middle East. The other three geographic areas did not differ markedly among themselves.

Since the care of children is related to the care of the household, another function almost universally assigned to the female world, the size of the household will have considerable impact on the part of a woman's life that is devoted to those responsibilities. The average size of households in 53 countries varied from 2.5 in the German Democratic Republic to almost three times that size (6.9) in Tongo; it varied also in the five geographic areas, though not so precipitously, from 3.3 in Europe–North America to 5.7 in North Africa–Middle East (Handbook, 191–92).

All four of these differences among females—in life expectancy, scheduling of childbearing, child care, and household size—reflect enormous disparities in the worlds in which they live in different parts of the globe. This diversity in uses of time shapes women in many ways. It influences their degree of literacy, education, participation in non-household activities. If women live in a world where early motherhood is the taken-for-granted norm, where the expected childbearing years will last over a large part of their lives, where a considerable part of their lives will also be consumed in child care, where household responsibilities will claim much of their time, they will become the product of these norms, of the culture—that is, of their world. These contrasting demographic structures, in brief, and the cultures that maintain them, help us understand the differences in the women they produce. The women in Europe–North America are older, more in control of their reproductive life, have more time in their early years for growing, maturing, learning, and in their middle years for expanding their sphere of activities. Reproduction takes a far smaller proportion of their total life span.

Whatever the nature of the life course in the female world may be, women everywhere are not only shaped by it to contribute their part to the pattern, but they are also shaped to find it tolerable. Thus

> a Hausa woman growing up in her [Nigerian] culture understands the demands made on her and is prepared to deal with them on her own terms. She knows there are certain social expectations to be met: marrying according to parental choice, bearing children and obeying the head

of the household. The fulfillment of these obligations gives a devoted woman a sense of security in knowing she has complied with the expectations of both her God and her community. . . . Polygamy . . . offers periodic relief from domestic responsibilities as wives take turns preparing the household's meals, doing laundry and attending to their husband in roughly three-day cycles. Thus co-wives experience a situation in which domestic chores ideally are shared among congenial companions. Of course this is not always the case; in any large household there are complaints about unequal work loads and jealousy among co-wives [Mack, 1984].

It may take a bona fide revolution to shake loose the accommodations women have everywhere been shaped to make to their world, as the Communist party in many parts of the world has found (chapters 4, 5). And, indeed, as the feminists in capitalist societies have also found.

I noted above that female literacy was related to life expectancy by way of its effect in reducing infant mortality rates. So also is it related to the female life course. Early marriage and childbearing cut short the time available for schooling, and even if the girl does not marry young she is often required to stay home from school to look after younger siblings and to take care of the household to relieve her mother for outside work. If she does go to school at all it will probably be for fewer years than her brothers do (Bachu, 10). So she is not likely in the course of her life to have much opportunity for education beyond literacy, if even that. Thus communication beyond face-to-face local contacts will be greatly restricted.

Illiteracy does not, of course, impede the development of practical, day-by-day know-how and the acquisition of leadership skills in the local community.[13] Nor does it imply lack of intellectual talents. But it does limit the grist for the mind to work on. The sociological importance of literacy was recognized in the laws governing slavery in the United States which forbade anyone to teach slaves to read. The ability to read could be dynamite to the slave system. It can be equally subversive in the female world.

Among the 102 countries included in the Handbook, ten as of 1969–71 had been able to reduce female illiteracy to less than 10 percent.[14] In 25 countries, at the other end of the continuum, illiteracy remained at more than 90 percent. Half (51) of the countries had been able to achieve a literacy level of at least 50 percent. There appeared to be three sticking points in the process of reducing female illiteracy: the first was getting it down to 80 percent, then passing beyond 60 percent, and then overcoming the last 10 percent.[15] Why reduction to less than 40 percent was so difficult cannot be determined by the data, but it is conceivable that the presence of more than three-fifths of literate women approached a kind of "critical mass" that seemed threatening to a status quo. Or it might simply be that achieving high female literacy levels was just too expensive for many countries. Girls were too badly needed elsewhere to waste their time in school (Bachu, 10).

Most—99 percent, in fact—illiterate women live in the developing countries. "Here, more than one-half of the female . . . population are estimated to be illiterate in 1980" (Ness, 1982). The contrasts among the five geographic areas in female literacy are as striking as in the life expectancy and life course data. The proportion of females who were illiterate, for example, was more than five times as high in Africa (85 percent) as in Europe-North America (16 percent). Samuel Baum, using a somewhat different grouping of countries, reported similar findings in the 1970s, when female literacy in developing countries ranged from 21.0 percent in Africa (excluding North Africa) to 68.3 in Latin America (1984). In a world where only about one in six or seven is literate, the pool for supplying teachers and leadership is limited, and education will be harder to achieve.

But there is evidence, fortunately, that progress is being made in increasing female literacy in developing countries. Thus Baum has found remarkably higher literacy rates as of about the 1970s among the younger—15- to 19-year-old—girls as compared with the older women, 35 to 39 and 55 to 59, especially marked among countries in North Africa–Southwest Asia and Africa, where the rates for the oldest women were exceptionally low. In some countries—Jordan, Tunisia, Cameroon, and Zambia—there was an increase of more than 50 percentage points.[16] Using somewhat more recent data, Shirley Nuss and Lorraine Majka in 1982 projected significant increases in literacy between 1975 and 1985 for the 15–19 age group. Still, despite this reduction in illiteracy there will still be an estimated 418 million female illiterates over 15 years of age. Nor will the sex ratio among illiterates improve by 1990; "two of every three illiterate persons are and will continue to be female" (1982). Still progress has, according to Baum, been accelerating.

The presence of a school system can be taken for granted in any modern society; it is a sine qua non of its existence. And when its curricula lead beyond mere literacy it has an even more encompassing impact on the female life course.[17] According to the Handbook, in 26 out of the 76 countries for whom data were available, females had had less than one year of schooling. These countries constitute, in effect, a universe in themselves in terms of the kind of life they provide women. The other countries distribute themselves according to an approximately symmetrical curve, about a third of them offering girls at least five years of schooling. Additions beyond that seemed a goal harder and harder to achieve. Perhaps the beginning of puberty seemed in many countries to be a suitable point at which to end female schooling. Nuss and Majka, reviewing more recent data on females, still find educational deficiencies, especially among African countries, and note that developing in and of itself cannot be expected to overcome them. They urge the need for more attention to the situation.

> Progress for female literacy and formal education is essential if women are to share decisions related to the rapid advances in science and technology which threaten to change the character of society the world over. Insurance of female progress in social growth and developing necessitates an expansion of policy-oriented research which addresses the relationship between female literacy and education and their participation in these areas (1982).

The aspects of the female world looked at so far deal to a large extent with the part reproduction—childbearing and child-rearing activities, including household care—plays in the course of women's lives. But in addition to these reproduction-related activities, there are also productive, or work-related, activities which take up a great deal of time in a woman's life. Before turning to these productive activities, however, a brief interjection on some of the current changes in the bodies of women and the consequences, not only for the course of their lives, but also for the female world.

Most of the 2.5 billion females we have been looking at—give or take a few million—are small children, girls, and fairly young women. They have been with us, literally, from time immemorial. But at the other end of the life span something brand new has been entering the historical stage with a new script. It is a cohort of human beings whose like has never been known before on land or sea. There have always been individual women who have achieved great age. Abraham's wife, Sarah, comes to mind, who gave birth at what seemed to her contemporaries the age of eighty. But the existence of a whole generation of women in, let us say, their fifties, sixties, let alone seventies, is such a new demographic event that recognition of its significance cannot be denied. We have not yet researched these new women in sufficient depth to understand what their presence is going to mean. We have tended merely to extend ancient lore and assume it was still suitable. There has not yet been a "critical mass" of such new women to reveal their impact. Having completed their childbearing and rearing roles these women are still youthful, healthy, energetic, increasingly well educated, creative, purposeful, autonomous, many still beautiful. In the United States they have recently become media figures, and the public is surprised to find how achieving women in their fifties can be. No conception of the future female world can ignore this powerful demographic fact. In the words of one of the most knowledgeable students of the life course:

> The world of the 1970s and 80s is . . . not that of the 50s and 60s. Women's life course is being transformed. . . . Women today make choices

and go through life stages in a radically different way from that of their mothers and grandmothers. The stage is set for feminist scholars to reexamine traditional assumptions about the biological and social imperatives that supposedly govern women's lives. [Beth Hess, June 1985, 6]

And there is, indeed, a great deal of such reexamination going on today not only with respect to reproduction but also with respect to its flip side, production or work. For, as Sarah Hrdy, a primatologist, reminds us, reproduction has not taken place unless the infants survive. Someone has to take care of them, a task almost universally assigned to women. So a considerable proportion of females—grandmothers, mothers, sisters, cousins, aunts—are engaged in feeding, cleaning, teaching, amusing, healing, protecting, quieting, disciplining infants and small children. No one can honestly say that these activities are not work, sometimes in fact, very hard work. Still, by a strange paradigmatic quirk they are not visible. In a study in Mauritania, for example, "most men stated vehemently that their wives did nothing" (Smale, 1980, 39). This invisibility of so much of the work done by women is perhaps one of the most important aspects of the female world. It may be invisible, but it is by no means ignorable, as Mao conceded in his statement that women held up half the sky. And, as a matter of fact, their half is probably heavier. The old folk observation implied as much: "man may work from sun to sun but woman's work is never done." Somewhere between the folk and the modern Mauritanian men a profound change had taken place in the conceptualization of work. With industrialization a totally different model was called for: productive activities were not work unless they were paid for.

Understanding work in the female world is harder to achieve than understanding reproduction. There is an inescapable set of activities standard for reproduction, however differently performed, however differently evaluated. A birth is a birth; a death, a death. But work is not similarly standardized. The same activity which is work under some circumstances is not recognized as such in other circumstances. It takes, for example, eight and a half pages in the Handbook just to explain technical and definitional problems related to indexes of "economic activity," that is, of "work" (304–12), and nine pages to explain "labor-force participation rates" (295–304). Eleven pages are required to define "industry" and "occupation" (324–35). The dates when the data were gathered differ. Different researchers classify countries into somewhat different groupings. In the case of industry, lack of data is not the only roadblock. Another has to do with the structure of the global female world itself, parts of which are in industrialized, technologically sophisticated economic systems and parts of which are still in preindustrialized societies. Thus in 54 out of 126 countries reported in the Handbook, questions dealing with occupations—white-collar, blue-collar, farm, and service—were "not applicable" in another study (Bachu, table 15). The Handbook distinguished eight industries, but only four—agriculture, manufacturing, commerce, and service—reported, on average, as many as a fifth of their paid workers as female (285–86), and in only two of these—agriculture and service—were as many as about a third of the paid workers women (286).[18] The World Bank is satisfied with three industrial categories: agriculture, "industry," and service (258–59). In terms of industrial composition, and therefore of occupation, this is clearly "a man's world." But tucked inconspicuously away, out of sight, are the millions of females keeping the work force on the job in good shape. For in all economies, developed or not, rural or urban, the unpaid work performed in the household does not count as work. Often we get a better picture of work in the female world to date from the insights of historians and anthropologists. And even when the technical research barriers to knowledge of the work aspects of the female world have been eliminated, the sheer speed of change taking place in many parts of the world often renders our research anachronistic. Data become dated almost as soon as they are published. With the rise of multinational corporations, for example, in the recent past young women in the Orient, in Latin America, in the Caribbean are attracted from rural to urban areas to work in the manufacturing plants in so-called International Zones established in cities to attract foreign factories (appendix B). New kinds of work multiply and produce new kinds of women. Old ways of looking at female work are no longer acceptable.

A review of the story of female work in agriculture has led Rae Blumberg to conclude that in most prehuman groups women were the primary producers and, on the basis of recent studies, that "women continue to produce approximately half of the world's food (1949, 447). In Africa, as of 1974, women were responsible for 70 percent of food production and half of animal husbandry. A similar situation prevailed in Asia and the Middle East. But, as noted above, in relatively few countries (22 out of 92) were females recorded as constituting at least half of all paid agricultural workers. Either the relatively small number of female paid agricultural workers were exceptionally productive or there were many farming women who were invisible. Other more recent studies have corroborated Blumberg's conclusions.

Nor does any of this work limit a host of other productive activities. Studies of village life in Azania (southern Africa), the Caribbean, and the Middle East report, for example, that women's working days are long: as much as 18 hours. . . . These women are involved in cultivation, food processing and storage, home-based commercial enterprises, out-of-home wage labor, child rearing, water and fuel hauling, animal tending, cleaning, repairing, educating, and nursing, all with a minimum of training, capital resources, or technology. [Goddard, 1985, 34]

The author of this study concluded that "if the unpaid labor of women in the household were given economic value, it would increase the world's annual estimated economic product by 33 percent, or four trillion dollars" (31).[19] Again:

In Africa, women do 75 percent of the agricultural work, in addition to domestic chores of caring for children, fetching water and firewood, cooking and cleaning. In Malawi . . . women do twice as much work as men on the staple crop, corn, in addition to equal amounts in the cotton fields and their domestic chores at home. . . . In the developed countries, it is estimated that women spend 56 hours a week on domestic chores; in developing countries it can be more. [Sciolino, *New York Times*, 23 June 1985]

And here is Dora Ayobga who lives in Kenya:

She wakes up at dawn in the bed she shares with her four children in a walled-off corner of the family's grass-roofed hut. Her husband, Silas, sleeps alone most nights in another bed, separated from his wife and children by a partition.

If there is any cornmeal left over from the previous day, Dora Ayobga builds a fire in a smoke-stained corner of the hut and cooks porridge for her children and her husband. By 7 a.m., if she can find the work, she is out hoeing weeds for a neighbor.

Silas, 28, who is looking for work, waits at home (his mother taking care of the children) until about 1:30 p.m. when Dora comes home with the corn and beans that her hoeing has earned. She fetches the firewood and water needed to cook lunch, feeds him and the children and cleans up. For the rest of the afternoon, she combs the village for greens or other vegetables for dinner, which she cooks and serves before dark.

Before Ayobga goes to sleep in the bed with her children she washes the one dress she owns and hangs it to dry above the fire where at dawn she will cook more porridge. [Harden, Blaine, *Washington Post*, 6 July 1985]

Even when allowance is made for undercounting of the work performed by the female world, its work load is staggering.

The second major industry in the female world—equal in importance to agriculture—is the household care of families. And it is anomalous that because they are not paid, those engaged in this industry are classified as "economically inactive" unless—as is increasingly the case—they have paying jobs outside the home. Few deny the importance of the services they contribute—almost everything can go wrong if or when the homemaker or housekeeper is not on the job—but that does not endow them with economic recognition. A major product of this industry is only health.[20]

One final point about occupations in the female world, about, that is, what "occupies" the time of women. Almost everywhere the female world is charged with the performance of a wide variety of services—religious, ritualistic, emotional, otherworldly—that may involve a considerable amount of time if not of energy. Here, for example, is Dzermianthes, a Greek village in Crete where

> women dominate the rituals connected to the life cycle as well as irregular, secret rites such as magic and witchcraft. As midwives, matchmakers and singers of bridal songs and, finally, as lamenters, they dominate the rites of passage, the perilous moments of transition from one realm to another. [Caraveli Chaves, 1980, 143–44]

These activities have little economic or productive relevance. They perform, rather, an integrative or sociological function.

Some years ago a U.S. economist, Kenneth Boulding, introduced the concept of "integry" (1969) which contrasted with "economy" and "polity" and served the function of holding the parts of a society together, of preventing the economy, for example, from self-destructing. The rules which govern the way the economy and the integry operated were almost polar opposites. The economy governed the production of goods and services for the market; the integry did the integrating work, that is, it built morale in the community; it "stroked," supported, tempered griefs, disappointments, and failures; helped individuals "manage" the heart (Hochschild, 1984). In addition, it performed such services as those reported in the Greek village—seeing to birth, marriage, and death rituals. Although Boulding did not specify the integry as a female world, "a good case," it has seemed to me, "can be made for the conception that historically the integry has been 'manned' by women. It has, that is, performed the integrating function of holding the whole system together" (Bernard, 1981, 27). To the extent that it succeeds, it is invisible.

Having now stripped the inhabitants of the global female world of all individuality, let us take time here to look at some of them as human rather than as numerical figures. Here are several vignettes in which we can catch glimpses of how they live their lives—here, there, anywhere; some in the fast lane, some in the slow.

We begin with an "economically inactive" Phillipine woman whose time is "occupied" with arranging patterns of consumption for herself and her family, based on imported luxuries:

The upper middle [Philippine] class and the traditional powerful families . . . live the following lifestyle: In the morning, they can eat cereals imported from the U.S. and ham with bacon from Australia, drink orange juice from California and coffee from Brazil, courtesy of the companies that import or repackage products from their mother conglomerates. After breakfast, the family is ready to dress for school and work. . . . The parents hurry up with their toiletry: the ladies using the scents of Paris. . . . The ladies, particularly entrusted with shopping, are scanning the papers for the latest in fashion, in housekeeping and in hosting parties. Hanae Mori is in town and the ladies who set the pace must be fluttering over her butterfly collection. Then they have to make appointments with the beauty parlour. Get the trendy hair stylist from New York and come out of the parlour looking like a Princess from London. . . . At the end of the day, the family is eating together in front of their video machines. . . . The evening wears out with the ladies putting the children to sleep in their soft cotton pajamas and their teddy bears. . . . The morning will be another bout of shopping. Perhaps it is better to go to Hong Kong. There are more new items there: must remember to call up the British airline. Might just fly to a short trip to Europe. Anyway, it is already spring. . . . Though they are only about two percent of the population, they [the elite] have created a market with their taste for goods produced by foreign companies. The advertising climate . . . is aggressive. . . . Women are deliberately selected as the prime multinational consumers. [Villariba, n.d., pp. 9–10]

For women like them there might well be an occupational category "consumer," because consuming is what they "do." Thorstein Veblen, a United States economist, did, in fact, recognize the validity of such a conceptualization. He described women whose time was occupied in the performance of what he called "conspicuous consumption" and "vicarious leisure" for their husbands. This was their occupation. They show up in all parts of the global female world. We will, indeed, run across them from time to time.

Here is a counterpart, a Philippine factory girl, whose time is occupied in paid employment—in her case, making doll parts:

Nena, [a 27-year-old Mattel employee in the Philippines] makes doll parts for a pay of P590 [pesos] a month. She likes working in the toy factory. For her, it is better than being a housekeeper. She gets paid for a specific task and has benefits like a vacation with pay. She gets to meet friends, for there are many women working in the factory and in the zone. . . . Nena is optimistic. She can still afford to see the movies or buy comic books. She is not married and her take-home pay is enough to meet her simple needs. Though she suffers from recurrent backaches and muscle fatigue, she can still pay for the minimum cost of medical care. Nena thinks that women must get an education. Hers was short, cut by necessity of earning a living. And women must work. For her, housekeeping is impractical; it has no definite hours, no pay, no benefits—and no union. Women should widen their perspectives. Nena is strong on women being economically active. No double burdens for her. But Nena's optimism is clouded by the mass lay-offs in Mattel. She has to work harder and longer to keep her job. She has to clock in at 6 A.M. and last up to 6 P.M. She has to meet her quota of a thousand parts. She must not get sick, for if she is absent for a single day, she may be struck off the list of workers Mattel will keep due to rising costs. If this happens, she will have to go back to the farm and raise pigs. It will be very difficult again. Farmlife is hard on women. [Villariba, n.d., 8] [See appendix B]

And here is another woman—a Palestinian rebel—who hates the boring and petty domestic activities that "occupy" her time:

> I am subjected to forced inactivity . . . confined within four walls. Just like a conventional housewife. I think of my friends and acquaintances, women who follow the traditional role of the Arab mother and housewife, presiding over her narrow little kingdom, rarely venturing outside except for the most immediate needs. Their way of life has always frightened me. Tied to the boredom and pettiness of domesticity, gradually sinking into inertia, with their horizons becoming progressively narrower. It is an awful fate, a vegetative existence without meaning or value. [Plexus, October 1981, 19]

Here are urban Uganda women "occupied" in white-collar activities or self-employment:

> One tenth of Uganda's female population is urban and better educated, typified by the secretary, the civil servant, the nurse, the worker in private industry, but also by the self-employed beer-brewer, charcoal seller and land-lady. These women have a higher level of economic independence and mobility than their rural counterparts. Some come to town because jobs for which they were educated could only be found in towns. [Akello, n.d., 16]

At the low end of the occupational totem pole, this is how women nomads are "occupied" in Somali:

> Daily life among the Somali nomads is a constant search for water and pasture in 100 degree temperatures. Historically, Somali women have been responsible for household chores, as well as for making baskets for milk and water, and milking and tending the sheep and goats (or, in agricultural areas, helping in the fields). [*Connexions*, no. 2, 1981, p. 27]

And, finally, a woman for all seasons:

> Thailand is . . . remarkable for the high percentage of women engaged in its labour force. In 1968 Gunnar Myrdal declared Thailand to have

reached the highest rates of female work participation in the world.[21] . . .
Thai women (like women in Burma, another Theravada Buddhist country) . . . for hundreds of years . . . have not only laboured in the paddy-
fields but have also conducted the bulk of marketing chores and controlled their households' purse-strings. Foreigners in the 1900s were usually forced to negotiate with 'elderly Siamese women' when they wanted
to open electricity plants, ice-factories, or tin mines. Today three times as
many women as men are evident in large and small businesses as owners
and managers, market-sellers, hawkers and market-gardeners. . . .
Women . . . also constitute a significant portion of labourers in construction work, transport and mining. . . . Women's role in agricultural
production . . . has been and still is the backbone of the national economy.
Thitsa, n.d., 5, 10]

They did all this but, as a recent survey on the status of women showed,
family needs came first; family welfare had the highest priority. Truly
supermoms. "Women's liberation is a foreign concept to all rural Thai
women and most urban women" (10). Who needed it?

These, then, are the inhabitants of the global female world, and this is
the nature of the world they live in. This is how they spend the years
they have to live, how their world schedules them for childbearing,
childrearing, and education and how their time is occupied, paid or
unpaid. Emphasis on the many differences among the lives of women
anticipates the argument frequently made that so much diversity invali-
dates any all-encompassing conceptualization of such an entity as a
global female world. Still, the effort seems to me worthwhile. For, as
Elise Boulding notes, "the simple act of working for uniformity and
comparability in the ways in which we conceptualize what people do in
order simply to . . . count them can aid in fostering social and political
change in the long run" (1976, 24). Adequate conceptualizing can itself
be, indeed, a cerebral form of activism in the direction—in the present
context—of a self-conscious female world.

The concept of the female world accommodates not only diversity
among women but also differences from the male world. The several life
courses traced here show that almost everywhere women spend a considerable amount of their lifetime bearing and rearing children and
that, although not specified in the records, they also do a considerable
amount of the work of the world. These are usually different from the
kinds of work men do (chapter 2). There is, that is, a sexual division of
labor. Chapter 2 shows that as a result of these differences men and
women inhabit quite separate spatial—as well as psychological and
sociological—worlds.

CHAPTER TWO

Separate Worlds

Not only does the life course of women differ among women in different parts of the female world but, within any of these different locales, so does it also differ from that of men.[1] And not only does the work women do differ among women in different parts of the female world, but so also, within any of these different locales, does it differ from the work men do. The sexual division of labor is, in fact, one of the most widely reported aspects of societies, historically as well as currently. Indeed, a considerable number of women worldwide would have to change their jobs in order to equalize the number of men and women in the same occupation or industry.[2] As a consequence of these two kinds of differences—within the female world itself and between it and the male world—there tend also to be varying degrees of spatial separation between the two worlds.[3]

A considerable proportion of the life course of women revolves, as we saw in chapter 1, around the part women play in reproduction. For reproduction involves more than simply conception, gestation, birthing, and the nourishment of infants. As Sarah Hrdy reminds us on the basis of primate research, reproduction involves the rearing—as well as the bearing—of offspring to maturity (1981). The group is not reproduced if too many of its infants and children die. And because women bear and lactate the children, the function of rearing them at least in infancy and early childhood is almost universally assigned primarily if not always exclusively to them.[4] Small children, male as well as female, remain with the mother or a surrogate—usually a female—during the first few years of their lives. "Women-and-children" come to be viewed as a distinct structural entity, different from "women" and "children" separately, but clearly part of the female world. Even work that has no genuine sexual basis becomes "genderized" into female work when it is assigned to women, and into male work when it is assigned to males.

The care of infants and small children is not the only kind of work that

20

is allocated on the basis of sex. Nor are the specific kinds of work assigned to each sex necessarily everywhere identical. The care of cattle may be assigned to females in one culture; in another, women may not even be allowed near the cattle. Among Somali nomads only men may tend the cattle, even though the animals are communally owned (*Connexions*, 1981, 27). "In Senegal women have complete control of swamp rice, whereas in Sierra Leone, this activity is a male prerogative, and women have responsibility for upland rice" (McNamara, 1979, 6).

This sex-based division of work may differ not only from one place to another but also over time. The specific kinds of work assigned to each sex will depend to a large extent on the way a society earns its living which, in turn, will itself depend on a host of sociological and technological factors, so that the sexual division of labor that prevails may change as technological, ecological, even political[5] factors change. Or as the environment itself changes as, for example, in the case of deforestation and land dessication.[6] Such changes may reassign certain old kinds of work or create new kinds. In the French town of Chanzeaux, to illustrate, before modern transportation came, the men brought goods from the city to sell or they bought and sold products of the community. By mid-century, middlemen were doing all this and the local men had become artisans, civil servants, or farm laborers, and "shopkeeping was limited to retail sales and delegated to the women" (Wylie, 1966, 142). In the United States, to take another case, the work of stenography was once a male occupation; today it is all but totally a female one. In the north of England and Switzerland men were once the weavers; elsewhere this cottage industry was female work (Smith, 1982, 311). Weapon making has traditionally been male work; child care, female.

Sometimes the male and female worlds may engage in the same kind of work but have different specializations. In the case of marketing, for example, in Ga—an urban population in Accra, Ghana—marketing was done by both men and women, the men dealing with—at one time— slaves, gold, and ivory and the women with small luxury items and food (Robertson, 1984, 198). Although there have been times and places where work was interchangeable between the sexes—either the men or the women might weave or tend the animals (Bell, 1981, 310)—still overall, complete ignore-ance of sex in the allocation of work seems to have been rare. In any event, a complex gender-oriented superstructure is built on this foundation, whatever its nature may be. It is not, therefore, necessarily the specific way the work is divided between males and females that gives rise to the two worlds but the mere fact that it is so divided.

Ester Boserup and other students of current development carry the point further applying it to whole economies as well as to specific occupations. They conceptualize the two worlds in some parts of the globe in terms of dual economies, a female subsistence economy and a male cash economy.[7] In Peru, for example, when "husbands and older sons are forced to migrate in search of . . . [waged] work in construction or mining, or of ambulatory vending in cities," women remain actively engaged in agriculture on small farms (Figueroa and Anderson, 1981, 8). Boserup, further, sees differences within the two economies. She speaks of predominantly male towns, predominantly female towns, and semi-male towns, the first common in Asia, the second in Latin America, and the third in Africa (85–87).[8] She also distinguishes two patterns in the subsistence economies, in one of which "food production is taken care of by women, with little help from men, and one where food is produced by the men with relatively little help from women" (16).[9] Africa is the area par excellence of female farming; it is also an area of female marketing. Kenneth Little, in fact, refers to the market in Africa as "virtually a woman's world" (1973, 49). To Schumacher the patterns of living in the two economies are as different from one another as two different worlds are (1973, 164). Even—perhaps especially—in industrialized economies, where sex-segregated work patterns are found almost universally.

Attempts to explain the existence of a sexual division of labor may rest on logical, economic, or biological grounds.[10] Work that is compatible with the female life course, especially work connected with infant and child care, for example, will, it is suggested, tend to be assigned to women; work that has to do with war—weapon-making[11]—will be assigned to men. In view, however, of the enormous variety of ways that the division is actually implemented, it is doubtful if any simple explanation is adequate. In the present context, it is less the specification of causes that is relevant than it is the separation of the worlds which the sexual division of labor has as a consequence, if not cause. For although it may be the sexual division of labor—including infant- and child-care—which constitutes the basis for the two worlds, it is the associated allocation of space that undergirds their separateness.[12]

The significance of space—in individual interactions, in crowded housing units, in competing uses of land in cities, in issues of national Lebensraum, among other contexts—has been a long-time interest of social scientists; it is now increasingly being looked at vis-à-vis the relations between the female and male worlds, both at work and in the household.

It has been noted, for example, that among those doing the same kinds of work there tends to be a sharing not only of work space but also of work attitudes and skills. A common work site facilitates among the workers an awareness of common interests. The mere fact that individuals are engaged in the same kind of work means they already have something in common. They are at least subject to common work-related rules and norms. Referring especially to African women's organizations in rural development, Kathleen Staudt notes that "women's solidarity patterns are often based on a sex division of labor in which women work on similar tasks, labor *separately* from men, and consequently, share related interests" (1980, 11, emphasis added).

Separate work sites mean almost universally that there is a difference elsewhere in turf also. Melinda Smale cites Cynthia Nelson (1974) to the effect that nomads define the tent as the women's political area, and the camp as the men's, where community matters are discussed (1980, 41). Almost universally the courtyard is female space (Boulding, 1976, 132–35), the streets, male. There are, in fact, streets where no decent woman may tread; there are areas where the presence of a man would be cause for suspicion. Almost universally certain kinds of leisure activities take place on male turf; within the household almost universally the cooking and cleaning space is female. The fact that work comes to be tied in with the work site means that it acquires an association with sexual identity (Bernard, 1981, 1983). Sharing the work site of males "desexes" females; sharing the work site of females "desexes" males. Separateness protects gender identity.[13]

The separating consequences of such different work sites may be of varying orders of magnitude. Smale illustrates the separating effects of different occupations among the Bidan of Mauritania:

> Although, in Mauritania, the tent is open to both men and women of any caste, men are absent both during the day, in herding and cultivation supervision, and during seasonal periods, in commercial herding enterprise. Men and women share no common workplace; men supervise the herds and conduct commerce while women supervise camp distribution of foodstuffs and household utensil maintenance. While men's and women's responsibilities are considered complementary, their work itself coincides only in the education of their children and administration of the camp at select points in time. [1980, 38–39]

She then adds a footnote: "One woman, when asked what mutual responsibilities men and women shared, replied 'the work of the night, and that's it' " (39).

Carcelli-Chaves, on the basis of a study of the Greek village Dzermianthes in Crete, sees such separateness as both a political and a power-balancing factor. Thus, in her village

> the spheres of activity of men and women are strictly separate and, in many ways, parallel to, and independent from, rather than subservient to each other. Men's power is restricted to the public, visible, and official realm. Though it provides them with opportunities for social domination, it limits them to a temporal sphere of experience. [1980, 143–44]

A study of the use of space in English and Australian houses in the nineteenth and early twentieth centuries found "the spatial location of male and female activities . . . frequently demarcated, with a clear distinction between the two domains inside and outside the house" (Lawrence, 1982, 129). The garden, the work bench, the garage were male turf; the kitchen and laundry, female. Arza Churchman and Rachel Sebba in a study of high-rise apartment dwellers in a middle-class Haifa neighborhood found not only clear-cut individual, shared, and "public" areas in the apartment but also in individual rooms (1985). A study of spatial patterns in the organization of households in Adabraka (a suburb of Accra, Ghana) illustrates how complex gender allocation of space may be (1982).[14] The men congregate with friends in bars or go to the soccer stadium for recreation; the women engage in church activities, associations, lodges, and the like in their own areas. "Husbands and wives have individual incomes and make separate decisions about their consumption activities and expenses" (Sanjek, 1982, 89). In Mauritania at least the "work of the night" is done in a common household. But in Adabraka not even this activity takes place in a shared household. "Sexual relationships between women and men who reside in separate households are the statistically normal pattern in Adabraka" (89).[15] This pattern is one of the most extreme forms of spatial separation of the sexes. But other studies corroborate some level of spatial separation elsewhere also (Lawrence, 104–30; Churchman and Sebba, 1985; Nordstrom, 1985).

The sociological "geography of space" is being increasingly researched, with results of considerable interest for understanding the two worlds. Joni Seager, summarizing some of the points being made in recent studies,[16] notes that

> space is gendered; that is, . . . the design and use of space is determined in part by ideological assumptions about gender roles. . . ; in turn, spatial relations help to shape and maintain culturally specific notions of gender behavior . . . women's perception of "safe" and "unsafe" environments . . . is markedly different from men's. [1985, 9]

The data do, in fact, show that women "have a geographical existence distinct from [that of] men" (9). Like so much of the female world, its geography remains as yet invisible. We are only now beginning to see the implications of this "female geography." But what we are learning from it shows an aspect of the female world only dimly sensed until now.

Spatial distance is augmented by psychological or social distance in some societies. The avoidance patterns of the Eastern European Shtetl for example, illustrated such a symbolic and ceremonial way of maintaining separation and distance:

A division of sexes at social functions follows naturally from the division of interests and responsibilities, as well as from the avoidance rule. . . . At weddings, the men and women stand in separate groups during the ceremony and sit at different tables for the feast. Such physical separation of the sexes is obligatory. . . . Most men . . . learn to glance sideways with a look that sees and does not see. . . . If a difficult social situation forces a very orthodox man to shake hands with a woman, he deftly slips his caftan over his hand to avoid contact. [Zborowsky and Herzog, 1952, 136–37]

Some inkling of how isolated from one another the two worlds are may be gleaned from the experience of a researcher in Iran:

When I lived in Urmieh, a city in Northwest Iran, I spent a long time looking for Kurdish women. I could see them well enough on the street and bustling through the marketplace . . . but I could not meet them, could not talk with them, could not find out the first thing about their lives. After much effort I met some Kurdish men. I expected soon after to be introduced to Kurdish women, but the men put me off by saying, unaccountably, that they did not know any Kurdish women. [Kahn, 1981, 4]

The intellectual as well as the emotional ambience of such separate worlds also came through:

The degree of sameness, the lack of opportunity or variety in a Kurdish woman's life is hard for women in the West to appreciate. . . . When I could not stand it any more I would go over to the other side of the wall and speak with the men. They would talk to me on any subject—news from abroad, the state of the economy, the pilgrimages they had made to Mecca—anything except the state of their women. [5]

Hanna Papanek, discussing purdah in Pakistan, where spatial separation has long prevailed, raises questions about its impact on the emotional relationships between men and women (1971, 528). And Cynthia Nelson, cited by Smale, points to the inherent distancing between husbands and wives in nomadic societies which results from segregative work sites. She found that "with the minimization of contact between spouses, distrust tends to widen the schism" (Smale, 39). Interviews confirmed this observation. Informants

revealed no knowledge whatsoever of their spouse's productive activities. Most men stated vehemently that their wives did nothing, although when women began listing their daily activities, they acknowledge that women worked. Others, recognizing their spouse's activities, were simply unable to describe them. This element of ignorance on the part of the men or attitude of deference on the part of the women, is crucial to understanding the persistence of work segregation. [39]

As well, it might be added, as to understanding the invisibility of the economic contribution of women everywhere.[17]

Nor does the spatial separateness between male and female worlds seem to be diminishing; it may, rather, be increasing. Berit Aas, for example, surveying developments in many parts of the world, notes that distances between the two worlds may in fact be expanding as a result of male migration in search of work:

> The economic mechanisms that are involved in such dissimilar areas as Central Europe and developing countries of Africa are different but the outcomes are similar. Commuting male workers [in Germany and Scandinavia] from the south of Italy and the outskirts of Turkey have left mothers, sisters, and wives behind in female dominated rural areas. "Planned development" has forced men away from their villages in African countries and left the women behind to pay the price of economic growth and to take care of the children, the sick and the aged there. [1981, 107–8]

Some indication of the size of this separating trend may be gleaned from the estimated six million women left in rural areas of southern Italy as the male relatives moved to towns to find work, many as "guest workers" in Central and Northern Europe (107). Nor was the story much different in rural Peru, where husbands and older sons migrate in search of paid work as noted above. Or in Morocco, Botswana, Lesotho, Central America, the Caribbean (McNamara, 1979, 10). Or in South Africa, or in Kenya, where, in answer to a reporter's questions about women working in the fields—"Where are the men?"—his interpreter replied: "This is the problem we face here in Africa. You see these women working hard in the fields? They suffer. Their husbands may be working in town, drinking beer, spending their wages, enjoying themselves" (Critchfield, 1982). The impact of separateness in these situations is compounded by the cultural differences to which the migrating men—as well as the migrating women who may also become "guest workers"—are exposed.[18]

Physical proximity does not, of itself, obviate the social space between the two worlds. Men and women working side by side on an assembly line are subject to different norms of behavior. Little children—male and female—sitting side by side in a school room are, similarly, subject to different patterns (Best, 1984); they are not attending the same school (Bernard, 1975). Nor are they even at the college level (Hall and Sandler, 1982).

As a result of these physical, psychological, and social separating processes, a host of cultural prescriptions, proscriptions, and expectations arise which constitute a reality of incalculable power to guide, shape, and control—that is, to "genderize"—behavior. So taken for granted are the walls of the world that surround each individual that they are rarely noticed and even more rarely breached.

Once such a separating two-world pattern of work and space allocation has been established, it tends to perpetuate itself. The way separation is maintained, not only physically but also psychologically and sociologically, is illustrated in the French community of Chanzeaux in the middle of the twentieth century. It shows how sex—a biological fact—was being psychologically and socially processed into gender—a psychological and sociological fact. From infancy on, a system of rules, mores, beliefs, attitudes went to work on little girls and boys to shape their behavior.

Case in Point: Chanzeaux

The whole educational system, which separates girls and boys at the earliest age, is designed to make girls aware of what women should be. Even a geography book contains such lessons as: "Little girls, patient, charitable, humble, and sweet; never lose your modesty and piety. . . ." When a priest criticized the "femme egoiste," the girls agreed that "a woman who does not receive will still give anyway." [Wylie, 1966, 311]

With such thorough gender indoctrination, the physical separateness becomes a matter of course. Gender identity itself has been made hostage to its maintenance:

The habit of association with people of the same sex is carried on without interruption from childhood to old age. Both in family and in school, boys and girls are separated from an early age. In adolescence this separation is reinforced by cliques and *classe* groups, rules that limit dating, and clear definitions of feminine and masculine qualities. . . . This pattern of associating with one's own sex, so important in childhood and adolescence, continues through adulthood. Married men spend their leisure hours with each other; married women work together, spend Sundays gossiping in each others' houses and shops, and even dance together when they attend a dance. [313]

Usually after Mass the farm women stand around in the square and pass on their news for the week. [143]

Religious functions are "women's work." The Church is female turf. Male intrusion is negatively sanctioned:

The authority of the church, which children first experience primarily through women, comes to be identified with women, and the model of religious behavior held up in the catechism becomes primarily a feminine model; thus a man who is overly devout may be considered effeminate. [313]

Anthropological studies from all over the world report an analogous "processing" of male and female children for separate worlds by rites, rituals, ceremonies; by sanctions; by rewards and punishments.[19] When the "curriculum" is completed, the genderized girl graduates into the separate adult female world and the boy, into the separate adult male world.

Before proceeding further, a number of illustrations are offered here to show the kind of lives women lead with one another in their separate world in several parts of the globe. The main emphasis is on their work-related group life.

The focus here is on the local world where women live. Panning in more closely than in the discussion so far, this focus offers glimpses inside that world in Africa, Peru, and Bangladesh, which show women as they relate to one another at the local grass-roots level, in the part of their lives they live together. The idea is to counteract the male bias in our thinking which has led us, women as well as men, to see women solely as, in deBeauvoir's term, the Others—to see them, that is, primarily in their relationships with men as daughters, wives, mothers, mistresses, servants, employees, slaves, priestesses, prostitutes, or in whatever other role they participate vis-à-vis the male world. Since most of women's time which is not spent alone or with children only is spent with other women, these relationships cannot be dismissed as trivial or unworthy of attention as they have so often been in past research. The following cases suggest the nature of the relationships women may weave among themselves in their separate worlds.

Tontines (Mauritania and Ghana).[20]

The tontine, or cooperative revolving-credit association, makes it possible for women to perform traditional services for one another and their families even when, for whatever reason, they are no longer able to provide them personally or individually.[21] The source of the contributions invested in these groups varies. In some cases it might be household money; in others it might come from business profits, as in the case of merchants or business entrepreneurs; in still others, from savings—or from dances, jumbo sales, and bazaars of one kind or another (Smale, 52).

The uses to which the money is put also vary. Some of it goes to support women through difficult times. Sick benefits and interest-free loans are among the services for which funds may be spent. For the divorcee, in particular, these associations provide critical support. One group with seven members "set aside 20 UM [the local monetary unit] per person each Sunday . . . and if one of the women's husbands does not support her or is unemployed, or if she has problems, the other six donate rice, oil, soap, and some money" (81). In some cases the money supplements a woman's allowance. When a woman has a baby, each member of one group gives her 100 UM (81). In one group the money might even have to be used to buy household necessities.

Helping members maintain ties with their native villages also seems to be an important use for these funds. Some associations consider the retention of village ties so important for urban women that among their services they even include funds for travel to and from their villages. Thus, "in response to the social exigency of returning to the village with gifts in hand, the typical association includes provisions for travel subsidies. One such organization, numbering over 100 women, or a majority of the women of the quartier" (82), disburses money for births, baptisms, marriages, and funerals, as well as for traveling (82).

Some of the associations become, in effect, producers' cooperatives. At the simplest level, they might merely buy thread and cloth which they could then tint or sew for sale (81). But some accumulate enough capital to purchase sewing machines and expensive materials to work up for sale. Or they may "rent" a sewing machine, paying for its use by sharing returns with the owner. In the Cameroon, groups of women operate corn mills, generating income, reducing labor burdens, and thus "acquiring public value for that labor" (Staudt, 9). One association, engaged in vegetable cultivation, was extraordinarily successful. The women were full of plans: to install a motor pump for easier access to water; to get better transportation for taking their produce to market (Smale, 71).[22]

While the so-called River Women in Mauritania do not work well together except in household and child-care duties, almost all of them can and do save together. "Because of her traditional knowledge of age-set and group associations," the River Woman was "comparatively well-prepared for the establishment of urban networks" and was "a master at making fifty cents grow" (80). These networks are usually located in "neighborhoods among women who share a common trust and interest, providing a unique base for small community action" (106). These savings groups among the River Women are not work groups or producers' cooperatives but they do provide "ad hoc support to and a continuous flow of information among women" (106).[23]

In Ghana, as also in Mauritania, the "rotating credit association," called Nanemi Akpee or Society of Friends, is an important structural component of the female world (Little, 1973, 52), and performs the same kinds of services for women. Other voluntary associations run maternity and child-welfare clinics and conduct classes for illiterate women, giving them a chance to learn English, the lingua franca, important in almost any kind of upward mobility since so many of the desirable jobs require it.[24]

Less structured are similar mutual-aid groupings in other parts of the female world. In Peru, for example, women are embedded in tight networks of families, neighborhoods, and friends who:

> exchange the information, goods, and services necessary to . . . survival or . . . to a measure of social mobility. A woman who faces the urgent need of leaving her children while she rushes to pay the water bill searches among the members of her informal network for another woman that can care for them. Informal networks compensate for the irregularity of income. A woman whose husband is temporarily employed in a construction gang, for example, makes a loan to a neighbour whose husband is temporarily out of work. When in the following month the tables are turned, the neighbour returns the favour. Women locate jobs for husbands and other family members in the information they pick up from other women in their informal networks. Their intense relationships with female friends and relatives compensate women for their frequently troubled relationships with their male compañeros. [Figueroa and Anderson, 1981, 9]

All these cooperative activities in behalf of other women take place outside of the male world, in separate female systems.

But separate worlds do not always mean cooperation within the female world, for not all women everywhere find organizing with other women, formally or informally, congenial. The black River Women in Mauritania have individualistic work backgrounds. In the city they do not even join women's associations or attempt to regulate their market activities:

> A Haratin [black] woman, for example, claimed that while she and several others sell cous-cous at the same location daily, they are competitors and never proposed purchasing a common cous-cous grinder, sharing labor or marketing tasks, or expanding their operation. Thus, while rural women customarily fabricate tents, mats, and cushions together with other family women, the urban women, once separated from their families, are distrustful of other women. Enjoying no tradition of informal associations that bridge families and castes, the migrant Biden or Haratin woman is often isolated from other women. [Smale, 91][25]

Egbe (Nigeria).

Somewhat different in function is the second case in point, the organization designed to regulate the market—generally conceded by a long historical tradition to be female turf in Africa—and, in West Africa, the chief source of income for urban women.[26] Here separation of the two worlds relates to market specialization in foods by sex. Although such voluntary organizations perform a variety of functions, including provision of capital for starting or expanding a business, a major one is regulating market practices to prevent undercutting:

> For example, in Lagos market there is a separate section for each commodity—fish, the different kinds of vegetables, cloth, etc.—and the women sit according to the commodity in which they deal. Each such section has its own such association, or *egbe*, which discourages competition between women trading in that particular article. Such is the sense of solidarity—the women gossip together, eat, drink, and spend the entire day in each other's company—that it is said to be unthinkable for a trader to disobey her market *egbe* in this matter. Any woman undercutting is ostracized by her fellows, who may even take a case against her, reporting it to the leader of the *egbe* and if necessary to the Iyalode (Queen of the Markets). It is said that this official is recognized chief, taking second place only to the *Oba* (king) at official functions. The *egbe* also sees to it that no male trader deals in certain commodities customarily regarded as the business of women. [Little, 50]

A somewhat more informal and less structured organization in Lagos is a kind of guild among the women selling charcoal. They refer to one another as "daughter" and "mother" and try to limit the number of women who may sell in the same area in order to prevent competition. Intruders are asked to leave. If a woman does not then leave, a native doctor is asked to remove her (50–51).

Some *egbes* engage in cooperative buying; some engage in production. In Nigeria some female associations—one of which has a membership of 80,000—run bakeries, laundries, calabash factories, weaving corporations (51).

Harambees (Kenya).

In Kenya, the *harambee* is a self-help group of urban or rural women who "cooperate in some activity such as building a community school or clinic, from which each expects to derive a tangible benefit" (Rogers, 1979, 105). Here is an on-the-scene reporter's account of a rural example:

> Often we [the reporter and his interpreter] joined a group of women working in the fields, perhaps threshing a mass of beanstalks with poles. Beneath the gossip and laughter there was a rustling sound as the grains popped out of the beaten sheaves onto the hard earth. Or women might be winnowing beans; sometimes the wind stilled and they would wait,

cursing, their wicker baskets poised to catch the breeze when it came back again. I asked why they worked in groups. "We like to, it gives us strength," they would say. This ethic of mutual help is extremely strong in village Kenya, one of the happiest legacies of the tribal past. Jomo Kenyatta called it *harambee*, or pulling together. Villagers in Machakos found it natural to build their own schools, dams and roads. [Critchfield, 1982]

Although not, perhaps, technically *harambee*, but certainly pulling together was the case—as reported by Nici Nelson (1982)—of the women in Methare Valley, Kenya, who were engaged in the illegal brewing of beer. It was an occupation with few required skills and could therefore be combined with domestic responsibilities, a special advantage since so many of the women were divorced, widowed, or unmarried. But the illicit nature of their work isolated them and rendered necessary strong protective networks which included kin and friends as well as other *buzaa* brewers. Business problems were met cooperatively; daily crises were weathered by mutual aid:

> . . . keen competition for a limited number of customers makes it functional for members of an effective network to cooperate by brewing alternately. A woman who is in the process of preparing a brew will notify members of her network (both affective and extended) that her batch will be ready on such and such a day. . . . Women utilize links in their effective networks to meet the numerous, inevitable, small daily crises: running out of salt at a crucial moment, a baby crying when several customers are clamouring for attention, needing someone to run an errand, or a cup of tea when one's *jiko* (charcoal stove) is not lit. These daily reciprocal exchanges are part and parcel of "neighborly" behaviour and also include gossiping, joking, mutual hair braiding, and sharing food. [Nelson, 1982, 85]

If these neighborliness standards were not met, sanctions might be invoked, including "deliberate withholding of warning during a police raid" or even eviction.

More familiar to women in the West are such urban groups as the Botswana Council of Women and the YWCA and church women's groups. They provide day-care centers; they build classrooms, clinics, latrines, bus shelters (Rogers, 1979, 105). Such social welfare groups in the female world undoubtedly serve useful functions, but a study in Colombia, Korea, and the Philippines cited by Rogers found that "the most successful groups stressed that nothing compares with 'the perceived economic gain or the accumulation of capital or cash' " (104). And the women of Bangladesh in a Women-for-Women group asked urgently for training aimed at making them self-sufficient (104), a request thoroughly understandable in view of the fact that these economic gains might also pay off in political clout.[27]

Among the Ibo and the Kom of Nigeria, for example, the women who are engaged in trading, marketing, and farming become used to "presenting and defending viewpoints, making and enforcing rules, learning to compromise, and in general developing skills useful in the political arena" (Wipper, 1982, 69). They become "bold, competent women who matter-of-factly handle their own affairs." They acquire skills which give them the self-confidence and self-image to engage in independent political action in what amounts to a dual-gender system. The author of this report concedes that her judgments are subjective, but she believes they are easily supported by observation of the women's behavior. "Any encroachment [by the male world] upon, or abrogation of, their rights, be it by chiefs, agricultural officers, colonial administrators or even the head of state, was met with righteous indignation and determination to resist" (69).

Especially impressive in all these joint undertakings, these working groups, is the extraordinary entrepreneurial skill the women show. Nonliterate in perhaps most cases, relying largely on their own resources and native wit, they constitute a resource of as yet uncharted potential. But only recently has it been recognized. "Colonial officials and early ethnographers were sometimes blind to women's authority structures, organizational activities, and solidarity networks outside the home" (Staudt, 11). Now that research has shown the wide scope of this structural component of the female world, it is becoming not only recognized but also appreciated. Thus in 1979 the then president of the World Bank, Robert McNamara, was recommending to his peers that

> efforts should be made to identify [female] local organizations that have traditionally been important sources of support for women, such as savings and loan societies, production groups, and societies for sharing equipment or tasks. More needs to be known about the dynamics of these organizations so that projects can work through them and enhance rather than destroy, their potential. [22]

This busy, industrious, active female world may continue to be separate but it will almost certainly cease to be invisible.

The emphasis here has been on the structural rather than on the personal aspects of the female world. But it may not be wholly irrelevant at least to nod in the direction of more personal, individual, emotional, intimate aspects. Thus, for example, today

> visitors to the Soviet Union often notice the open physical affection between people of the same sex. It is common to see women holding hands, walking arm in arm, embracing and kissing. Close friendships between women are the norm; given the lack of mobility in Soviet life,

these ties may extend from grade school to old age. As recent films . . . indicate, female friends provide support through crises in relationships with men and in some cases remain closer and more trusted than spouses. Such closeness does not necessarily indicate that lesbianism is accepted or widespread. [Mamanova, 1984, 135]

And Asoka Bandarage reminds us that

while sisterhood may be a new discovery for Western, middle-class house-wives . . . it has long been a reality for women in many sex-segregated societies whether in Asia, the Middle East, in the female-headed, kin networks of the Caribbean and perhaps even in working-class communities in the U.S. . . . Lesbianism, when it exists in these situations, is not politicized either. Nevertheless it must be recognized that the conjugal role relationship is not the central relationship for women in many of these communities and that their emotional needs are met primarily through their relationship to other women. [1983, 8–9][28]

The author then concludes that these women "may be psychologically freer from men, especially their spouses, than their Western, middle-class counterparts."

Separation in these illustrations does not mean that the two worlds described were polar opposites to one another nor imply independence. The separate worlds are, in fact, two sides of the same coin, one the flip side of the other. For although the division of labor does, indeed, separate the two worlds, it also integrates them into organic, as distinguished from mechanical, solidarity. As does also joint parenting of offspring. Nor does the well-nigh global spatial separation of the two worlds imply that they relate to one another everywhere in identical ways.[29]

The actual relationship between the two worlds at any given time or place has reflected the day-by-day, ad hoc adjustments required to meet the encompassing circumstances—political, economic, technological, ecological—that impinged on them. In some parts of the world the separation has been wide and deep, the disparities of status incalculable, the power balance heavily weighted. At the other end of the spectrum have been societies in which the separation has been minimal, disparities of status relatively minor, power more nearly evenly balanced. For the most part, however, the outcome of these adjustments has rarely, if ever, been one of equality between the two worlds. Almost always it has been one of varying degrees of subordination of the female world vis-à-vis the male world. Although in some parts of the world moral superiority might be willingly and happily conceded to the female world, political—in the broadest sense of the term—subordination to the male world has almost universally been incorporated into the female role—in oral tales, prayers, or traditions, or written into laws.

Explaining—usually justifying—such differences in the relationships between the worlds has long been the crux of a considerable amount of male thinking. Either divinity or nature was usually invoked as the basis on which the subordination of the female world rested. Although there have been rebels—Vashti,[30] for example, and the Nigerian women described above—most women have become reconciled, have even colluded with men in maintaining their subordination (Lipman-Blumen, 1984, 52). Since, when change was relatively slow, each generation, born into an ongoing, already functioning system, accepted—as in Chanzeaux—whatever form the status relationship took as natural or even revealed. It might not even be noticed, let alone challenged. Separation was nonpolitical for the most part—but naive in the sense that it was consensual, taken for granted, not based on sophisticated, deliberated policy. It was the way things *were*. It was not an issue. The female world went about its own business and the male world its own, whatever their relative status happened to be. Even when it was painful to women, they learned to accede to the stern Victorian commandment: suffer and be still (Vicinus, 1973).

The number of women worldwide who suffered remained great well into the twentieth century; but the number who were remaining still about it was rapidly declining. The swelling number of protesters in many parts of the globe turned out to be one of the major "news" items of this—and perhaps even of the next—century, part of one of the several recent revolutions in process over the last two centuries as the extrinsic forces that had shaped the relationships between the two worlds in the West were beginning to reshape them.

It had all begun rather inconspicuously, unimpressively, almost shabbily, two centuries ago as sheds were thrown up to protect new machines that could spin faster than human fingers could and both women and children were being taken to work in them. The impact this seemingly insignificant movement was ultimately going to have on the relationship between the two worlds was to take some time to reveal itself, first in the countries where it started and then, finally, everywhere. But in time it did become clear that there was indeed a revolution in process. It was even called "the" industrial revolution. Actually, it was only the first in a train of what was to prove to be many industrial revolutions.

Among the accompaniments and consequences was the restructuring of the female world, facilitating the emergence of women who could earn money, who could be part of the labor force, whose work took them away from the home. In time many became literate and educated. Little by little they began to learn about themselves, a knowledge which was to be an indispensable instrument for shaping their relations with the male world. Cumulative experience in organization, national and international (part III), began to create a ferment that was having an explosive impact in the female world. The relations between the separate worlds which had been so taken for granted, seen for so long as in the very nature of things, came no longer to be carved in stone; they were challengeable. In time they became challenged. They became an issue.

Issues do not appear suddenly, fully sculpted, shaped for all to see. The issue of the relationship between the two worlds emerged from a complex bundle of forces, few more important than the growing awareness by more and more women in more and more places of their own gender identity, of their common concerns, of their potential autonomy vis-à-vis the male world. As women from all over have come into contact with one another, discovered commonalities, the costs as well as the rewards of separation have come under scrutiny. A kind of global female consciousness was emerging. Women were "getting to know" one another. A Feminist Enlightenment was taking place (chapter 6) through whose beams women were also "getting to know" the nature of their oppression (chapters 4, 5, and 6). And something new was being added. They were beginning to be heard, though not necessarily understood, in an international forum, the United Nations.

The Second Committee of the United Nations' World Plan of Action for the Decade of Women[31] included a draft resolution which specified among its objectives the integration of women in all development activities. It recommended that

> International Women's Year 1975 should be devoted to intensified action
> . . . to ensure the full integration of women in the total development
> effort. . . . The U.N. should provide increased assistance . . . to encourage
> and promote the further integration of women into national, regional and
> inter-regional economic development activities . . . and the integration of
> women in development should be a continuing consideration.

Integrationism—the "ism" implies its political nature—was "in."

But what kind? The answer to this question was hinted at in one of the recommendations—tucked away inconspicuously, among the activities calling for special attention—namely, that all agencies in the U.N. development system "ensure that women are included on an *equitable* basis with men on all levels of decision-making which govern the planning and implementation of these programs" (emphasis added). It was this recommendation that was really revolutionary.[32] After centuries, if not millennia, of general consensual acceptance, or at least toleration, of whatever the inequitable status quo relationship happened to be between the two worlds, it was now to be equitable.

As it turned out, the issue—equitable integration—transcended development, transcended even the United Nations itself. It spilled out over all aspects of many societies, it popped up in academic halls as well as in revolutionary councils. The U.N. recommendations for the relations between the two worlds sounded right on key. These were the words to use. These were the sentiments to express. These were the goals to aspire to.

PART TWO

Relations between the Two Worlds: "Equitable Integration"

INTRODUCTION

Equitable integration might, indeed, be "in." But what, actually, did it mean? Did it mean the same thing in Sierra Leone as in the United Kingdom, both members of the U.N. Committee that was recommending it? And how to achieve it? Answers, obviously, would vary from one part of the world to another. The United Nations was not dismayed. Its 1975 World Plan of Action included ideas about how to bring about equitable integration. Since the U.N. was an organization of governments, it addressed itself to governments. It recommended that national machinery such as women's bureaus, advisory committees, commissions, ministries, offices at all levels and in all administrative branches be established to look after women's concerns.[1] Actually, as these recommendations were implemented, they proved to be simply a male-defined form of separatism. The innovations were limited by poor financing; inadequate staffing, and old cultural attitudes validated rather than countered the traditionally inferior status of the female world, often restricting their programs to mere welfare projects which had low priority and were usually subject to control by the male world. Their recommendations could be ignored with impunity.[2] Definitely not models of equitable integration.[3] They could even be counterproductive.[4] In any event, many women soon learned that governments could not be relied on to give women's concerns attention unless female-oriented "non-governmental organizations both influenced and assisted governmental bodies" (Humphrey Institute, 1984, v). Provision had to be made for a separate "women's monitoring and resource-allocation structure" not only where there were women's bureaus, but also in *all* ministries," as complements to such bureaus (Staudt, 1980, 61). Equitable integration was going to be easier to recommend than to implement. It

39

sounded better than it looked.[5] Nevertheless, with some modification, the idea lingered on.[6]

If government agencies were the keystones in the U.N. approach to equitable integration, "projects" might be said to be the keystones in the "modernization" or "development" approach. World War II had left enormous economic dislocations all over the globe. The Marshall Plan of the United States for the restoration of Europe was established to reconstruct technologically advanced societies; and, for societies not yet at that level, there were also plans for their "modernization" or development. Much of the thinking that guided these plans stemmed from President Truman's Point Four policy of 1949, which stated that "greater production was the key to prosperity and peace, and that the key to greater production was wider and more vigorous application of modern science and technical knowledge."

Truman proposed that advanced nations pool their technical resources to help free people of the world to produce more food, clothing, housing, and mechanical power. The problems, as he saw them, were technological, not "people"—certainly not "women"—problems. Implicit was the idea that the people in developing countries were just like people in Western societies, ready, and needing only the training and resources to "catch up."[7] The method for implementing this goal was to be by way of "projects," which varied in many ways. New countries longed for prestigious items like air lines, paper mills, power transmission lines, highways, fertilizer complexes, locomotives. The impact of such projects on the female world was derivative rather than direct. They attracted men to cities leaving women and children back home in rural areas, increasing the spatial separation of the two worlds. They also left the farming work of women relatively unaided.

It would be diversionary to delve further into these early male-oriented modernization efforts. By the late 1960s the results had been disappointing. Great expectations were collapsing into depressing dislocations. In the late 1960s there was, in fact, among theorists and activists a veritable orgy of self-castigation for their "ethnocentric myopia," their "Westernized ethnocentrism." A leading sociologist concluded that we did not in any systematic way know "why some programs succeed by the developers' own standards, while other programs fail" (Sanders, 1969, 173). Four years later the same charge was being made by others:

> . . . development professionals do not know how to carry out an effective program either a big one or a small one. No one knows how—not the U.S. Government, not the Rockefeller Foundation, not the international banks and agencies, not the missionaries. I don't know. You don't know how. No one knows how. [Paddock and Paddock, 1973][8]

And five years later there was "a veritable consensus among scholars in the field that the study of the new nations has reached a state of acute crisis" (Hermassi, 1978, 239). It lacked a compelling paradigm.

The mea culpas of the researchers were doubtless overwrought. Whatever the failures of modernization efforts may have been, the causes were far too complex to be accounted for by their inadequacies. It would take a long time before all the currents impacting on modernization in the middle of the twentieth century could be traced and their part in the disappointing results, if not failures, assessed. Among them, as it is becoming increasingly clear, will surely have to be recognition of the policy errors made in dealing with the female world's part in development.

"Equitable integration" took a different tack in postcolonial contexts. World War II had not only left great economic dislocations but it had also ushered in a time of epochal changes in the political foundations of the world. Great historical forces were blasting through old structures, great empires had fallen; former colonies had become autonomous states struggling to identify themselves out of the rubble; old ones were trying to make a transition from medieval to modern structures. Some of the earlier anticolonial and liberation movements had become revolutionary movements. Great ideologies—socialist and democratic—were competing for the minds and hearts of people everywhere. In many parts of the world leftist movements were wooing the support even of women. For women were needed for a variety of services indispensable to these movements for success—for example: couriers in reconnaissance, nurses in medical centers, links in communication chains, suppliers of food, providers of hideaways, teachers, recruiters of other women, doctors, intelligence agents, even diplomats and fighters. Integrating them into liberation movements was essential (chapter 4). And all the while there were acts of God, like droughts of historical dimensions, to contend with. And a resurgence of religious fundamentalism. Equitable integration had to compete with many survival issues in this bubbling cauldron. Selecting priorities among them became crucial.

The Oxford English Dictionary (OED) defines *integration* in several ways, and it makes a difference which definition one has in mind. It means: "making up of a whole by adding together or combining the separate parts or elements; making whole or entire." It does not distinguish between integration "into" and combining "with." Thus, unless the parameters are suitably defined, integration might well become: absorption, incorporation, assimilation, cooption, enslavement, or disappearance as an individual entity. Nor does it distinguish between integration individually—tokenism—and, more relevant in the present context, collectively.[9]

The OED defines *equitable* as characterized by "equity or fairness" and *equity*, as the "quality of being equal or fair; impartiality; evenhanded dealing; that which is fair and right." It means, however, also: "tolerable; passable; average." *Fair* can be discarded at once. What is considered "fair"—just, legitimate, tolerable, passable, average—is almost wholly a matter of cultural training. What is viewed as "fair" in one society is considered outrageously unfair in another. Or in another time. The growth of civility defines more and more acts as "unfair." The feudal system came in time to seem unfair. So did slavery. The privileges accorded to human beings because they have male bodies are coming to seem unfair to more and more people. The work overload which women all over the globe endure is increasingly being viewed as unfair. Thus it is coming to seem "fair" to people that—if women are to continue to bear and nurse infants and care for small children—the occupational and professional costs of such time out of the work force be recognized and compensated for. Although equality, impartiality, or evenhandedness are not proving easy to achieve, it is still considered important that the words specified for integration by the United Nations—"on an equitable basis"—be there, ready to be used when a society is ready for them.

Problems of equitable relationships are not limited to those between the two worlds. For oppression, however different the forms it takes, can occur on any human stage. Status inequities within the female world may take characteristic forms but they are no less oppressive than are those in its relationships vis-à-vis the male world[10] (appendix B).

Part II looks at equitable relationships in both development (chapter 3) and in the anti- and postcolonial contexts (chapters 4 and 5), and also within the female world itself (chapter 6).

CHAPTER THREE

Separatism and Integrationism in the Context of Development

Not everyone had gone along with the Point Four idea of modernization as an exclusively technological problem. In 1955, for example, the World Federation for Mental Health had published a manual, edited by Margaret Mead, designed to show that it was also a "people" problem. It was designed to show how to introduce new crops, new systems of public health, or other projects without too seriously upsetting native cultures, including their version of the relationship between the two worlds. It emphasized the importance of going slow, of not upsetting the applecart. Change in one part of a culture could reverberate widely, with unanticipated consequences. The thinking was in terms of indigenous development rather than of technological modernization imposed from the outside. Change could certainly not be imposed by fiat. Cases from the Tiv of Nigeria and from Palau were used as illustrative.

The British colonial administrators among the Tiv, for example, had thought it safe to declare that "women were now free to choose whom they would marry, and free to divorce a man who was unacceptable; or so, at any rate, the Tiv women interpreted the ruling" (Mead, 1955, 123). Now that British law had given women "claws to scratch with," they were becoming uppity. "A woman could leave her old husband since the British had said that 'women could do as they wished' " (124). Because of the detailed sexual division of labor in the household and in the field, anything that threatened the breakup of a marriage in this way was harmful to productivity.

If the Tiv case showed a change that enhanced female power, the Palau example showed one that detracted from it. When men's work had become the major source of cash income, as it had in the early modernization projects, "the traditional opportunities of women to acquire wealth . . . have been circumscribed or eliminated, which in turn . . .

43

reduced their social power" (141).[1] Clearly any tinkering with a given status quo was like crossing a minefield.

In 1970, as noted in chapter 2, Ester Boserup was introducing a new perspective into thinking about economic development. The whole approach to date had been misguided, filled with errors resulting from ignoring or misreading or misinterpreting the contribution of the female world to productivity, especially of food (chapter 1). She threw into the hopper a new model for thinking about—especially rural—development. Despite the anthropologists' warnings against prematurely imposing Western lifestyles and patterns on developing countries, the planners had brought their Western gender roles with them and had tried to impose them on other countries. They had, essentially, all but painted over half of the producing population in these countries, the women, that is, who did a large part of the world's farming, who, in fact, produced half—in Africa, probably even more—of the world's food (Blumberg, 1979, 447). A continent that had once been able to feed itself was now a basket case, having to import food. Women researchers became involved and began to document the results of such policy errors, which showed

> exactly how discrimination against women, planned into almost all rural development programs, not only greatly damages women and children but often leads to the failure of the programs. They explain why after more than 30 years of internationally financed development in many countries women are worse off than before and why per capita food production is decreasing, especially in Africa, with terrible results for women and children. [Hosken, 1984, 8]

Something new and special—concern for women—was being added. Development would never be the same again.

It took some time for Boserup's ideas to seep in. But in time they did.[2] By 1974 the reorientation of thinking about development which Boserup had introduced in 1970 was beginning to have an impact. Projects of a different genre came to the fore, oriented not necessarily toward immediate profitability but rather toward development of "human capital" and thus ultimately toward profitability. Some were funded by governmental and U.N. agencies such as "the U.S. Agency for International Development (AID); Women in Development (WID); the U.N. Food and Agricultural Organization (FAO); the U.N. Education, Science, and Culture Organization (UNESCO); the World Health Organization (WHO); and the U.N. Voluntary Fund for the Decade for Women (VFDW), and some by private agencies such as foundations and funds (Carnegie, Rockefeller, Ford) and small voluntary groups, especially of European and U.S. women.[3] The emphasis came in time to include small, mainly rural projects. The purposes were usually twofold: to increase the productivity of female work, thus increasing income, and to increase "human capital" by way of education, training, skill acquisition, improved health. The two purposes were not mutually exclusive; often the process of increasing income involved increasing human capital.

The beneficiaries of these projects were to be among the roughly three-fourths to four-fifths of the women we met in chapter 1 who live in rural areas. But also in some cases, poor women in urban slums, for example the Madras credit project to be described below. Now the projects were smaller and closer to home, such as a community health or nutrition project, a well to make potable water available, a latrine, a family garden, better food preservation and processing techniques. Low prestige items, of little or no interest at all to international banking establishments with eyes on large-scale operations.[4]

Such changes in the character of projects did not come without opposition, especially from the male-world financial establishment. Robert McNamara, one-time head of the World Bank, had had to make a strong pitch for them:

> Is it a really sound strategy to devote a significant part of the world's resources to increasing the productivity of small-scale subsistence agriculture mainly carried out by women? Would it not be wiser to concentrate on the modern urban sector in the hope that its high rate of growth would filter down to the rural poor? The answer, I believe, is no. Without rapid progress in small-holder agriculture throughout the developing world, there is little hope either of achieving long-term stable economic growth or of significantly reducing the levels of absolute poverty [report at the Annual Meeting of the World Bank, Nairobi, *Washington Post*, July 1981].

In 1977 the World Bank added to its staff an adviser on women-related decisions.

It was to take a long time for students of development to recognize the errors in policy that had hamstrung their programs, especially policies dealing with women. Not until Boserup called attention to them did the matter attract research as well as policy attention. When it did, women scholars examined the cache of data that had been generated by experience to date, pinpointing the separatist-integrationist issue as it showed up in that experience and teasing out the pros and cons of both options.

Whatever the relationship between the two worlds may have been indigenously in the past, in areas where development projects were planned, that relationship was likely to be, in varying degrees, one of subordination for women. Christian missionaries all over the globe had, for many years, been bringing with them—along with the schools and

GOSHEN COLLEGE LIBRARY

GOSHEN, INDIANA

hospitals they established for women—Western models of this relationship, including female subordination. Colonial administrators had also brought Western patterns with them. In Senegal, for example, the daughters of the elite had been trained to be suitably subordinate wives for "chiefs, notables, and functionaries"; other women were trained to be skilled in household arts, hygiene, and child care (Hardy, D., quoted in Barthel, 1975). So achieving equitable integration was not going to be easy. Certainly not by fiat. How then?

The characteristically U.S. reply was: let's find out by way of research. Study the experience with different kinds of projects—separatist and integrationist—and judge how well they have achieved specified goals. These grass-roots projects were not, of course, nor were they intended to be, scientific experiments strictly speaking. But there was a modicum of control in the sense that they were planned, innovative, sometimes creative, and offered stages on which the relationship between the two worlds—separatist or integrative—could be played out and observed in the process.

> Much of the assessment of action programs is irregular and, often by necessity, based upon personal judgments of supporters or critics, impressions, anecdotes, testimonials, and miscellaneous information available for the evaluation. In recent years, however, there has been a striking change in attitudes toward evaluation activities and the type and quality of evidence that is acceptable for determining the relative success or failure of social-action programs. . . . A scientific approach to the assessment of a program's achievements is the hallmark of modern evaluation research. [Wright, 1968, 5: 197, 198]

It was inevitable that much of the research called for in assessing success or failure of projects would fall far short of such high standards for evaluation. No claim for such scientific adequacy was made by the researchers. But beginnings were being made. The projects could at least supply data for helping to evaluate the relative advantages and disadvantages for women of separate or integrated projects.

It may seem inconsistent or illogical to look at separate projects as building blocks of equitable integration. Actually they may be viewed as aspects of "affirmative action." They prepared members of the female world to participate as equals with the male world in all relevant decision making situations. Without such preparation the odds were that they would be out-talked or silenced in discussions of policy.

Although the U.S. Agency for International Development (AID) had been attempting since 1974 to improve the role of women in development, it was not until 1979, when a report on evaluation of projects for women became available, that there were enough data to make feasible an assessment of the impact of projects on women.[5] Even then, however, most of the projects were too recent to have proved—or not to have proved—to have helped women. Furthermore, measurement techniques for judging results were inadequate.[6] Still, it was something to start with. Ruth Dixon, of WID (Women in Development), was among those who took up the challenge (1980).

Using intended beneficiaries as a basis, she classified into four categories 32 of the available studies where there was at least a modicum of data: (1) women-only or separatist projects in which women were specifically named as beneficiaries; (2) general projects, with a women's component; (3) general projects, with no specific women's component; and (4) men-only or separatist male projects (98). The second and third would fall into the integrationist category, the first and last, into the separatist, but not necessarily reflecting identical definitions of separate. When the research challenge came it was not so much the separateness per se that fired its motor as it was the specifications that defined it, or the ostensible purpose of the project.

One of the definitions of *separate* in the OED is "kept away" from, implying exclusion imposed by others; unless the parameters are suitably defined it might well become imposed isolation, segregation, deprivation, even exploitation. The second definition is "withdrawn or divided . . . so as to have independent existence by itself," but it does not specify autonomy. As in the cases of "integration" noted above, the issue inhered in the distance imposed between the two worlds; on whose terms the rewards and penalties were assessed; who defined its parameters and hence their consequences for power; who benefited and who suffered from them. In brief, the political nature of the relationship between the separate worlds.

The separation of the two worlds illustrated in chapter 2 might be characterized as "natural", not in any deterministic or genetic way but as the product of a long and checkered history which included adaptations to Acts of God and man. It was imposed on each generation by culture; it was also cherished by the female world itself. In the context of development projects the concept was of separatism emphasizing the positive aspects, not "keeping out" (category 4) but "autonomy within" (category 1).

Dixon noted, however, that the actual participants did not always conform to the intended beneficiaries. Thus, for example, in Paraguay a general "livestock training project" offered to farmers with no specific women's component became a de facto women's project when an unanticipated 90 percent of those enrolled in the course turned out to be women (98). The planners, perhaps on the basis of Western role patterns, had probably taken it for granted that most of the participants would be male. And sometimes the beneficiaries of projects were male, not by design of the planners, but because of the relative status assigned to their work.[7] The application of research to improving food crops which women grew lagged behind its application to cash crops which men grew (Nji, 1980, 7). Thus when irrigation or other projects extended cultivatable land, it tended to be allocated to the male cash crops and the female-cultivated food crops were pushed farther into the less suitable soil (8).

Regardless of the complexities involved in any classification, the issue was reduced to the relative benefits for women as between women-only or separate projects and mixed-gender, general, or integrated projects. On the basis of a careful analysis of the relative benefits accruing to women in these two kinds of projects, Dixon found that the pros and cons of each added up to sometimes equivocal conclusions.

Despite Finsterbusch's relatively low emphasis on participation, Dixon viewed it as a basic criterion of success in achieving equitable integration. For no matter what the specified goals of any project might be—productivity and income or increased human capital in the form of better health and nutrition—participation was a first step in benefitting from it. In general, Dixon found that projects in which women themselves played an active part in designing, planning, and implementing tended to attract more female participation in decision making at both staff and beneficiary levels than did those in which they were passive "targets" for projects designed, planned, and implemented by outsiders. Unless a project specifically designated women as beneficiaries, participation was unlikely to be actively sought (99). The women were, in fact, loathe to take part. Even when women were specifically named as beneficiaries, participation could not be taken for granted; it had to be stimulated, encouraged. In effect, for many women it was either participation in separate projects or no participation at all.

When the women did participate, however, the rewards were substantial. Leadership skills developed. The women were in a position to present their point of view and they learned how to do it. They were, so to speak, given the floor. The audience paid attention to what they had to say, recognized their issues.[8] In Afghanistan, for example, a proposal to establish " 'women's houses' with nurseries attached, where women would assemble for income-earning activities such as rug weaving, milk and cheese production" (Hunte, 1978, cited in Staudt, 1980, 31, 41) would not likely have occurred in male-run projects or, if proposed by women, have been accorded much attention. The skills thus developed in women-only projects served also as training in skills for later participation in general or mixed projects (30).

In some parts of the world where separateness meant isolation, women-only projects could mitigate it. Women could participate in group projects with other women, giving them at least this much access to a wider world (Piepmeir, 1980, 29). There has long been recognition of the negative aspects of one of the most highly structured forms of separatism—purdah—but Hanna Papanek has reminded us of some of the positive ones. Where it has prevailed, for example, there have had to be women trained in the professions to serve in the female world as teachers and physicians, and now—as is happening today in some separatist countries—even as bankers for women.[9] Although currently most of the female staff for women's banks are foreigners, the hope is that in time they will be "Saudi-ized." Hanna Papanek has also noted the qualities and attributes such professionals may achieve as well as the self-confidence women may acquire when they are accustomed to strong support from their world. Urban Turkish women, for example, whether or not they observe purdah, "are able to maintain a poised detachment when working with them [men], because they are accustomed to a situation in which colleagues and companions are other women" (1971, 523).

A final pro is the fact that, as we saw in chapter 2, women in many parts of the global female world already have a considerable amount of experience in autonomous groups which provides a basis for expansion in development projects (Dixon, 1054; Hoskins, 1980, 40–41). It also shows the value of such experience for women. Piepmeir suggests that where they do have strong groups, women may achieve a considerable amount of power:

> A comparison of four preindustrial societies suggests that women's collective utilization of their economic and labor resources is a prerequisite to public participation. Among the Mbuti and Lovedu, where women's productive activities are *collective* and extend beyond the household, women are relatively equal to men. Women represent themselves in legal proceedings, participate in socializing opportunities and hold political office. [1980, 8]

In contrast, "Pondo and Ganda women who work *individually* and produce for the household alone, face active discrimination in a variety of spheres" (8). The existence of common individual problems and interests among isolated individuals does not seem automatically to produce a shared perception of them to serve as a basis for organized action. Introducing women-only projects might well create such a shared perception—as well as greater access to and utilization of resources. Confirmation comes from a quite different source, namely China:

> The value of separate women's groups in defining the separate interests of women and establishing their own power base from which they could confidently and collectively participate in the political affairs of the villages had been definitely established by a document published in 1948. It reported that in areas where there was an absence of female solidarity

groups, women felt uncomfortable in the presence of men and few had spoken at any of the village meetings. The women themselves had admitted that if "we are speaking with men present those who ought to say a lot say very little." In contrast it was found that only in those areas where solidarity groups had been established did women attend meetings enthusiastically, lose their reserve in speaking publicly, and participate in political affairs. Their establishment had encouraged women to speak out for themselves and openly and directly participate in village affairs. [Croll, 1982, citing Davin, 1973]

Piepmeir's data raise a question. Did women-only projects succeed because they were able to attract the participation of women, or did women participate in them because they were accustomed to joint group behavior? Perhaps women like those among the Mbuti and Lovedu, used to collective activity, would be ready for making themselves felt also in general projects, even in men-only ones?

However beneficial participation in women-only projects might be to women, there were also cons to it. Women-only projects were, first of all, likely to receive relatively little funding (Dixon, 99; Staudt, 39; Rogers, 105). They were, nevertheless, charged with more responsibilities than it was possible to carry with their limited resources; expectations were greater. They could, further, easily become isolated and marginalized or coopted or forgotten (Staudt, 39; Basch and Bruley, 1981). They were likely to be technologically weak and lacking in a macroeconomic perspective (Hoskins, 40), a weakness which, however, could be fairly easily overcome. But if it were not, they were vulnerable to male takeover (Dixon, 31–32; Blumberg, 1979). Also on the debit side was the potential for male-female conflict when women-only projects were too successful. In western Kenya, for example, one male-initiated effort to mobilize women "developed into such a successful judicial and political representational system" that the men could not tolerate it (Staudt, 29).[10] It collapsed because the "male elders withdrew their support" (42–43).

From a wider cultural point of view was the con argument that the social costs might be too great, that any tampering with the gender-related status quo would "adversely affect the survival balance of those families near the margin of subsistence" (Staudt, 40). We noted earlier the case of the Tiv, which showed that if separatism empowered women, however minimally, it was surely a con. It might even invite state intervention and control (Staudt, 40). The cure might be worse than the disease. In reply to such fear of disruption posed by segregated organizational strategies, the experience of the USSR was invoked:

> The dangers that sex-segregated organizational strategies divide communities appear to be slight. An analysis of the unsuccessful Soviet attempts to polarize Central Asia during the 1920s indicates that sex

[gender] roles are less susceptible to polarization than are class roles. [Massell, 1974, 397]

In Staudt's view this fear was unfounded in the first place because "women's intimate relationship and residence with men and the bonds of children, forestall polarization between men and women" (42; chapter 6, this book). A final con argument was that accepting sex-based organizations rather than challenging them merely perpetuated sex and gender disparities (41).

These gender-related criticisms of separate women-only projects raised basic questions about criteria. What standards of effectiveness should be applied in evaluating projects?[11] How much improvement in benefits to women should be sought? How much change was acceptable? How "uppity" was it sociologically tolerable for women to become? The answers were not easy to come by. Degree of success was "unanswerable by scientific research. It remains a matter for judgment" (Wright, 201). But whose judgment? If a project is so effective for women that it upsets a particular gender status quo should it be viewed as successful?[12]

Yes was one reply. Projects are successful only if they do upset a particular gender status quo, especially if the kinds of change approach those suggested by Dixon as ideal goals of projects, namely the achievement of equitable integration by way of a "Bill of Rights" for women. Without ignoring economic well-being[13]—including economic independence, which women themselves rank high—she states physical[14] and social well-being as ideal goals. Social well-being is broadly conceptualized as including knowledge, power, and prestige. Knowledge included specific skills as well as general knowledge measured in terms of literacy and numeracy, vocational skills, and understanding of the "interplay of socioeconomic and political forces in the household, the community, and the larger society" (71). The radical implications of this benefit for the female world are suggested by Dixon's comments:

> One could . . . consider the impact of the project [with this knowledge goal] on women's general knowledge, or world view. In societies placing severe restrictions on women's physical mobility, the limits of their social world are likely to be narrow and their social and political dependence on men is intensified. How does a project affect their access to knowledge and experience of the outside world? Are there deliberate efforts to "conscientization" among beneficiaries, that is, of stimulating a critical understanding of the dynamics of household and community social structures and of possible strategies for change? Do these reach women as well as men? [73]

Even more revolutionary was Dixon's second component of social well-being—power—including autonomy, as expressed in self-reliance, freedom from coercion, freedom of physical movement, and especially "participation in household and community decision-making . . . and mobilization for group action" (73). The benefits of group action could be measured "by the number and strength of linkages among individuals and groups, the degree of shared self-interest or group consciousness, and the capacity for group action" (73). Dixon's third ideal benefit—prestige—refers to a newly emerging "demand" now spreading through the female world and to a recognition of its denial as part of female oppression. Prestige includes self-esteem, a subjective belief in one's own value as a person, "the esteem of others as measured by the degree to which a person or group is 'objectively' valued by other household or community members" (76). Project designers might well ask "how does the project affect women's feelings about themselves?" (76). Lack of sensitivity to the possibly negative consequences of projects for women's self-feeling, status, or prestige illustrated "how even the best intentioned projects can have unanticipated deleterious consequences" (78).[15] Dixon recognized that "some tradeoffs are probably inevitable in any development project: one cannot usually move effectively on all fronts at once. The major issue here is to ensure that the costs are not paid disproportionately by those least able to pay them," usually women (79). In this quiet, unostentatious call for a bill of rights guaranteeing equitable integration, Dixon was making statements no less revolutionary in their context than those made by United States men in Philadelphia in 1783 in a quite different context.

Just as there were pros and cons for separate women-only projects as ways of achieving equitable integration, so also were there pros and cons for integrationist projects as ways of achieving it. It is, perhaps, a fallacy to refer to the general projects as integrationist since, as one of the major defects they showed was that women were not actually integrated into them. Still, for the sake of consistency the idea of including them, in whatever form, is accepted here as representing an integrationist position, however well or poorly implemented.

The integrationist, as well as the separatist, projects garnered both favorable and unfavorable evaluations on the basis of grass-roots development experience. In some cases the pros and cons of the integrationist projects were the flip side of the cons and pros of separatist ones.

The pros of joint or integrated projects are easily summed up. Because separate women's projects were, on the basis of traditional biases, so poorly funded, women were "likely to benefit more extensively by being fully integrated into general schemes" (Dixon, 99) which were larger and better funded (Rogers, 105). Better technical information was also available in such general projects (Hoskins, 40–41).

A common form which more theoretical arguments for the integrationist policy has taken is the plea for a humanistic rather than a feminist point of view, a lessening of emphasis on differences, and more emphasis on a "blended" world—a good life for all human beings, not just for women. Not emphasis on male and female worlds but on a shared world. Emphasis on a shared world has, in fact, been the documentable position of women, at least in the United States. An examination of their voting behavior, of their political activism, of the record of women legislators shows that the issues they have tended to support have, indeed, been humanistic or humanitarian—food, health, peace—rather than strictly feminist ones (Bernard, 1981). The difficulties lie in the outcome. When the humanitarian goal has been achieved—there is, let us say, more food—women are still less well off than men, girls less so than boys. Such an approach, however it is intended to work, tends almost always to turn out to be a male-oriented one.

Among other pros of the integrationist policy is that it sounds so fair. It is, in a way, a form of the Hegelian thesis-antithesis-synthesis, best-of-both-worlds paradigm. It seems to solve the issue or, at least, to put it to rest. All too often it turns out to be the best of the (coopted female) lamb inside the male wolf.

A major negative for integrationism is, in fact, the hazard it presents for cooption. In the United States in the nineteenth century one of the strategies used by large corporations against labor unions was to hire away their leaders, that is, to "coopt" them. A cynical or disillusioned leader might justify his defection by the cliché that "if you can't lick 'em, join 'em." Or that he could "bore from within" more effectively than attack from the outside. In the female world, cooption may not be so barefaced, but the results are similar. Leaders of women's groups, coopted into a male-oriented system such as those recommended by the U.N., became dependent on it for survival. "Such dependency complicates goal attainment and strains leader-member relations. Indeed, cooption can result in considerable exploitation of members" (Staudt, 36). For coopted leaders tend to identify with those who hold the power and to neglect the membership of their own group. They come to function, rather, "as an appendage of the coopting institution" (39). In such groups there is, not unexpectedly, a loss of solidarity or community consciousness among the members themselves.

Kenneth Little offers a case in point from Kenya. There a study of women's organizations found that there was, in effect, a "Government-patron alliance serving to block the militant women's efforts to force the Government's hand" (1973, 196). The leaders in the women's organizations were recruited to perform trivial political functions—attending embassy parties, presenting awards, making speeches, officiating at prize-giving days, teas, hand-shaking—which fit in "nicely with the Government's 'do-nothingness' and propensity for ceremony rather than actions" (196). Little was writing in 1973 and he concluded his discussion with the question: will these coopted elite women "fight for women's rights or will they . . . be co-opted into the political elite, succumb to the role of patron, and lose any deep commitment to women's goals?" (198). When the coopted women serve as official representatives in national and international meetings of one kind or another they may, indeed, in Little's 1973 words, "lose any deep commitment to women's goals".[16]

The cons of integrationism are magnified in highly separatist societies, for just as an existing separating status quo is a plus for separatist policies, so is it a minus for integrationist strategies. In highly separatist societies, participation by women in mixed-gender groups is viewed as inappropriate:

> In a Tanzanian pilot project which used dialogue to develop a participatory approach to solving grain storage problems, special efforts were made to attract women to discussion groups, to little avail. Women viewed these discussions as formal meetings in which they do not customarily participate. [Staudt, 41]

Staudt comments that "separate meetings for women should have been tried." She cites the case of Mothers' Clubs in Korea as an example of the need to provide peer support for such risk-taking activities as participation in mixed groups.

One overriding con for mixed-gender projects is that, in general, the experience in development corroborates the findings from experimental research in the United States which has shown that in mixed-gender groups, unless there was a great preponderance of women, men tended to outtalk and out–influence women by way of both spoken and body language. They seemed to interrupt more than did women. Their style of discourse was more combative; that of women more collaborative. The vocabulary permitted to men was more forceful than that permitted to women. Body language—"the way we sit, use space, stare, cock our heads, or touch one another" (Henley, 1977)—was also biased in favor of men. The men were larger and had louder voices.

> Male domination is experienced through various verbal and non-verbal controlling behaviors, such as interruption, staring, touching, and postural displays of superiority by males. . . . Those are part of women's non-verbal experience, the experience of external domination. Another aspect of women's non-verbal experience is the internal prescription, often non-conscious, to behave in certain ways. Examples of this prescription are the non-verbal norms of condensing the body, taking up little personal space, lowering the eyes, smiling, cocking the head, and canting the body. . . . A third aspect of women's non-verbal world . . . is that of behavior not associated with external domination of internal prescrip-

tion—the behavior emitted by women for their particular needs and expressing their particular attitudes and values. [Henley, 1985, 216]

Lockheed and Hall summarize some of the research work on male and female behavior in mixed-gender groups in the U.S.

> Men are more active than women; that is, the average man initiates more verbal acts than the average woman. . . . Men are more influential than women. . . . Men initiate a higher proportion of their acts than women in task-oriented categories of behavior, while women initiate a higher proportion of their acts in social-emotional categories [1976, 121].

Lockheed and Hall do not, however, explain these findings on the basis of sex per se. For they found that in separate one-sex groups, there were no differences between males and females in verbal activity (119). Thus, in another study they found that disproportionate male leadership in mixed-gender groups at the expense of females, was susceptible to intervention (1976, 59). Susceptible, but not overwhelmingly so. "Eliminating the source of status differentiation requires the re-evaluation of men and women in society, a formidable task which is not likely to occur overnight" (121). Certainly no more so in developing countries than in the United States. In Zimbabwe, for example, there was "a very strong tradition; we are told we are women and should stay in the back; we should not speak out; we even look down upon our own women who would speak up. This is how we are brought up" (Zimbabwe Women's Bureau, 1981, 45). And even in ostensibly egalitarian contexts, the male advantage prevails. Thus a Hungarian Marxist notes that even "in movements where men and women work side by side, women are not able to free themselves from century-old traditions. Women are silent; men speak. Women accept men's domineering role and their intellectual leadership, even if they oppose it on a theoretical level" (Heller, 1982, 29), thus colluding with men (Lipman-Blumen, 1984).

As a result of such interaction patterns, as well as other physical and institutional advantages men have in mixed-gender groups, and because so much of human thinking has been from a male perspective, it is usually the male point of view which tends to pervade and to prevail in mixed-gender groups, whatever the issue that is being dealt with. Thus, for example, when the women in one project were opposed to buying a pickup truck "because they had no experience with one and felt renting these services would be cheaper, the men from the union talked the women into buying it" (Dixon, 23). From this and other examples, Dixon concluded that "when women's programs are affiliated with larger male-dominated institutions, decision making on major policy issues tends to be transferred to men in the parent institution" (23). In Bolivia, even in cases when projects were decided on and implemented by local female staff, the "overall guidelines . . . were set by men at the national level" (24). In India, as in Bolivia and Africa, gender-integrated "cooperatives rarely permit women to develop leadership and management skills because men tend to dominate those roles" (Dixon, 41).

In addition to depriving women of the opportunity to acquire leadership and management skills, mixed-gender projects gave them little "access to the forum," the opportunity, that is, even to present their case or to get differences recognized. Or, if recognized, to be given high priority. In mixed-gender groups "women's interests are often given low priority, regardless of the society's ideological persuasion" (41). And, whatever priority was assigned to women's issues, they were likely to be watered down by the time they surfaced (58). In any event, the uniqueness of their needs was not recognized or adequately dealt with. In brief, unless women had support and were given fully autonomous space of their own, their point of view was ignored, buried in the overall program (Piepmeir, 24–26). To the disadvantage of the project as a whole: "Without sufficient resources and power to press claims and acquire bargaining leverage, those resources [that] women bring to organizations have often been appropriated by existing [male] leadership" (Dixon, 41). The result has been not equitable integration but loss of influence by default.

Policies with respect to separatism or integrationism are related to ideological positions with respect to sex and gender differences. Judith Lorber has analyzed this relationship in terms of "minimalism" and maximalism," the first referring to an ideology that plays down sex and gender differences because they have been used to justify male oppression of women, and the second referring to an ideology that emphasizes such differences because they may be a source of general enrichment (1981, 61). Lorber states some of the hazards for women of minimalist—integrationist—policies such as: loss of identity, absorption into the male world "without group social support and without a means of defense against subtle, informal types of discriminatory treatment" (62). In the long run maximalism—separatism—might increase social power by giving women a critical mass. Specifically, in the short run this involves "affirmative action," that is separate female organizations, coalitions, and networks as means for creating political, professional, economic, and cultural power (64). In this conclusion Lorber agrees with Staudt that separatism may be a necessary transition at least until the final goal of equitable integration becomes feasible.

Just as most human knowledge is based on the male perspective, so also is much of contemporary knowledge based on Western experience. Thus most of what we know about development projects is from the perspective of the donors or sponsors. But since turnabout is fair play, it is worth looking at projects from the point of view of the women for whom they are designed.

Female separate projects are at a competitive disadvantage in regard to male projects vis-á-vis potential donors. Thus, at a 1981 feminist meeting of Latin American and Caribbean women, Figueroa and Anderson pointed out that:

> Women's grassroots organisations are much more fragile than men's. The men have far more experience in labour unions and political parties; they can read and write and keep accounts, and they know parliamentary procedures better than women do. Their greater mobility and more wide-ranging work experiences give them greater "savvy" when the issue is analysing the motives of a potential donor. The very nature of the problems the women's committees address makes it easier for them to be "bought"; it is difficult to refuse a package of aid which includes milk rations for children, whatever the conditions for acceptance may be. [1981, 14]

From Zambia has come a severe feminist-political criticism of the whole project approach to development. Too many projects concentrate on welfare and ameliorative changes "rather than on alternatives in the structural position of women in the economic, political and social spheres" (Muchena, 1985, 16), as though one could solve women's problems by way of knitting, sewing, hygiene, nutrition, and income-generating activities. Reliance on this "project approach" has meant that most women are not integrated into development but are left out of mainstream growth. Other reasons why they are excluded are "ideological, cultural, and in part due to women's own negative self-images and their responses to marginal positions" (16). Women must abandon the piecemeal project approach; more attention should be given to planning, monitoring, evaluating. They should learn to exert pressure, realize the power of the vote and how to use it to bargain for "equal political, economic, and social opportunities" (16) despite the male "defensiveness towards efforts to emancipate women."

In Peru, the dangers of cooption by donors were often contraproductive. "With restricted budgets at their disposal and the constraint of having to justify the work they do to the financing institutions, these groups have become 'clubs for insiders,' regarding new women who would like to become involved [in the project] as a threat and a strain on their limited resources" (Fuller, 1983, iv). These women allay their guilt by helping poor women; the result is "compromise and—survival." A far cry from Staudt's project ideals.

The Second Latin American and Caribbean Feminist Meeting in Lima, Peru, in 1984, included a workshop on development programs

with participants from (mainly European) donor agencies, private institutions or centers dealing with projects, and academic and exiled
women. They objected to projects dealing with women only as mothers;
they called for new criteria for project proposals, implementation, and
evaluation. Some projects dealt with social welfare, urban planning,
health services and were usually directed by men. There was much
concern among these women about dependence on outside financing.
European participants suggested that contacts with European feminist
groups which, though able to supply only small funds, were more
feminist in organization and perspective than larger, wealthier hierarchical international aid agencies. Ideally development would be autonomous: "Feminist work depends much more on the initiative of the
women involved, who find their own answers to their problems through
organizing themselves. Women must become aware of their situation as
a first step towards real development" (21). Time was essential for
women; "affirmative action" was needed.

> Managing development projects is a challenge for women. They are at a
> disadvantage because of lack of practice in having responsibility for large
> sums of money and staff movements. Research to support projects . . .
> should provide grassroots women with the conceptual and analytical
> tools to help them determine their own development. . . . Development
> agencies in general seek "cheap development," involving a minimum
> investment in agents or promotors of change. In view of this we must seek
> ways of bringing about the elaboration of new evaluation criteria which
> we ourselves propose and which are capable of recognizing subtle, but
> deep and long-lasting changes. [22]

Another feminist critique was the charge that

> even to this day, the most ardent proponents of integrating women into
> development have not realized that neither mainstream nor Marxist mod-
> els have room for women. . . . Society's acceptance of male-domination
> has pervaded development work. Though much lip service has been paid
> to the equal participation of women in the male-dominated development
> circles, this has remained by and large "integration" without much
> thought or attempt towards genuine sharing with women. [Anand, 1983,
> 6]

Then there was the critique of the "pseudo-feminist myth" that
women necessarily wanted to integrate into a male system illustrated
by the South Yemen woman who did not want to integrate into the
intellectually undeveloped world of the men (Molyneux, 1977). It was
"important to realize that development also means knowing when to
reject bad solutions which are imposed on us" (Second Feminist Meeting, Lima, 1984, 22).

So what do all these pros and cons add up to? All these criticisms and critiques? What's the score?

Since both separation and integration are inherent in any society, there is no alternative to some kind of modus vivendi between the female and male worlds. Because the extinction of neither is imminent, both are destined to share the same earth. The issues become one having to do with the nature of the accommodation, of the integration which, until today, has tended in most societies to be asymmetrical, favoring the male world. Still, for a variety of reasons—economic, political, sociological, technological—this accommodation is no longer appropriate or acceptable in many parts of the female world. Nor is the male world consistent. It may look on integrationist attempts by the female world as an unwelcome invasion of its turf. When, however, separation becomes separatist—a deliberate policy of withdrawal by women of essential female support from the male world—it is rejected. Equitable integration in brief is not an easily achieved goal. The most realistic conclusion that one can arrive at for the present is that there is as yet no all-purpose solution. But research, theorizing, experimenting, paradigm construction are now going on in many parts of the female world which are seeking to arrive at suitable new answers and, given time, may approach acceptable ones.

In view of the ambiguities of the results from grass-roots experience, Staudt concludes that the idea—equitable integrated programs—must be compromised or at least tempered:

> Although sexually integrated organizations are ideal, the need to support a transitional period of sex-separate organizations has been emphasized. First because separateness is a strong tradition in many societies, and second [because] such separateness provides women with the opportunity to develop leadership skills and to accumulate resources for leverage and coalition building with other groups. . . . Until women are integrated into mixed-sex organizations and institutions at all levels, they will remain marginal to the mainstream. In the meantime, however, separation permits the development of organizational capacity, skills, and resources for leverage in mainstream interaction. [58, 42]

Separation is thus seen by Staudt as a transitional phase on the way to an ultimate integration, a time-limited accommodation to an unsympathetic, at least inauspicious, status quo. Without such a plan, lacking structure and resources, attempts to integrate women equitably will lack focus. Some form of "affirmative action" is called for.

Several kinds of such affirmative action have been proposed. One is suggested by Dixon, who envisions a form of integration in which the position of women is protected. According to her review of the evaluations of Women-in-Development projects, if every general project were to include a women's component commanding half of the resources to be allocated among beneficiaries, the intensive and extensive qualities of both separatist and integrationist approaches could be maximized (99). In 1982, the U.N. Economic and Social Commission did, in effect, urge just such a form of affirmative action on its Development Programme, requesting it "to allocate funds from their existing budgets to promote the economic development of women" (Resolution 1982/19, 2). A "quota" solution has also been recommended, this time by the Zimbabwe Women's Bureau in a somewhat different—political—context:

> Since the integration of women into the decision-making process is an absolute prerequisite to the social as well as economic development of the rural areas and the country as a whole . . . the conservative attitudes that continue to prevent women from exercising their capabilities [must be counteracted. It was therefore] recommended that a minimum number of seats on the local councils be set aside for women. [Zimbabwe Women's Bureau, 1981, 43]

The Zimbabwe affirmative action took the form of counteracting the "conservative attitudes that continue to prevent women from exercising their capabilities," not only in the male world but in the female world as well. Consciousness raising was one form of such counteracting; so was so-called assertiveness training, that is, giving women opportunities to learn how to make their case. For presumably integrated groups would not be mere assemblages of individuals in which (from what we know from research about the behavior of women and men in mixed groups) men would prevail, but joint councils of members representing the female and male worlds, each voting as separate blocs, sometimes in coalitions, sometimes not. Successful coalitioning, if it was to avoid cooption, presupposed strength, autonomy, self-confidence, leadership skills. And developing these qualities calls for a limited period of separation during which the female world could acquire them in addition to the conviction of the validity of its own perspective. The female world might, thus, also learn how to use the strength that this knowledge and understanding could generate. This might be the most effective form of affirmative action aimed toward equitable integration.

Granted that there is no all-purpose strategic solution to the issues involved in equitable integration, whichever strategy is used, some level of solidarity in the female world or at least consensus must be posited if it is to succeed. A host of isolated women may live in worlds that are separate not only from the male, but also from the female, world. Efforts to join hands in behalf of common goals will be difficult for them even locally, let alone internationally. Without some degree of consciousness of the reality of their existence, joining hands will be impossible. It may be that in many parts of the globe the present is precisely the transitional period Staudt calls for in which the female world can develop the assurance to cope with the challenges of equitable integration, to establish the reality of its existence. It may be, in fact, that the women-only projects in development and feminist activism in the West are parts of the curriculum in that school and that the benefits it offers may supply the qualities needed for success in that different process. As the following success stories illustrate.

These modest conclusions from the experience in development may not call for dramatic flourishes and ruffles. But neither do they call for discouragement. Especially when there are some successes like Markala, a cooperative project in Mali, and the Working Women's Forum in Madras, both of which seem to have achieved the benefits derivable from a project established by women, managed by them, salvaged by them when they made mistakes. Their courage, their pride, their endurance, their style, their demonstration of what is possible for poor, non-literate women seem clearly to "vindicate the rights of women"[17] to equitable integration.

> When resources are given to groups (and care is taken to see that the individual members are full participants and that the group has control over the resources), and the members have the social or peer group support necessary for individual change, the concept of self-help can be implemented and there is the possibility for some power and leverage or greater political participation to accrue to the group [Piepmeir, 1980, 29].

Success Stories

The Markala Cooperative

In 1975, a group of twenty poor women in rural Mali joined together in an effort to learn marketable skills and thus to be able to earn a regular income. They were launched by grants from several voluntary agencies,[18] but they financed their own training by their own earnings. Their experience was valuable not only because it proved to be economically successful—achieving its avowed purpose, income generation—but also because it illustrated the growth of "human capital" in the skills acquired, an outcome not part of their original purpose.

A dam, a canal network, and dikes providing irrigation for large-scale agriculture had changed the occupation of the men in Markala from farming to wage labor. But the training programs that had made this change possible were not available to the women. Severe drought in the late 1960s and early 1970s had exacerbated the situation. So the women "decided to join together in a form of economic organization—a cooperative" (3).

A major incentive to undertake a cooperative business was the desire to learn new trades. Many economic activities in West Africa are the province of certain ethnic groups or families, the necessary training passed down from one generation to another. The women viewed the cooperative as an opportunity to receive new skills training just as the men had received training through the irrigation project.

In a series of meetings that took place over three months [in 1975], the women discussed their problems and what they might do to earn money. Before beginning any business activity, they agreed on some ground rules:

  a. The group would be open to any woman in the town who wanted to participate.
  b. The membership fee would be low, so no one would be excluded because she had little money. (The initial fee . . . was lowered . . . when it was discovered that many women otherwise could not afford to join).
  c. The main purpose of the cooperative would be income generation. From the onset members rejected activities such as literacy training and health education as irrelevant in light of their financial needs.
  d. All important decisions would be made by the group members. The women would not call on local political or government officials for leadership. . . . Though they would be careful to discuss their project with local authorities, the members would retain responsibility for decision making. . . .

Approximately two hundred women expressed an interest in joining the cooperative, and most attended one or more of the planning meetings. However, community skepticism and the prospect of a long training period dissuaded most of them from continuing with the cooperative. By the end of 1975, twenty determined women began working in borrowed rooms in the back of a local school and the Markala cooperative was in business (3–5).

A grant from the U.N. supplied the cooperative with the initial capital to buy cloth, dyes, and string, and to hire a specialist to train the members in cloth production. The losses from cloth production during the first two years were chalked up to training costs. Not until 1979 did the women feel they had achieved good quality standards. They then underwent similar training in soapmaking. And in time—with help from Femmes et Development—they completed the complicated bureaucratic procedures for registration as a producer cooperative under Malian law. By now membership had grown to fifty, a permanent workshop had been acquired, community skepticism had changed to admiration, applications for membership had increased. "Local officials, astounded that a group of illiterate women owned a major building, began to consider the cooperative as a genuine business venture rather than writing it off as a social club as they had in the past" (8).

The style of organization was tailored to the needs of the women themselves. It did not always conform to standard systems; in fact it almost defied "commonly accepted business practices." Thus, regardless of individual productivity, each member originally received the same monthly salary, on philosophical, not economic, grounds. Some members "felt that equal salaries were necessary to promote group unity and discourage jealousy and quarrels." But others "resented the inequity of a system that rewarded all members equally— even those who were less talented or hardworking" (9). After months of discussion a compromise was arrived at. "A small sum is subtracted from the monthly salary of any woman who does not meet minimum production and attendance" requirements (9). Although the issue—between "those who prefer to sacrifice some profit in order to keep the group alive and those who view the equal payment system as exploitation"—continued, "through solving problems together, the group became loyal and cohesive" (12). Their persistence and initiative "demonstrated that poor nonliterate women can collaborate successfully on economic ventures" (15).[19]

The Madras Working Women's Forum Organization for Credit and Change

Credit is a widespread need almost everywhere in the female world, from top to bottom of an economy. It is especially crucial in developing areas. We have already noted (chapter 2) how many women in Africa solve the problem by way of their revolving credit associations. Another kind of rural credit project was established in Bangladesh by a U.S.—trained man which has had spectacular success. Many housebound rural women participate, accounting for about half of the loan recipients (Claiborne, 1984).

What is especially encouraging about another credit project, this one in Madras, India, is that it was initiated by a woman, for women, and is operated by women. The initial beneficiaries were women considered risks too poor for banks to bother with. And, indeed, they did not look like a profitable constituency.

> Many were vendors of one kind or another: vegetables, fruit, greens, fish, peanuts, snack foods, sweets, and groceries, as well as firewood, aluminum utensils, silk, ornaments, hay, lime, salt. . . . They were small-scale operators and could devote only a limited amount of time to their businesses because of their heavy domestic responsibilities. [Chen, 1983, 5]

Such female projects were lacking in prestige; their profits, if any, were minimal. They were too insignificant for banks' attention; it would be embarrassing for them to have such a clientele.[20] Such petty trading activities had not been recognized as legitimate businesses. When the women needed credit, therefore, it was the moneylender who extended it, at usurious rates. Only when a woman leader, Jaya Arunachalam, confronted the banks on the matter did it occur to them that bank policy might apply to poor women as well as to poor men. But even when the Indian government nationalized banks and prescribed social concessions to the "weaker section of society," it did not occur to women that they might be eligible. When they did learn they were eligible, they found the formality, inhospitality, impersonality, and lack of help in filling out forms intimidating, offputting, and were therefore inhibited from applying.

To meet this obstacle, a "credit and change" organization called the Working Woman's Forum was set up by a group of women in Madras to serve as intermediary between the women and the banks. The "key element in the Forum structure" was the neighborhood loan group. These groups, each consisting of from ten to twenty women, look remarkably like the *tontines, egbes,* and *harambees* of Africa. But here, apparently, they had to be built up from scratch.

This is how it was done. First, group meetings and discussions were held to acquaint the women with the program. From there on it was in the women's court:

> A usual pattern is for a potential leader to approach a Forum staff member. She then is told to bring together a group of 10–20 women and explain to them how the Forum works. When a sufficient number have committed themselves, they elect a group leader. On some occasions Forum staff will approach a woman and encourage her to put together a group. . . . A woman may become either a full member or an associate member. . . . The membership requirements are simple: a member must attend group meetings regularly, repay loans consistently, and act as a mutual guarantor for the loans of all group members. [6–7]

In effect, the Forum was performing, in a more female-oriented manner, a good deal of the administrative work for the banks, thus relieving them of having to deal directly with such nonprestigious customers. Loans were limited to those to be used for productive purposes, but the Forum included in its definition of "productive" both child care and housework, even critical consumption needs—health care, for example. In addition, then, as an intermediary between the working women and the banks, the Forum has been able to develop a flexible repayment system that takes into account the realities of poor women's lives" (8). Further, like the revolving credit groups in Africa it recognized the legitimacy of expenditures for marriage and religious festivities which were perceived by the women to be social and economic investments" (8).[21]

The results proved to be reassuring. One of the most appreciated benefits reported by the women themselves was better nutrition, two meals a day instead of one. But the benefits extended further:

> An estimated 2,800 new jobs or businesses have resulted from the program and earnings have increased an average of 50 percent in existing enterprises. It also has assisted many women to expand and diversify their economic activities. [10]

As seen by its staff the Forum was just a beginning. Urban social service projects were also being developed, including: day care centers, night classes, skills training for the unemployed, health and family planning; and expansion to rural women was also in the cards for disseminating technological know-how to them to improve their productivity. It had helped landless women acquire livestock and, with it, training in animal husbandry; it had arranged credit facilities for rural fisherwomen and lacemakers.

Further, social action—mobilization—was seen as the essence of the Forum. It united women formerly divided by caste, religion, party politics. It "empowered" women. They came to "feel more confident to confront political forces that might be threatening to them as individuals (civic authorities, police, middlemen, money-lenders, wholesalers)" (14). It was liberating just to know that they did not need male cosigners for their loans. The upgrading of their petty trading enterprises increased their "bargaining power" and strengthened "pressure groups to demand greater access to and control over government goods and services" (17).

And even beyond all this, the Forum was engaged in the female revolution, feminist style. It was undermining the caste system.

As one member put it: "after joining this Forum, we do not have caste differences that much" (14). It was striking a blow against the dowry system which had encouraged extralegal unions in cases where the dowry made marriage impossible. At mass weddings of its members, attended by government officials, the Forum had been able to "publicize its anti-caste and anti-dowry position and to put pressure on the government to institute the economic incentives for inter-caste marriages that it has promised" (14). From such small acorns, who knew what great oaks might grow.

Among the several lessons learned by the experience of the Forum was that it was "preferable to begin a program by supporting women's existing economic enterprises rather than attempting to train them and create new jobs. Technical assistance, skills training and enterprise development can be added later" (17). Another lesson was that it was advantageous to activate government programs that had existed only on the books even if it meant setting up parallel—separate—"delivery systems to guarantee that established programs would reach poor [as well as other] women" (18). And, most relevant here:

> A program for women is more likely to succeed if it adopts at least two elements: (a) a strong, pro-women ideology to instill a spirit of solidarity and self-confidence in the women, and (b) a commitment to grassroots leadership as a means of strengthening and nourishing the dormant power of poor women. [18]

This positive judgment on the Madras Forum was confirmed by a more detailed and scholarly study of similar projects in three Indian cities:

> Our study suggests that women-specific interventions are beneficial at the grass-roots level but not, or not to the same extent, at the bureaucratic level. The key to success appears to be grass-roots women's organizations. This is not to imply that anyone could embark on such an undertaking. The existing organizations in three Indian cities are run by competent, energetic women with long histories of involvement with urban poor. The challenge remains to organize the vast majority of poor self-employed Indian women who so far do not have access to development programs and services.
>
> In summary, we have found that programs targeted for self-employed poor women may actually benefit various intermediaries as much as (or more than) they benefit the women themselves. This is because development programs do not eliminate the hierarchical structure in which poor women exist. More program benefits flow to poor women when they are mobilized as members of grass-roots organizations. Such organizations, in turn, may help challenge the hierarchical structure itself. [Everett and Savara, 1985, 290]

The secret of success was the "establishment of neighborhood borrower groups" which "enabled women to develop a sense of collectivity and to discuss a variety of issues" (290). They were free to talk, to make themselves heard. Such projects might not be a royal road to equitable integration. But they seem to be a serviceable, pedestrian, and apparently successful one.

This, then, was the experience with projects in development, and these, some of the lessons derived from it. The curriculum was by no means complete. More and more "courses" will no doubt be added to it as new approaches are used. And as literacy increases, as beneficiaries themselves gain a wider perspective, learn from other women, they will be in a position to make their own contribution to development. We are still only in the "affirmative action" phase of the process toward equitable integration.

At the same time, as all these changes were going on in the design and implementation of projects in the West, other revolutions were also going on but in a totally different context. Events overtook not only the Point Four approach to development; they also overtook colonial empires. Anticolonial movements, liberation movements, revolutionary movements were shaking up old systems. The overthrow of empires had left whole areas without stable governments. Revolutionary parties (Marxist, Leninist, Maoist, among others) rushed in to fill the vacuum. Regime succeeded regime. The female world was not left untouched.

CHAPTER FOUR

Relations of the Two Worlds in a Postcolonial Context

If government agencies were key concepts in the U.N. model for implementing equitable integration (chapter 2) and "projects," in the development models (chapter 3), *political priorities* might be said to be the key words in the postcolonial leftist liberation and revolutionary models for equitable integration. The course followed by the female world in these situations was strongly influenced by the kind of colonial treatment their countries had received earlier. Some empires had paid more attention than had others to the preparation of their colonies for self-government; they had at least trained civil servants. The British, for example, had envisaged as a successor to the Empire a great commonwealth of willing constituent member nations. Some, like Portugal, had neglected their colonies, leaving them without a well-trained cadre of civil servants to take over.[1] Some former colonies remained dependent on their erstwhile rulers as recognized or unrecognized "spheres of influence." The whole postcolonial scene was a hodgepodge of political experiment, aggression, regression—socialist in some areas, capitalist in others.[2] It would be diversionary for our purposes to trace out in every case what the specific colonial and postcolonial situation was. So we begin with a brief glance at the leadership in the female world during these transitional times.

We are again truly at the margin of history and news. So much has happened and is, at this moment, happening, that often the on-site reporter's story has as much credibility as the historian's careful and scholarly documentation. In some cases we can almost hear the television reporter's "Hang on! There's talk of . . . a coup, a takeover, a new coalition."

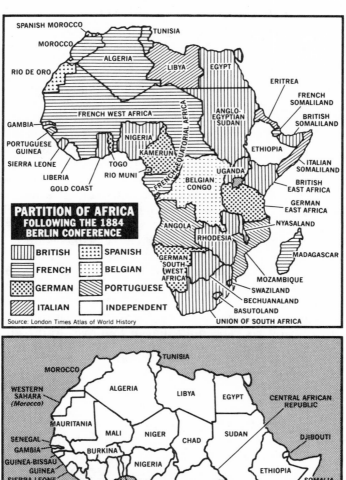

Reprinted by permission of *The Washington Post,* maps by Dave
Cook.

> If men [sic] are to remain civilized or
> to become so, the art of associating
> together must grow and improve in the
> same ratio in which the equality of
> conditions is increased. [Tocqueville,
> 1835]

Tocqueville's statement might be turned around to read that equality of conditions is a prerequisite for the growth and improvement of the art of associating together. Whether equality was antecedent to or consequent to the art of associating, and whether or not this was an art needed for becoming or remaining civilized, it was viewed by the U.N. as essential for equitable integration. "Women's organizations are the principal institutions for integrating women into national life" (United Nations, 1981).

The right to associate and assemble freely was so uncertain when the U.S. Constitution was drawn up that its protection was specifically spelled out. It is still far from assured in many countries today. For there is, or can be, considerable power in the right to organize, as we saw on a modest scale in chapter 3. When or if such a right is granted some regimes maintain strict control over the groups that result; their autonomy is narrowly limited. Especially that of feminist groups. In some countries the Communist parties themselves organize women as, in effect, arms of the party.

In the United States autonomous women's groups are old (Bernard, 1981, 310–12). Today there are so many that merely listing them requires a whole volume. What is "news" today has been their bourgeoning in other parts of the female world as well. Their proliferation is, in fact, one of the most important trends on the world stage today (part III). Not that women's groups did not exist before the 1970s, but their character in many parts of the world has changed. Even in Africa there had long been women's business and professional groups, philanthropic groups, Red Cross groups, and other elite groups, Christian or Islamic (Little, 1973, 73). They had provided hospital services, staffed orphanages; they had supported vocational education and child care (Staudt, 1980, 12). In Iran there had been such groups led by the Shah's sister, under whose tight control they had "played much the same role as the phony trade unions that were supported and controlled by the state" (Tabari, 1980, 3).

The politically innocuous nature of such groups could be inferred from the fact that, although they existed in almost all the member nations of the U.N., only forty governments provided information about them for the 1980 review of progress that had been called for at the Mexico City Conference in 1975. The official appraisals of those in the forty countries gave them passing marks but noted that they tended to be parochial, limited to welfare issues rather than seeking social transformations. And in some cases, as in Singapore, for example, they were still limited to the traditionally smug elitist urban women without dynamic leadership skills. "Women," the appraisal continued, "are, like any other social group, differentiated by class interests and backgrounds. A significant number of [urban] women's organizations do not therefore necessarily represent the interests of all or even the majority of women" (U.N. Review and Evaluation, 1980, 15). And certainly not of most rural women. In Senegal, for example, a Dakar woman, when asked which she preferred, urban or village life, replied disdainfully, "It's not even comparable. The women in the bush, eh!" (Barthel, 1975, 14). Not an auspicious stance for national leadership.

Corroborative of the U.N. appraisal was the portrait of a typical urban leader in many such groups, such as this example from Africa. Such an urban leader would typically have come from a fairly well-placed family:

> She will have attended mission-run primary and secondary schools and this means that she knows the Bible and is probably a Christian convert. She has had between eight and ten years of schooling, during which she was introduced to the Girl Guides and the YWCA; later, she was a member or the executive of one or another of these organizations, the Girl Guides being an especially important training ground. From secondary schools the typical leader will have gone on to a teacher-training course or to the former Jeanes School, which was designed to give training in leadership, social work, and the technical specialties, and played an important part in training Kenya's social and technical workers. Ages range from the mid-twenties to the late forties, and most such women are mothers of large families even though many are employed full time. [Wipper, 1971, cited in Little, 74–75]

Groups led by women with such conservative family and educational backgrounds held conferences, explored practical problems, and served as safe pressure groups. Their leaders, according to Little, were peculiarly susceptible to cooption. In Iran they were in the pocket of the Shah's sister, Ashraf. Hardly well qualified for the UN's assignment for them, to integrate women equitably into national life. Still, when there were no government agencies to perform the services they supplied, they had a legitimate role.

But they could do more for integrating women politically. They could perform three functions: mobilize women for change at the grass-roots level—including those we saw in chapter 3—to influence national policy; monitor and evaluate government policies, plans, and programs and initiate new ones; and act "as a forum and provide a support network among women, raising their consciousness and instilling in them confidence in their capacity to influence the processes of change" (U.N. Review and Valuation, 14–15). The words sounded fine.

But there were beginning to be some women who sensed danger in accepting government initiative and support vis-à-vis women's activities. Government support for such organizations might be viewed as a way of taking care of all the needs of women who could thereafter be ignored in social and economic plans and programs (Piepmeir, 1980, 25–26), a premonition which later proved to be well grounded. In country after country the problems of women identified by such organizations were given low priority on government agendas. To this extent, the women's traditional national organizations, thus "integrated," did not achieve great success in implementing their goals.

By the 1970s, however, a great sea change in thinking about equitable integration was taking place. A different kind of integration was beginning to be called for. The traditional picture of an essentially elite, conservative, urban membership and leadership among women's groups was becoming dramatically altered. A new kind of leader was emerging.

Even in the early 1970s, Little had reported that there were now militant women in Africa who, without privileged family position or relations with the political or professional status-quo elite, had nevertheless secured an education and were now employed. In Senegal, for example, some women as early as 1975 were already being reported as strongly feminist in orientation. Complete—equitable—integration was the idea that motivated them. Some insisted that "woman's role was exactly the same as man's, as wide and as comprehensive" (Barthel, 1975, 14). Even more of them felt women should be politically active "whether through the women deputies in the assembly . . . or through the organized activities of all women." Complete and equitable integration was the goal:

> Now women and men do the same things. Men shouldn't say any longer that a certain job is for men, another for women—we now have equality— almost. . . . It's crazy to say there are occupations which women can not do. Women can do all the jobs that men can. [14]

A thirty-year old lawyer commented:

> Personally, I don't like it when one speaks of the role of women—I think it's the misogyny of men. Men and women can play the same role. What I don't like is when one says "men," then "women." I don't like this term "the role of women." Women can do as much as men. In the city we're not talking about physical work but rather the work of the mind. [15]

Nor were the Senegalese women alone. Peggy Antrobus, of the University of the West Indies, had found the first UN Decade for Women Conference in 1975 a watershed in her own thinking about the contributions of women:

> We've had women's organizations for many years doing mostly traditional things, social welfare programmes. As a result of 1975, people started thinking and focusing on the fact that women were not only beneficiaries, not only subjects for social welfare programs but [also] in fact had a very important and significant contribution to make to the social and economic development of their countries, as producers and decision-makers. [1981, 8]

She subscribed to the goals of the UN-initiated Decade for Women and was eager to incorporate them into the national organizations of her country. These goals included

> equality between the sexes and the integration of women in the process of development . . . including more vocational opportunities, opportunities for employment, better levels of salary, getting women into a wider range of skills, allowing them to climb the promotional ladder, even opportunities for women to get into decision-making positions, like more female permanent secretaries, more judges and more women in politics [8].

Women like these were ripe for the UN 1975 message. Many traditional women were becoming radicalized by it. They were becoming part of the "women's movement" destined to have enormous impact on the female world in many parts of the globe.

But in another part of the forest a different game was being played, a different kind of equitable integration was being sought. The course followed was therefore different.

The services of women were essential in anticolonial, liberation, and revolutionary movements. There was no way they could be excluded from the struggle. Recruiting them was therefore crucially important. Even in Guinea-Bissau, where female life expectancy (33.5 years) was near the lowest in the world:

> Mobilizers went into the countryside in 1960; they spoke of the need for women to participate equally in the revolution and thus end their own dual exploitation. A PAIGC [African Party for the Independence of Guinea and Cape Verde] directive of the early '60s states: "Defend the rights of women, respect and make others respect women. . . . Persuade the women of our country that their liberation must be their own achieve-

ment on the basis of their work, dedication to the Party, self-respect, personality and decisiveness toward everything that can act against their dignity." [Urdang, 1978, 34]

The rewards promised for such service were to be complete and equitable integration. In southern Africa, for example:

> Because women have chosen to fight side by side with men in all three fronts of the struggle—diplomatic, military, and political—you find that they are accorded great respect by men. It's obvious that men, especially in African countries, have customs which hinder the progress of women and which look upon women as weak. But today you find that our men in the camps don't look at women just as women, to be separated out to do the cooking. But work is divided up among groups irrespective of sex, whether it's gardening, cooking or any of the work of the camp. If you look at the leadership of SWAPO today, you find that both men and women are coming up to be members of the Central Committee, the Executive Committee. [Musialela, interview, 1981, *Isis*, no. 19]

In addition, the party organized women into national groups to take care of the special problems of women. These were not voluntary or autonomous groups like those described earlier in Africa (chapter 2) nor sponsored groups like those set up in development projects (chapter 3), nor the social welfare groups described above, but they served, in effect, as arms of the party which, like the Women's Union in South Yemen, acted strictly "according to party directives" (Mohsen, 1977, 7). What all this meant for the female world was a question that came increasingly to engage the attention of women scholars.

In 1981 a group of Western women historians were asking: "How can we look at the relationship between women's movements and leftists' movements?" and "Do we know enough today to say something substantive about the nature of that relationship?" (Smith-Rosenberg and Freidlander 1981). On the basis of considerable research on a generation of experience with such relationships, they were answering in terms of "involvement and marginalization." Their own research "gave superb, if distressing and repetitive, detail about how women joined and promoted the cause of the leftist parties, receiving support for women's issues, but more usually finding themselves forgotten in the wider struggles for emancipation."[3] The picture seemed clearly to be one of cooption rather than of equitable integration.

It was not only the scholarly historians in the West who were asking questions about the relationship between women's and leftists movements. Activist women in the Third World were also. To them the questions were not merely academic. They wanted to know what *should* be the relationship—separatist or integrationist—between them. The issue had assumed enough importance to warrant a call for an international workshop of women on the subject. Thus, in June 1980, such a workshop on Women and Development was, in fact, held at the Hague in which women from countries from A to Z had participated.[4] The central question was:

> Do women, who are necessary for the success of any liberation struggle, also gain their own liberation during and after this struggle? Historical and contemporary evidence is to the contrary. After liberation, women often have to return to the old sexual division of labor. . . . The main question is therefore: "What happens to women once national liberation has been won?" [Isis, no. 19, 1981]

Both the researchers' scholarship and the activists' experience suggested the answer to this question: the women were left with unpaid promissory notes they had been given for participation in the leftists' movements, often uncollectable.

An enormous amount of research is going to be called for before definitive answers can be offered. The story of Marxism, Leninism, Stalinism, or Maoism as it wove its way through the Third World, the varying situations it found in each country, the organizational experience, skills, and know-how of the women it encountered and trained, the weight of cultural "patriarchy" embedded in prevailing laws, customs, traditions, attitudes, mores, and other agencies of control in the female world, will all have to be traced. But the historians suggest that we are beginning to know enough to say something, however minimal, about that relationship.

Lip service had always been paid to women as mothers. But male leftist groups learned early on how important women were—or could be—for any ongoing enterprise, how essential their taken-for-granted services were for their own activities. Prototypically they began to recruit women for their anticolonial, liberation, or revolutionary movements by promising to attend to their (women's) demands when success had been achieved. They organized the women as working groups under the aegis of male groups. Under such tutelage there was a veritable explosion of women's national—anticolonial or national-liberation, or revolutionary—organizations in the female world altogether different from the voluntary groups commented on above.[5] Only recently has the smoke begun to clear enough to give us a glimpse of the part played by women in these leftist movements. But the promised rewards were not to be forthcoming. The leftist leaders, once success was achieved, reneged on their promises. The promissory notes were not paid. The relationship was, as the women historians finally concluded, one of "involvement" by women and their "marginalization" by men. A far cry from equitable integration.

In a way, however, the leftist movements were among the best teachers of women, for—quite aside from Marxist, Leninist, Stalinist, or Maoist ideological grounds for recruiting women—revolutionary experience itself supplied their minds with food for thought. Further, the leftist movements provided women with a vocabulary of oppression, a language with which to express their frustrations; they raised among women a consciousness of female oppression along with a consciousness of class and/or racial oppression. They rendered visible to women dozens of aspects of their oppression that had never been visible to them before. In the process they emphasized the importance of literacy, of organization; they extended horizons. The female world would never be the same again.[6]

With a Marxist-Leninist-Stalinist-Maoist vocabulary at the ready women became prepared to think in terms of the feasibility of throwing off their chains. Their actual status might not yet have changed very much, but they were now becoming aware of it. They could now see that they were oppressed. They redefined their situation as not intractable, inevitable, unchangeable. It could be changed.[7]

The Chinese Communist Party is given credit for pioneering the process of recruiting and training women for revolution. From the time of its establishment in 1921, it had begun to think through the best way to do this. One way was to clarify the special form female oppression took, as distinguished from oppression shared by men. It began by nurturing

> separate organizations of village women on the basis of their special experience of oppression.
> The special oppression of women, which was identified as different from that of the political, clan, and religious oppression shared by the men of their own social class, distinguished them as a separate social category. The common identity of women was based on the sexual division of labour and the inheritance of male supremacy. . . . The Communist Party . . . forecast that while a government could provide the legal and material conditions favourable to improvements in female status it was the women themselves who must recognize their common interests and negotiate a new collective role in society. Female solidarity groups were to be assigned a major role in encouraging women to evolve a collective sense of identity, translate the individual experience of oppression into a coherent analysis of oppression, and redefine their position within individual families, villages, and factories. [Croll, 1982, 52][8]

Separate social category? Common identity? Common interests? Female solidarity? *Negotiate* a new collective role in society? (emphasis supplied). It sounds like a letter-perfect prescription for the equitable integration of two strong autonomous gender-defined entities.

In the 30s, 40s, and 50s, as villages in China began to be liberated by the advancing Communist armies, women's groups were established as part of a nation-wide movement in which they were linked to practical objectives such as agricultural work teams, cooperative handicraft ventures, or literacy classes (55). Such party initiatives brought urban women into contact with rural women, but especially young women into contact with other young women, so that the movement was disproportionately a youthful one.[9] In areas under Communist party control during the anti-Japanese liberation movement and the civil wars that followed, women, in the absence of men, were badly needed in the war work programs, which called for collective action in their new economic roles.

But practical goals did not preclude ideological ones. In their groups the women were taught to "speak bitterness" and admit their suffering and oppression, a powerful technique labeled "consciousness raising" when it was taken over in the West. Participation in such groups not only raised consciousness about common grievances but also contributed to mutual emotional support. In the discussions the women engaged in after study or work, they were encouraged "to tell us themselves what things had been like before, how they were now and how they ought to be in the future" (55). New opportunities now becoming available were contrasted with such old practices as seclusion, arranged marriages, and bound feet in the bad old days.

It looked like equitable integration when the women's groups even changed the attitudes of some of the men: "the village elders began to admit that 'the Women's Association doesn't seem so bad after all!'" (55). What they were learning was quite useful—not only reading and writing but also industrial skills. Like these useful accomplishments, the promise of equality was part of a strategy for upgrading women's ability to participate in the revolution.

But equality was hard. Wrestling with it, the women concluded that "within the family, men and women are equal. We help the men when they work in the fields and they should help us in the house" (55–56). Nor were the promises of equality wholly reneged. New marriage and work laws in 1950 and 1951 did grant women equality and protection, and although they defined women's interests as separate from those of men, they allowed women for the first time an opportunity to challenge male authority both in the family and in the work force.[10] The idea was to help women acquire the requisite skills and then to overcome opposition to the redefinition of their economic roles (57). And, incidentally, to ease the transition from individualized to collectivized peasant production by way of land reform (58).

While it was important to teach women to "speak bitterness" and thus become aware of their oppression in order to promise redress, it was also important to keep female oppression in perspective. Women were oppressed by the status quo—colonial, imperialist, capitalist, whatever—and, in addition, by sexism, patriarchy, male domination—again, whatever. In Guinea-Bissau, the Portuguese had oppressed both men and women, but women had been oppressed twice. "We had two colonialisms on our hand: we had the Portuguese in our country and our husbands in our house" (Urdang, 1978, 41). In many parts of Africa women suffered triple—class, race, and sex—oppression, as workers, as Africans, and as females (Unsigned, paper at African National Congress, Havana, 1979). All this was freely granted by the leftist movements. "The aim of the revolution is the ending of *all* forms of exploitation and oppression" (Resolution of the 2nd OMM [Mozambican Women's Conference] 1974. Emphasis supplied).

But all oppressions were not equal in seriousness. Some were "more equal" than others and therefore took priority over them. Sex oppression was low on the priority list. In southern Africa, the party had politicized women on a class basis; the African National Congress, on a race basis. In both cases, sex took a place far lower than either class or race (unsigned, Feminist Newsletter, n.d.).[11] True, the liberation or revolutionary movments and the women's movements were inextricably tied to one another—neither could succeed without the other—but since the status quo, whatever its form, was the most inclusive oppressor, affecting both men and women, black and white, overcoming it deserved top priority. All oppressed groups should unite to destroy it. All separating internecine differences should be set aside in an integrated assault on it. Once that battle had been won, other forms of oppression could then be addressed. And redress was promised.

The leftist women's groups took the priority argument at face value. It appeared and reappeared in their program statements everywhere. It became, in effect, the basic integrationist statement.

Cases in Point

Thus, for example, in Chile though women carried on "a double struggle, the struggle for freedom alongside our people and the often tiring and wearing struggle for our own emancipation," experience had shown that "our struggle is only part of the battle to regain dignity, to once again become protagonists in, instead of mere observers of, history" (Diaz, 1979). Doubly exploited as they had been,

> oppressed since time immemorial, relegated, misunderstood, and for the most part ignored when it . . . came to important discussions . . . still we see the women's struggle, our struggle, in the context of the class struggle, and therefore we consider the struggle of our people to be a priority; that

is why we conceive of exploited men and women as a group, as one single class.

This was one of the strongest statements of the integrationist position.

In Nicaragua, the Association of Nicaraguan Women argued that "full equality for women, the full integration of women into society, can only be achieved through the consolidation of the revolution" (Isis, no. 19, 1981, 6). Women must therefore combine working for the general reconstruction of the country with overcoming their own inequalities as women. But "the *main* aim is to maintain the mobilization of women around the defense and consolidation of the revolution" (7, emphasis supplied). Even measures taken specifically in behalf of women—such as Child Development Centers—were not for the sake of women themselves but to help them become more useful for the revolution.

So also in El Salvador women proclaimed a dual purpose—one was to make women better fighters for liberation, the other was to achieve women's goals. The first recruitment, which had top priority, was to "provide an organization through which women such as housewives, nurses, and secretaries could participate in the liberation struggle" (Galdmez, 1981, 11). The second goal, liberation from a machista or sexist society would have to wait; it could not be achieved until national liberation had been won, since both national and women's liberation were integral, not separate, movements. Thus, by helping national liberation, the goal—establishing their own rights, carrying out their own aspirations—would come much faster.

In southern Africa, where both black women's and black men's oppression was so all-encompassing, where both women's and political liberation movements were up against such an implacable and intractable regime, the integrationist argument would seem to be persuasive. It was, in fact, widely used. The race issue did indeed transcend gender issues. The oppression of black men equaled that of black women, and there were women among the white oppressors. Here liberation would seem to be a first priority for both women and men.

> We are left with one option only, and that is to fight side by side with our men for National Liberation. This all-encompassing oppression of the white man has got to go first; the dignity of our men has got to be regained; our national heritage and our self-determination has got to be restored to us. [Rennie, 1982, 86]

Again:

> Despite the traditional barriers between men and women, women have started to understand that we have to fight together to fight the system,

because we are oppressed as women, and we are oppressed as blacks—both men and women. [Misialela, *Isis*, 1981, no. 19]

And in Namibia:

> In seeking to resolve this centuries-old [class] problem, SWAPO [Southwest Africa Political Organization] proceeds from the proposition that women's oppression should not be regarded as an independent problem which can be solved through a [separate] feminist struggle isolated from the main world revolutionary currents, i.e., the struggle for national liberation, democracy and classless society. It can only be genuinely resolved through [an integrated] revolutionary transformation of society. [Unsigned, in *Namibia Today*, n.d., 24]

As well as in Azania:[12]

> . . . the plight of the Azanian women cannot be and must not be seen in isolation from the struggle of the entire oppressed, exploited and dispossessed people of Azania. Their lot can only and genuinely be free if the oppressed, exploited and dispossessed Azanian people attain genuine national liberation. . . . The women took their rightful place in the Pan Africanist Congress of Azania as full and equal members. . . . There are many Azanian women currently carrying out important roles and duties . . . [such as organising peasants, serving as combatants, workers, trade unionists, students, organizing self-help community projects, and serving in refugee camps]. [Sifuba, *Azania News*, vol. 21, no. 1, n.d., 23]

And in South Yemen:

> We are against the idea that there is a contradiction between men and women. We're against bourgeois slogans which claim this, or say that women must struggle separately because their struggle is isolated from men or is against them. We might think that men are the cause of women's situation; but men are not the cause because they are themselves governed by the feudal and tribal social relations of the society itself. [Aida Yafi, interview with Molyneux, 1977, 6]

There were, nevertheless, some women who argued that even in these drastic circumstances, women's issues could not be ignored. They had to be dealt with along with all the other liberation issues. They could not be blotted off the agenda. Thus the Federation of South African Women (FSAW), organized in the 1950s, to express "the needs and aspirations of housewives, wage earners, peasants and professional women of South Africa" declared in its manifesto that although they would stand shoulder to shoulder with their male liberationists, they were also determined to "teach the men that they cannot hope to liberate themselves from the evils of discrimination and prejudices as long as they fail to

extend to women complete and unqualified equality in law and practice" (Snudge, 1982, 66). They planned to build and strengthen organizations in the trade unions as well as in the liberation movement itself.
From liberation they demanded the right to vote, equal opportunity in
employment including equal pay, equal rights in marriage, property,
along with a host of other welfare programs.[13] FSAW was banned
sixteen years later. But its message had been heard. And continued to be.
Although the impact of apartheid was so great on everyone's life that
there was strong pressure to "relegate 'women's issues' to a remote
priority . . . feminist issues must nevertheless be dealt with con-
currently because after the 'political struggles' are over, the women tend
to be forgotten" (Chabaku, 1982, 68). As, in fact, the history of many
countries had by now so well documented.

Still, however brave the words in support of the priority of national
goals, the hearts of many of the women were not in it. However much
the Association of Nicaraguan Women, for example, might be working
to carry the revolution forward, at the local grass-roots level the discussions among the women themselves often dealt not with the defense or
consolidation of the revolution but with the miserable conditions of
their daily life, with such issues as ways to keep their children healthy,
what was best for them to eat, and the causes of machismo, none of
which were on the agenda of the revolution (*Isis*, no. 19, 1981, 7). In El
Salvador, too, the women sought the right to maternity and an end to
forced sterilization; they wanted safe family planning right now, free
child-care, education and training (Galdmez, 1981, 11).[14] In a word, the
kinds of human rights that political rights were designed to ensure—but
did not always guarantee.

The problem of relative priority among goals was by no means limited to postcolonial countries; it was not unknown even in the United
States. In order to discourage the organization of separate labor unions,
women had been told that after the overall labor union movement had
succeeded the (lesser) female issues, such as gender differentials in pay
could be taken care of. It was taken for granted that the interests of
women, however legitimate, had low priority. In the civil rights and
antiwar movements of the 1960s also many young women had rebelled
against the low priority accorded their grievances when they found that
the leftist men, theoretically most dedicated to egalitarian principles
and most eloquent against racial discrimination, were most insistent
that old gender-role patterns which subordinated women's issues be
maintained.

In the case of Ireland, after many years of effort to win priority for
women's issues, the women gave up. Ireland had been engaged in an
anti-imperialist struggle for a long time, and it, too, had had to confront
the separatist-integrationist issue. More than seventy years ago one

commentator, James Connolly, had seen the matter as an issue of priority between the struggle against British imperialism on one hand and the women's movement on the other. The issue had remained divisive. It had split the women's movement. Now, "out of recent struggles within the Irish women's community has reemerged the traditional separation between those who believe the primary task is the struggle for the resolution of the national question and those who believe the interests of women deserve priority" (Casey, 1981, 8). The Belfast Women's Collective dissolved in 1980, concluding that "there is precious little common ground on which feminists and socialists can meet." With little hope for improvement, "for all watchful Irish women, the resolution of the conflict between feminism and nationalism remains a struggle" (8).

We have already met the Latin American and Caribbean women who also marched to a different drummer, who protested the whole donor-project relationship (chapter 3). They also rejected the patronage of the leftist groups and sought autonomy. The first Latin American and Caribbean Feminist meeting in Bogota, held in 1981, "succeeded in convincing all the different groups which participated of the necessity for the feminist movement to be autonomous" (Fuller, 1983, iv). They knew where their priorities lay. The women's section of the Trotskyist Workers Revolutionary Party "broke away from their male comrades and some of them later founded the Women's Autonomous Group" (iv). Other less radical groups also arose, such as the Association of Progressive Women, composed of lower-middle-class housewives dedicated to consciousness raising and a Women's Institute interested in education for women and research on women's organizations. Both were feminist and autonomous.[15]

South Africa represents a special case, definitely sui generis. Here there were several levels of radicalism among resistance organizations for women to choose among, ranging from the Pan Africanist Congress which had chosen armed struggle to, in effect, take over the whole of Africa, to the Federation of South African Women (FSAW), consisting mainly of black African, Coloured, and Indian women, but including also some white women.

South Africa had had a different kind of colonial history. Fought over by white—Dutch and British—trading companies for centuries, fought over by armies early in the twentieth century, not until 1948 did it arrive at the current ethno-political status in which the Dutch or Afrikaner strain took over the government and instituted racial apartheid as government policy. This became a situation in which the priorities of the female world were clear and unambiguous. Under a system as brutal and inhumane as the apartheid regime there could be no issue of priorities (appendix C). Racial liberation had to come first. Apartheid had to be dismantled. Black women were among the most active in resistance to it.

In the early 1950s the Federation of South African Women (FSAW) organized protest movements, especially against the pass system. They were, also, along with members of other organizations, demanding the rights of women, as well as other reforms.

> While stressing that they did not form a society separate from men and would stand "shoulder to shoulder" with them in the struggle for liberation, the women of FSAW were also determined to "teach the men that they cannot hope to liberate themselves from the evils of discrimination and prejudices as long as they fail to extend to women complete and unqualified equality in law and practice." To this purpose, they aimed to build and strengthen the women's sections in the liberation movements, and the organization of women in trade unions. Included among the demands for the right to vote, to have equal opportunities for employment with equal pay, and for equal rights with men in relation to property, marriage and children, were the demands for "the protection of mother and child through maternity homes, welfare clinics, crèches and nursery schools." And, not calling for a return to the original traditional laws, the FSAW instead called for a change in the laws of marriage . . . and property laws. [Snudge, 1982, 66]

Reformist rather than, like the Pan Africanist Congress, revolutionary, FSAW recognized that although men and women shared certain kinds of oppression, women had, in addition, unique forms of oppression to contend with (chapter 10).

As it turned out, in some cases the promissory note by which leftist movements had enticed the support of women's groups had proved to be a cynical ploy. It was paid for with a bogus check. The story of Algeria became the classic example, a cause célèbre that had a disillusioning effect in the female world. The women had participated in the liberation movement wholeheartedly and successfully. They had supplied moral support as well as food and shelter for resistance fighters, served as intelligence liaisons, aided the families of fighters and prisoners. They had even borne arms. A great deal had been made of this participation as public proof to the international community of their liberation. In the end victory had been won. Algeria was no longer a French colony. The liberation movement had achieved its goal. Now, as promised, it could turn its attention to the issues of the female world.

It did not. The position of women did not improve. If they had been such active participants in the liberation movement—some even condemned to death for it—what, some French feminists were now asking, had been the payoff?

> Once national independence was achieved we were sent home and we are actually being threatened by a feudal family code. . . . We are Muslim but we refuse to let the integrists send us back; it is not in the name of Islam that we liberated Algeria. [Ouzegane, 1982, 84]

So what had the women achieved? If they had contributed so much, what had been the reward? Why had the promissory note not been honored?

Of course, payment had not been expected to be immediate. But after twenty years? Why, after so long, did women still hold no leadership positions in the government? Why were so many women still illiterate?[16] Still forced into marriage? Still wearing veils? Still working in their homes without pay? (Dufrancatel, 1981, 21).[17]

The bitterness expressed by these Algerian women echoed the bitterness that had been expressed by women in the United States in the nineteenth century when they too had felt betrayed in their fight for the suffrage. They too had been asked to delay their suffrage activities, to invest themselves in the abolition movement instead. They had. And they too felt that they had been doublecrossed. In the words of one of the leaders, Elizabeth Cady Stanton:

> Our liberal men counselled us to silence during the [Civil] war, and we were silent on our own wrongs; they counselled us to silence in Kansas and New York (in the suffrage referenda), lest we should defeat "Negro Suffrage," and threatened if we were not, we might fight the battle alone. We chose the latter, and were defeated. [quoted in Freedman, 1979, 516]

They had learned their lesson. Such betrayal would never happen again:

> Standing alone we learned our power: we repudiated man's counsels forevermore; and solemnly vowed that there should never be another season of silence until women had the same rights everywhere on this green earth, as man. [Ibid.]

Attempts to integrate women's movements with men's were doomed to failure:

> We would warn the young women of the coming generation against man's advice as to their best interests. . . . Woman must lead the way to her own enfranchisement. . . . She must not put her trust in man in this transition period, since while regarded as his subject, his inferior, his slave, their interests must be antagonistic. [516]

In the case of Algeria, though the differences in female literacy between Muslim and non-Muslim countries were, indeed, substantial (Bachu, 1983, 9),[18] Dufrancatel did not accept the religious explanation as adequate for the failure to pay the promissory notes. She had a more sinister explanation. She saw the male liberation movement as having perpetrated an enormous fraud on women, exploiting them for its own ends, namely the preservation of "Algerian Islamic culture and social structures against the onslaught of French modernization" (21). The much-touted participation of women in the anticolonial movement, it was now alleged, had not in fact been a bona fide feminist movement but rather a male-created public relations ploy, a case of "progressive trickery." Stories and pictures of women in parades had been used to create a popular public image for outside media consumption: "The theme of the participation/liberation of women was exploited for the benefit of foreigners in order to solicit international support for the resistance" (Dufrancatel, 21). It had been especially useful in attracting the support of French radicals and liberals. How could they resist statements like: "The Algerian woman is already free, because she participates in the liberation of her country, of which she is its soul, its heart, and its claim to glory." Or, "in the National Liberation Army all sectors are open to women" (21).[19] Actually the contribution of women, however essential, had taken the form of performing traditional female roles such, for example, as the care of resistance fighters and their families, roles with little panache or ability to attract foreign interest. And when the need for even that role ended, the women were dispersed and the demand for payment of the promissory note was now being seen as a sign of loose morals.[20]

It will, of course, take a considerable research effort to corroborate or discount Dufrancatel's interpretation. But whatever the reason might be—different perhaps everywhere—the situation of women all over the globe was still far from what had been promised in the name of equitable integration. There were many "raisins in the sun,"[21] that is, hopes deferred around the world, many variations on the theme of betrayal.

Cases in Point:

Ireland

Irish history shows that women have always played a significant role in the national struggle. Their energies have been poured into fund raising, welfare work, providing accommodation and campaigning. Women, however, have seldom risen to positions of authority except where they have adopted the male ideals, aims, and discipline of the movement. The failure of feminist issues to emerge as part of the overall policy of any of the movements is proof of this (unsigned, *Connexions*, no. 1, 1981, 10).

Palestine

There is a popular Palestinian expression: "The honor of our land before the honor of our women." As Israeli attempts to crush the Resistance intensify, more women are joining the Resistance, risking death or imprisonment. . . . Armed struggle has liberated these women to a large extent. Women are expected to participate in the struggle in a variety of ways. Still, there is a distrust that what happened to Algerian women after their revolution will happen to Palestinian women. . . . An Algerian woman who has been active in the Palestinian resistance since 1967 describes her experience. . . . "For the men the only worthwhile issue is the Palestinian struggle against Israel, and they are unwilling to put any effort into the liberation of Palestinian women. . . . All the militants agree that women should be liberated, but if one asks a militant why his wife is at home? his answer will be that "His wife is his wife, after all" . . . Women have begun to struggle against this mentality, but how long will it take to change it? Without this struggle Palestinian women could end up in the same condition as Algerian women (unsigned, *Connexions*, no. 2, 1981, 22–23).

P.L.O.

There had been a "failure to implement seriously resolutions to promote women's rights and equality within the PLO and society" (Sayegh, 1981, 34). Women "are still tremendously constrained by Arab men's mentality which has not changed."

Iraq

The Arab Left is in total contradiction to the declaration of the rights of man. Their slogans of equality are only words, never implemented at all. In 1963 the Baas socialist party of Iraq declared that the "liberation of women is a priority task of the national socialist revolution." But when they achieved power women were returned to their ancient status. In most Arab countries which have achieved national independence, society still suffers with respect to sexual equality (unsigned, April 1982, 20).

Corsica

The people of Corsica are engaged in national liberation from French colonialism. And we Corsican women are taking part in this struggle but we think that it is as . . . a movement of female liberation that it ought to be led. When we were struggling for the liberation of our imprisoned brothers, sons, fathers, we were respected. Today we want to take our [own] independence and we are told that we divert the struggle, that we are traitors (Canale, April 1982, 30).

Uganda

As in other parts of Africa, missionaries and colonial administrators had imposed a male sex-role ideology on Uganda, resulting in subordinate status and a sense of inferiority in women. Between 1900, when the colonialist and the Ugandan woman met, and the time of his departure in 1961, nothing effectively had changed her status. Thus, at independence it was said, that a woman was regarded as inferior, she herself felt inferior, and because she saw her mother and all the women around her accepting this position of inferiority, she accepted it too. There were, nevertheless, some women active in campaigning for improved status. Little changed, however, since no political party was prepared to take women's issues seriously. The structure of power and decision-making was still heavily weighted against women's specific needs which were, in any event, seen as secondary to those of men. Women remained far enough away from the power structure not to be taken seriously. (Akello, n.d., 11–12).

Some of these stories deserve closer attention, for they tell us how the processes for achieving equitable integration actually worked. For, in all fairness, it must be conceded that even when policy makers—imperial or socialist—meant or even tried to pay their promissory notes and grant rights to women constitutionally or legally there were strong currents of resistance among both male and female traditionalists who fought any changes which altered relationships between the two worlds.[22] We look at some of these stories, especially those of Zimbabwe, Iran, and Oman—in chapter 5.

CHAPTER FIVE

Relations of the Two Worlds in a Postcolonial Context: Cases in Point

In Algeria the leftist groups had won, as they had in Zimbabwe. But in countries such as Iran and Oman, they had not. The resulting patterns differed, but in none of these cases had equitable integration been achieved. In the case of Zimbabwe the new government did make an effort to implement it when it took over, and in some countries the leftist parties almost succeeded in achieving it at least within the party.

Thus the Chilean compañeros in exile were amenable to change.[1] The women were having some, but not total, success with them. The account by one woman suggests some of the difficulties involved in achieving equitable integration in exile. She had not expected it to be a gift that would be automatically forthcoming with socialism. The struggle was going to be a long one. Still, there was a note of disappointment in her account of the behavior of the compañeros in exile on the way to the revolution.

The women in the resistance had been successful at every level, passed every test, achieved high positions, endured exile, grown, as the men had. But their burdens were not yet equal:

> Women party members, because of our experiences, had more self-confidence on reaching exile. We expected more of ourselves, and also more of our compañeros. . . . [But] there was no coherent response to our expectations . . . from the compañeros. . . . It was taken for granted that the compañeros had advanced; they washed the dishes, set the table, went out with us to shop. The compañeros helped, but did not commit themselves wholeheartedly. Tasks were not equally divided, they were merely lightened a bit. The women continued to bear the major responsibility. Responsibility for what? For accepting everything twice over,

> double exploitation, doubly difficult exile, because while we face the
> same difficulties as the exiled men, we also have had to face the job of
> integrating *all* our roles, of coordinating them. Once again women have
> had to make a double effort in order to meet our responsibilities, so as not
> to be obliged to opt for one role at the expense of another. [Diaz, 1979]

They still had, for example, to make a choice between career and family:

> We aspire to be integral women, to have children while fighting on the
> front lines or in the rearguard, to bring them up, to be part of a revolu-
> tionary relationship, to be workers, to have homes. We women have had to
> work much harder than men to fulfill our responsibilities, but when we
> do we blame ourselves because we are always giving our time to one role
> to the detriment of the other.

This was a kind of equitable integration no revolution had wholly
succeeded in achieving as yet. Still the author was hopeful. After all, the
compañeros *were* washing the dishes, setting the table, going out with
the compañeras to shop. However slowly the men might be moving, the
women were certainly making strides. "Millions of women all over the
world have already begun to move." And the future looked good.

> History begins anew each day, when in some corner of the Resistance a
> woman ceases to be a simple courier because she has won the right—by
> working twice as hard—to organize, to create, to lead. The history of our
> emancipation begins each day that a woman in Chile, in Latin America, in
> any part of the world, joins the struggle of the exploited and learns to
> expect that if she falls, the generous hands of the people will raise her
> children, learns to walk beside her compañero, at the same pace as he,
> toward the definitive victory.

It was, indeed, going to be a long haul. But victory was surely going to
come. It was not going to be a raisin drying in the sun.

The story of Zimbabwe showed how hard it was going to be to pay the
promissory notes in the coin of the realm—even by those with the best
intentions—when equitable integration had to face a reactionary foe.

> When Zimbabwe became independent nearly four years ago . . . its
> leaders expressed a determination that things should be different here.
> Women had fought in the guerrilla war to overthrow white minority rule.
> They had occupied prominent positions in the liberation party. . . . They
> were respected "comrades." . . . Prime Minister Mugabe sought to give
> substance to his promises by immediately establishing a ministry of
> women's affairs. Soon afterward he passed a law . . . giving women equal
> legal rights and the right to override tribal traditions and arrange their
> own marriages. [Sparks, *Washington Post*, 31 December 1982]

The saga of the women in Zimbabwe falls into four rather clear-cut stages: the guerrilla period before liberation in 1980; a brief honeymoon of several years; then a great letdown; and in 1984 a violent backlash.

The first stage was one of high hope and expectation. A 1980 Report on the *Role of Women in the Struggle for Liberation in Zimbabwe, Namibia, and South Africa* had stated the standard priority issue:

> In all three societies, women's struggle for equality with men has historically been subordinated to the wider struggle for national libera- tion. Thus the main goal for African women in Zimbabwe, Namibia, and South Africa has been to achieve national liberation working with men as the essential prerequisite for any real change in the social status of women in general. The two are seen as complementary and the participa- tion of women is seen as a way of ensuring that liberation of women will also come with national liberation [3]. . . . The common oppression of African women and men as well as their common fight for freedom have helped forge the movement towards sexual equality. [6]

The opportunity to participate in the armed struggle had been "the biggest blessing for the Zimbabwean women. It had speeded up the process of opening doors that, without it, might have taken years to achieve.[2] In the words of Teuri Ropa Nhongo, later to be made Minister for Community Development and Women's Affairs, "The struggle for national independence has opened our womenfolk to a world even they would not have dreamt of" (6). Their involvement in the struggle had been total:

> Our women's brigade is involved in every sphere of the armed revolu- tionary struggle. . . . In the frontline they transport war materials to the battlefield and . . . fight their way through enemy territory. . . . They do politicization work among the masses. . . . They teach the masses how to hide wounded Comrades, hide war materials and carry out intelligence reports behind enemy lines. . . . They are engaged in administration, health work, production and construction, educational work, etc. . . . At the rear, our women Comrades' tasks are even more extensive. They are involved in the work of every department of our Party, ZANU. They work as commanders, military instructors, commissars, medical corps, teach- ers, drivers, mechanics, cooks, in logistics and supplies, information and publicity, as administrative cadres. There is no department where their beneficial presence is not felt. [Ropa Nhongo, 1981, 7]

This was the crest of the wave, a high point. "In many parts of the country women Comrades, together with their menfolk . . . [were] re- constructing a new social order" (7). And they intended to succeed.

Independence was, indeed, achieved in 1980, and a honeymoon period began. When Teuri Ropa Nhongo and Naomi Nhiwatisa—minister and deputy minister, respectively, of Community Development and Women's Affairs—were interviewed a year later, they reaffirmed the goals of the women's movement. The minister proclaimed her ministry's plans for women:

> The Government has categorically asserted that men and women have equal rights, and that it will take steps to bridge the gap by accelerating the development of woman. I think many of these things are easier said than done. But the Government has set up the Ministry of Community Development and Women's Affairs to guarantee that whatever we proclaim we can actually carry out in practice. [45]

This was a momentous first step. It guaranteed achievement of equitable integration, something admittedly far easier said than done. But Zimbabwean culture had neglected women, and it was high time that they "should come together and solve their problems or else find the reasons why women are being left behind." Actually, the reasons were not all that hard to discern:

> Our society has a very strong tradition; we are told we are women and should stay in the back; we should not speak out; we even look down upon our own women who would speak up. This is how we are brought up. . . . It will be very difficult to overcome those cultural traditions, because of the oppression we've gone through and the difficulties we've had. That's the best we knew then, but now Zimbabwe is growing. It's a member of the international community and the Zimbabwean woman must be as developed as any other women. [45]

The ministry would have to supply leadership, encourage a kind of consciousness-raising form of affirmative action, actually to tell women it was all right for them to participate. For without such reassuring support it would be "very difficult to overcome those cultural traditions because of the oppression we've gone through and the difficulties we've had" (45).[3] So whatever a ministry—separatist or integrationist—instituted to help overcome those cultural traditions would be a plus.

When this seemingly separatist policy was challenged by Tendi Ndovu, the acting director of the party's publishing house, who asked: Did the establishment of a Ministry of Community Development and Women's Affairs mean that women were going to become isolated, segregated, and not have input into other ministries? The reply of the minister was clear and unequivocal. No way. "We won't allow it." The goals were not limited to changing the women themselves. The ministry would "encourage [both] the private sector and [the] Government to employ as many women as possible, as well as try to improve some statutory laws which deprive women" (44). There need be no structural disadvantage women would have to face in the future. The minister represented the "compleat" equitable integrationist point of view. "What we don't want is to have the Ministry of Women's Affairs be the only ministry for women. What we want is to have women as representatives in all ministries, and that the men should come and work with us to know what we are thinking, and give us their ideas" (Kelso, 1984, 13).[4] In the meanwhile, the women were talking, making themselves felt, in the trade unions, in education, in employment. They were refusing to take second place (interview with Ropa Nhongo, 46).

As a token of their planned achievements, the ministry in 1981 ordered a survey made of 3,000 rural women, most of them farmer-housewives, who had been left behind in the subsistence economy without new technology, credit, or know-how when the men had left for employment in the growing urban areas—a scene reported many places and many times since Ester Boserup called attention to it in 1970 (chapter 2).

The findings showed that land was a big issue and, among these women, so—ominously, as it proved—were the inequalities within the household. So also was employment an issue. "That women need to earn money was one of the strongest facts to emerge" from the survey (40), money for their children's education, nutrition, hygiene. The obstacles in the way of earning money were: lack of financial resources, transportation difficulties, and market know-how. They wanted also better access to the mass media so they could be reached by them and be kept informed on government plans. They suggested setting up "mobile 'agit-prop' vans . . . to reach" rural women who did not have radios. All this was necessary to teach both men and women in rural areas to "understand what we are fighting for." They wanted women's organizations to play an important part in all this. Otherwise there might well be regression to traditional culture, so exploitative of women (Kelso and Metz, 13).

Among the recommendations of the survey was a "quota" form of affirmative action in rural areas to encourage participation by women in decision making:

> The discriminatory attitudes that have prevented women from holding any positions of responsibility in Local Government should urgently be redressed at District Council level. To counteract conservative attitudes that continue to prevent women from exercising their capabilities, it is recommended that a minimum number of seats on the local councils be set aside for women. The integration of women into the decision-making process is an absolute prerequisite to the social as well as economic development of the rural areas and the country as a whole. [43]

Apparently the survey had consequences. After the publication of its findings, the government promised that bills "dealing with these discriminatory practices will be presented to Parliament early in the new year" (43).[5]

But the path to equitable integration was far from open. The honeymoon, it soon became clear, was over. Women found, as the minister had anticipated, it was going to be far easier to put words on the book than to plant new ideas in the minds, especially of males. Preparing men was going to be even harder than it had been to prepare women. It had proved to be easier to train female guerrillas to fight than to get noncombatants to accept them.

Military experience had given women a taste of independence and power, a chance to discover and exercise talents they had never known they possessed. In the words of a former combatant, the deputy minister herself, given the structure, the women could do whatever had to be done:

> When women were in the battlefield, they could command men. The line of command in the military is a relatively easy one: there is the commander, you follow the line of command. Women combatants learned to take leadership, to give commands and to expect commands to be followed. [47]

Women had even become instructors, had trained men, so the men *had* to accept them as equals (Kelso and Metz, 12–13). Party teaching had prepared the way for such change; it had taught men as well as women that women were equal so "the men also had to accept this and [in turn] teach the women that they were equal with men." Here, it appears, there was equitable integration.

But now, instead of enjoying the prerogatives of earned rank, women were being told, "No, you sit on the floor while the men sit over there" (47).[6] Even worse. They were now being punished, downgraded, rather than rewarded for their military service. Among the guerrillas, in a structure that had needed all the requisite talents, whether housed in a male or a female body, the men and women had understood one another. But the noncombatants, accustomed all their lives to a structure that subordinated women, did not understand what military experience had done to the women. The image of the female combatant was of her, allegedly, "the most cruel of the guerrillas, crueler than men. . . . So men were afraid to approach guerrilla women" (Kelso and Metz, 13). Further, in Zimbabwe, as in Algeria, the military experience of women destroyed their status as virtuous women. In the words of one former combatant, Stella:

> We played an important role in the struggle, putting up with countless sleepless nights and other privations. . . . But now we are treated as if we had committed a crime. Most parents would not have their "clean" sons

marry an excombatant. They think . . . we are undisciplined and will not make good wives. Some people regard us as prostitutes. . . . I feel very strongly about the way our society is ostracising us—it shows a society riddled with prejudices. [13][7]

Only four years after independence there was a violent backlash against women as the implications and ramifications of equitable integration began to show up. In the 1980 interview mentioned above, the minister had been asked if lobolo, or marriage dowry, was being phased out.[8] She had replied that since it faced so much opposition by nonprogressive men and even "women still imprisoned by their culture" (47), she did not think it important to stop it at once. The deputy minister had been more upbeat. It was, she granted, a complex problem. Still, she hoped that "as the income level and standards of living increase . . . parents will stop looking at their children as sources of income" (46). The minister was nearer the mark.

The new prime minister, Mugabe, to make good on his promises, had had a law passed, the so-called Legal Age of Majority Act, which gave women equal legal rights and the right to arrange their own marriages, thus overriding tribal custom, including lobolo. In the implementation of the new agenda, the government ordered Operation Clean-up, a crackdown on prostitution. This turned out to be an opportunity for male resentment to express itself in a violent backlash. There were indiscriminate raids—on beer halls, cinemas, a football stadium, even homes—picking up women and demanding proof of marriage, thus creating an "atmosphere of hysteria."

> . . . police raided at least ten major towns and cities. They picked up women walking in the streets; they pulled them out of cinemas, beer halls, and, in some cases, out of their own homes. Students, nurses, schoolgirls, teachers, married women and mothers with small children were among those arrested. The entire female work force at a canning factory in the eastern town of Mutare was picked up and held. . . . Once detained, the women were screened. Those who presented marriage certificates, or evidence that they had regular boyfriends or jobs, were freed. They had to depend on husbands, friends and employers to come forward with this evidence. Those who failed the test were sent to a resettlement camp. [Sparks, *Washington Post*, 31 December 1982]

The Minister of Community Development and Women's Affairs, Ropa Nhongo, was outraged at this "unpardonable violation of human rights." Even the acting minister of justice admitted in a placatory speech in Parliament that "mistakes were made." And when Mugabe returned from abroad two weeks later, he released all the women.

But a Women's Action Group was formed to "find answers to the question: why had the raids happened?" They did not blame the government. Its antiprostitution intentions had been good. But some members of the group felt that while the government's position suited the middle-class elite, it was "out of kilter with the masses of the African population," including even those charged with implementing it. Enforcement of Operation Clean-up "had gone out of control because of deeper, pent-up feelings against women on the part of those responsible for executing it." It "opened the floodgates for this resentment to vent itself on urban women, a class that represents a threat to the old ethical codes." The government, however willing to deliver the equitable integration in payment for the promissory note, was going to have to walk a fine line. It was going to have to follow the time-honored political path of compromise. And compromising with the inertia of history took time.[9] The Women's Action Group concluded therefore that its major task was going to have to be to educate the public about women's rights. True liberation faced many obstacles. It was likely to be a long struggle. Truly the understatement of the year,[10] or decade.

In the case of changes of this kind, no less than in cases of technological changes, Margaret Mead's questions were still relevant: "How much destruction of old values . . . must there be? How slow must we go? How fast can we go?" (1954, 2).

In Algeria and Zimbabwe, the leftist groups had won. In Iran they had not, and the experience there of women's groups with leftist groups left a bitter taste in their mouths. Both the women's and the leftist groups were defeated, but the women felt they had also been betrayed.

Unlike some of the other Third World countries, Iran had an ancient written history; it was already a great empire in Biblical times. It had also a recent history of attempted modernization, or Westernization as it was sometimes called. But it was an unlikely scene for a successful women's movement. Among the fourteen states of the Middle East, Iran ranked among the lowest in female literacy rates.[11] There were thus great numbers of women unreachable by the written word; and even by the spoken word, couched in a sophisticated vocabulary they had little way of understanding. The Shah had introduced numerous reforms in behalf of women, but there were not many who could use or appreciate them. Few women were in the labor force, and among those who were,[12] only a tiny proportion (5.8 percent) were professional, that is, educated or trained, workers. The professional women came from upper middle-class families with several generations of educated professionals behind them, accustomed to life in the modern world. Most (56.7 percent) of those in manufacturing, on the other hand, came from families of small businessmen and, like first-generation immigrants anywhere, they were ill at ease when they entered the work force, a world that was so new to them. Like the peasants (22.7 percent of the work force) these women were strongly conservative. The lower-middle-class women were conservative because adhering to Muslim customs protected them against frightening modern innovations[13]—including equitable integration—and the peasants were conservative because they had never been exposed to modern ideas at all.

As in so many other parts of the globe—the Phillippines, Singapore, Hong Kong, the United States—there were also some women whose major function was to perform conspicuous consumption for their wealthy husbands, the products consumed being Western, that is "modern." It was not among these "modern" women that leftist groups recruited members but rather among the small number of primarily urban educated women like themselves. They suffered defeat in two revolutions, first vis-à-vis the male leftist organizations, which acted exactly as the male leftist organizations in so many other countries had acted with respect to women, but also vis-à-vis the Khomeini-led government, which took over soon after the imperial regime's downfall.

As in other developing countries, as also in the United States, there had been a tradition among middle-class women of active participation in social and charitable organizations (chapter 4). In fact, the Shah's sister had sponsored them. The more activist women, however—some of whom had been influenced by the Western feminist movement—rejected such groups, viewing them as they viewed the trade unions, as designed, that is, to contain and stifle genuine class struggle. Most of the "socially conscious and intellectual women remained outside such organizations and the more militant and politically advanced among them were largely absorbed by the underground revolutionary anti-regime activities" (1982).[14]

A number of political parties had recruited these avant-garde women and organized them into support groups.[15] But, the women felt, their support was not reciprocated. In a pinch the leftist groups did not support them. Thus when they "resented and protested the blatant restriction on, and interference with, their most basic personal and social rights," the leftist men were not there to back them up. They were still making promises, "but in reality they have done little to implement them" (4).[16] They tended to see socialism rather than women's demands as the solution to women's problems. Not a promising stance for equitable integration.

The failure of both the organizational and the ideological components of the male leftist groups to recognize their issues constituted an almost traumatic shock to radical feminist Iranian women. Years of underground struggle had left the radical male groups with a "one-sided and inflexible outlook on the problems of women." They reduced everything to economic relations; they were unable therefore really to grasp the nature of female oppression which included, but went beyond, economic oppression; or to understand its cultural and ideological components. With this blind spot they did not "acknowledge the validity of women's struggles" (Az, 1980, 4–5). With no support, these women were forced into temporary retreat, but they had "by no means surrendered" (4). Some went to the United States where, as students, they carried on, though now they were fighting a different battle. And their message was now one of female separatism; the male world could not be depended on. They had found that they could not rely

> on any of the existing [leftist] organizations to acknowledge and act upon the specific needs and demands of women. The social, political, cultural and personal rights of women—dress, the right to work at any occupation, reproductive rights, etc.—will only be won by militant, active and self-acting women, and these rights will be won by organized women. [1982, 7]

And then the pitch for separatist, autonomous, independent women's groups:

> Clearly, what is needed is a genuinely independent and militant women's organization to organize and mobilize Iranian women around issues specific to women as well as democratic rights as a whole. In addition, the existing left organizations must make the struggle for women's right central to the struggle for democratic rights as a whole. A correct analysis of the important role played by women in the production and reproduction of class society, and the significance of domestic labor will put the overall struggle for democratic rights on the right path. In the final analysis, though, it will be women themselves who will liberate themselves. [7]

There was a "happy" ending to the failure of the leftist movements to support the women's groups. "Some sections of the revolutionary left are re-assessing their position vis-à-vis the question of women's oppression" (2). And conceding the necessity and value of separatist organizations, acknowledging "the need for a separate and independent organization to represent women and lead the woman's struggle, and within which Iranian women could gain the necessary consciousness to resume the struggle for democratic rights as a whole" (2). It was the rationale for a self-organized form of preparatory affirmative action.

After having rebuked the leftist movements—for their neglect of the special needs of women, for their rejection of women's separate organizations as divisive, for their one-sided and inflexible outlook on women's problems, for their inability to grasp the nature of female oppression, for their failure to support the women's 1979 demonstrations—the women were glad to hear of the male change of heart. Better late than never. They might have reminded the men that a victory delayed was often a victory betrayed. But they acknowledged the male statement appreciatively. Better luck in the next revolution against an adversary more difficult to deal with than a mere shah, namely the cultural inertia among the uneducated and a powerful fundamentalist backlash.

In some countries successful leftist groups were too poor to pay their promissory notes to women. Droughts, world depression, loss of revenue from exports, rising costs of imports had impoverished them. They were having a hard time just surviving. But in the case of some countries there were plenty of resources. Oman was one of them. Its government was wealthy enough to offer women more than any revolutionary movement could. It could at least outbid whatever material demands Omani women might make, or any leftist group promise. Its tide—of oil—could lift a lot of boats, including the boats of women.

Five years after the British had found oil in Oman in 1954, women were participating in a revolt against the British occupation, a revolt that marked the beginning of a national liberation movement. In 1975, after three years of armed revolutionary struggle in the south, the occupation was defeated by the combined efforts of the shah of Iran and eight other countries supporting the sultan. The military defeat of the People's Front for the Liberation of Oman (PFLO) was hard enough on the men but, trained and experienced, they could retreat to the borders of South Yemen to reorganize and continue their political education and rebuilding programs (*Isis*, no. 19, 1981, 29). But it was devastating for the women. Their participation in the liberation movement had been primarily in the lower echelons of the military, mainly in relatively unskilled positions. They had not had the education or political experience or the reading and writing skills required to participate at the ideological level. Thus, when they were demobilized they just left the schools of revolution, married, and "relapsed into their traditional role" (29). But a convinced and dedicated female remnant survived, however insignificant in terms of numbers; they became ideological keepers of the (separatist) flame.

In 1975 they organized the Organization of Omani Women (OWO) specifying as its tasks "to make demands in their capacity as women, and to defend the right to, for instance, maternity and child-welfare programmes, the reduction of housework" (*Isis*, no. 19, 1981, 29). They would also strugggle against "the incorrect ideas that women's only role is marriage and the production of children." For the less educated women the task was to be to establish a "special agitation department" to raise their consciousness and encourage their participation in the revolution. Brave words in the face of the oil tide that was working against them.

In 1970, a new sultan, Qabus bin Said, had come to power.[17] Awash in oil revenue and aware that the country was "acutely short of trained manpower," the new government accorded top priority to developing its human resources, including women, through education and training.[18] As recently as 1970 there had still been "almost no medical facilities, only three primary schools, and only the most primitive communications in Oman." The new Sultan inaugurated two massive five-year development plans for health and education. Hospitals, schools, clinics, welfare programs were to be established. By 1975, at the end of the first of the five-year plans, a "sizeable economic and social infrastructure" had, in fact, been established. Qualified women had begun to fill important positions in government, in the social services, in commerce. In 1981 the second plan began, and a year later there were 2,000 hospital beds.

But it was in education that the growth was to be most striking. Beginning with 900 boys and 30 teachers in three primary schools in 1970

> there are now 431 primary, preparatory and secondary schools with 138,170 pupils of both sexes and 6,500 teachers. . . . The second five-year plan seeks to provide at least a primary education free for every Omani child by the end of 1985. To achieve this, another 140 schools will be built, some in remote rural areas (72).[19]
>
> The English Language Department in the Ministry of Education . . . is headed by an Omani woman (73).
>
> The education authorities believe that during the period of general education, it is important to expose a child to different opportunities in order to develop his or her natural talents. Pupils who show an aptitude for technical studies can subsequently join a technical secondary school and continue tertiary education in engineering.
>
> Three more teachers' training institutes will be established as Oman is acutely short of trained Omani teachers. Two of the Institutes will train women teachers.
>
> One of the basic aims of the education system is to provide equal opportunities for girls, who now make up about one-third of the present enrollment of 125,000 students. Three of the new secondary schools are to be for girl students. At the preparatory level, all girls' schools will now have domestic science wings.
>
> Among Omani students studying abroad are girls taking up engineering, electronics, medicine, education and other specialist disciplines. Girls enjoy equal job opportunities with men on qualifying (74–75).
>
> Adult literacy will also receive increased attention in the current development programme. Under the slogan "Education for All," the government holds literacy classes which are attended by more than 6,000 men and women. Over 5,000 others study at adult education centres. For those who are unable to attend these centres, there is a free study-at-home programme which provides participants with textbooks and other educational materials (76).

> Women's centres combine literacy lessons with training in domestic
> science and the basics of public health. [Oman Ministry of Information,
> 76]

A picture of three Western-dressed women working at modern technological equipment—under a male supervisor—projects the image of a
modern well-trained female worker (37). And, not restricted to security
checks at the airport as she was before 1972, "the police woman today
performs duties similar to those of her male counterpart, including
traffic control and criminal investigation" (34). Omani women had
moved almost overnight from a medieval to a modern society.

By 1975, the sultan's first five-year plan was beginning to make itself
felt. A revolution against a colonial power in a poor country was altogether different from a revolution against a native regime flush with
oil in the throes of an acute shortage of trained manpower calling for
education and training even if it meant education and training for girls
and young women if necessary, even if it called for coeducation, even if it
called for training young women in engineering, electronics, medicine,
and other formerly male disciplines and professions. Even, at least
verbally, if it meant equal job opportunities for women. A very hard act
for a competing revolution to keep up with. OWO could only counter it
by downplaying it:

> The liberation of women is not indicated by the percentage of female
> workers or employees in government departments or corporations, nor
> the number of employees or secretaries in ministries, nor by the number
> of educated women or university graduates. [1981, 29]

Nor could the liberation of women be "achieved through men making
concessions to women" but only by "constant organized struggle by
women on the economic, social, and political levels." And OWO was
engaged in just such a struggle:

> The Organization of Omani Women is at present working to train
> women cadres who can lead the Omani women's movement as a whole,
> and form a women's vanguard. It will in no way compromise on women's
> demands for equality with men. Nor will it allow anyone to pacify
> women, or to stop them after the completion of the liberation struggle.
> We are well aware that traditional ideas remain in the minds of many
> people for a long time—even after a transformation of the social system.
> We are building a cadre force in order to lead women towards their
> liberation, so that they will reach the end of the road and not stop half
> way. [29]

The military setback which took place soon after these brave words
were uttered as well as the apparent success of the Five-Year plans

seemed to have led OWO to a greater emphasis on strictly female issues, where they might have had a competitive edge. Thus, included in the second OWO congress in 1979—in addition to the standard political and economic rights—there were

> the right to choose freely one's partner and the right to apply for a divorce. . . . a reduction of the bride-price, and prohibition of humiliation and corporal punishment of women. . . . special privileges in connection with pregnancy and parturition, and for the establishment of nurseries and kindergartens all over Oman. [30]

Although OWO pledged itself to implement its original program, giving high priority to the work of the PFLO, working hard "to engage women in its activities," concentrating in the ideological and organizational fields, consciousness raising, and educational activities, and expanding its publication activities by way of a monthly magazine, it nevertheless remained dedicated to its major priority, a kind of affirmative action, namely, the preparation of women for their own liberation. For although men had an important contribution to make to women's active struggle for her legitimate human and social rights, "the responsibility for this struggle belongs to the Omani woman herself" (30).

> It is clear that an understanding of the significance of the women question coupled with an understanding of the importance of the participation of women in the national struggle is a *first* essential step towards women's emancipation. The *main* task of the women's and of other organizations is to explain to all women their basic human rights, how they can fight for these rights, and what major role women can play in reconstructing society. [29, emphasis added]

In view of the powerful inertia inherent in the lack of literacy in the population to whom these views would seem threatening, among the specific tasks OWO set for itself was a special agitation department "to meet the specific problems of the less educated women, to raise their consciousness, and to lead them towards participation in the revolutionary struggle."

Although OWO granted the male world's premise that women could not achieve liberation without the liberation of their society at large—the standard priority issue—it recognized that the reverse was also true. Full liberation of society was impossible without the full liberation of women. Placing obstacles in the path of Omani women was the same as placing them in the path of all Omani society.

Still, they knew they had a powerful competitor for the minds and hearts of Omani women. A wealthy government that needed trained women and was willing to pay well for them in the form of concessions was a formidable foe.[20]

Worthy of at least a passing nod is the case of Kuwait, where it was not a party-sponsored group, but the head of the Women's Cultural and Social Society that was supplying leadership. In a country where even men were waiting for the franchise she was seeking the right of women to vote (Ottaway, 1984). "It is very important for women to be in parliament. . . . There are so many issues that deal with women—the family and such." Brave words. Nor was the idea unthinkable, for both the ruling emir and the crown prince—though not his wife—supported women's suffrage. If women did gain the right to vote in parliamentary elections they would constitute a majority (52 percent) of the potential, though not probable, voters, for "so far as one can glean from the public discussion, a majority of women is still either indifferent or actively against the idea—not to mention the men." The women's antisuffrage lobby, better organized than the liberal women's movement, thought it was too early to enfranchise women. But their leader, Lulwa Gattami, was undaunted. Of course opposition was natural, still the lesson being taught and learned everywhere was that it was "a matter of mass education. Our job is to raise the consciousness among women."[21]

Although the experience of women in the United States vis-à-vis a leftist group—the Socialist party—in the early years of the century is not consonant with the postcolonial theme of this chapter, it is, nevertheless, relevant in showing some similarities in a quite different context. The Socialist party was hardly revolutionary, nor was the ambience the same as in postcolonial countries at mid-century. But, as in the countries we have been glancing at there was no "acknowledgement of women's special needs nor any particular stress upon reaching them and enrolling them into the Party" (Buhle, 1971, 68–69). It was always male wrongs, male needs, male audiences (71). Nevertheless, at the 1904 national convention of the party, "a small group [of wives of delegates and single women] held several sessions in a separate hall for the purpose of organizing a [separate] Woman's National Socialist Union" (69). Although this union had little national impact, separate women's branches of the party did spring up across the country.

> . . . if the Socialist Party was to speak for the most progressive forces in the nation, it could not easily stand aside when women, conscious of their new political and economic roles, were organized into non-socialist reform movements. . . . Thus the reassessment which marked the period indicated a development of intent among socialists toward the neglected problem of women's liberty. [69]

The men justified their position by their professed belief in perfect equality for women, but, as one man admitted, when it came "to practice, we are not always in accord with this highly respectable principle of ours" (69). Women had to be the support of men in their party work;

they had to be taught the nature and importance of that work. But the emphasis was on a kind of preventive cooption "to prevent advanced women from being siphoned off into reform groups and ordinary wives from dragging their socialist husbands into inactivity" (70). But separatism grew.

A new journal, *Socialist Women*, was established as if to emphasize this trend. The founders wanted to make it clear to male socialists that members of separate women's branches were not mere passive housewives seeking enlightenment about socialism but active spokesmen of women's rights. Their approach was more dynamic than the standard merely verbal one. They were hopeful about the party "but believed the nominal 'equal rights' plank was insufficient" so long as it remained merely in the form of "cold, printed words" rather than in "real pulsating life" (71). Liberation was not something granted by others; it was a do-it-yourself achievement. This situation justified separate women's clubs. "A woman . . . could never gain freedom and equality as long as she was satisfied being in the 'dishwashing contingency,' even to the Socialist Party. . . . Even under socialism, women could not be free until they had developed the power of freedom within themselves" (71).

Africa, Latin America, the Persian Gulf, the United States. . . . Nowhere was equitable integration guaranteed so long as its terms and implementation were specified by the male world. The male specifications too often had meant, in effect, incorporation, cooption. In some places leftist movements had created and then absorbed the women's movements. The cons of equitable integration which had shown up in development projects (chapter 3) had also shown up elsewhere. Women's issues were not listened to, or, if they were, they were downgraded; in the words of the women historians, marginalized. And everywhere the "dead hand of history" blocked even the sincerest efforts to achieve equitable integration.

So almost universally governments—socialist and capitalist alike—continued to have to explain away persisting inequalities between the two worlds with such euphemisms as "tribal resistance," "undeveloped ideas," "remnants of the past," "feudal remains," "Victorian hangovers," "bourgeois relics," and the like. It was precisely these vestiges which feminists were learning how to expose, verbalize, protest, resist, conceptualize as issues, render visible, demystify. Sometimes, as we saw in Zimbabwe, at their peril.

Regimes fell, regimes rose; governments succeeded governments; cabinets followed cabinets. Discrimination against women, marginalization of their issues, persisted. Constitutions and laws proclaimed equality; inequality remained. At full tide, as at the ebb, the women were below deck. As the women historians had said: "Women joined and promoted the cause of leftist parties" only to find "themselves forgotten in the wider struggle for emancipation." The rewards of their involvement had been marginalization. Or, as in Algeria, even worse—regression.

One need not extend to all leftist movements Dufrancatel's cynical interpretation of the misogynist and exploitative motives of the Algerian national liberation movement (chapter 4). It is conceivable that the failure of new regimes to pay the promissory notes to women might in some cases have been due to a lack of understanding of what they had promised. Only with time did the meaning of the promises become clear, even to the women themselves. For a strange thing happened to many women on the way to national liberation. In the process of thinking about one of the major recruiting themes of the leftist movements—the dual oppression of women—they worked out new ways of interpreting their own oppression that were filtering in from the West, new ways of looking at it from their own perspective, not that of the male world. It generated a greater awareness in the female world of its own unique self-defined identity and self-formulated characteristic issues. And, incidentally, a new kind of female-defined separatism.

Despite the failures of so many regimes vis-à-vis women so widely deplored in the female world, on a strictly verbal level, most of the liberation movements had actually done quite well. Almost universally the correct promised words were included in constitutions and placed on the statute books. In many countries there were now services for women, including provision of child care, primarily, to be sure, to keep mothers in the work force. It was not, therefore, in verbal or even legal recognition that the new governments had failed to pay their promissory notes.

The oppression women had shared with men new regimes could understand, and they could write laws against it. Or when women's issues came to their attention in standard form and dealt with concerns they were used to, they could respond. The right to participate in elections, of course. To participate in the work force, naturally. They were not only permitted, but in some places, actually encouraged—as, for example, even in Muslim South Yemen. Training for and access to all kinds of jobs, equal pay, the right to run for all kinds of office. Anything you could pass a law about—whether or not you could enforce it—could be acceptable. One might resist granting everything, but at least one could see what the issues were. When women asked for potable water or better roads, that was understandable too.

Even some forms of emotional oppression and psychological humiliation they could also understand. Thus when the former president of South Yemen, Salem Robaya Ali, in a 1974 speech deplored the "extreme forms of humiliation, degradation, oppression and exploitation to which women were subjected under colonial and reactional rule," the men could see it. They had themselves had the same destructive experiences. They had themselves been despised, considered worthless things, beaten grievously. When the former president deplored the custom that defined women as having half the virtue of men in law, property, and employment, he could understand such female oppression even when he had not himself experienced the impact of this particular custom. He, like the women, was against arranged marriage, the selling of women like sheep. He was opposed to a status in which suicide, disobedience, or flight was the only escape for many women. Men had also suffered in that status. He was glad that "now a more positive end was in sight." All these evils were to be taken care of by law, education, and employment opportunities (Molyneux, n.d., 2). Polygyny was to be prohibited, divorce equalized, bride-price limited. True, the new laws still permitted some inequalities, and many changes had met with great resistance. There were plans, nevertheless, to extend legal provision for equality and to eliminate anomalies. Anything that could be dealt with by passing a law could be granted. It would, of course, "be a long time before women's rights . . . could be effectively guaranteed since the power of traditionalist ideologies and family pressures combine to limit the degree to which women are able to attain them" (3).

But it was precisely traditional sexism itself that was inching its way forward in the female world as target for attack. And this was an issue much harder for the male world to understand. What, some men might have mused, was all this about "a new type of relations within the family, between husband and wife, relations of equality, possibilities to discuss, mutual respect?" (Moiana, 1981). What was all this about "recognition of her [woman's] dignity?" (Akello, n.d., 18–19). What was all this about women being "not only a quantitatively important sector, but also a qualitatively vital one?" (Diaz, 1979). About "women's belief in her own abilities?" About her feelings about herself? (OMM, 1976, 28). About "Society's contempt for the single woman?" Complaints about the painful words fathers, brothers, and husbands used against them? Complaints that men talked but did not listen? That they took for granted that their views should prevail? What was all this hullabaloo against the traditional ideology that "conceives of the woman's role as serving men—as an object of pleasure, as a procreator and as unpaid worker?" (OMM, 28). *What*, for heaven's sake, did women want? What kind of law could you pass to achieve it?

Was this what all the fighting had been about? Was it really necessary for us to have to turn our attention to these trivia? None had been on the agenda of the liberation or the revolution. Did we *have* to take time to discuss them? We had, after all, a socialist system to build. Or a trade policy to implement. Or an election to win. Or a war to fight. As already noted, however sincerely a new regime might give lip service to the issues raised by the female world, such issues were given low priority. There was always something more urgent to deal with.[22]

The puzzlement—and resistance—of the male world was understandable. For along with all the other anticolonial, liberation, and revolutionary movements taking place there was also going on in the middle of the century another revolution of equal if not greater magnitude and ramifications. A Feminist Enlightenment was taking place in the female world which was changing the way the world was seen and tackling not only the standard structural targets of revolutions—political and economic systems—but also the very way the mind worked, the way gender relationships were conceptualized, the language that defined them.[23] It was attitudes, feelings, thinking itself that the female world was seeking to change. Women were talking about things one didn't talk about; calling attention to things one didn't call attention to, rendering them visible for all to see. They were inventing terms like *sexism*, and they were raising the consciousness of women in ways analogous to those Marxists had once used to raise the class consciousness of workers. They were holding up an unflattering mirror to the male world. They were downgrading machismo, making it something one should be embarrassed about rather than proudly glory in. They were, ominously, redefining themselves rather than automatically accepting a male definition. They were discovering that the personal was political. It was this "personal" that male leftist movements had a hard time swallowing. How could it have anything to do with the political?

In the West this revolution had even taken the name Women's Liberation Movement, giving it the dignity and validity and legitimacy of the male liberation movements all over the world. Despite differing backgrounds, its ideology was spreading everywhere. Thus a woman in South Yemen, when asked, "Do you have any knowledge of, or views on, the women's liberation movement in the West?" replied: "Yes, we know about their struggles concerning work, wages, children, and other things. Our society is, however, a backward one: while our tactical struggles are [therefore] different, our aims are the same" (Molyneux, n.d., 11). An emerging Feminist Enlightenment was teaching women to see themselves not as the Other—not as the object but as the viewing, observing, even judging subject. It was supplying a vocabulary, a perspective, a critique. Concepts. Paradigms. Tactics might differ but even in South Yemen, "the aims were the same." Even when women opposed the new ideology, the very act of having to challenge it meant it was having an impact. In some parts of the female world the flyers, the polemics, the conference papers, the articles, sounded like applications to specific local situations of the vocabulary of this universal liberation language.

One can imagine even an honest and sincere male revolutionary rubbing his eyes: was this really the kind of oppression the women had felt they were fighting against? Confronted with a whole array of issues only now becoming articulated—male chauvinism and sexism among others—he might be able to see reflected an image of the male world as it looked in the female world, a world in which it was men like them who were among the oppressors. It had been easy to see oppression of women when the oppressor was a government, an employer, or a white man, the same one that had opressed them. It was different when they were themselves seen as the oppressors, when they looked at the oppressors and found that they were them.

An anticolonial, Marxist Frenchwoman, Simone de Beauvoir, had begun a train of thought in 1949 that was to reverberate widely everywhere in the female world. A great deal of the momentum for spreading it was to come from the thinking of women in Europe and the United States, where the historical "women's movement" was to give rise to the so-called feminist movement. The two movements were not mutually exclusive, but, in general, participants in the women's movements specialized in the standard political and economic issues—political and economic and legal rights. And participants in the feminist movements added the characteristic and uniquely female—even biological—issues as well. There was usually considerable overlap in membership, and divisive issues of ideology existed in both. It was the feminist issues that were so puzzling to men, in leftist movements as well as to men everywhere when they were confronted by them.

Beauvoir's book *The Second Sex* had painted an unflattering portrait of women in the middle of the twentieth century. Every weakness was admitted. But—and this was the overall thrust of the book—these defects were not viewed as intrinsic but rather as the result of women's position in the social and economic structure. This did not mean that female liberation could be achieved by economic change alone. A wholesale revamping of the whole sex-socialization process was called for.

> We must not believe, certainly, that a change in woman's economic conditions alone is enough to transform her, though this factor has been and remains the basic factor in her evolution; but until it has brought about the moral, social, culture, and other consequences that it promises and requires, the new woman cannot appear. At this moment they have been realized nowhere, in Russia no more than in France or the United States. [1949, 683]

But the new woman was beginning to appear soon after.

Beginning slowly but with increasing power, these new women in the West were refusing to wait for the transformation which their economic conditions under socialism would produce. They were going to liberate themselves. As so also were women in the Third World. There had been a change in the way things were seen, a paradigm shift; a seed had been sown which was now bearing fruit. Women were now conscious that they need not remain passive. They may not yet have broken with the old schemas, but they had started (Mendoza, 1981, 8).[24] No longer as part of male movements but as activists in their own behalf, women were beginning a new kind of (ideologically self-defined) separatism as, perhaps, a kind of affirmative action on the way to equitable integration.

The new activists delineated new kinds of issues including control of their own bodies; the right to abortion; protection against rape in or out of marriage; protection against domestic violence, including painful words; against irresponsible paternity; against, in brief, whatever advantages men have had on the basis of sheer physical size or muscular superiority. They sought cultural bulwarks against any biological odds against them at the most primitive level of force, as one more step in the civilizing process which has tamed "nature" in behalf of civility. They wanted, in brief, civility as well as equitable integration. Manners as well as morals.

Even more, they sought liberation from the male bias in male mentality, attitudes, feelings toward women. Liberation from the male bias in all human knowledge which had resulted in the denigration of female experience, of the female perspective.

So much, then, for some of the issues that in one form or another, on a trivial or on a vital matter, were coming to invade and, in some places, to pervade the global female world. Much of the success of the effort toward an equitable integrationist revolution depended on the emerging character of the female world itself. On what strengths it developed. What resources it achieved. What weaknesses it overcame. Especially its vulnerability vis-à-vis the male world. For the female world was not unified, of a single mind, or without its own separatisms.

CHAPTER SIX

The Feminist Enlightenment

Knowledge is Power. [Francis Bacon]

Difficult as it has been for the female world to achieve equitable integration with the male world, it has been only slightly less difficult to achieve it within the female world itself. Even learning how to conceptualize it is problematic. Does it mean solidarity? Does it demand homogeneity? Discouraging diversity? Of racism? Of classism? Of ethnicity? Rather than engaging in theoretical specifications of equitable integration in the female world, the discussion here deals with racism, classism, and "status impediments" in the relationships among women in different parts of the world. Underlying the question of equitable integration with the male world is the assumption that such integration depends on equitable integration within the female world.

A considerable amount of the thinking about equitable integration vis-à-vis both the female and male worlds and within the female world itself has so far, as a matter of historical accident, been done by U.S. feminists, especially by those who lived through the 1960s, when antiwar and civil rights movements were raging at crisis levels. On the basis of participation in these activities women's consciousness of their position in the social structure was raised and greatly illuminated. Thus just as the leftist movements in postcolonial areas of the world were supplying the female world with a vocabulary to describe and illuminate its oppression, so also were these women performing an analogous role in the West, especially in Europe and the United States.[1]

This movement emerged about two centuries after an eighteenth-century intellectual movement which came to be known as the French Enlightenment (because France was its source and center) arose and cast its rays far and wide, even as far as the Russian Empire. This movement gave the Western intellectual world a new view of its history; it rejected the old status quo, especially its old authority structure, and installed one based on reason, on science. In these respects the twentieth-century Feminist Enlightenment resembled it in many ways.[2]

In 1970 a book entitled *Sisterhood Is Powerful* appeared in the United States. It was an anthology that embodied the experience of a group of U.S. women during the 1960s, a period when the country was being raked by antiwar and civil rights activism at a high pitch. In both of these movements women had participated along with men. They found, much to their dismay, that although the men were ideologically dedicated to equality in all human relationships they nevertheless relegated women to second-class status in the movement. About the same time, in another part of the forest, under the leadership of the President's Commission on the Status of Women, set up in 1961, there was a revival of political activism among women which led to a succession of organizations and activities to extend women's political rights.[3] And out of all this excitement and activism women in the colleges and universities began to produce a body of research and writing that led to a monumental rethinking of most of the inherited body of human knowledge, until then an exclusively male prerogative.[4] This Feminist Enlightenment—child of theorists, activists, researchers—began to cast its beams in all directions as its eighteenth-century predecessor had done. And just as the earlier one had been felt all over the Western intellectual world, so also was this one being felt. Terms like *sexism, male chauvinism, the personal is political* began to show up in many languages, whether as weapons or as tools.

Many of the activities, writings, and research findings of these women aroused enormous hostility in the 1960s and 1970s. They were viewed as destructive, threatening radicals. They became the whipping girls not only of conservatives in the male world but also of many women in the female world. There, as "white, middle-class" radicals they were widely rejected. For some in the Third World they became surrogates for colonialism as the enemy.

Whether they were guilty or not, the Feminist Enlightenment did make clear not only that separation—psychological, sociological, spatial—characterized relations between the female and male worlds but that so also did geographic and political separation exist among constituent parts of the female world itself. Equitable integration might be the eventual solution to the question of the relationship between the female and male worlds—after a preparatory period of affirmative action in the female world—but it was not the answer to other relationships (racial, class, ethnic, national) within the female world itself, either locally or globally.[5] For the concept of a global female world did not imply a seamless entity equitably integrated for the achievement of shared goals. The 2.5 billion females on this planet differed not only demographically (chapter 1) and culturally—in material and nonmaterial cultures that shaped them within any given community (chapter 2)—but also historically, which meant politically, and hence in the consequent impact of centrifugal political, nationalistic, and economic forces.

Just as it was the historical position of France in the eighteenth-century and the universality of its language that had led to the wide spread of the teachings of its philosophes, so it was also the historical position of the United States in the second half of the twentieth century and the universality of its language—English, "American," Pidgin English—that facilitated the wide spread of the teachings of its feminists. The impact was astonishing and not always appreciative, at home[6] or abroad:

> The reforms that the founding feminists fought for have created conflicts and contradictions . . . for poor women, women of color, working-class women. . . . who by and large did not define themselves as feminists in the first place. . . . To our knowledge no one has developed a definitive theory of world systems that takes into account all oppressions and that has an unerring crystal ball that will direct us to radical social change. . . . [So] how do we create a feminism that speaks to the realities of *all* women? [JET, introduction to "Movement Buiding," vol. 5, in *Quest*, vol. 5, no. 4 (1982), pp. 5–6, emphasis supplied]

Thus it was that these women, by no means a homogeneous category, became, as the "white, middle class" Western (read "American") feminists, the targets of the slings and arrows of critics everywhere. So, it is legitimate to ask not only who they were but also if they were guilty.

They were the brilliant, talented, creative women who, beginning in the mid-sixties had been evolving and providing the vocabulary for modern feminism.

Their perspective was both personal and political. They could see not only that personal problems had political diminsions but also that political actions had personal impact. They could, that is, perceive the impact on individual women of the great social and economic forces turning around them. They were diverse in temperament, class, and racial background as well as in physical attractiveness; they were rebels, some rebelling against their own demons. They were brave. They were antagonistic, antagonizing, and antagonized. They had had different apprenticeships—in politics, in lobbying, in civil-rights activities, in antiwar activities, in media communications, in academia, in the work place. They had followed different paths, arrived at different theoretical positions. Some were activists skilled in street theater, in demonstrations. Some were cerebral activists, that is, primarily writers. They differed in ideology, in explanations, in definitions, and in the goals of feminism. Some emphasized the victimization of women, their oppression; some exalted the achievers. But whatever their apprenticeship had been or where it had taken place or where it had led them, they had all had their consciousness raised. They could see what had been invisible to them before. Like their eighteenth-century forebears they were inaugurating new ways to see the world.

Many women and men, both in the United States and throughout the world, rejected the new reality the feminists were uncovering. They were often characterized as "man-haters," as well as "crazies." Many seemed trivial, irrelevant, frivolous, arrogant, "bra-burning" rebels.[7] It was held against them that they attacked what they called sexism, the whole syndrome of verbal and body language, attitudes, customs, mores, laws, court decisions, regulations, which they insisted demeaned women. The implication of the three charges against these women was that they were racist, insensitive to the poor, and ignorant of the situation of non-U.S. women. How guilty were they?

Actually, to the extent that they were guilty of these defects, it was not for lack of trying to overcome them. That a disproportionate number of them were white could not be gainsaid. But they were not racist.[8] Indeed, they had made great effort, had leaned over backward, to be antiracist.

> We simply cannot continue to deny or ignore the fact that feminism as a movement has been and is predominantly white and middle-class. It cannot remain so if it is to be a progressive force for social change. Fortunately, there are some encouraging signs that white feminists are beginning to understand that an analysis of sexism is incomplete without an analysis of racism. . . . The growing understanding among white feminists that racism exists within us as individuals and in our organizations, and the escalating leadership of women of color have the potential for the creation of a women's movement that is truly revolutionary. [JET, *Quest*, vol. 5, no. 4 (1982), pp. 6–7]

In order to minimize race differences, to show their sensitivity to black women they had, entre nous, deliberately taken on the language and dialect of black women until they were taught by the black women themselves how patronizing this was, how insulting. That was not the way to go. They cringed when reminded that they shared the privileges of white men while black women endured the hardships of black men. In time these women came to understand what racism was and that they themselves were guilty of it.

Indeed, the author just quoted believed that women of color held "the key to yet another 'new wave' of feminism—one that embraces more women by examining, speaking to, analyzing the experiences and realities of women of color" (7). The "escalating leadership of women of color" did, in fact, show itself increasingly in the 1980s. Their work was becoming a "textbook classic, [which] clearly demonstrates the body of information and theory being developed by women of color, and the practice on which it is being built" (7). The author concluded that any feminism that did not take into account the special oppression of women of color would be incomplete.[9] And all over the globe, women of color—Black, Asian, Hispanic, American Indian—were now reviewing and researching their history and developing ideological challenges to the intellectual, theoretical hegemony of white women in the female world, and especially of the white, middle-class, U.S. women.

The charge that feminists were "middle-class" implied that their interests were not relevant to poor women, to lower-class women, to working-class women; that they were insensitive to the issues important to these other women. They had probably never seen anyone who was involuntarily hungry. They could afford more expensive grievances. Sheltered as they were from the hardships of life, how could they empathize with working class women? Or with women in poverty anywhere?

Actually these feminists were as rejecting of classism as they were of racism. They worked hard to free themselves of such antifeminist defects when accused of them. A lively literature of charges and ripostes arose in the 1970s on the subject. Mistakes were made as, for example, engaging in the practice of "downward mobility," an attempt by middle-class feminists to abolish class differences by deliberately taking on the life style of poor or working class women, by depriving themselves of amenities poorer women could not afford. No more than in the case of blacks, was this the way to go.[10] But the impediments to genuine feminism posed by class did have to be dealt with:

> The question for each upper and middle class woman is how to change class oppression in her life, in the movement, and the society. Behavior and privileges can be examined to see which are destructive to other women and how to change those. Skills and privileges that are gained from class connections can be used to advance all women, not just oneself or women of your class. Each woman can teach what she has gained from her class position and in turn learn from other women those strengths which she has been denied by her middle class socialization. Finally we must all work to break down the barriers of class as well as of race and sexism. [Bunch and Myron, *Class and Feminism*, 1974, 11][11]

Middle-class women would have to be shown their own classism, how they enjoyed certain privileges because they were "attached to or . . . had been attached to some male along the way (father, boyfriend, husband) and got the privileges from him" (39). They would have to get rid of their classism by recognizing that the privileges they enjoyed derived from their white male connections. It would not be easy. There were many ways to avoid this recognition.[12] But liberation from such escapism was possible:

> Start thinking politically about the class system. . . . Stop being immersed in political idealism and abstractions that have little or nothing to do with your life or anyone else's. You are an enemy of lower class women if you continue destructive behavior, based on your sense of middle class superiority. But you will become an ally in the feminist revolution if you will examine that behaviour and change those patterns. If women start forcing confrontation with their own class, race, and heterosexual privileges, then they will both oppress other women less and begin to confront a whole system based on power and privilege. [Myron, 41][13]

The U.S. feminists of the '60s and early '70s were, then, accustomed to a wide variety of charges against their position on race and class. But, whatever their defects may have been in the areas of race and class, these "white, middle-class" feminists were determined to overcome them. Neither racism nor classism was acceptable to them. To the extent that they were guilty of these defects it was inadvertent, unwitting. When alerted to either one they tried to overcome it. By understanding racism and classism they believed they could train themselves "to be rid of them" (Karen Schiller, "Morality and Feminism: Creating Laws We Can Live By," *Plexus*, October 1981, 15).[14]

By the mid-70s the feminist stage had become international and the "white, middle-class" feminists were confronted with another charge that encompassed both race and class. They were "American" or "Western." And by a curious twist of logic their feminism became for some women of the Third World a unique form of (intellectual) oppression, a surrogate for "neocolonialism," attempting to impose on the rest of the female world paradigms and conceptualizations that were in no way congruent with the lives and issues of women elsewhere.[15] Meetings and gatherings were planned and run in ways that censored or prevented different feminist perspectives in, for example, the Third World.

In the 1950s in the United States, movements to improve race and other minority-group relations had sometimes operated on the assumption that prejudices could be mollified by more contacts under appropriate conditions. In a popular musical, *The King and I*, one of the songs was called "Getting to Know You," and it implied that getting to know one another meant getting to like, even love, one another. This happy process did not, however, necessarily occur.[16] Indeed, in some ways it could be said that the more some women in the Third World learned about women in the West, especially in the United States, the more angry, hostile, suspicious they became.

> At every intellectual women's gathering the divisions of race, class, nationality and ethnicity erupt, tearing at the unity that brings women together. . . . We can pretend that differences do not exist, or we can explore them and, in the process, reformulate feminism itself. The latter is more difficult and painful, but indispensable, if sisterhood is to become more than a slogan. [Bandarage, 1984, 6]

Painful, but indispensable it might be, but the participants at these meetings did try. It was not always easy. Sometimes intellectual accord might be achieved, but without supporting emotional conviction.

Thus the reporter of a 1983 conference of a thousand women commented on the contrast between the thoughtful scholarly papers—by an Arab woman examining sexism in schoolbooks in her country, by a South African woman explaining her struggle against apartheid, by women publishers exchanging ideas about feminist writing—and what she remembered about the meeting later. The papers showed women thinking along the same or similar lines, having similar thoughts, similar ideas, similar problems no matter where they lived, whether in Latin America, Africa, or Asia (Rieder, 1983, i). It was not, however, these commonalities, nor the important intellectual contributions these women were making that stuck in her mind. They were drowned out in her memory by the "vocal arguments" and "fights."

> Listening to both sides of an argument I often thought that although they were actually talking about the same issues, they were unable to listen to each other and thus unable to understand each other's point of view. . . . Euro-, Afro-, Asian-, and Latin-American feminists had their arguments. They lost out on the opportunity of a constructive dialogue that is going on between all these other women who represent 94 percent of the world's female population. Women who have so much to say and whose voices are rarely heard.

Thus common differences—the stated topic of the conference—were drowned out by separating issues.[17]

One persistent charge against Western feminism running through the relations of women on the international scene has been the lack of fit of its paradigms elsewhere in the world. Attempts to impose them constituted a kind of cultural colonialism. Though "couched in universal terms," actually "the analytical categories and social-change strategies produced by Western feminists are derived from the unique historical experience of their own social class and culture" (Bandarage, 1984, 7). They did not fit everywhere. Nor were they based on universally valid theories. There were many paradigms for looking at the female world, not just one (Rihani, 1983). "The general rejection of traditional, Western, and/or Marxist models and analysis by Third World women, although countered by other speakers . . . provides us with . . . a needed redefinition of analytic and research priorities." Experience had demonstrated the inadequacy of Western paradigms. Wage work, for example, had not trickled down and emancipated women, as anticipated. "Rather, young, new wage-working women can be and are coopted into the traditionally conservative male system" (May, 1983).[18] Nor had "the expected expansive and progressive effect of 'emancipated' women entering the work force in Islamic countries . . . occurred. . . . The western approach to 'liberation' was inadequate because it did not account for the fact that wage work does not produce trickle-down emancipation effects" (May, 1983). There just was no uniform model valid for women everywhere; the different positions of women in different societies precluded a globally valid model for the liberation of women. Issues differed too much in different parts of the world.

In the West, for example, acceptance of female employment in the labor force even after marriage, even after motherhood was not an issue. It had been resolved, but for women in many other parts of the world that was not a much-desired goal, not a genuine issue:

> Integration into the wage labor force entails at best working as a factory or field laborer and at worst as a maid or a prostitute. Can absorption into the prevailing structures of employment bring liberation to most women? In the absence of changes in those hierarchical structures at the international and national levels, integration results merely in prestigious careers for a few women and men but continued underpaid and undervalued work for the majority. Data now available indicate that unequal integration further deepens the class, racial and national cleavage among women rather than helps build sisterhood. [Bandarage, 8]

Certainly not an issue for poor women who were forced into paid employment against their wishes because there was no alternative and who resented making such a right an issue. Black women who had to engage in paid employment because their husbands could not support their families without such help also saw this feminist issue as fallacious: in the United States the real issue for them was employment for black men. Such issues seemed trivial and were alienating to many women who felt the consequences were negative for them. No wonder they showed "great antipathy and resistance to feminism" (Bandarage, 1984, 6).[19]

Even *equitable* integration was not an issue in some parts of the female world. Not, for example, for some dissident women in the Soviet Union who were opposed to "compulsory equality" (Rothchild, 1983).

Or for Japanese women (Atsumi, 1985). Nor was even equitable integration the cup of tea of women in South Yemen if, as we saw earlier, the male world was backward and benighted:

> When we declare that we want to be equal to men, we want to be equal in rights but we don't want to be equal if men are trapped in underdeveloped thoughts: in an underdeveloped society men have underdeveloped ideas and we don't want equality in this. We have to fight with, not against, men to eradicate these backward social relations. [Aida Yafi, interview with Molyneux, 1977, 6]

Even where there was verbal acceptance of the goal of equitable integration, actually integration was rarely equitable. The charge of parochialism—including in it the erroneous definition of issues—in Western feminism seemed justified. Western feminism could not be a uniform exportable ideology. The different positions of women in different societies precluded an internationally valid model for the liberation of women. It had to be defined and achieved "contextually," for

> women of different regions, histories, and cultures have different objectives and strategies in mind for their "feminist" work and research, and . . . accept the fact that women do have different—sometimes opposing—interests. Until we do this, we will be driving blind-folded. . . . With a thorough, shared understanding of our situations and differences, we can better assess our common situations. [May, 1983]20

We will then be in a position to launch an international feminist revolution. In the meanwhile, however, the small-group discussions at international conferences were needed as preparation, as in effect, a form of affirmative action.

It was not, however, as Bandarage noted, that most women were opposed to the broad ideals of feminism. Where there was resistance, it was to Western—again read "American"—white, middle-class feminism. For a distinction had to be made between "feminism as a universal ideology potentially acceptable to most women and . . . middle-class, predominantly Western feminism" (7). This distinction was "at the root of many of the conflicts that break out among different groups of women at international women's conferences" (7).

It was admittedly true, then, that the same feminist paradigms were not yet suitable for the female world everywhere. Perhaps an international, let alone global, feminism was premature before local, national, regional stages had been mastered. Western feminism was only the first; others would follow with their own paradigms suitable for other places. Already local women's movements were emerging. This did not, however, mean that the separate women's movements must necessarily be isolated or antagonistic toward each other. Feminism today is an international issue. Women's subordination is a systematic feature of the world political economy and ideology. The struggle against women's subordination must also be international in character. It is in this common struggle against those aspects of women's subordination rooted in the "world system" that different groups of women and their culturally specific movements come together. If feminism is truly to be internationalized it must have the flexibility to become a distinct but interconnected struggle within a wider and holistic movement toward social change and human freedom [Bandarage, 1984, 12]

And at bottom were the status differentials between these white, U.S., middle-class feminists and feminists in the Third World. Not the inequitable existence of differences per se, but the nature of these differences were what was "problematic." There were oppressive "inequalities and conflictive interests" based "on the hierarchies of social class, race, nation, ethnicity, etc." Then straight for the jugular:

It is obvious that imperialism (Western, economic, political and cultural hegemony) has given white women a higher social status in the world over Third World women (woman of color in Asia, Africa, Latin America as well as the racial minorities in the West). Similarly, women from the privileged social classes in the West and the Third World, though themselves subordinated to their men, are placed in relations of dominance vis-à-vis poor women and men. [7][21]

Ironic as was the charge of neocolonialism against Western or "American" feminism, it did have a kind of substantive base which inhered in a phenomenon which has been labelled "status impediment" in contacts between men and women from different parts of the world. It had to do with the "asymmetry and dependency" which was often "the heritage of colonialism" (Angell, 1981). In the female as well as in the male world. Although by and large women had not participated in the male world expansionist movments of the fifteenth century, they had, in due course—as missionaries and missionaries' wives; as wives and daughters of colonial administrators, military officers, of business men, and industrialists; as teachers, doctors, nurses, and health workers bringing their western religion, and ethos to thousands of women in all parts of the globe—come to participate in some of the sequels. They had felt they were doing good, helping men carry the "white man's burden."

But whatever the relationship was—positive or negative—between them and the women they were teaching, healing, helping, employing, it was hierarchical,[22] one of superior and inferior, superordinate and subordinate. A wide status disparity was built into the relationship.[23] In the homes of colonial administrators, industrial developers, imperial representatives, "native" or colored or black women served white women. In the mission school they would teach under white supervisors, though it must be said that the goal of missions was to turn them over to "natives" in due course. In brief, contacts between women in the West and those in the rest of the world have taken place in circumstances of vastly unequal status, in which Western women have shared with men the power and the prerogatives of high status vis-à-vis "native" women. It was this status disparity that served as an "impediment" in global relationships among women.

These Western (mainly U.S. and European) women had the advantage of other status prerogatives as well, in terms, that is, of literacy, education, skills in communication technology. They were the ones who, like any other intellectual elite, were in a position to conceptualize the female world, formulate its issues, create the models or paradigms for interpreting it, to enjoy, in brief, the privileges and perquisites and status of leadership. We have compared them with the eighteenth-century French Encyclopedists or philosophes who put the Enlightenment into books that could be read everywhere by any literate person. They wrote, discussed, published. The stream of books, pamphlets, articles, that issued from their typewriters was spectacular. Their words and deeds, especially in the 1960s, were, like the storming of the Bastille or the shots at Bunker Hill, "heard round the world." It was to take some time for the words to reach some places, but, in time, they did. The shock waves were widely felt, and by now they are becoming audible and visible in the remotest precincts of the female world.

It is among this highest elite, the women oriented toward research, that the status impediment plays most havoc. It is among them that the "asymmetry and dependence" factor is most obvious. Many researchers have been coopted by funding agencies; they have to "adapt" their work to the objectives of national and international—European and North American—donor agencies (Second Latin American and Caribbean Women's Meeting, 40). At the Kerala Women's Studies Conference in 1984 the importance of avoiding the status-oriented relationship between researcher and researched was emphasized. It looked to many Third World women as though Western feminists were viewing them almost exclusively as subjects for research. Thus at one international conference a Third World woman asked if she and other Third World women had been invited primarily as sources of data about their societies. They felt that they had been invited to attend a conference where

> mostly American "scholars" were interpreting for us our condition, our cultures, our religions and our experiences. . . . The absence of papers on American women restored for us the hardly-healed colonial experience

wherein the detached outsiders define your world to you. [Sadawi, Mernissi, and Vajarathon, "Organizers' Dialogue." *Quest*, winter 1978, 103]

The Third World women felt reduced to being passive, accomodating audiences rather than participants. "After repeated clashes, it became clear that the organizers expected us to sit quietly and listen respectfully to the papers, no matter what their content" (105). The status relationship between the U.S. hostesses and their Third World guests resembled that between men and women. This was the "status impediment" referred to above.[24]

Nor were the challenges of the Third World participants unfounded. One male observer of the international research scene has attributed the strain to

> a mixture of academic ambition and a certain degree of arrogance on the part of American and other Western researchers who have used their research grants and privileged university status to enter foreign cultures, collect data on topics of their choice, and bundle it up to take back home for use in publications about the cultures they have studied. Years of this kind of academic habit in India understandably turned the Indian government against the whole idea of United States-financed research on the problems of Indian society [Harold Taylor, 1982, 302].

In any event, it was not helpful to have the female world researched only by people trained in the West, to have research everywhere conceptualized in terms of a Western perspective, to have topics selected for study determined by those in the West, to have women from other parts of the world feel defensive at international meetings.

Actually, such strenuous efforts were already being made in the female world. Research was rapidly becoming a major arrow in the feminist quiver. I noted earlier how in many parts of the postcolonial world the leftist parties were teaching women a vocabulary with which to express their oppression. In the West a different kind of education was growing up. A branch of knowledge, including so-called women's studies, was evolving that provided a new perspective on the female world, one emphasizing research: its content, its methodology, its teaching, and its organization. This new field of knowledge provided a feminist critique of science and philosophy (Basch, *Feminist Forum*, 1983, iii) and their relevance for women.

Although the male tradition in research has remained, the female world was also beginning to have some impact on research. Its contribution has been

> in bringing to light new theories, new questions, and new interpretations of data. Feminism has also brought to the analysis of the research process: the importance of situations and context, and the value of commu-

The Feminist Enlightenment Takes Time.

Courtesy of the *United Nations State of the World's Women 1985*.
Illustrator, Wendy Hoile.

nal methods [Carlson, 1972]. While . . . no method is inherently feminist, feminism can lead us to a true and equal marriage of agentic [often male-preferred] and communal [often female-preferred] inquiry in which both are utilized and perhaps lead to a more creative science [Wallston, 1985, 231].

And not a moment too soon. For the hunger for knowledge about the female world had become voracious. Women's studies courses in universities became insatiable for research-based knowledge. All angles of the female world were eagerly explored. By the 1970s research was beginning to show up in all kinds of specifically women's activities. All kinds of programs for research findings dealing with women were receiving increasing support—not only data collection, important as that was, and fact finding, but also analytic and interpretive research to support feminist activism and thinking.

Women, in brief, were learning how to use the growing armory of research technology—historiography, anthropological field work, statistics, demography, content analysis—and how to ask relevant questions. They were no longer to be in the vulnerable position vis-à-vis the male world of having to receive the male canon as unimpeachable. The sociology of science was showing them how to conceptualize their own problems. Research-oriented meetings now began to appear in many parts of the female world. This training in scientific research was to prove one of the most important trends on the current world scene. Its use by women was a rebellion against the necessity—because of lack of training—for accepting the male view of themselves and their world. It rendered possible autonomous participation in the creation of knowledge, not only about their world but also about the male world. With training, they developed the skills for asking their own questions, mapping their own reality, formulating their own paradigms, making their own interpretations, for handling their own archives and documentation. In brief, for using the tools of research to make their own discoveries about themselves, who they were, what they did. It was, indeed, a female counterpart of the French Enlightenment. Like that one, it was also casting its beams in many dark corners. This research push was one of the most important aspects—as antecedent and as consequence—of this Feminist Enlightenment. It was a long step toward female empowerment.

So much, then, for equitable relationships both between the male and female worlds (chapters 3, 4, and 5) and also within the female world itself (chapter 6). In part III we turn to ways the female world is achieving, by way of "affirmative action," the experience needed for equitable relations among themselves and hence also with the male world.

PART THREE
"Affirmative Action"

INTRODUCTION

The second half of the twentieth century may be said to be one of the great moments in the history of the female world, equal to, if not greater than, the human transition from hunting and gathering to agriculture. We are indebted to Elise Boulding for one of the first histories of the female world. Although, admittedly, of necessity such a history must as yet be based almost exclusively on male scholarship and therefore be incomplete, it does appear that the female world has been one on which extrinsic forces have operated almost exclusively. There are few accounts of the intrinsic forces (those generated among women themselves), of the dynamic that has characterized their world. Elise Boulding feels the need for overcoming this paradigmatic inadequacy. She emphasizes "the active role of the individual rather than treating the individual [merely] as an object of the social process" (1976, 24). She shows how "structural differentiation enlarges or constrains the social learning spaces for women," but also "how and when constraints have been transcended" (20). The relevant point here is that the present moment is one, par excellence, in which the female world is in process of transcending its inherited constraints, in which women in many parts of the female world are pushing back farther and farther their boundaries until they now approach international boundaries. Women in many parts of the world are getting to know one another. Part III shows where and how.

Several forces, demographic and technological, have contributed to this epochal movement in the history of the female world. Demographically, as we saw in chapter 1, a brand new kind of woman has appeared on the scene, a woman in her prime, educated, with childbearing and childrearing responsibilities fulfilled, vigorous and ready to go. True, these women are more likely to show up in the West, especially in Europe and the United States. Their thinking, therefore, is based on experience that does not always seem relevant for many other parts of the world (chapter 6) but which does, nevertheless, recognize numerous

commonalities (chapter 7). Contributing to this expansion of consciousness, of perspective, of knowledge, of self image, of intellectual
skills—including research skills—is the proliferation of contacts among
women personally (chapters 7 and 10), by way of the media (chapter 8),
and by way of networks (chapter 9).

The female world has been swept along with every kind of historical
revolution—technological, industrial, occupational, political, ideological. Relevant in the present context are technologies in transportation and communication. In the fifteenth century men had gone down to
the sea in ships and sailed away to find the Orient. They had ridden away
across deserts to find China. Thus, their spatial world had become
enormously extended. New peoples, new wonders, new horizons. It was
an age of expansion. Half a millennium later an analogous expansion
has been taking place in the female world. Women are now boarding
airplanes and flying east, west, north, south, finding new people, new
horizons. It is an age of expansion for the female world. Especially
notable is that to a large extent this expansion is intrinsic—initiated,
that is, by women themselves so that they participate as initiators
rather than, as in the case of so many other revolutions, as willy-nilly
beneficiaries or victims.

Equitable integration calls for preparation in the female world for
dealing with the male world, for the acquisition of appropriate skills
and knowledge. It calls also for efforts by the female world "to get its act
together." As we have already seen (chapter 3),

> in many countries, where traditions make it difficult for women to pre-
> sent their viewpoints and discuss their problems together in organiza-
> tions which include men, it is valuable for them to find their own forum.
> This may prepare them for later expressing their opinions and ultimately
> for common action with men. [*Styrel für Utveckling*, 1974, 74]

Part III looks at the experience women are gaining not only on a
personal level but also at international women's meetings, ranging from
relatively small ones within a shared culture to mega-meetings on a
global scale (chapters 7 and 10); at the messages they are communicating to one another by way of the media (chapter 8); and what they are
achieving by way of networks (chapter 9). In a sense, these experiences
and activities may be viewed as forms of "affirmative action," one of
whose definitions, the Oxford Dictionary tells us, is "assertion," which,
in turn, means "an action setting free." As a policy in the United States
it implies positive efforts to invite into the mainstream groups and
individuals who, without such encouragement, would not have known
they were eligible. Part III is devoted to ways the female world is
discovering, cultivating, sharing, and using its own resources of talent

and skill. Perhaps an even better term than *equitable integration* would be *equitable separation*.

Before continuing, a caveat. Not many of the women we met in chapter 1 are likely to participate in the international contacts to be described in part III. For the most part those who do are a small elite, women relatively free to move about. But they cast a long shadow. They include those who are exploring the emerging global female world, rethinking the relations among themselves as well as the relations between their world and the male world. This relatively small elite includes members who are literate, who are in a position to participate in international meetings. Small in number as they may be, they are important far beyond their number because they supply the vocabulary, the paradigms, the perspectives, the strategies, the policies, the visions for many less privileged women everywhere. They are by no means representative samples of their native lands. They probably have more in common with one another than they do with the non-literate women of their homelands. A woman judge from the United States, that is, is probably on more nearly the same wavelength as that of an African woman judge than that of a Chicana agricultural worker in the U.S. Southwest. And the African judge, similarly, is probably more nearly like her U.S. counterpart than she is like women in the bush at home.

CHAPTER SEVEN

"Glad to Meet You"

We are moving into a new period in
our history when people will
understand that our problems are
global problems and that to deal with
them we have to develop new channels
for person-to-person communication
world-wide—a new kind of
international diplomacy. [Jane Threatt,
Media Report to Women, January–
February, 1985, 5]

The knowledge that women around
the world are experiencing . . . [an
awakening similar to their own] and
discovering new ways of associating
together towards common goals is very
important. . . . This very need for
reinforcement and support may be
what will impel women to a higher
level of organization. Once together
and comparing their past experiences,
they may convince themselves that
action is possible, and that change can
come about because of their action.
Here, again, knowing about the
experiences of women in other parts of
the world is important for making out
possible routes. . . . We make this call
for exchange and sharing across
national boundaries in solidarity and
mutual respect. [Figueroa and
Anderson, 1981, 16]

This chapter is about these "new channels," "this new kind of international diplomacy," these "new ways of associating together." They may
take place on a wide variety of stages, some of which are more relevant

than others for raising consciousness of a shared female world. They may involve participants with a wide variety of class backgrounds and encompass a wide variety of formats, ranging from pleasure excursions to serious political gatherings to marches and parades, with a wide variety of objectives, sponsorship, and locales. There is, for example, a long tradition of "pleasure excursions" in the West, as scholarship is married to pleasant learning experience.[1] There are also great global meetings every four years at the Olympic Games, where a different kind of international diplomacy takes place. Robert Angell, speaking of academic fellowships for foreign study, tells us that there is solid evidence that they "increase international amity, understanding, and cooperation" (1982, 248). An increasing number of such person-to-person, face-to-face contacts are taking place among women in the current age of expansion in the female world. They include academic seminars, summer courses for foreign students, fellowships, scholarships, special cultural tours, and the like, and they may range from small, almost intimate, contacts to large bureaucratic meetings.

In addition to standard personal contacts stimulated by international academic fellowships, one feminist group—Isis-Wicce (Isis Women's International Cross-Cultural Exchange)[2]—has innovated a program of international "sisterships" which makes it possible "for women activists to have more direct contact with each other" (1983, 5). Scholarships are offered to young women to come to Geneva for a month of feminist orientation followed by three months of training in receiving countries.[3] Their comments on their experience illustrate what the contacts these women had made meant to them and the kind of female world this program was oriented toward:

> I want to thank you for the love shown to each woman, and the welcome which made me feel that I was in Nairobi, Kenya, where I meet people I know and who are relatives and friends. I have found the same thing here—where I've met people who behave like sisters and I've felt very much at home. [Florence, p. 8]

> This was my first exposure to feminism, and it has broadened my concept of what a woman's programme should be in the context of the Philippines. In the Philippines, we are in the process of finding out what is really meant by "women's programmes," and this is something I will take back with me and discuss back home. [Delia, p. 8]

> We have an idea that women in the West are quite liberated. Yet I came here and learned that we have many problems in common after all. [Rekha, p. 9]

> We are here to build a new era in international solidarity among women. Until now international contact has been the work of an elite—through this programme we are trying to build another way of international exchange—that is, on the grassroots level. [Kistna, 10]

Another innovation for encouraging women to learn about one another in warm and sustaining environments is the International Feminist University, the brainchild of Berit Aas, which takes the Friends World College as its model. It envisions small groups of students who will travel to places of interest and work in cooperation with local female inhabitants. Aas anticipates that such areas as Galicia, Crete, Lesbos, and Lappland will be especially interesting places for such groups. Contacts had already been made with women's high schools in Denmark and Sweden and with special women's universities in Sweden and with the Women's Proletarian University in Italy. For academic women lecturers it would be a revitalizing experience—a kind of revitalizing sabbatical—and offer them a different way of teaching, especially for those "who feel that the existing university systems are inadequate both for women teachers and for teaching women."

> The University will be open to all women from the age of 18 upwards and it should be a goal that women with [only] primary school education can attend as well as academicians. Another goal of this University is to combine education, research and action within particular areas. The goals of the University are to relocate women's past which has been neglected and to strengthen bonds between academic and nonacademic women of all ages.

Of course the university will be a poor one economically "in that it cannot count on any financial assistance from any partriarchal organization. It will have to learn how to operate on a subsistence level." It would have to count on the enthusiastic support of women which, apparently, it did have,[4] from local women's organizations at Loten, where the campus, "Rosenlund," two hours north of Oslo, was located.

There are doubtless dozens of such small-scale projects in progress by which women are "getting to know" one another in ambiences of their own design, engaging in a "new kind of international diplomacy," sharing the Feminist Enlightenment. But equally impressive and perhaps more ramifying are the meetings—large and small—taking place all over the globe at which women meet, discuss, teach, and learn from one another.[5]

There is, no doubt, great potential for depth in such personal contacts that cover a considerable period of time. But there are briefer personal contacts that may also have reverberations in the female world. In small international group meetings, for example, personal contacts may also generate proto-solidarity among participants. In contrast to the meetings described in chapter 6, where differences were confronted—sometimes with hostility—is the atmosphere of warmth in other international meetings of women as the participants discover commonalities among themselves. Reports of such meetings, for example, often include comments on the ambience surrounding them such as:

> "There was generally a feeling of friendship, sisterliness, vitality. . . . The Conference gave women ideas and inspiration";
> "International sisterhood was constantly in evidence. . . ."
> "[There were] literally hundreds of attempts over coffee, meals, and drinks to bridge the gaps between us. There was an atmosphere of friendly sisterly effort to comprehend each other. . . . We came away strengthened and warmed by the knowledge that so much is going on everywhere."
> "There was deep and meaningful exchange among participants, with little or no antagonism or hostility which can so often plague such encounters. The richness of exchanges between women from developing and developed countries was especially remarkable. In spite of enormous differences politically, culturally, socially and geographically, women found that there were many areas of common concern. . . . This was a truly feminist international meeting characterized by a warm feeling of solidarity."
> "At a fundamental level [there] was a commonality of experience among women which [transcended] differences in ideology, class and culture."

The latent agenda included morale boosting, inspiration, the reduction of separateness and isolation.

We turn next to examples of meetings of several kinds of special interest groups, classified under four U.N. subthemes: employment, health, education, and peace.

Under the heading of "employment" might be listed three meetings of union members which took place in Israel, Nairobi, and Turin. In 1977 a U.S. labor organization, the Coalition of Labor Union Women (CLUW) organized a seminar for 24 women from 15 countries to be held in Israel (Nelson, 1978). The goal was "to learn from each other, share strategies, problems and successes." The subject selected for study by their unions in Sweden, Israel, and France was to be child-care programs. But they did more than just observe. "They shared experiences and ideas" (14). Equally important were the strong bonds forged among the women, bonds "important to women in leadership positions who too often find themselves isolated from information and easy peer support of their male associates" (14). They were not attempting to find an all-purpose solution to the labor problems of women in different countries everywhere; they were fully aware that each country had to arrive at its own characteristic remedy. They were surprised therefore to find how much they actually did have in common, how the same kinds of discrimination existed in both developing and industrial nations and that working women in both had the same practical needs to ease their burdened lives: housekeeping equipment, child care, jobs that could be fitted around their family schedules and the chance to train for upgrading, facts that have been rediscovered wherever working women have met since then. [14]

Including in Africa. Thus, "in the summer of 1977, a ten-day Pan-African Conference on the Role of Trade Union Women was conducted by the African-American Labor Center, AFL-CIO, in Nairobi," at which the participants were asked to answer two questions: Why do women not participate more actively in their unions? What can be done about it? "You would think" the questioner reported, "that the same person had written all the answers,". . . . "Union women's problems are the same all over the world and union women understand they are all part of the world together." [Nelson, 1978, 14] The author concluded that

where the Third World is concerned, international and United States agencies may be overlooking one of the best possible liaisons to rural women: women trade unionists. These women were not elitists; they often came from rural homes themselves. They wanted to work to bring the spirit of collective action to rural women. Women unionists may be the best friends any government organization could have for reaching women in the countryside. [Nelson, 1978, 14]

Many of the more than 700 women from 15 countries—Europe, United States, Australia, Japan—who attended the First International Conference of Women from Industrialized countries in Turin in 1983 represented women's sections of their trade unions. The main themes discussed covered the waterfront: wage earning, self-employment, domestic labor, new technologies, social services and services run by women, sexual identity and self perception, culture, sexism at work and in politics, feminism and power, women in publishing, a press agency for women. There were no stars; any woman could speak at any workshop. "International sisterhood was constantly in evidence" (Zmroczek and Cockburn, 1983, vii). In plans for the second conference, hope was expressed that it could include women from nonindustrialized countries also.

Among special interests everywhere in the global female world health is, understandably, a major concern. Thus at one conference on health it was noted that

it is almost universally true that women do not have control over their own bodies, health and lives. Choice of contraceptives which are not damaging, restrictive, or abusive abortion laws; prescription of nocive drugs, inadequate or inappropriate health systems, were issues which women from all countries could speak about and relate to. Especially valuable was the exchange of knowledge and ideas on herbal, natural, and alternative methods of healing. . . . We felt that perhaps for the first time this was a truly feminist international meeting characterized by a warm feeling of solidarity [Isis Report, no. 20, 1981]

Thus, after two conferences on Women and Health (Rome, 1977 and Hanover, 1980) at which only women from the West had take part, the organizers of the third one in Geneva in 1981 wanted to "benefit from the experiences of, and exchange our ideas with, women from Latin America, Africa, and Asia" (*New Directions for Women*, March–April, 1981, 10). So "all women who would like to share their knowledge and practice of health care were invited." At this third Geneva conference, 250 women from 35 countries gathered to discuss 17 themes, selected by the participants themselves. As in so many women's meetings, they had a plate running over with topics to discuss.[6] But that did not preclude a party with music, dancing, and films. And warmth. The idea of meetings devoted to women's health was appealing. The first Regional Meeting on Women and Health in Latin America met in Colombia in 1984 with 70 participants from ten countries.[7] These several conferences on women's health reflected the protests of the rising international women's health movement against the absence of women's perspectives and participation in male-world health-policy decisions. This movement was beginning to "provide a platform where more women can redefine the problems, offer new analyses, and hopefully become a significant force for change" (Media Report, 1 October 1981).

In a certain sense all the meetings glanced at here are enlightening. And certainly education is a major theme for the United Nations, especially in the Third World. But at this point let us look at only two examples of meetings with education as a theme. The first, a conference of the International Council for Adult Education, took place in Paris in 1982. At this conference on adult education, between a fourth and a fifth of the 600 delegates from 110 countries were women, and in the course of the meetings the Women's Policy Working Group took it upon themselves to make themselves visible.

We discussed such issues as the subordination of women, the work we do and the division of labour, women's differing positions in their societies (as mothers, housewives, peasants, low-paid workers, prostitutes, illiterate/literate/professional women, etc.), violence against women, what kind of educational provision exists/is needed, the role of international agencies; and the need for men to be educated about the changing relationships between the sexes and the implications of this in their societies. [Mary Kennedy, reporter, *Feminist Forum*, 1983, vol. 6, no. 3, p. ii]

An excellent project in adult education.[8]

The second example of a meeting on an educational theme should probably be viewed as training-oriented rather than education-oriented inasmuch as the emphasis was on research which, as noted in chapter 6, is rapidly becoming one of the major tools of enlightenment. This was a conference in Toulouse in 1982 on women's studies at which almost a thousand women from 34 countries participated. The program and workshops were organized around three themes: the first was on "contents of research, methodology, structures of women's studies." The second "included a feminist critique of science and philosophy, particularly around the problem of the differences between the sexes." And the third dealt with the teaching of women's studies and the organization of research (Basch, reporter, International Forum, 1983, iii).

A special kind of educational meeting is the academic gathering at which research by disciplinary specialists is presented to peers. There are probably scores of such academic meetings every year in which dedicated women researchers, scholars, students, quietly intent on finding and analyzing the major themes of the female world engage in the processes of creating the knowledge to keep the torch of the Feminist Enlightenment supplied with fuel. They range in size from small, informal groups not too different from the one-on-one contacts looked at above to large, formally organized ones. Although many of them are feminist in orientation, neither ideological debate nor activist consciousness raising characterizes all of them. They are engaged "in serving the public," but in a most cerebral way, asking the crucial questions, seeking the most suitable answers, learning from, and teaching, one another.[9] There is little one-upmanship among them.

A case in point is the vintage three-day conference of women historians at which five European countries and the United States were represented. These scholars were, as Robert Angell has noted about academic meetings in general, "talking shop with their . . . [consoeurs] from other nations, making friends, becoming stimulated by ideas and practices in their field stemming from different cultural backgrounds" (1982, 238). Here, as among participants in similar groups, powerful intellectual forces were quietly being generated, ideas proposed, perspectives enlarged, questions asked that in one way or another, extensive or limited, would in time impact in subtle ways on the global female world. Participants were seeking to understand the effects on women of war, of depression, of fascism, effects on the family, in the work force, and in the political arena. The contradictions in public policies with respect to the social mobilization of women during war and depression, cross-nationally and across class, also engaged their attention.[10] As did government attempts to influence fertility patterns and family life and the cultural productivity of both working-class and middle-class women. The preoccupation with political issues did not imply an activist perspective.[11] Still, sooner or later, the contents of these discussions will find their way to the desk of, say a member of some U.S. Congressman's or state legislator's staff and have some input into national or state legislation relevant for women in the Third World or even at home. These scholars, ostensibly a quiet little group of women just talking to one another about their research were perhaps the most "activist" of all, for they were "engaged in the slow but integrating work of transforming social institutions through scholarship" (Gelpe, *Signs*, 198), adding perceptibly to the transcultural orchestration of ideas, helping the female world clarify its own concerns.

The political thinking going on in this meeting of Western historians might have been relevant for women actually facing the "involvement and marginalization" issue the historians had been discussing except for the political obstacles that kept them separated. There was, for example, in 1972, a meeting in Dar es Salaam (Tanzania) of 300 women from 41 countries including women from India, North Vietnam, and Chile to discuss what women could do for a liberated Africa. How could they achieve legislation against certain customs, traditions, and practices which were incompatible with women's demands for equality (Styrel für Utveckling, 1974, 2). We have seen what the situation of these women was. Words were put into the constitution or in the law books, but nothing changed in the lives of women (chapters 4 and 5). In the same year, 1972, 39 women from 16 Arab countries met in Cairo, at the first conference on another puzzler: What was the role of women in Arabian national development? Thirteen years later the question was still moot (chapter 10).

The crucial issue for equitable integration—what should be the position of the female world vis-à-vis revolutionary movements—had assumed enough importance in the female world by now as to warrant a call for an international workshop on the subject. So, in June 1980, such a workshop on national liberation and development was, in fact, held at the Hague. Here women from all over the female world—from Azania (Southern Africa), Angola, Mozambique, Zimbabwe, Namibia, Rep. of South Africa[12]—analyzed their liberation experience and contributed what they had themselves learned from their own participation in liberation struggles. The central question was, again, Do women, who are necessary for the success of any liberation struggle, also gain their own liberation during and after this struggle? What happens to women once national liberation has been won? On the basis of historical and contemporary evidence the answer seemed to be that all too often women return after liberation to the old status quo (chapters 4 and 5).

The political thinking going on in this meeting of Third-World women actually facing "involvement and marginalization" could have been potentially of great value to the Western historians trying to understand what the female world was really like. More fuel for the torch of the Feminist Enlightenment would have been created. Unfortunately, however, among the major rifts in the female world today remain the political (nationalistic) barriers which prevent contacts between and among women who otherwise would be "glad to meet" one another.

At a 1983 Vienna meeting of six women from the USSR, Mauritania, India, Brazil, Poland, and the United States "it was generally agreed that peace was an all important and all encompassing subject . . . paramount to all other concerns" (U.N. Expert Group Meeting, report, 1983, 15). There was already a long record of contacts among women in international settings when, in 1915, there was a meeting of women, not in the form of the traditional do-good mold, to which the public was accustomed, but in the form of a bold, even brazen, intervention in male-world business, war. Here are "Some Particulars" from the International Congress of Women from both sides of World War I which convened at the Hague:

How the Congress Was Called

The scheme of an International Congress of Women was formulated at a small conference of women from neutral and belligerent countries, held at Amsterdam, early in February, 1915. A preliminary programme was drafted at this meeting, and it was agreed to request the Dutch Women to form a Committee to take in hand all the arrangements for the Congress and to issue the invitations.

Finance

The expenses of the Congress were guaranteed by British, Dutch and German women present who all agreed to raise one third of the sum required.

Membership

Invitations to take part in the Congress were sent to women's organisations and mixed organisations as well as to individual women all over the world. Each organisation was invited to appoint two delegates.

Women only could become members of the congress and they were required to express themselves in general agreement with the resolutions on the preliminary programme. This general agreement was interpreted to imply the conviction (a) that international disputes should be settled by pacific means; (b) that the parliamentary franchise should be extended to women.

Conditions of Debate

The Congress was carried on under two important rules:

1. That discussions on the relevant national responsibility for or conduct of the present war, [and]

2. Resolutions dealing with the rules under which war shall in future be carried on, shall be outside the scope of the Congress.

[Jane Addams, Emily Balch, Alice Hamilton. Women at the Hague. *The International Congress of Women and Its Results.* New York: MacMillan, 1915]

This was not the first international congress of women,[13] but it was certainly one of the bravest and most endearing. There were 1,111 attendants from both belligerent and neutral countries; 180 others had been kept away by the military closing of the North Sea. It was emphatically not envisioned as a debating event where one made verbal points, nor as one catering to male propensities. Women only, and only women favoring pacifism and women's suffrage, were welcome. "Proceedings were conducted with the greatest goodwill throughout." Among the resolutions adopted were a protest against the madness and horror of war, including their odious wrongs against women; a request for inclusion of women at the peace conference; the universal enfranchisement of women; disarmament; an International Federation [League of Nations]. Although this congress was the butt of patronizing jokes in the world press for months, the participants themselves considered it "extremely successful." They were nearer the mark than the belittlers.[14]

Neither a congress nor a conference was the meeting of a small, six-member "Expert Group" of women who came as nonofficial individuals,[15] under U.N. auspices, to discuss "The Participation of Women in Promoting International Peace and Cooperation." In addition there were five observers from U.N. organizations, four from U.N. special agencies, and 26 international nongovernmental organizations. In 99 paragraphs this expert group reviewed women's participation at the decision-making level in political institutions concerned with international peace; and in nongovernmental peace-related activities; research on women and peace, especially on women's contribution; and women's role in education of societies for peace. There followed "recommendations on forward-looking strategies" for national, regional, and international levels of both governmental and nongovernmental institutions. The group also recommended an International Year of Peace. The report was a thoughtful resume of the current position of women in the search for international peace. It was not original, but it did bring together a useful body of data. There was little, however, on the "metabolism"[16] of the group to show what the emotional impact of its product was intended to be.

Totally different in design and concept from either the Hague or the Vienna approach to peace as a concern of the female world were the sensational Marches of Nordic Women in the early 1980s. The personal contacts these women made were sui generis.[17] They reduced the distance between women in the USSR and the West, as evidenced by reports of two of the participants in one such march, describing their experiences in Moscow.[18]

I have just been talking for hours with English-speaking students. We could talk about everything. Everything was news to them. They knew hardly a thing about nuclear power. I had to tell them about the catastrophe in the Urals. We understood their fears about their contacts with us which it took time to allay. That meant we had a hard schedule all day long. Some of the meetings lasted so long that there was little time for discussion. They had to be cautious when they met people from the West. We functioned as seminars even out in the streets. We were asked about how we live, and so on. On our side, we also asked questions. We asked about the sixteen dissidents, and I believe that our persistence influenced their own way of thinking. The very free and open debate between us when we had disagreements surprised them. The way we played theater, with English songs, with flutes stood up well in contrast to their rapid-fire propaganda. I had very many good contacts, including some with women along the road. They cried. I cried. So many things are now at stake.

THE MARCH OF MY LIFE. . . . We rapidly took the initiative and asked questions about: the work for disarmament, the isolation of the Soviet Union, its war in Afghanistan, the submarines in the Baltic Sea. We asked how the Peace Movement was working. . . . We engaged in one march every day. And what marches! Thousands and thousands of singing and applauding people met us. . . . And every evening the march of the day was shown on television. Many older women who had experienced war cried with us. We felt both sorrow and anxiety, but energy and trust, too, against the nuclear arms threat. All the meetings ended in dancing in long rows. We could hardly stop. We could hardly leave. We walked with the Soviet's first woman astronaut, a member of the highest presidium. She thought as we thought. How exciting to be able to deliver pamphlets in Russian, look people straight in the eye and feel that we understood each other! To speak in Moscow to thousands of people! To exchange buttons with all those young people and give them our names and addresses! . . . And to receive a tiny bottle of perfume from an old woman, a bottle almost empty.[19]

It was, to the participants, a moment of profound significance.[20]

As more and more women have come to engage in face-to-face contacts with one another in self-initiated formats, a considerable amount of thinking has come to be invested in learning how to organize and run international women's meetings. What, for example, should be the political orientation of such meetings? How, considering economic and political constraints, can they be truly international? How much autonomy should they enjoy? How much party or other outside support should be acceptable? Awareness of the importance—present as well as future—of such learning, as representatives of the female world in all its diversity, has led to attempts to systemetize experience. Leaders have sensed that whether the international women's meetings were to be intellectual, theoretical, or activist in orientation, confrontational or consensual in modus operandi, it was important to give them high research priority on the agenda of the global female world.[21]

Aside from the theoretical issues that must be dealt with, organizers initially had to deal with the banal nuts-and-bolts problems, including the monetary and political constraints that hobble them. Few women anywhere can finance their own participation at such meetings out of their own resources. Like so much else in the female world, such participation has to be done on a shoestring. Scrounging for support is therefore a major problem. The disappointment entailed in such parsimonious support is painfully felt by would-be participants who would enormously appreciate the contacts possible at such meetings but who find their resources inadequate. The result is often limited spread of knowledge. Almost equally painful is the heartache and disappointment of those who organize meetings only to find so many who could profit from them missing. At an International Women's Conference on feminist methods and strategies in educational work called in 1983 in Bergen,[22] the recorder tells us that it was like having a party at which more than half of the invited guests did not show up.

As a result of the difficulties of funding, some participants to international women's meetings come as subsidized nationals, as in the UN-sponsored Conferences of the Decade for Women (1975, 1980, 1985), rather than as autonomous representatives of the self-defined interests of women. Government-supported meetings especially suffer from the hazards of cooption. Even funding from nongovernment sources[23] can invite suspicion as a public-relations or power ploy.[24]

There are also political as well as economic constraints. The location of an international meeting may run up against a host of such restrictions. Promising cities may have to be cut out of the running because their national governments will not issue visas to women of certain countries.[25] Currency restrictions may also create barriers.[26] Hosting a conference is costly, and some countries who might be willing, even eager, to undertake such a project, cannot afford the amenities such a luxury would entail. Such monetary and political constraints have their impact on the composition of conference participants. They do little to eliminate the status gap among participants and much to expand it.

But even assuming success in mastering such extrinsic chores as finding a home for international meetings and funding them, there still remains the task of mastering the actual intrinsic, internal dynamics of group interaction. As illustrated in the following case in point.

Second Latin American and Caribbean Feminist Meeting— Lima, Peru, 1983

We have already met the women who were in charge of this meeting (chapter 3), where they were criticizing the project approach to development. Profiting from the experience of the first such meeting in Bogotá two years earlier, the organizers had specified that the second meeting would be "on an individual" basis rather than by delegation. They wanted to conserve the event as a gathering, not as a conference where "it would be decided by majority vote 'what the correct feminist line is' " (unsigned, 1984, 3). And it would be a feminist meeting.

> The use of the word "feminist" to define the meeting was a political decision and the result of much discussion. Many women in Latin America are prejudiced against this word, which has been so distorted by male dominated media and institutions. Some feminists felt that it would alienate women, especially the more marginalized ones. However, we have chosen to reclaim the term and identify ourselves as feminists. We conceive of feminism as much more than two or three specifically women's demands. The feminist movement is political; it is struggling against the root causes of women's oppression. . . .

Among the workshop topics planned were: patriarchy and the Church in Latin America; feminist research; domestic work; women in exile; alternative communication; health; history; literature; the Third Age; methodology; development programs; sexuality; power; violence and sexual slavery; peasant women; paid work; family; psychotherapy; feminism; everyday life. As in so many such women's meetings, a very full plate. And, again as in so many such meetings, this one was more easily planned than carried through. True, there were successes: the feminist cause became less frightening to many participants; and many "passed from skepticism . . . to conviction." But it hadn't been easy.

The organizers of this meeting took their responsibilities seriously. A great deal was at stake. There were lessons to be learned. So several months after the event and the euphoria and stress had died down, four members of the Organizing Collective met for several hours and, "spurred on by the provocative questions" that had been raised, took the meeting apart, expressed their doubts and worries and what they had learned from their mistakes that could be used in the next meeting in São Paulo, planned for 1985. Although for the most part the general plans had been successfully designed and carried through, still there had been mistakes. There had been unanticipated mundane housekeeping difficulties resulting from lack of experience. Who would have expected so many at a meeting to be devoted to such important themes? For example:

> . . . we felt a bit lost during the first part of the meeting. We only became reconciled with this at the end. The level of pressure and anxiety was so great that we were unable to transfer any of this responsibility, to make it more collective. We were behaving in an almost patriarchal way: "here is the organizing committee and it will take care of everything." Then, strange things happened; for example, a woman came up to us asking for a lock for her suitcase so it wouldn't be stolen. This at a time when we had to see about the lighting, air a room for the evening plenary session, when we were under pressure from people in workshops who wanted something different or to find a place for the new workshops on racism and lesbianism. It was mad. There came a moment on Thursday night when, while running to and fro, I ran into Cecelia and Fresia [other members of the organizing Committee] and we began to cry out of helplessness, from wanting to participate more in the meeting and being unable to, and because of all the work we had to do. As feminists we are always coming up against the problem of the balance between democracy and efficiency. . . .

Some facilitators appointed to run workshops had not allowed time for full discussion. Some actually silenced participants had "tried to create a division by asserting that the meeting was 'petit bourgeois' and that they themselves were with the masses" (58). Nor was activism allowed enough in-depth consideration. They had tried to do too much. Too many—21 workshops and 63 papers—sessions had been scheduled. Participants varied widely in feminist knowledge. The physical setting, while attractive, was dispersive. . . .

And the nemesis of so many feminist meetings, the issue of structure vs. structurelessness:

> I was . . . tremendously bewildered. . . . It was an incredible whirlpool. At a certain point we found ourselves caught between two fires, and I think this is what really wore us out. Some of the women wanted something much freer, with more feeling, looser, less structured. . . . We also heard from women who were unsatisfied and who wanted a different kind

of meeting. I don't think it is possible to fulfill entirely everyone's expectations in this kind of meeting. . . .

It seemed to one member of the group that "sometimes women need and demand to be anarchic." This may have been inevitable since "the issues of democracy, freedom, openness, sharing and searching for new forms lead to unstructured practices" (57). Structurelessness at the first meeting in Bogota in 1981 may have been permissible. But since it sometimes resulted in chaos, at least a bare minimum of structure came to be seen as essential.[27] "We cannot completely set aside all structures." Effective action called for guidelines. Creative alternative forms of organizations had to be found (58).[28] From the hard-driven achievement oriented: "It might help us to have a good time together, but . . . we have a big responsibility to build alternatives in the direction of social change" (58). Still there were others "who were really very satisfied and happy, feeling that they had found a way of understanding feminism."

After subjecting themselves to hours of mauling self-criticism, the women felt it permissible to explain their errors. And perhaps even to allow themselves some satisfaction for "one positive outcome of the meeting," namely, that "the feminist cause is becoming less alien and increasingly less frightening to the large number of women who passed from skepticism or ignorance to conviction after their encounter with feminism at the meeting" (3–4). All told, a vivid picture of the metabolism—serious, responsible, but also joyous and liberating—of such meetings. The thoughtful analysis by the organizers of the conference provides insight into its dynamic, revealing how the pioneers in this new frontier of the female world were facing the challenges so new to them—nondefensively, eager, and anxious to avoid in the future any errors they had made so far. They seemed to be fast learners, their actions clearly affirmative.

Most of the personal and group international meetings described so far in this chapter have been fairly modest in size and fairly homogenous in culture and racial, if not national, composition. The consequences, one by one, may not seem significant. A woman here, a woman there; groups here, groups there. They do not necessarily add up to an impressive global movement. Because their sociological impact may be cumulative and take years to reveal itself, it is easy to dismiss them. And because many meetings leave no records in the form of minutes, programs, or reported observations to base analyses on, it is difficult to learn much specifically about their potential or latent impact. So systematic knowledge about them is as yet fragmentary. In any event they are minuscule against a global backdrop. The activities of most such meetings, further, are slow-breaking news, so that they are not likely to be widely reported in the media. Like so much else in the female world they remain as yet almost wholly invisible.[29]

Still, personal contacts at international meetings do plant seeds, even where they are not yet harvesting the fruits, of global female consciousness. Steps, however small and faltering, are in process toward a global mind-set, if not consensus, the implications of which are not yet predictable. Still, out of the brief moment of sharing as women that does take place, small tentacles may develop which can result in wide-scale networks (chapter 9). Even transitory exposure to one another for a few days may raise feminist consciousness and have a radicalizing impact. Thus, for example, after one international meeting one Caribbean woman began to challenge women's traditional goals. She became aware of the fact that "the structure of economics" did not "suit women at all." So, she had concluded: "what we really should be talking about and beginning to think about, is how we can transform those structures. But we're not going to begin to do this until we develop that kind of perspective which I call a feminist perspective" (Antrobus, 1981, 8). Such diffusion of ideas cannot help but have extraordinary significance.[30]

Whatever the format, such contacts are often proliferating: "sharing information at such . . . events can have far-reaching effects. . . . Participants return home with ideas of networking" (Nelson, 1978, 15). Thus, at the Turin conference referred to above "various international networks were started;[31] an international newsletter, a data base on women and technology . . . and a press agency run by and for women were proposed" (Zmroczek and Cockburn, 1983). Angell feels, in fact, that sometimes it is not the subjects discussed—at meetings of International Scientific and Professional societies—that are significant . . . but rather the very fact that the participants become part of a web of intersocietal and intercultural contact which can make for understanding and cooperation (245).

On a different scale were three global meetings of women sponsored by a coalition of International Non-Governmental Organizations (INGOs) in the UN-sponsored Decade for Women (1976–1985).[32] INGOs, Elise Boulding tells us, are by definition "identified with interests that transcend national boundaries" (1977, 186–87).[33] They see problems in global terms, consider human interests and needs all over the planet. The only power they have to carry out their aims inheres in shared values and concerns, not political dominance.

> Since they [INGOs] are emergent structures, we may . . . assume that they will reflect new perspectives of planetary society, and of appropriate social roles for individuals and groups. In short, we might look at them

for new definitions of problems based on global frames of reference, and new ways of thinking and working.

Boulding believes INGOs constitute especially suitable channels for the participation of Third-World women in international conferences, a fact which facilitates the process of rendering "the women's movement truly worldwide in its membership" (1980, 26).

Since to achieve "consultative status" with the United Nations, a group must not only be identified with issues transcending national boundaries, define them in global terms, and deal with all kinds of human needs, but also be nonprofit and receive financial support from more than one country (Boulding, 1977, 186), such a group will almost of necessity be broadly humanitarian in perspective. Only the third and last of three INGO-sponsored Decade for Women conferences, the 1985 Nairobi Conference, is looked at here.

At the opening meeting of the nairobi conference, Nita Barrow, a Barbadian woman in charge of the Forum, promised her audience that they were "part of one of the greatest meetings of the century" (Battiata, *Washington Post*, 11 July 1985). "Of all time" would not have been an exaggeration.

> The women on whose backs all civilization and commerce has depended, who were said not to be able to speak for themselves ten years ago, are here today. . . . It is a meeting of the minds of women. You are having the first taste of a glorious adventure. [Battiata, *Washington Post*]

Some of her listeners had scrimped to pay for this experience, others had been sponsored by their unions, by women's groups, by foundations; and one had come by bus paid for with the help of eight local women to whom she would report what she had learned.

> Elizabeth Wanjara heard about the Decade for Women Conference on a transistor radio at home in the town of Bungoma in western Kenya, 450 miles from here. With eight local women, she saved up by selling honey and knitting sweaters and bought herself a bus ticket. Mrs. W. doesn't know exactly how old she is or how many grandchildren she has. She speaks only her tribal Kiswahili dialect and cannot read or write. But she knows exactly why she came to Nairobi. "I have to go back to all the women in my place and tell them the stories on all the happenings here," she says. "I have to tell them how we can be ourselves—no longer just have babies and have babies dying." [Sciolino, *New York Times*, 18 July 1985]

Only one of literally thousands of women "glad to meet" others who spoke to their condition.

For many other attendants also the Forum was a "joyous adventure," an "audacious, cacophonous, often inspiring smorgasbord of open workshops, displays, films and demonstrations" (ibid.). And much activism in the form of petition pushing, buttonholing, calls for or against support of: clean water, electricity, basic health care and food in Africa; female circumcision and infibulation; right-to-life; South Africa liberation movements; prostitution tourism in Southeast Asia; release of Ukrainian political prisoners in the USSR. . . . There was a human chain of African and Western women leading a procession singing "We Shall Overcome." There was a folk quilt that had taken 46 women from nine countries around the world two years to make; it described "women in struggle." There was much collecting of badges, booklists, posters, T-shirts, names and addresses. There was much sweetness and light. There was an audience, for example, of Chilean, German, Dutch, Vietnamese women listening to a Soviet professor of Social Science at the University of Moscow, Zoya Zarubian, expressing her loving sisterhood.

But there was also anguish.

> . . . the exchanges between Arab and Israeli women ranged from vituperation to intense, personal, sometimes moving, dialogue. One Forum workshop that was meant to explore the role of friendship between Israeli and Egyptian women . . . dissolved into chaos, and the police were called in twice to restore order. Panelists and members of the audience shouted back and forth, with Israeli and Arab women accusing each other of thwarting efforts toward peace. Before the workshop was scheduled to end, participants and observers gave up and left. [Rule, *New York Times*, 26 July 1985]

But even this calamitous event marked an inch of advance over the 1980 conference in Copenhagen, where they had nearly come to blows. In Nairobi "they still fought in public, but there were cordial talks behind closed doors" (Battiata, *Washington Post*, 19 July 1985).[34]

There were also field trips scheduled at which there was a meeting not only of minds but also of hearts. One group of women—lawyers, librarians, educators, among others, from Fiji, Australia, Botswana, and California—visited a female project at Kabiro. Confronted with the problems faced by these women, the visitors responded with the promise that they would spread the word.

> [Some of them] said they would spread the word. Some contributed money, others gave advice on marketing techniques. They exchanged addresses and hugs—one rural woman said she was "adopting" a black American journalist among the group. The local women rode part of the way back with the visitors, singing and rocking the bus as it wound through the bleakness and optimism that is Kabiro. "My eyes have been

opened," one Japanese woman said. "I will do whatever I can and I think that the others who see the fight in these wonderful people will do the same. I hope so. [Rule, *New York Times*, 24 July 1985]

For most of the estimated 14,000 to 17,000 women who attended the Nairobi Conference, it was indeed a joyous adventure. It was also an intellectual one. It was enlightenment in the truest sense. An enormous amount of research had gone into the papers, lectures, panels, workshops on ecology, feminism and peace, child care, battered women, lesbian women, female employment, development planning, women's studies, to name only a few.

When the conference came to an end, one U.S. leader, Sissy Farenthold, told the women what they had already felt. What they were seeing was "the birth of a real international women's movement" (Battiata, *Washington Post*, 20 July 1985). In keeping with the forum's "resolute chaos," there were no official pronouncements, but a great many personal ones, most of them positive.[35] No farewell speeches. But there was singing when three South African men "got the crowd to its feet with a song about freedom." Many gathered at the Great Court to "sing and stomp and congratulate each other for having survived and prospered at the greatest and possibly most chaotic gathering of women that the world had seen" (Battiata, *Washington Post*, 20 July 1985). "It was like the end of summer camp, women embracing and crying, exchanging addresses and bits of jewelry, exhausted and aware that something momentous was coming to an end."

Or just beginning. Unless women themselves put into practice what they had been learning it would be little more than an exciting memory. More was expected of them. In the words of Letitia Shahani, secretary general of the official U.N. Conference, "It is all up to you. . . . You will need the enthusiasm, the love for truth.and integrity that you have shown here, and the sense of sisterhood."

CHAPTER EIGHT

Never Another Season of Silence

We must not suffer in silence . . . for "a silent cause is a lost cause." [Torild Skard, quoted by Margaret Gillet in "Strategies for Power," Groningen, 1984]

Early in this century a sociologist was hailing a century of progress in communication in this panagyric:

> The changes that have taken place since the beginning of the nineteenth century are such as to constitute a new epoch in communication, and in the whole system of society. . . . In a general way they mean the expansion of human nature. . . . They mean freedom, outlook, indefinite possibility. The public consciousness, instead of being confined as regards its more active phases to local groups, extends by even steps with that give-and-take of suggestions that the new intercourse makes possible, until wide nations, and finally the world itself, may be included in one lively mental whole. . . . Social contacts are extended in space and quickened in time, and in the same degree the mental unity they imply becomes wider and more alert. The individual is broadened by coming into relation with a larger and more various life, and he is kept stirred up. . . . The change . . . has involved a revolution in every phase of life. [Cooley, 1909, chapter 8]

If such a revolution characterized the beginning of the last century, an even more extended one has characterized the following years, expanding the number of messages that can be communicated, the geographic territory that can be covered, the speed that can be achieved, the numbers and kinds of recipients that can be reached, including, in the present context the most relevant, namely women.

But so has come not only Cooley's emphasis on freedom but also fear

145

of its loss as the implications of the control of the media of communication—whether by official or unofficial censorship—have become clear. For if control of the means of production became the key concept in Marx's analysis of class, control of the media of communication, especially of the mass media, might well be said to be a key concept in analyses of modern societies. Even on the international scene—perhaps even more on the international than on the national scene—there are gatekeepers who control what messages may have access to the media with the result that "the public channels of international communication are highly selective so that some message flows are let through the system while others are turned back through choices made by 'gatekeepers' located at various points in the transmission chain" (McClelland). One result has been that the female world has had little access to the means of communication.[1] It is only now that it is beginning to create its own media, disseminate its own messages, and thus share in the revolution Cooley described.

Before modern communication had entered the scene much of what even women in the West knew about "darkest Africa" or the "inscrutable Orient," or, for that matter, the United States or Europe,[2] came from travellers' books, lectures, and slides, or from missionaries' reports or anthropological monographs. The illusion was created that all those faraway societies were fixed, stable, established systems as old as history. It wasn't until newspapers began to send correspondents to cover distant news and political moves that the time perspective shortened. And with the advent of radio and television, "wide nations, and finally the world itself, . . . came to be included in one lively mental whole," as Cooley had foreseen.

The female world cannot easily follow the standard course of coups and revolutions, that is, by way of capturing communication systems—radio and television stations or the established press—but it has sought to create its own. In Yemen as in Mozambique as well as in the United States and Europe, it is learning how to use the media, both print and electronic, and is loading them with its messages.

There has, actually, been for over a century in the United States, a "dissident press" agitating in behalf of women's rights:

> Eight generations of American feminists have refused to keep quiet about inequality and discrimination. . . Ignored, ridiculed, or stereotyped by the conventional media, they could not use this traditional forum for the presentation of their ideas. Instead, they formed separate organizations, initiated lecture tours, called for demonstrations, and established their own journalistic voices. Only through these alternative means could feminists be assured an outlet for their ideas. From the first

women's crusade of the 1840s to the current movement of the 1980s, feminist newspapers and periodicals have been the backbone of the on- going women's movements. Serving as organizational tools, morale boosters, consciousness-raisers, philosophical and political forums, and propaganda organs, hundreds of these journals have helped wage the battle for equality. [Kessler, 1984; present citation, *Media Report to Women*, January–February, 1985, 13]

A considerable amount of attention in these media today is directed to overcoming false stereotypes about women in all the media, to correct- ing the biases in reporting news about the female world, and to over- coming its invisibility. And just to learning about one another, to finding out what's going on elsewhere in the female world. In brief, news.

We have already noted the newsletters that have sometimes arisen among women as the result of contacts at international meetings (chap- ter 7). The simplest were little more than letters. In the case of the participants in a 1975 seminar of women union members in Israel, for example, although they wrote "an official statement of the issues impor- tant to working and union women," more interesting was the fact that they were still writing and exchanging news with one another three years later, letters which constituted, in effect, a sort of proto-newsletter (Nelson, 1978, 14). At the other end of the spectrum were the carefully planned newsletters, often with no-nonsense agenda, designed to facili- tate the implementation of the purposes of some special-interest group. They were methods for facilitating cooperative activities. The purpose of one such newsletter, the Women-Make-Movies Newsletter, was, as with many others, to make available "information to each other, and, therefore, aid international cooperation" (*Media Report to Women*, 1 October 1981, 11). The Nigerian Association of Media Women, organized in 1981, was interested in better media coverage of women, especially of the nonelite, and welcomed for their newsletter "publications and other appropriate documents from women in other countries" (6). A quarterly newsletter of the International Council of African Women, *African Women Rising*, was working "towards the unity of all African women and seeks to build a network of women of African descent around the world" (5).[3]

Even outside of such ready-made newsletter-created readerships there were eager audiences waiting for news about women in all parts of the world, even among Marxist and left-leaning women. In 1976 a group of women in Birmingham, England, had conceived the idea of a *Newsletter on Women in Eastern Europe*, to be supported by their university's Centre for Russian and East European Studies. They had contacts with women in other countries and would like more. Their idea of a news- letter took the form of a debating platform.

We are a group of women who believe that to study the position of women in Eastern Europe is important to us both as socialists and as feminists. The women's movment has not traditionally paid much attention to Eastern Europe, partly because there are no organized women's movements there. Yet the countries of Eastern Europe call themselves socialist and assert that they have solved "the woman question." It is up to us to demonstrate that this is untrue, that the subordinate position of women is as integral to the political systems in the East as it is in the West, and to use the discussion of the position of women in these countries to inform the debates within the women's movement. [*Media Report*, 1 January 1982]

They criticized the position of both the Church and the government in Poland, where "the rhetoric of socialism has been coopted by the establishment," which wants a return of women to the family and to femininity. It speaks of women as a delicate plant but also permits women to sweep the street in bitter cold. Writing before 13 December 1981, the editors ask, "would it be over-optimistic to hope for the foundation of an independent feminist movement" in Poland? As it turned out, it was.[4]

But before it was nipped in the bud there had, in fact, been some first steps toward feminism in Poland. Thus, in November 1980, there came a call from Sigma, a student group, for information about Western feminism:

We have learned about the experiences of Western feminists . . . and we are adapting them to our particular situation in Poland. . . . We want as much information as possible about the women's movement in other countries. We have plans to publish a woman's newspaper and to start a women's theater. The history of women, their ideas and lives must be known. We're the ones who will have to do it. Presently we are planning a seminar on Polish women who have managed to escape the narrow traditional women's roles to become artists and scientists. We also want a feminist gallery to display their works. [*Media Report to Women*, July 1981, 1, 10]

Their agenda sounded like vintage feminist issues: female work overload; inferior pay; education. They were dedicated to raising feminist consciousness, to extending the Feminist Enlightenment. They wanted interdisciplinary women's studies in the university. The whole gamut.

Nor did the national trauma in their country between 1981 and 1983 dampen their enthusiasm. In the spring of 1983 these indomitable young women were reorganizing:

Our organisation, which was developing previously, at present is starting all over again. Our planned activities (some of which were already in preparation) had to stop last year. Now we are once again at the beginning and in a different situation. . . . All our material on women in Poland is based mainly on our own personal observations, and from this we see that the burden of the crisis is being carried by women. . . . Our seminar at the University on feminism is still running, but even there the passivity of the participants is noticeable. We're trying to do some more theoretical work, i.e., extend our scope of knowledge and hopefully . . . start on a research project on women in Poland. When this is done, we'll inform you of the results. [Krystyna and Barbara, 1983]

The news component of newsletters was especially important for special-interest groups. Indeed, the wide dissemination of news is held by some to be a sine qua non of the women's movement itself, certainly for reducing separateness among women everywhere. But more encompassing news required a less specialized medium than newsletters, a medium, that is, reaching a broader readership.

The Women's Institute for Freedom of the Press was founded by Donna Allen in Washington, D.C. in 1972 to stimulate the diffusion of news about women not only among women themselves but also in the general public. It sought to overcome the invisibility of the female world. Neither technical information nor research nor entertainment nor features but news was the grist for its mill. It sought also to avoid the demise that had overtaken earlier women's movements when they had lost their means of communicating among themselves. The Women's Institute was to find "ways to protect and expand the present communication system among women" (program, 1979 conference, 3). Women now had expertise in modern technology, training in its use, and know-how for applying it. They also had an extensive base to start with, a system that reached

millions through a . . . multitude of networks in our many communities of professional organizations, churches, political parties, government offices, public interest groups, unions, farm organizations, libraries, women's studies . . . in every form of medium: music, film, print, art, audio, video and cable, theater . . . in the newsletters and journals of our thousands of women's organizations . . . in conferences and rallies, demonstrations and marches . . . by our mimeographed fliers, posters, bumper stickers and buttons . . . in our clubs, our kitchens, at work . . . by word of mouth, by telephone. . . . This vital communications system is the key to our survival.[4]

In 1982, the WIFP became international and vastly expanded the reach of that system.[5] The informational contents of this system included: news about health and safety as well as economic, political and international information, the indispensable "basis to a mutual support network for women."

More formal than the newsletter and broader and more general in scope than the newsletters of special-interest groups have been the periodicals springing up everywhere which serve as channels of communication not so much of news as of the new ideas and ideologies bubbling up in the female world everywhere. Since they do not, like newsletters, have a ready-made readership, they must "sell" their messages. Still their number and variety, ranging from scholarly and academic journals to magazines modeled after traditional women's magazines but with a more feminist slant, have multiplied.[6] The proliferation of such channels reflects the need women have been increasingly feeling "to have their own journals, newspapers, magazines, etc., to explore their own problems and put forward their own ideas however new or tentative" (*Isis*, no. 16, 1980) rather than to remain passive recipients of male statements of their position. It reflects also encouragement from the UN-sponsored Decade for Women. In 1984 the International Women's Tribune Centre published a directory—Decade for Women Information Resources for 1985—showing that the number of women's periodicals and newsletters which had appeared since 1975 was "one of the most encouraging and promising outcomes of the UN Decade for Women (1976–1985)" (*Media Report to Women*, January–February, 1985, 6):

> Because of the important role played by women's alternative media channels as connecting and supporting links in the women's movement worldwide . . . this directory will enable women to expand their existing dissemination channels and also allow women activists everywhere to obtain greater visibility for issues and activities of concern to us all.[6]

The next year, in 1985, the Women's Institute for Freedom of the Press published *Media Reports to Women* which listed even more channels and resources.[7]

After early flurries of experimental attempts in both Europe and the United States which foundered because of lack of experience, periodicals with styles and formats that were more appealing to readers of general women's or homemakers' periodicals were evolved with hope to cover costs at least if not to make large profits.[8] And, in addition, there were literate publics emerging ready for the feminist messages.

Unfortunately there is no universal language that women everywhere can communicate with. French was once such a universal language for the elite, and today some version of English—American or pidgin—has almost achieved that status in speech. But few women in most parts of the female world feel at home in languages other than their own. Translations are therefore important for them, especially for U.S. women, few of whom are multilingual. One feminist English-language periodical, *Connexions*, was established in the United States in 1981 to be a journal "of translations by, for, and about women." It was to be, and has remained, "the collective product of feminists of diverse nationalities and political perspectives committed to contributing to an international women's movement" (Summer, 1981, no 1, p. 1). The first issue included articles about women in India, the Pacific Islands, Ireland, Nazi Germany, Argentina, South Africa, Holland, France, Copenhagen; there were articles on international prostitution and women organizing against violence.[9]

The general editorial thrust was in the direction of sisterhood among women everywhere:

> *Connexions'* editorial policy is to focus on and make heard the voices of women from beyond U.S. borders. This is because we . . . feel closely linked to women around the world and are often dismayed by the lack of contact we have with them in this country [United States]. While this policy has satisfied our goal of redirecting the flow of information from the "inside out" to the "outside in," it does, indeed have to accept the political boundaries that imperialism has defined for us. . . . These delineations must be questioned and . . . the redefinition of our communities must be a priority if self-determination and stronger links between us are to be achieved. [no. 15, 1985, 31]

It called on women "to organize as women and to support each other's causes," to profit from one another's experiences, difficulties, and successes. It urged that help be proffered to oppressed women in such countries as South America, Asia, and Africa who had fewer possibilities than U.S. women "to disseminate their ideas and actions." Women had to organize against "such urgent problems as rape, militarism, political repression and housing shortages." Women, they reminded their readers, "do not live in a vacuum, but in what is still largely a man's world. It is essential for us to understand the workings of that world if we are to understand each other." The hope was that *Connexions* would "be one step toward building an international women's movement!"

Connexions is oriented toward the larger swells on the current historic scene, whereas the French feminist news biweekly, *des femmes hebdo*, is oriented toward the more immediate, choppier waves, using the news to make its points. Thus, when on Women's International Day, 8 March 1982, its offices were vandalized, a full-page advertisement five days later made an appeal for solidarity. "We appeal to the solidarity and intelligence of women and men who cannot help but be indignant at this behavior. . . . You know what Solidarity is in Poland. You know what the Liberation Front is in Salvador. Do you know what the Women's Liberation Movement is?" Replies in the form of a shower of yeas came from all over the world.[10]

WIN, Women's International Network News, a quarterly, was established by Fran P. Hosken in 1975 as "a world-wide open communication system by, for and about women of all backgrounds, beliefs, nationalities and age groups" to serve the general public, institutions and organizations by transmitting internationally information about women and women's groups" (vol. 1, no. 1). Its motto was to include "all the news that is fit to print by, for and about women." In commemorating its tenth year, *WIN News* reminded its readers of its priorities, "as reflected in the pages of every issue":

> To raise the consciousness of women and men everywhere about the true facts and the injustice of the status of women in all parts of the world, based on the principle "I am my sister's keeper";
>
> To join hands all over the world and work together towards fulfilling the basic needs shared by women and our children in all societies, regardless of country, color, or political "ism." They are: reproductive freedom of choice, economic equality in the family and marketplace, equality before the law and personhood;
>
> To assert and implement human rights as indivisible for all people, regardless of sex and without man-made prejudice, discarding all man-made customs or traditions favoring the male sex. [vol. 10, no. 2, 1984, 1]

The range of coverage, both substantively and geographically, has been astonishing, including female circumcision or genital and sexual mutilation, the media, health, peace, Moslem fundamentalism, human rights. . . . Nothing dealing with women has been alien to WIN News, no part of the world has been outside its beat.

Isis was established as an International Bulletin[11] in 1974 in Geneva by a women's collective to gather material from local women's groups everywhere and make it available to other women in the feminist movement. It invited notices and information about the activities of women in other countries and continents and welcomed exchanges with those producing newsletters, magazines, and other materials. Its success was phenomenal. In its tenth year it introduced an expanded program including not only the Women's International Cross-Cultural Exchange, WICCE (chapter 7), but also a *Newsletter* and *Dossier*, or *Report*, which, together, constituted *Women's World*.

> ISIS was born in response to the needs of women in different parts of the world to be able to communicate with each other, create networks, and share ideas and experiences. Ten years later, these needs are even more urgent. . . . These ten years have witnessed a revolution in communications technology, a revolution that has forged global links for large corporations and governments, but left women on the sidelines. . . . The mass media continually fail to portray women as participants in the

world's important events or as significant contributors to the world's economy. . . . The women of the world need their own communications revolution, and women's groups everywhere are springing up in answer to the challenge. [March 1984][12]

Not all periodicals were as successful as these. To whatever extent the numerous periodicals succeeded—some were short-lived—they did contribute to the considerable seepage of feminist thinking into many parts of the globe, including, surprisingly, the USSR (chapter 9). The global female world was rapidly becoming acquainted with itself.[13] The torch of the Feminist Enlightenment was burning brightly.

Not technically a periodical is WIRE, Women's International Resource Exchange which publishes articles on specific countries relevant for women. It is a collective of nine women who base their selection on extensive discussion. Among their publications have been a collection of papers on women in South Africa (Spring 1980), South Yemen (1977).

Periodicals—the print media in general—call for a modicum of literacy. In this sense they are elitist. But we know that most women in the global female world are not literate (chapter 1). They are therefore cut out of many channels of communication. Until recently the situation looked discouraging. Now, however, a new application of modern technology by way of electronic media enters the scene and the lights turn on for them. These women now become reachable. And even in culturally nondistorted form.

> Women are communicating with each other through audio-visuals: slides, tapes, videos, films, posters and photography. They have become an important means of communication, consciousness raising, and organizing for action. . . . Many of them have been produced with few resources, but with great integrity, attempting to reflect a real image of women's situations. Many of them could be useful to other groups of women who are working on the same issues. Therefore *Isis* has produced a *Resource Guide on Audiovisuals for Women*. [Women in Action, no. 1, 1984, 36]

It is not the use per se of modern technologies that is new in the global female world. They have long been used to spread commercial messages. Dr. Nawal El Saadawi of Egypt has excoriated the sexism of the messages in films and television, their insistence on the use of cosmetics and other consumer products. She notes that "the modern woman in Baghdad, Cairo or Tunis does not wear the clothes she wishes to wear, but rather puts on what a capitalist fashion king in Paris or New York considers suitable for her" (*Media Report*, 1 September 1981, 12).

Although until now the messages diffused by commercial electronic media, especially film and television, have not been feminist in content but, in fact, even antifeminist, still, the basic premise of many of the newly evolving channels of diffusion is that their messages can be made to enhance rather than degrade women. It is the messages that are now new, and the recipients.

Resolution 6 of the 1980 UN Copenhagen conference had asked governments and INGOs to "encourage and support the cultural, economic, and technical cooperation between rural women in developed and developing countries and among developing countries. Such encouragement and support are hardly problematic among women in developed countries; books, periodicals, newsletters can find their way to them fairly easily. Not so in developing countries. Rural women are not always reachable. But now a project called the Village Network—already tried in Canton, China—has appeared and shows a wholly new way for women to reach one another, a way that makes it possible for village, as well as urban, women to teach and learn from one another. Here, for example, is a project that

> set out to train villagers in twelve different countries in three years to use and produce their own videotapes. Exchanges among the countries will allow a new form of communications to take place. Small-format videotapes used in combination with the national television, can stimulate an unprecedented degree of exchange within a country, giving people of diverse cultures and backgrounds a way to know each other. This exchange can happen at a village, national, and international level. The Village Network Project allows villagers in Mali to learn about life in Indonesia, from Indonesians. [*Media Report to Women*, 1 September 1981, 9]

The use of video technology makes possible an entirely new kind of transfer of information. "It provides a means by which small-scale, locally-inspired, village-centered development solutions can be transferred from place to place without losing the spirit that animates the practicalities." Groups otherwise disconnected from one another can nevertheless experience the exchange usually limited to those in close physical proximity. Although only one such project has as yet been completed (in Canton), the potential for webs of village communication systems for the sharing of solutions to common problems is heartening.[14]

Equally revolutionary but at a different level is the use of the teleconference:

> The first international teleconference was the on-going monthly teleconferences held by women in some half dozen countries in the South Pacific, Fiji, Papua New Guinea, Vanuatu, Tonga, and others, on a dif-

ferent subject each month, chosen by the women in each nation in turn,
such as: infant formula, a nuclear-free Pacific, food preservation and
storage, independence movements, etc.; the teleconferences began when
the membership of the Pacific Women's Resource Center found they could
not travel such long distances to meet and decided to communicate by
satellite, using university-based facilities in each country. (Media Reports
to Women, August 1, 1981, p. 9)

The choice of subjects in these conferences was freewheeling, including,
be it noted, "independence movments" as well as "infant formula," a
"nuclear-free Pacific" as well as "food preservation and storage," all
recognized as equally important female issues in substance, all equally
feminist in slant.[15]

The basic premise of many of the newly evolving channels of diffusion
is that electronically diffused messages can enhance rather than degrade women as women themselves gain expertise in using the new
media. As they were, indeed, doing. In Japan, for example, Haruko
Kojima Watanabe was using the training received in the United States
to build an international women's videotape library (*Media Report*, 1
August 1981, 9). In Amsterdam about 300 media women, representing
more than 30 countries, met at the First International Feminist Film
and Video Conference, to work out ways to expedite international communication and cooperation. The messages sent by the media operated
by these women are not so likely as are those sent by commercial
channels to subvert the concerns of women.

Periodicals, videotapes, teleconferences were, then, little by little
creating among women a transcultural way of looking at themselves
and their world. In slow, circuitous ways they were creating relationships among women from many parts of their world, even at the
grass-roots level, but also at the level of the intellectual elites at the
vanguard of change. The results may not always be immediately striking. But there they are, women-to-women messages of all kinds racing
from one part of the globe to another.

And, in addition, there are networks.

CHAPTER NINE

Networks in Action: Cases in Point

"How many legions does the Pope
have?" replied Stalin as he rejected the
warnings of his advisors against a
certain policy, secure in the knowledge
that without legions the Pope could be
ignored. [Story told by USSR defector]

The female world may have no more legions than the Pope. But networks can prove to be excellent surrogates.

Formal organization in the female world in the West has until recently tended to follow the male style. There have been constitutions
and bylaws, rules of order, agenda, the whole package. But, it is coming
to be seen, this male model does not make the best use of the assets of
the female world. Elise Boulding, who has traced the history of both
national and international organizations in the female world, reminds
us that although its nongovernment organizations have accumulated a
"substantial knowledge resource," this knowledge has not been well
used. Their low level of power should have led women "to examine the
age-old skills that women have exercised in operating from positions of
lesser power, in terms of organizing resources differently" from the way
men have (1977, 214). She is referring to their traditional networking
skills.

Although networks are among the most researched topics in sociology
in the United States today, the part they play in the global female world
is only now being studied in much detail. Even so, it is already clear
that they vary in format and style, ranging from simple grapevines and
word-of-mouth gossip to fairly structured systems; that the messages
they spread may vary from "intelligence" to news; and that they may
even lead to action.

Kathleen Staudt has described traditional networking skills locally among women farmers in Kenya, showing how, though deprived relative to men of all kinds of agricultural services, they have nevertheless

> managed to maintain farm productivity largely without the aid or encouragement of the government's agricultural service. . . . The diffusion of agricultural information was found to occur not by way of such government services but by way of women's networks, particularly among the numerous women's communal agricultural and mutual-aid associations. [*Rural Africana*, no 29, 1975–76][1]

Nici Nelson argues that the female world would do well to learn how to expand to a wider scene these microskills of communication so useful locally:

> One of the most important activities women have undertaken to advance their cause is linking with each other and forming women's networks, those formal and informal contacts among women whose homes, occupations, and backgrounds may differ, but who call on and are called on by those in the network for advice and assistance. [1978, 14]

And Boulding specifies extension of such networks beyond the local, even to the global, scene (217–18). One U.S. group, On Our Side, has for its motto, "Act local, think global." Such experience in working together according to their own style may be excellent practice in preparing the female world for equitable integration, a kind of affirmative action which helps it get its act together to deal with the male world eye-to-eye—that is, on an equitable basis.

It is, however, one thing to diffuse knowledge, information, and advice among women who speak a common language and share a common culture. It is quite a different thing to extend the process to encompass women who do not speak a common language or share a common culture. Still, one way and another, the female world is actually in process of doing precisely that and finding that this network-style of organization, in which there are just self-structuring participants with varying levels of involvement, is more congenial to many women than hierarchical male-style formal structures.[2] This does not mean that networking has been reduced to a fine art; there is still a great deal to be learned about it. And cases to be learned from. For networks are beginning to sprout everywhere, in both the female[3] and male[4] worlds.

In 1975 the United Nations officially recognized female networking as a method of achieving equitable integration. In that year, Resolution 3520 recommended the establishment of an International Research and Training Institute for the Advancement of Women as an "autonomous body within the framework of the UN," to serve as a vehicle for research, training and information to help ensure the integration of women into the mainstream of development, particularly in developing countries. . . . The Institute works through existing networks of women's organizations, research institutes, centres, as well as by establishing national focal points throughout the world. . . . The Institute is funded solely from voluntary contributions made by governments, nongovernment organizations, philanthropic institutions and individuals . . . in cash or in kind. [*Media Report to Women*, January–February 1985, 6][5]

When the International Women's Tribune Center was incorporated in 1978, its modus operandi was to be one of "collaborative teamwork of a small group of women professionals who maintain close contact with colleagues worldwide" (undated flyer). What the women farmers in Idakho were doing autonomously, as reported by Staudt, was to be formalized, structured, and turned over to specialists far away.

Some feminists outside the UN ambience saw the shadow of cooptation hovering over this embracing of the network idea. They feared it could be used subversively as well as constructively.[6] But, in any event, networking proved to be too flexible and amorphous to be contained in any single model. It proved to be widely adaptable.

Only three cases in point are offered here, all of them subverting some aspect of a particular status quo. One is the International Feminist Network, dealing with specific individuals oppressed by a national government; one is a group of women protesting oppressive conditions in the USSR in a periodical, *The Almanac: Women in Russia*; and one is a group of women referred to in chapter 7, who organized a series of peace marches against the militancy of governments both East and West.

The International Feminist Network

In 1976 an International Tribunal on Crimes against Women had been organized by feminists to raise the consciousness of women with respect to the international scope of violence against women and the silence that everywhere protected it. More than a thousand women from every part of the world assembled in Brussels to participate.

They spoke of the physical violence they experienced as women: by rape, battering, genital mutilation; of being imprisoned for defending themselves against physical attacks. They told of the suffering imposed on them by governments and institutions which refused to let them freely choose whether or not to bear children and of many more violations of their rights. For many women this was the first opportunity to break their isolation and to speak out openly of these crimes. [Karl, 1980, 5]

If they could find no forum at which to protest these crimes against them at home, they found one here. And they found a continuing forum in the International Feminist Network that grew out of the Tribunal.

The modus vivendi that the new network evolved was to serve as a receiving center for appeals for support by women through so-called contact women and to distribute these appeals by way of a network of such contact women.[7] A common appeal for help called for supportive telegrams, letters, demonstrations, or other forms of publicity in a specific case of oppression. The idea was to "give support and solidarity to women everywhere in combating injustices against women," to exert pressure on governments or other agencies of power by way of international public opinion in cases damaging to women. International support did make a difference. Acting together women could be strong.[8]

In the first three years of operation the IFN dealt with more than fifty cases. One had to do with a television programmer in Portugal who had shown a program on abortion; one had to do with South Korean women who had organized and elected women to leadership in their union; one with a Chilean woman who had participated in a peaceful demonstration on International Women's Day. Such appeals for support circulated by the IFN generated responses from all over the world in the form of letters or other forms of support.

Here are several examples. A Belfast woman in prison for killing her father, who was guilty of incest, had been refused an appeal. A committee of the IFN gave notice that unless she received the Prerogative of Mercy, "actions would be raised in five European countries and in America, Canada, and Australia." Evidently giving some consideration "to the reputation of British justice," the officials released the woman.[9] In Portugal a woman was facing a sentence of two to eight years of imprisonment for an abortion three years earlier, and the women who had found the abortionist for her were also subject to four years in prison. "On the date of the trial several hundred women demonstrated in support of . . . the woman, bearing a 3,000-signature petition of women who said they had [also] had abortions and who demanded to be prosecuted." She was acquitted. In an abortion-bill case in Israel, support was received from women in about a dozen countries, including letters from "famous individuals whose letters we could use to obtain local publicity for our cause. . . . Because of these women we made local headlines." The government took them seriously enough to reply to all of them.[10] Still on the docket, so to speak, as of 1980, were appeals to the IFN from women all over the world—Greece, Ireland, Peru, Namibia, Japan, the Phillipines, India, Copenhagen—and among the issues raised were family law, prison conditions, workers' grievances, South African sexual as well as racial oppression, sexism in broadcasting, contraception—the gamut.[11] It is not likely that the IFN will exert the kind of power available to the male world. But its influence had made itself felt even against great multinational corporations, as in the case against Nestlé for its promotion of infant formula use in the Third World.

Sometimes the calls for help were simply for release from feelings of isolation, as in the case of an appeal from Israeli feminists who often felt isolated, "the knowledge that our sisters all over the world are ready to assist us by responding to our requests for letters . . . gives us the strength to go on." At Copenhagen in 1980 women spoke of how important it was for them to learn that there were other women and groups in the world working for the same ends and supporting their work.

The IFN network was an idea whose time had come, not only in the West but also elsewhere in the female world. As recently as 1985 women in the United States were being asked for support of a woman at Kuwait University,[12] and almost a decade after the IFN was established in 1976, a feminist think tank called Sisterhood Is Global was set up (1984) by representatives from more than thirteen countries to reinvent this wheel. Its plans included an "Urgent Network Alert System to organize international campaigns of support for women censored, jailed, tortured, exiled, or otherwise persecuted for activism on behalf of female human rights" (*Ms.*, 1985, 46).[13] At about the same time Amnesty International USA was also beginning to pay attention to the special—female—kind of human rights that needed protection. It was "beginning to focus on women and human rights abuses in a more in-depth way, something that has been a long time coming. . . . There is a lot more work to be done in researching and presenting cases of women" (Paula Jackson, personal letter, 19 February 1985).[14]

Equitable integration was clearly not self-enforcing. Some kind of networking was clearly a sine qua non for its implementation.

The Almanac: Women and Russia

The second feminist legion was a less formally structured network than the IFN; its center was the feminist community in Paris; it was addressed to the support of a dissident group of women in the USSR.[15] They had set up a periodical, *The Almanac: Women and Russia* in Leningrad and its first issue appeared in September 1979.[16] It contained articles, poems, and fiction describing the lives of women in the USSR, including the situation of unmarried mothers, the conditions in the kindergartens, and in the abortion clinics, which the writers called "butcheries." It had items on male drunkenness, on the lack of help by husbands in the home and the resulting overload for wives, on the endless queues at markets, where they had to stand after a long day's work. In the USSR, as elsewhere (cf. resolutions of the United Nations), whatever the official proclamations of equality might be demands for the "rights of women were regarded as presumptuous" (*Isis*, 1980, no. 17, p. 22).[17] These were familiar issues, echoing back and forth from many parts of the female world, from the Chilean compañeras to Mozambican revolutionaries.

The statement of the aims of the *Almanac* reflected the raised consciousness of women in a country zealously attempting to keep such subversion out:

> Attention! Dear Sisters! We have scarcely begun living when we become conscious that all the burdens of life are kept for our shoulders. At first, everything which is painful and harmful to us—containing us in a dense circle—seems to happen by chance. It is impossible to believe that life can punish completely innocent individuals just because they are born female. All suffering is felt to be so unbearable that it surely must disappear of itself, dissolve as would a nightmare. But nothing changes of itself. And we are convinced that no-one will help us except we ourselves. Only when we write, talk about our sufferings, our bitterness, only when we have made our experiences known to each other, politicized, can we find a way through, can we help ourselves and thousands of women suffering as much as ourselves.
>
> Precisely for these reasons we have decided—in our free country—to put out a magazine for women. On the pages of this magazine, we are reporting on the situation of women in the family, at work, in the hospital, in childbirth, on the situation of our children, on the position of our theoretical reflections. . . . We hope that we will, with our strength united, set ourselves in motion and, with that, the liberation of women. When that which is concealed is revealed, then it will become clear.[22]

An editorial stated that "the situation of women in society is the most important question of our time" (22). An appeal was made to free women from male criteria, male standards.

> Values remain male-oriented; the woman is appraised by the society she lives in and she is forced to measure herself by those values. Her worth is dependent on how much like a man she has become. The falseness of this position always demands a sacrifice from the woman but it is society which has caused this: what is known as the "woman question" is the most important element in the common struggle for the revolutionising of the world. [22–23]

Another editorial struck the same note:

> . . . male culture excludes women, it is saturated with misogyny. . . .
> The brutal pressures of a phallocratic culture represses everything female

in the world and at the same time makes them misogynistic. . . . Woman, who cannot obtain true knowledge, who is filled with misinformation, cannot see her real enemy. While she turns away from herself, she must wander about in the dark corners of an alien culture. This contempt of women leads to . . . the division of humanity and to the isolation of women from each other. The common experiences of the women of society are not respected and new experiences do not develop. New ideas are prone to be discredited from the start. The voice of truth is difficult to hear in the middle of parade-ground music. [23]

It was inevitable that sanctions ultimately would be invoked against women who so brazenly demanded the rights guaranteed them and who could even challenge the military with such obviously subversive statements as "there is much talk of military defense, but before someone is defended, the vitality of the whole society should be ensured. That is, the woman, who gives life, comes first, and then military defense, not the other way round" (23). The familiar old priority issue once more, more than sixty years after the Revolution.

Inevitable as it was that sanctions would be invoked, what is relevant here is that they were not invoked immediately. The women themselves felt that support garnered from European feminists by way of a network postponed, if it did not finally deflect or vanquish, sanctions. One of the women, Tatiana Goritscheva, noted that although the women had been frequently taken into custody—she herself, about ten times in one year—they had not been formally arrested. Why had they not? Because, she replied, "we had great support among European feminists. Without that support we would have been arrested in November."

As it turned out, not until 20 July 1980, did the guillotine blade fall. The women and their families were boarded on a plane for Vienna and expelled from the USSR. A week before the opening of the Olympic Games which were attracting international crowds, the women had been given an ultimatum: emigrate or be imprisoned. The support of their feminist network outside the USSR had made them too dangerous to tolerate any longer.[18] This legion, like Carthage, had to be destroyed.

But the idea of the network did not die. There were always new victims to be supported. In April 1982, Natalia was writing from Paris: "We should like to create an International Feminist Union which would . . . offer help to the women of Eastern Europe and to all struggling feminists in the world" (*Media Report*, 1 April 1982, 3). And, apparently indomitable, she was organizing the Defense of Repressed Women in the USSR from her Paris address. And in 1985 Tatyana Mamanova was planning to establish a Russian feminist press in the West, where Soviet women could get their ideas published and presented to Russian women (Costello, 1985, 6).[19]

The Women's Peace Network

When the anti-freeze campaign of the Women's International League for Peace and Freedom was sanctioned by the State Department in a July 1982 Special Bulletin (no. 101), the league commented:

> Evidently, the aspect of WILF that scares the Administration most is the aspect of which we are most proud: our international contacts and our sisterhood with women all over the world, including the Soviet Union. The global perspective reflects the ideals of Women Strike for Peace as well. . . . WILF's very history started with an international women's delegation to The Hague to demand an end to war. We have continued that legacy. There is something powerful in sisterhood and solidarity. [Frank, 1982, 3]

As they had shown a few years earlier (chapter 7).

In late October 1979, the WILF in Geneva had announced the news of the deployment of American-controlled middle-range atomic missiles in Europe. This was the first public knowledge about these missiles. The league sprang into action. It asked its branches in the different countries to protest to their governments about this development. News spread rapidly along the network. "Before the 12th of December, a demonstration of between 40 and 50 thousand Europeans had gathered in the streets outside the NATO headquarters in Brussels," and the antimissile campaign was launched.

In response to the League's alert, the first march of Nordic women through Europe—this one from Copenhagen to Paris—to make their demands about disarmament and nuclear war in person was planned in Oslo.[20] These women were highly motivated. And they had a clear idea of what the character of their action should be. It had to be an action by women and among women. It began with a peace resolution, written in two days, translated, and distributed, and at the U.N. Copenhagen Conference for Women in 1980 it was presented to Kurt Waldheim, U.N. Secretary General, with half a million signatures, followed by 60,000 supporting signatures from women in West Germany, 16,000 from women in Switzerland, and more still from women in other European countries as well as from women in Japan, Tanzania, Lebanon, and Latin American countries. A good beginning. But more was needed. A peace march, for example.

The next year a peace march from Copenhagen to Paris did, indeed, take place. With disappointing results.[21] Instead of garnering kudos, it was ridiculed, negatively criticized, condemned. But at least it attracted attention; it stimulated discussion. "Why march in Europe?" the women were asked. "Europe does not want war." Then, challengingly, "try to march in the USSR!" The women accepted the challenge. Very well, they would. The next march would be to Moscow.

Peace organizations in several countries were asked to appoint representatives to plan the march. Church-related and housewives' organizations,[22] as well as labor unions and U.N. chapters, were asked to discuss whether they wanted to participate. Seventy persons from each of four countries (Sweden, Norway, Denmark, Finland) said they did. They were well briefed. To avoid the charge that they were Soviet collaborators or stooges, or at least funded by the USSR, every woman paid her own way. Great effort was made to see that the participants were politically representative.

The women were instructed on how to behave in the USSR. In private conversations every question that individual women wanted to discuss could be taken up; in official speeches, official slogans were to be respected. The trip was to be by train, though others could follow the designated route in buses, boats, or even on foot. Some participants wanted more aggressive tactics. "Why should we use trains?" they demanded. They warned that "the March could be totally controlled in that way." Why couldn't they just walk? That would give them greater freedom. Some did, in fact, walk. Some wanted more contact with dissenters in the USSR and members of oppositional groups. Agreement was finally reached on all the crucial issues.

But the carefully planned composition and briefing of the group bred skepticism among their Soviet hosts. Under no circumstances was the Soviet Peace Committee willing to accept the group's firm statements that peace and disarmament were the sole objectives of the march. During the first days in Moscow the women were accorded diplomatic courtesy; they were offered a tour of the city. They were expected to conform to protocol and accept the usual invitations to see the usual tourist attractions. But the women refused to use their time for these irrelevant time-consuming activities. They told their hosts that they intended to remain in the same room with their USSR negotiators until mutual trust was established. Only then could the hard work begin. It finally did.

The major issue dealt with the nature of the slogans to be carried in the march. Those finally accepted were: "*No* to nuclear weapons in Europe—East and West." "*No* to nuclear weapons in the world." "*Yes* to disarmament and peace." Unfortunately, as soon as this hard-won agreement was reached, the chairman of the Soviet Peace Committee died. Back to square one, almost. When the group reformed, every item that had already been settled would have to be taken up again. The new Soviet chairman had to feel his way. The women, pressed for time, did not give him much opportunity to get used to his new role. With too much to do in such a short time, tension rose. Another stalemate ensued.

Discouraged, the women concluded that the march might not take place in 1982 after all. But they told the Soviet chairman they were willing to continue some other time. In 1983. Hours elapsed.

The next day when the women came back they were presented with the USSR proposals. The women had seen them before. They were, in fact, the very proposals they had themselves submitted in the first place. Apparently, in the meantime, the chairman had been the speaker at a meeting of Party members and told them what the Soviet Peace Committee was proposing. When he was applauded, supported, and rewarded by his Party peers, he was reassured. He felt secure. And, said one woman, "he won *our* victory."[23]

In any event, whoever won the victory for whom, the march was a great success among the thousands of watchers, as we saw in chapter 7, and a joint statement was drawn up for presentation to the UN by the Nordic Women for Peace and the Soviet Peace Committee:

> To the United Nations, governments, parliaments and the people of the world: The Peace March, 1982, Stockholm-Helsinki-Moscow-Minsk, July 13–29, 1982, is completed. Women stood up to act and men joined them in a common endeavor to save the earth from destruction. Representatives of public organizations from the Nordic countries and the Soviet Union have carried through a common project, a peace march. The march is showing the world that growing peace movements—in the East and West—declare together:
>
> > Our common march has shown that it is possible for representatives of organizations in different countries, East and West, to work together and reach an agreement on the most vital problem of all times, to save humanity from extinction.
> >
> > We call upon the United Nations and all the governments, parliaments and people of the world to act together as we have done during the peace march, 1982, to reach an agreement.
> >
> > The time has come for the governments and parliaments to proceed from words to deeds in the field of disarmament.
> >
> > Together we shall overcome!

So much, then, for this legion in (peaceful) action.[24] The emerging global female world could add one more notch to its belt. This was Feminist Enlightenment at its best.

The Pax Romana and the Pax Britannica were maintained by ships and legions. The Pax Femina will not have ships, and its legions will not be armed with guns. The power its legions will have is not yet entirely clear. For it is only in the last historical moments that there have been enough literate, let alone educated, women with the time and training even to think about the resources available to the female world and the most suitable tactics and strategies for their deployment. It has been said that no government has ever been toppled by women. They could therefore be safely ignored. But, on second thought, could they be? Most of the world press thought they could. It ignored the Nordic women *en marche*. From a currently journalistic point of view a march by women was not newsworthy. The activities of women are slow-breaking news. They supply few scoops. They require time to show impact on policy. But these marches were more nearly like the kind Stalin might well have understood. He might even have coveted the kind of organization and spirit that could set them in motion. He might have even feared them,[25] for if or when global solidarity is achieved by the female world it might well rest on its common goal of peace. For war is the ultimate cooption of the female world by the male world.

PART FOUR
A "Decade for Women"

INTRODUCTION

The knowledge that women around the world are experiencing . . . an awakening similar to their own and discovering new ways of associating together towards common goals is very important. . . . This very need for reinforcement and support may be what will impel women to a higher level of organization. Once together and comparing their past experiences, they may convince themselves that action is possible, and that change can come about because of their action. Here again, knowing about the experiences of women in other parts of the world is important for making out possible routes. . . We make this call for exchange and sharing across national boundaries, in solidarity and mutual respect [Figueroa and Anderson, 1981, 16].

Since the history of the female world has only recently become visible, bit by bit, by way of scholarly research, it is not always easy to know how to assess it on the current scene. From one point of view the UN-sponsored Decade for Women (1976–1985) discussed here takes on critical historical significance, as a time when global female consciousness-raising took on unprecedented scope, when the beginning Feminist Enlightenment made clear how little we actually knew about the female world beyond the parochial local scene. If even that.[1] The male world had engaged in far-flung world trade, had sailed the seven seas and conquered continents. Its exploits had defined human history, excluding from it the female world almost completely. Now, in a seemingly casual gesture, the male world was inviting the female world to participate—on its own terms, as it turned out—in one of its events, a world-wide Conference dealing with its issues. The time was the early 1970s when the Feminist Enlightenment had just begun to embolden some of the more privileged women, East and West to think in global terms. Although much of the drama to be presented in part IV re-enacts much that we have already seen in the struggle for equitable integration, it is played on a larger world stage and with an enlarged cast of characters. The protagonists—most of them women—are representatives of the male and female worlds. The priorities are also déjà vu; they have to do with the relative importance to be assigned to male and female issues (chapter 5). Unlike the international conferences women were learning how to organize (chapter 7), those dealt with here were under the sponsorship of an agency of the male world, the United Nations General Assembly. A slightly different point of view is therefore called for here, one that pays more attention to the male world, especially as represented in the UN General Assembly.

The UN-sponsored Decade for Women came at a most inauspicious time, a time of great transformations in the UN General Assembly. The U.N. itself, beginning as, in effect, a gentlemen's club of member nations, most of whom shared a cultural, legal, political, and diplomatic history and tradition which, if they did not necessarily assure agreement, let alone consensus, at least made clear what the unwritten rules were. So "during the first 15 years of the U.N. . . . countries sympathetic to the U.S. enjoyed comfortable majorities in the General Assembly and Security Council, thus making the organization an instrument of American foreign policy" [Frank cited by Sciolino, Washington Post, 1985].

By the early 70s, however, a host of newly minted African and Asian states became members of the U.N. and the composition of the U.N. General Assembly became radically altered.[2] Since many of the new members were client states of the USSR and the U.S. (chapter 3), the General Assembly became "a free-fire zone for rhetoric" between representatives of the two great powers. By the early 70s the General Assembly was controlled by a new majority of small countries representing small populations, many of them following the Soviet paradigm.[3] The results seemed dangerous to Western delegations reared in the Western parliamentarian tradition.[4] In time, recognizing the validity of the principle "autre temps, autre moeurs," the U.S. delegates came to seek common ground with the newcomers. They assumed a tolerant attitude of noblesse oblige; it was beneath their dignity to fight with the new majority.

The relevance of this change in the General Assembly lay in the power it gave to the Soviet Union, its client states, and even to so-called nonaligned states. They could twist the lion's tail at will and with impunity. They could show "selective outrage," or "selective name-calling," almost always vis-à-vis the U.S. or Israel. By the 1980s, however, "the common feeling was that many members were trying to take advantage of the United States and that this country had gone too far in seeking to accommodate them" [Editorial, Washington Post, July 2, 1985]

By this time a new administration had come to power in the U.S. and there was a new Ambassador to the U.N., a woman who did not accept the old "noblesse oblige" stance of the late 70s. The times had, in fact changed. And this time it was the hostile delegates of the General

Assembly who had to bow to new customs. The new Ambassador protested Third-World tactics in the UN which she labelled abusive. She
referred to "the practice of singling out particular countries for special
criticism" almost always the U.S. and Israel [Washington Post, Feb. 2,
1985]. There was also a reaction in the U.S. against the General Assembly's "blame America first" point of view. She stopped the patronizing,
demeaning practice of taking the "gratuitous political assaults" lying
down. She was not, as the men had seemed to be, "too proud to fight."
Criticizing the assaulters was not beneath her dignity.[5] The U.S. public
supported the new position. Thus one newspaper editorialized that
there was:

> an argument for being patient and forbearing at the U.N. when, as so
> often happens, American interests, friends and values come under gra-
> tuitous political assault. It is that Third Worlders are sensitive and frus-
> trated and it does no particular harm to let them sound off at American
> expense [Washington Post, Feb. 2, 1985].

But it was, the editorial continued, a specious position:

> Self respect and self-interest demand that the United States take the U.N.
> seriously. Those who want to use it as a political playpen demean the
> organization—and then wonder why its processes do not serve them
> better.

The years 1975 to 1985 constituted a critical time in the history of the
female world as well as in the history of the Third World. In 1947, the
UN had established a Commission on the Status of Women and five
years later one of its members and one-time Chair—Helvi Sipila, a
Finnish lawyer—became Assistant Secretary General for Social and
Humanitarian matters, an office she held for eleven years, 1972–1983.
No women had ever before been named to any such high-level position
in the U.N. Nor had any period in the story of the U.N. been more
relevant for women. The U.N. had always been concerned with women
as beneficiaries—as refugees, that is, or as victims of catastrophies—and
its several agencies—WHO, UNESCO, UNICEF, ILO—had always included them in their programs. But something new and different was
now being added to the scene. New kinds of women were looming up on
the horizon. They wanted to be activists as well as beneficiaries. They
were writing a new script. The scene was changing.

In 1972, two years after Ester Boserup had taught scholars about the
female side of development (chapter 2), the General Assembly—probably at the suggestion of Helvi Sipila[6]—almost absent-mindedly, proclaimed 1975 an International Women's Year, to be devoted to
promoting equality between men and women, to fully integrating

women into the total development effort, including at the international level; to recognizing women's increasing contribution to the development of friendly relations and cooperation among states; and to the strengthening of world peace.[7] But their heart was not really in it. Half of the member nations did not even ratify the idea. And 16 out of 138 did not pay their part of the expenses. There was, in brief, general apathy and the sponsors had a hard time selling the idea. The U.N. had already done a great deal for women. In 1945 its Charter had affirmed its faith in "fundamental human rights, in the dignity and worth of the human person, and in the equal rights of men and women." Two years later its Economic and Social Council had established a subsidiary Commission on the Status of Women, and in 1952 a Convention on Political Rights of Women prepared by that Commission was adopted by the General Assembly. In 1979 it also adopted a Convention for the Elimination of All Forms of Discrimination Against Women. So why an International Women's Year?

It took a considerable amount of prodding by activist women even to begin to implement it.[8] Still, despite such lack of enthusiasm, even apathy, a conference celebrating the International Women's Year did take place in Mexico City in June, 1975, and in December of that year it was extended into a decade and the years of 1976–1985 denominated a Decade for Women.

All told, as it turned out, there were to be three such conferences, the first the 1975 IWY Mexico City meetings, the second or mid-decade conference in 1980 in Copenhagen, and the last one in 1985 in Nairobi (chapter 10). There were, rather, to be six conferences, for parallel to each of the three U.N. sponsored conferences there was to be a non-official women's conference by female International Non-Governmental Organizations (chapter 7).

CHAPTER TEN

A Drama in Three Acts

The Mexico City Conference celebrating the International Women's Year got off to a bad start. The president of Mexico in his opening remarks recognized the oppression of women in many countries, an oppression which he attributed to the poverty inflicted on them by an unfair world economic order, by colonialism, neo-colonialism, imperialism, and a long litany of other grievances standard in many General Assembly documents, including the UN's own charter.[1] Since the UN was an organization of governments it saw the situation in terms of the political relations among nations, and a call for a New International Economic Order (NIEC) became a prime component of the conference agenda. Obviously the redistribution of world wealth came before female equality could be achieved.

Feminist activists were taken aback. They were being confronted with issues they viewed as purely political—unjust economic relations, colonialism, poverty, Zionism, the occupation of Palestine among others—and irrelevant to the day-by-day struggles of women. Nor were they prepared for this nationalist statement of their case. They rejected it. They had come to Mexico City with Sipila's vision in mind. Sipila had envisaged the conference as one at which women from rich countries would mingle with women from poor countries, the most exploited of human resources, and both would learn from one another how the lives of women everywhere could be improved. The feminists wanted to talk about what they saw as the genuine female issues: discrimination, inequalities in all aspects of women's lives including health care, economic opportunity, education, overwork, the whole female agenda. Their indignant protests rendered them personae non gratae to the official delegations,[2] to whom these irrelevant items were not what the conference was about. Almost from the sound of the opening gong, the issues were joined.

Olof Palme, then Swedish premier, stated the priority issue as he saw it. Improving conditions for women was vitally tied to improving the lot of all mankind. Many Third-World women agreed. Mexican and Chinese women argued that without redistribution of world wealth and power, equality with men was unimportant. And delegates representing the USSR and the East European bloc stated that women in their countries were already liberated so world peace and disarmament should be the major focus of this conference.[3] Even the (woman) lieutenant governor of New York, presumably a feminist, seemed equivocal; she straddled. She urged the women not to be sidetracked by political issues; she referred to the bickering and endless political rhetoric that had bogged down the proceedings so far but hoped that the conference could yet be salvaged. She noted that whereas women from advanced countries sought equal opportunities and equal pay, women in poor countries could not even hope for equal food or medical care or education. They were therefore correct to give top priority to social and economic re-forms to provide for their basic needs. This did not, however, conflict with the values of the Western world, where many women suffered the same hardships.

The head of the U.S. delegation, Patricia Hutar, vehemently denied the theory that redistribution of the world's wealth and power was a prereq-uisite for female equality. Women must participate as partners with men for social and economic betterment rather than wait for the world's male-dominated leadership to accomplish such improvement first. Women could not wait, for example, with arms folded for men to achieve a new international economic order which might take years to achieve. Women delegates from Sri Lanka, Iran, the Philippines, Great Britain, and Egypt agreed with her that the conference was ignoring genuinely feminist issues in favor of nationalistic ones. It was con-centrating on political issues that reflected a male mentality. This rift between male-oriented and female-oriented issues, erroneously charac-terized as "political" and "women's," was to dog all three Decade-for-Women conferences.

The accompanying cartoon (Gary Brookline, *Richmond Times Dis-patch*, in *New York Times*, 28 July 1985), illustrates graphically the seemingly irreconcilable differences between the "political" and the "female" issues. In the tall urban buildings with world-wide perspec-tives really important political issues—unfair economic relations among nations, Zionism, colonialism—were to be discussed. Invisible from that high perch were two oppressive hard-working mothers sur-rounded by their fifteen children. As compared with the sweep of impe-rialism, colonialism, neocolonialism, and unjust international economic relations—all worthy of male attention—the petty little female issues such as potable water and available firewood were minor.

The argument for separate projects for women in development pro-grams (chapter 3) had proved to be a sound one. They gave women a

By Gary Brookins, *Richmond Times-Dispatch*, 1985. Permission
of News America Syndicate.

chance to state their problems, uninhibited by the presence of males.
That was doubtless what Sipila had had in mind in her welcoming talk
at Mexico City. Actually, the conference was separate only in theory. It
turned out to be a meeting in which women in many delegations were
being told what to do, what to say, how to act, how to vote. And one of
the casualties of this turn of events was that issues came to be viewed as
either "political" or "women's." With most of the 219 items on the
agenda few countries had difficulties; they were the kind that any
country could write a law about, and many of them had (chapter 4).
They were of no particular relevance in the great game of global politics.
It was the "political" ones that were important; they could be used to
humiliate the United States. And to disarm the feminists by accusing
them of refusing to deal with "political" issues.

It was a kind of Alice-in-Wonderland situation when feminists who
had long since been proclaiming that all issues were female issues and
that all issues—even personal ones—were political came to be charged
with refusal to deal with political issues. The feminist expression "the
personal is political" had, in fact, already found its way around the
world in many languages. Still, queried one woman, "can we honestly
ask Third World women to discuss their problems without taking into

account the international context in which their countries exist?" (Navarro, *Signs*, 1982, 716). To which the answer was no. Nor was that what was asked of them. Indeed, even more discussion of women's problems in international contexts was needed. Every issue that impacted on women called for concern in international conferences; women should be represented in every U.N. organization or commission in whatever field—food (FAO), education (UNESCO), children (UNICEF), work (ILO). Women "must insist that the issues of women's special needs are inserted in every relevant debate: women and food production, . . . women and muilti-nationals, . . . household energy needs of women" (Tinker, *Signs*, 1981, 534). If there was no forum at which women could state their specific problems and ask for redress, such forums should be created. As, at least theoretically, the Decade-for-Women conferences had been. The point was not that women should not engage in discussion of political issues along with the male world, but only that care be taken to choose the appropriate forum. Not in a forum specified by men which, in fact, deflected the discussion away from the problems of women (chapter 3). Nor as mere messengers of the male agenda, as surrogates for a male presence. Although a separate conference for women to deal with the issues close to the hearts of women had, however unenthusiastically, been granted, as Tinker had recommended, it had become clear at the outset that these Decade-for-Women conferences were not to be women's conferences but to a large extent conferences of female proxies for male government representatives. The bodies of the delegates from most countries were, indeed, female, but their minds were well briefed in the male agenda. The major emphases were not those Sipila had dreamed of but those the well-controlled stooges chose. It was not that female problems were ignored; they were, in fact, admirably specified. It was rather that political issues overwhelmed them. It was the political issues that were useful to the male world. They could be used to deflect blame from the male world itself, as it impinged on women personally, to some distant practitioner of imperialism or colonialism or neocolonialism or supporter of an unjust international economic order.

The logic against incorporating the discussion of women's issues into a "framework of the major political and economic issues of the world" took this form. Yes, world trade, for example, was indeed a women's issue, just as food was, as energy was, as potable water was. All these issues had powerful repercussions on their lives. Still, there was the experience in liberation movements which had promised anything in order to recruit their services but which, upon liberation, had not paid their promissory notes (chapter 4). Suppose, for example, Israel did withdraw from the West Bank. Was there any guarantee that this would, indeed, change the attitude of, let us say, Palestinian men toward women? (chapter 5). Would a New International Economic Order—a goal that ran through all three conferences—when achieved actually equalize the economic status of men and women? Or would women still be left at the end of the line? Would it guarantee that the education of girls would become as good as that of boys? Or their nutrition? Or that the work load of females would be no greater than that of males? That all political and economic inequalities between males and females would disappear? That oppressive laws, attitudes, mores would change? That, in brief, sexism would disappear? And, confronting all these issues, would the male world recognize itself as the oppressor?[4] (chapter 5).

If the IWY Conference did not resemble the conference Sipila had seemed to have in mind, she was not one to be discouraged. She summarized the benchmark contributions of the conference, and they were not unimpressive:

> Never before have women and men representing 133 governments, 31 intergovernmental, and 113 non-governmental organizations and 7 liberation movements, come together to deal with problems of women. . . . Never before have 891 women represented 131 governments at any conference of the U.N.. . . . Never before have there been so many high ranking women present at and participating in the U.N. session. . . . Never before have so many Heads of State and governments sent messages to a Conference expressing their particular support to its goals and objectives. . . . Never before has the world seen so much data collected and analyzed. . . . Never before have so many women been in the front pages of the newspapers. . . . Never before has a U.N. Conference attracted the mass media and the non-governmental circles to such an extent. . . . Never before has there been such a world-wide mobilization of human and material resources. . . . [Reported in WIN, 1975; Boulding, 1976, 763]

Even so, she continued, important as these achievements were, "what happened in Mexico City itself is of minor importance. It is the continual building of the case for women in policy making that is of major importance" (762). The document that issues from that conference, the so-called World Plan of Action, was "an important priority-setting document" (763). It included 219 items, most of which dealt with much-sought-after female oriented goals and almost all of them unanimously endorsed by the member nations. But the World Plan of Action was not signed by the United States. It could not endorse several items, namely one that identified Zionism as a form of racism and one that recognized the PLO.[5]

The IWY Conference was a benchmark, a great consciousness-raising event. It was more than that. It was a great learning experience as well. Women learned more not only about the male world but also about the coopted female spokesmen for it. Everyone learned how little was yet really known about the female world, its diversity, its strengths, its flaws, its issues. Women learned about the definition of salient issues of the female world and how easily their own formulations could be neutralized. So also was the IWY Conference a learning experience for the male world. It had learned how to sidetrack the issues of the female world, how, in fact, to use women's conferences for its own ends, including ways to humiliate the United States. It learned that it had a powerful secret weapon in its armory, little words like "zionism as a form of racism," which the United States could not endorse and thus suffered obloquy in the eyes of the world.

If preparation for the 1975 IWY Conference had dragged its feet, preparation for the mid-decade conference in Copenhagen in 1980 did not. The mid-decade conference had two goals: to assess progress in the first half of the Decade for Women and "to develop strategies and action programs for the remaining five years of the Decade through a Programme of Action" (Department of State Press Release, 15 October 1980). For some women, unfamiliar with the Mexico City story, the prospect of the conference was a tremendous challenge. Women were now being allowed to play with the big boys, participate in global political discussions such as the New International Economic Order. What the Copenhagen conference demonstrated to them was that "women are not afraid to deal with the issues of world politics and its effects on their lives as people" (Lenore Dorsett, Trinidad and Tobago's Deputy Permanent Representative to the UN, *International Women's Tribune Centre Newsletter*, no. 11, 4).

But there were others who were fearful when they learned that the same issues as those that had undone the 1975 conference were again to be highlighted. As, indeed, they were. The feminist breach in the global female world was, in fact, to reach its nadir in the 1980 Copenhagen conference. As in the IWY conference there were plans for both the official UN and the unofficial INGO sessions at which women would meet and discuss women's issues. The official meetings were, as before, of government representatives, mainly but not exclusively women, selected to state the positions of their governments.[6] The INGO conference had a forum rather than a tribune, but its function was the same.

There had been forewarnings, based on the experience at the 1975 Mexico City meetings that there would again be attempts to exploit the mid-decade Copenhagen conference for nationalistic purposes. Thus, in July, a French-initiated statement by a group of distinguished women appealed to all participants to avoid such exploitation:[7]

> This conference provides us with the opportunity to make known our views on questions which preoccupy women: social life, equality, educa-

tion, health and employment. We know that actions are envisaged to use this conference for partisan ends thus diverting it from its initial aims. Politicizations have no place in this encounter. It is to be hoped that this conference, which rallies women from all countries, preserve its universal character. [Lilith, no. 8, 1981, 32]

The National Coalition of American Nuns also issued an appeal to women of all faiths to "join hands as sisters in an effort to make the International Women's Conference in Copenhagen what it is supposed to be—an opportunity for women to dialogue about the women's agenda" (32). It deplored the plans to "politicize this women's conference."[8] Both appeals failed. The head of the U.S. delegation conceded that "the Conference was subverted from focusing on women's real issues by the political polemics of the Middle East crisis" (33).

The media, observing the scene, recognized its political nature. Thus, for example, the *New York Times*, which had devoted almost five columns to the 1975 conference, summarized the Copenhagen meetings in little more than one column:

UN World Conference on Women opens in Copenhagen; political clashes expected over Middle East because Palestine Liberation Organization and supporters have won three-day agenda on issue. . . . Denmark offered to host conference after Iran withdrew. . . . about 1,000 delegates from 118 countries attend. . . . Non-governmental Organization Forum also held in Copenhagen. . . . politics becomes major topic at conference. . . . Jihan el-Sadat raises Mideast issues and prompts walkout by Palestinians. . . . Bella Abzug urges women appeal for release of American hostages held in Iran; is answered by Iranian delegate demanding return of Shah. . . . Arab and some African delegates walk out as Israeli delegate Hava Hareli speaks; Eastern bloc, Arab and some African delegates walk out as Cambodian Ieng Thirith, representing ousted Pol Pot regime, speaks. . . . Natalia Malakhovskaya is ejected by police from conference when she attempts to protest to conference, under pressure of Third-World delegates, plan that would ignore sexism and call only for new international economic order. . . . Conference ends . . . with discordant conclusion for delegates from U.S. which refuses to sign plan of action equating Zionism with racism; plan of action is also rejected by Canada, Australia, and Israel. . . .

Strange agenda for an ostensibly female conference.[9]

The women at Copenhagen attending the unofficial INGO conference (chapter 7) saw quite clearly what the "hidden" agendas were—expressions, that is, of "the tussle between those delegates who felt that women's problems must be discussed within the framework of the major political and economic issues of the world and those who contended that women's problems were women's problems" (Earle, 1980, 4).[10] Specifically, problems of women. Granted that the conference sensitized women to the importance of international issues and heightened their awareness of the economic forces impacting on their nation and on their world, still the minuses of giving such issues priority outweighted the pluses:

> When, in the last hours of the 16-day deliberations, the Conference "gagged" on the word "Zionism", many women became more conscious of the fact that the Conference had been politicized to the extent that women's issues and the proposals for their advancement took second place in the international debate, as representatives of countries carried out their mandate and voted in accordance with their countries' position on controversial issues. These actions confirmed the worst fears of many a delegate. . . . The Conference to them had lost its focus on the concerns of women and was out there somewhere making statements on the Palestinian question, the New International Economic Order and the North-South dialogue (4).

Summing up the pluses and minuses of the Copenhagen conference, a press release by the Department of State found among the pluses the Programme of Action which resulted from the proceedings, addressing some of the major inequities faced by women. Among the serious minuses, as far as the United States was concerned, was the inclusion of items which the United States could not accept.[11] They included "references to UN documents which question the Camp David accords"; listing "Zionism with imperialism, colonialism, neo-colonialism and racism, as an impediment to world peace and cooperation among states; and calling for financial assistance for Palestinian women by UN organizations, specialized agencies for organs and funds to be provided 'in consultation and cooperation with the Palestine Liberation Organization, the representative of the Palestinian people.' "

There were other pluses and minuses, but most relevant here was the acceptance into the U.N. lexicon of the concept of sexism.

> The Draft Programme of Action listed imperialism, racism, colonialism as barriers to women's equality, but did not mention sexism. The inclusion of sexism was resisted by many nations (Latin American, Asian, African and East European), who insisted that sexism did not exist in their countries. After extended debate "discrimination based on sex" was added finally to the Programme qualified by a footnote, "which in a group of countries is called sexism"—the first time the concept has been specifically mentioned in a U.N. document. (The word sexism did not appear in the World Plan of Action adopted by consensus in Mexico City). (Press release, U.S. Department of State)

The director of the U.S. secretariat for the conference concurred in the importance of introducing into the vocabulary of discourse this basic concept. This reluctant concession—in a footnote—was so important because, though it did not, of course, solve the question of the decade— namely: what were women's issues?[12]—it did make a solution possible. True, defining sexism for the reluctant male world would prove as difficult as validating women's issues. But it was worth the effort and useful to have the conceptual tools.

> Virtually all U.N. conferences of the past decade have focused on the Middle East, Southern Africa, and the New International Economic Order, but the World Conference at Copenhagen marked the first time that the concepts of feminism and sexism were discussed seriously. . . . The concepts of feminism and sexism are now part of the United Nations lexicon (1980, 45).

The third and final Decade-for-Women conference met on schedule in 1985 in Nairobi, even better prepared for than the one at Copenhagen had been. A consultant in international development, Anita Anand, had briefed participants on what to expect:

> Women delegates will pore over background materials, take notes, negoti- ate, meet late into the night. At times the process might break down. Often women delegates have not had much experience at such meetings and need time. We must be patient. Tolerance is an essential ingredient for the conference. [Reprinted from Development Forum, 1985, 4]

She had even drawn up suggestions for what might be called "con- ference etiquette":

> Between delegates, individuals, nations and organizations there must be mutual respect for concerns, agendas, styles and priorities. When political considerations and differences begin to dominate the conference, all must remember that women and the cause of women must come first, over national, political and racial loyalties. Differences are to be expected and disagreements will occur. [Reprinted from Development Forum, 1985, 4]

But creative ways of dealing with them were possible and the results worth striving for. A great deal rested on success. "The decade" had been "an opportunity for women to begin to define their destiny and design the means to achieve it. Nairobi in 1985 could well be the start of the era in which women begin to shape the future" (4).[13] With so much at stake, success was imperative. She may have been whistling in the dark.

For, with two failures behind them, there was so little hope among many women for success at this conference that some of the outstanding women leaders—including the recent U.S. ambassador to the UN, Jeane Kirkpatrick—did not attend, although Ms. Kirkpatrick reassured the head of the UN delegation that if needed at any point she would come. One male columnist was saying that only failure could result from the feminist fantasy embodied in the conference. Women did not constitute a special political class with special interests of their own. Feminists were wrong to harbor such a delusion. "The only thing all women have in common is their differences from men." That difference made for many good things such as delight, romance, and drama (Podhoretz, *Washington Post*, 18 July 1985). He even invoked the cry of vive la différence!—overlooking the fact that difference could also make for anguish and babies and that, among other things, it was the anguish women shared and the care of babies that created issues for them. In any event it did not seem likely that the Nairobi conference was headed for success.

All the old issues were at the ready. They had proved so successful in the first two conferences, why would they fall short this time? It would be like a replay of an old record. It was not at all surprising then that the third conference began almost exactly as the first one had. This time it was also about issues. But now it was a U.S.-born woman, wife of the prime minister of Greece, Madame Papandreou, who threw down the gauntlet. Upon arrival she challenged the stance of the U.S. delegates: "no one group of women can determine what are women's issues and foreclose discussion on non-women's issues, as that group defines them . . . and I am talking about the United States" (Battiata, *Washington Post*, 15 July 1985). It might have been a decade earlier. Already déjà vu, except that now it was the wife of the prime minister of Greece and not the president of Mexico. Again it was to be men wielding power.[14] Blatantly, without even attempting subtlety:

> What it came down to, at the end of the United Nations conference on women, was men. What would the men allow? Would the Palestinian men permit the excising of the word "Zionism" and its equation with racism from the conference document? Would the Palestinian men persuade the Iranian men to go along? Would the Soviet men, who'd written the language in the first place, back down and give the Palestinian and the Iranian men, and all the other men who listen to the Soviet men, their blessing? If not, would the American men and the Israeli men order their female delegation to walk out? Or could the Kenyan men keep the rest of the men talking and thereby save the day? For the ladies? [Battiata, *Washington Post*, 26 July 1985]

Perhaps a reporter's exaggeration. But there was corroboration from other observers. A United Press International item reported that men participated in negotiating the wording of items dealing with political issues; they were highly visible as advisers to women on matters of policy. "Men on the Egyptian, Syrian, and Palestine Liberation Organization delegations dominated the conference proceedings at times and engaged in most debates and rights of reply" (*New York Times*, 28 July 1985). Same issues. Same male input. So why bother?[15]

But something new had happened. There was a different U.S. policy on ways to deal with assaults on the United States in the General Assembly. So now, although U.S. delegates were going to Nairobi, as one of them put it, "with humility, affection and respect" for the women there, she was not going to "have that 'kick me' sign around" her any more (Battiata, *Washington Post*, 3 July 1985). She was not going to kick anyone, but neither was she going to accept kicks herself. Interestingly enough in this new ambience the old hostile gambits did not seem to work. But although there was still a considerable amount of hostility at Nairobi,[16] the preparation had been so extensive and intensive[17] that much of it was nullified.

One newspaper summarized the results of the Nairobi conference as follows:

> The real news at the close of the U.N. Decade for Women was that the women's movement has achieved a breadth and power that the 157 nations represented here could not afford to ignore. . . . The final document to come out of this . . . conference . . . is a manifesto of more than 350 feminist proposals demanding that the world's women be given their fair share of power in government, commerce, and in their families. . . . True, the U.N. . . . cannot force governments to implement any of the proposals that their delegations agreed to. But approving them constitutes a "moral commitment" buttressed by international consensus. Feminists believe the document gives them leverage with their own governments. [Harden and Battiata, *Washington Post*, 28 July 1985]

Although most of the more than 350 items in the final document dealt with women's specific issues, there were also "political" statements, several of which tacitly criticized the two superpowers.

Despite differences among the women with respect to the success of the conference, there was general agreement that the Decade had improved the position of women. Little may have changed politically, said a member of the Israeli delegation "but on the women's issues, one can certainly notice that in the past ten years the consciousness of the world has been raised. There is a unanimous demand for equality" (Harden, *Washington Post*, 20 July 1985).[18]

Success had not come easy. Some delegates from Arab countries and the USSR had come to Nairobi seemingly intent mainly on vilifying Israel; the U.S. delegates had had to threaten a walkout; it also showed that women had learned how to play the political game, how, that is, to use their own interventions by labeling terrorism by "a small group of out-law states" a female issue thus justifying its condemnation by a

U.N.-sponsored women's conference. Such tableturning had its intended effect. Many women delegates who until then had been intimidated by male disciplinarians now feared that the intrusion of political male-type issues would deprive their own preferred issues of attention. The presider, Philippine diplomat Leticia Shahani, knew that a certain amount of political activity was inevitable but, along with many other women, hoped to keep it down and make it possible for the participants to concentrate on what she defined as the basic female issues, namely "the dismal social and economic conditions that remain the common lot of most women" (*Washington Post*, 14 July 1985).[19]

The hard-core male-defined female issues that had been so successful in breaking up the earlier conferences—the long litany of such female issues as imperialism, colonialism, neocolonialism, expansionism, apartheid, racism, Zionism—were still being used. The debate between female and the political issues went on and on. Compromise was elusive; some alleged it was not even wanted. Not until the eleventh hour was it achieved. The Kenya host delegation finally did not want a failed conference on their record, so they replaced "Zionism" with the phrase "and all other forms of racism and racial discrimination" (*New York Times*, 27 July 1985). Even that other time-tested disruptive issue, the New International Economic Order, lost out this time. It was dropped when it could no longer muster a two-thirds majority in a vote from the floor.[20]

From a distance the whole performance looked absurd. All the sweat and tears, disappointments, pains had been poured out over a single word? It was this easy to solve the deadlock? To detonate the secret weapon? Alas, was all the female world could say. Apparently that was the way it had looked to the male world. It sounded very much like the Nordic women in Moscow allowing the men to win their victory for them (chapter 7).

From near rout in the 1975 IWY conference in Mexico City to the achievement of a Bill of Female Rights in 1985 in Nairobi was something well nigh revolutionary. To be sure, this Magna Charta was not a body of law that could be enforced. Nor was Nairobi a Runnymede. But a threatened third failure had been forestalled, and great strides had been taken. The significance lay in the support it gave women in their own countries. They could draw up programs and say to their governments, "You signed this. Now make good on your signature."[21] However iffy a gambit, UN resolutions had proved to be powerful chips in the case of PLO-Israeli relations. Conceivably they might be again.[22]

In any event the last of the Decade for Women conferences was over. This official, tightly controlled U.N. meeting, ostensibly for women, so many of whom were closely monitored, was certainly not the joyous, jubilant, celebratory conference of the INGOs (chapter 7). But there was relief among many of the participants, and even hope. A start had been made. It had not happened without pain and suffering. Nor were there guarantees of success. It had been nip-and-tuck until the last moment. But at the end the words were finally put on paper to be signed by 157 countries. They were words providing leverage for women, at least in those 157 countries, in their struggles to achieve their goals. More decades would certainly be needed before all women could feel as renewed as many of the women participants in the Nairobi INGO conference had felt.

Nairobi, then, had been at least a qualified success. How about the Decade? Did the success at Nairobi undo any damage of the earlier conferences? The overall judgement was equivocal. There had been pluses in some parts of the world, minuses in others. When it took more than 350 items to deal with all the difficulties of women that had to be addressed, the complexity of trying to evaluate the decade became clear.[23] Replies to an NGO questionnaire by 124 NGOs, representative of more than three-fourths of all governments,[24] considered the main achievements to be: "greater awareness of the vital role of women in development, a higher level of consciousness, and progress in the legislative field" (UN Decade for Women, special conference issue, July 1985, 2). Where there had been failures they were due to the economic crisis and the global recession during the decade, "as well as prevailing negative stereotyped attitudes about women."

Although tempered by the caveat that improved attitudes were not always translated into action, there was a belief among some of the NGOs that the major achievement of the Decade had been an attitudinal change on the part of governments. Plans for the advancement of women were now incorporated in national policies though much discrimination remained. Substantively the greatest progress had been in reaching higher educational levels and better economic opportunities, somewhat less gains had been made in health services and efforts for peace. And the future? The four most frequently cited objectives specified were: education, consciousness raising, economic and employment opportunities, including credit, and advancement of women into political decision-making positions. Some international NGOs wanted recognition of the value of women's work done in the home.

One evaluator, Maria Riley, felt that "one of the most important outcomes of the UN Decade for Women has been the development of statistical and sociological information about women that was never available before. . . . Women were, and in all too many cases continue to be, invisible" [Development Forum, 1985, 7]. Other examples of the hitherto invisible "anti-woman bias which shapes women's lives worldwide includes the facts—among others—that: four times more female than male children are malnourished; two-thirds of the illiterates of the world are females; that female-headed households are creating a new class of the poor worldwide. . . ." (7–8). Data like these "helped to focus public opinion and policies on the inequalities of the sexes, and in so doing exposed weaknesses in statistical information on the situation of women. For statistics are an essential ingredient of planning and policy evaluation" (unsigned, Development Forum, 1985, 17). Recognition of the importance of knowledge was, indeed, an important achievement of the Decade.

Related to such recognition of the importance of the Feminist Enlightenment was the lesson of the importance of being able merely to state problems, of having a suitable vocabulary to render visible problems long buried in cultural invisibility. The mere invention of the word *sexism*—and its acceptance for the first time, however reluctantly at the Copenhagen conference—made possible the statement of a truly timeless and universal problem of the female world—the sexism that had blinded the male world for millennia—rendering it also deaf to attempts to explain it to even well-meaning males, even those who had themselves taught women to see their shared economic and political oppressions (chapter 4). The male world could clearly see the perpetrators of the oppression they both suffered from; they could now see themselves as perpetrators of sexist oppressions.

Although overall judgments tended to be upbeat, there was still recognition of a lot of failure. In the NGO study, three-fifths said plans for women were still not adequate; half still found continuing discrimination in inheritance and family law; a fourth still found political, civil, and economic policies discriminatory. Still needed were more consciousness raising, economic employment, credit, and promotion of women in policy making (Development Forum, 1985, 5).

In general it seemed to evaluators that the Decade had taken two steps forward and one backward. Improvements in verbal recognition of women's problems in the laws and constitutions, but deeply flawed implementation. And almost everywhere complaints of "repressive traditional practices and the cultural attitudes of both men and women" (McParland, 1985, 5). Again and again, "traditional attitudes," "customary practices," "ancient beliefs," or some variant of mental and emotional devaluation of women. The Decade for Women did not solve that problem, but it began to do so by recognizing its existence and accepting a name for it, *institutionalized sexism*.

L'Envoi

> It is in the nature of culture that
> visions (whether they offer hope or
> despair) organize people's perspective
> on themselves and their societies and
> provide a lens through which they
> interpret the world. [Cynthia Fuchs,
> Newsletter Eastern Sociological
> Society, June, 1983]

> I have now, albeit reluctantly, closed shop on this book. I am finally
> surrendering to the imperative that some time or other one has to write
> finis. I have been rewriting this book so long that I am loath to stop now.
> Tomorrow, a research report will cross my desk that will illuminate an
> aspect of the female world quite new and arresting, and I will want to
> make room for it somewhere or other; . . . some chapter will have to be
> torn up to include it. A book is an organic entity with a life of its own; it
> can take over one's life. Still, the time does come when one must call a
> halt. [Bernard, 1972, 290–91]

These words appeared in a book on marriage published almost a decade
and a half ago; I have only substituted "female world" for "marriage."
The story of the two books is the same. My experience has been the same
with both of them. I prescribed no ideal solution for the future of
marriage in that book. Nor do I have an answer to the question of
equitable integration between the two worlds to offer here. But, as I was
then, I have been impressed by the potential of the Feminist Enlightenment, which was only then beginning to shed its light.

In the late 1960s I sat in my study and, with eyes wide in astonish-
ment, read the mimeographed papers circulating in the underground
feminist dissident press in the United States. They were written by
young women from all parts of the country, all with the most mind-
boggling contents. I followed with some excitement the ideas being

discussed and debated and wondered how such obscure young women could dream so big. And how could such unimportant young women, however talented—as they so obviously were—hope to make any kind of dent on the public mind.

Less than a decade later the ideas had emerged from the underground and were reaching a large part of the public, and hardly anyone recognized the source of those extraordinary ideas. They no longer even seemed all that extraordinary. In the mid-1980s I again sit in my study and read the words of young—and not so young—women, now from all parts of the globe, asking the same subversive questions, expressing the same radical ideas about women's place in the scheme of things. I read the same statement that the personal is political, the same attacks on sexism, the same demands for role sharing. But also, and increasingly, I hear more cheerful notes, of joy and excitement as women discover one another and come to share "visions of hope." I no longer ask myself how such unimportant women can expect to have any impact on a world filled almost exclusively with male preoccupations, with wars and the alarums of war. For in the context of the last two decades I do not doubt that they will. The Feminist Enlightenment clarifies the lens through which they interpret the world. The undergirding "continental plates" beneath the two worlds are moving.

The prolegomena to this book was written for the nth version of this book, the one that was completed a year before this one was. Since then I have learned a great deal about the female world, some of it disappointing. The expectable "I-told-you-sos" and, sometimes, patronizing comments on my naiveté have been received and absorbed. Still, having shielded myself in the prolegomena, I feel I need not defend myself further here. I did not promise a vision nor even an impeccable version of an easily attainable reality. Nor a strategy for achieving global solidarity in the female world. My optimism rests on humbler, grass-roots bases.

I have been impressed by the plucky women in Mali who taught themselves how to operate a business; by the Zimbabwe women doing their best, against great odds, to carry through the promises of their revolution; by all the women organizing and attending meetings and trying to learn by their mistakes; by the thoughtful women trying to learn how to deal, in ways consonant with their dreams, with the emerging world they will be called upon more and more to share the government of; by the extraordinary women who lighted the torch of the Feminist Enlightenment and all those who carry its flame far and wide. I am no less impressed by the teacher of girls down at the grass roots in Africa, trying to bring at least some of the Feminist Enlightenment to them before tribal inertia spirited them away and she lost them to early motherhood.

The discussion here began with two-and-a-half billion faceless females, the emphasis being on the demographic differences among them. At this point I would like to recognize one of those many women, a woman of Nyeri, one of the nonelite, faceless women, a woman quite innocent of ideology, pro-or anti-feminist—but no longer faceless as Perdita Huston describes her:

> When, much later, I emerged from the building with the last inter-
> viewee, all the women with whom I had met hours before were still there,
> standing in the rain, without shoes or coats, shivering in the winter
> cold. . . . As I moved toward the group, they began to sing and dance. The
> interpreter explained that they wanted to make me an honorary member
> of their tribe and to give me a tribal name. In the midst of the ceremony, a
> seventy-year-old woman . . . rushed out of the crowd and took me by the
> arm. . . . Shaking her finger in my face, she said, with authority: "Now
> you go back and tell the women in your place that the women of Nyeri
> *care* about them. [Huston, 1979, 14–15]

I am one of the women in that place. I am one of the women the women of Nyeri care about. The potential they represent is enough to supply a vision of hope rather than of despair. It explains why I am so much like the little old lady who said she tried to be philosophical, heaven knew; but cheerfulness kept breaking in. I can clearly see the powerful centrifugal forces at work in the global female world. I try to be philosophical about them. But cheerfulness keeps breaking in. Those women in Nyeri standing in the rain help to keep philosophy at bay.

So I do not accept the crabbed and cynical Preacher's obiter dictum that all is vanity, that everything that has ever happened is going to happen again, that everything we do has already been done, that we must go on repeating our mistakes, for "there is no new thing under the sun" (Eccles. 1:9). The female world now in process is new. A world in which increasing numbers of women have decades of vigorous years ahead of them beyond childbearing and rearing is new. Their minds are new. Their ideas are new. Their potential for autonomy is new. There have always been individual women with these qualities; but not a whole worldfull of them, a worldfull of women becoming well prepared to achieve equitable integration with—not into—the male world.

APPENDICES

Because my own perspective is slanted in the direction of the female world as an entity in its own right, with an intrinsic logic of its own, rather than primarily as a foil, so to speak, of the male world or as a pawn of extrinsic forces, many relevant aspects of the male world have been omitted. But several of them deserve at least a once-over-lightly glance. Three are looked at here. One is related to war or conflict, one to world markets, and one to the black female work force in South Africa. The first deals with populations, mostly female, of refugees, displaced persons, asylum seekers uprooted as the result of natural catastrophe or war; the second looks at the "migration" of jobs as a result of worldwide market forces in the male world, a process that has the effect of putting women in one part of the female world in competition with those in another part; the third, the black female industrial work force of South Africa, has been relatively unscrutinized by Western researchers until today because the racial system it reflects so overwhelmingly overshadows it.

Uprooted Women

Flows of people fleeing persecution and violence have proven endemic to the modern world. (Rubin, 1984, 1).

The nature of the refugee crisis has changed drastically since the Second World War. Today we have grown accustomed to flows of hundreds of thousands, even millions of people on the move across international borders (Hartling, 1984, 17).

On a global scale, more than two-thirds of the world's refugees are women and children, often the victims of tribal and international conflict. (Fraser, Arvonne, 1985).[1]

In most [refugee] areas . . . women and children suffer more. (UN, 1980, 17)

I noted in the prolegomena that a considerable number of women were not included in the world we have been looking at here, namely the "tribals," or women living on reservations or women in actual if not official colonies or in unrelinquished mandates or protectorates or in territorial enclaves of one kind or another.[2] But there are millions of uprooted women and children in areas which are included who, for one reason or another, live in a kind of sociological limbo. They escape the researchers' eyes until urgent political issues demand attention. We may then—or may not—get reports about them supplying (wholly inadequate) data for policy decisions but rarely enough to tell us much about the worlds they live in. More data might be "too political" even to gather (Clay, 10). Their story is, therefore, inadequately known; and some wonder if the data are even worth gathering (37). Still at least a nod in the direction of this aspect of the female world seems called for.

Although—because of the deficiencies in human history as we know it—there is no way to state it categorically, there does seem to be an archetype of the female world as an anchored one, as representing what is stable in human life in contrast to the male world in which there is much wandering, crusading, marching, exploring, warring. So there is relatively little in the study of the female world about its experience with uprooting. Still, at least a glance at this aspect of the female world seems warranted.

The uprooted are by no means a homogeneous population. Some are members of a high-level elite, exiled by their governments or self-exiled women needing asylum, as in the case of the Iranian and Chilean women we glanced at in chapter 5. Others are women from societies that practice female seclusion, a fact which, as among the Afghans in Pakistani refugee camps, may multiply the trauma but may, contrariwise, make for liberating changes. Some are migrant workers. And some are war-related refugees. Some are victims of political decisions that call for mindless transfers of whole races or ethnic groups. However diverse in background these women may be, most are probably simply women seeking only to survive and protect their children. Without any theoretical presuppositions, but simply to avoid the impression of a casual miscellany, five illustrations of uprooting are presented here: refugees, "guest" and other migrant workers, political and military "pawns", exiles, and the women forcibly returned to "homelands" in South Africa.

There are two definitions of *uproot* in the Oxford English Dictionary. One is "to tear up the roots from a fixed position." The other is "to destroy as by tearing up, to exterminate, eradicate." The first may refer to a sought-after choice, a longed for escape from boredom, responsibilities, suffering. It is less likely to be experienced by females than by males.[3] There are few, if any, records of large scale voluntary uprootings in the female world.[4] Nomadic societies, to be sure, include women, but they carry their roots with them—that is, their established relationships, their groups, languages, ceremonies, beliefs, technologies, their social infrastructure, in brief, all of the elements that provide continuity and stability in their lives. The second, more violent, definition seems less applicable to the female than to the male world. It is true that historically women have been included in holocausts, archetypical uprootings—as they were in the Nazi holocaust—but this term is rarely applicable in the female world.[5]

Separation trauma is no doubt universal and timeless in the case of either kind of rootlessness. But it is probably more common in the female than in the male world. In patrilocal societies, for example, small girls may be married to their future husbands and forced to leave their homes to join them. Some societies may wait until the brides are older, but the trauma may be equal or even worse, especially when the home she goes to is not a receptive one.[6] The ancient and almost universal injunction that wives went where their husbands went has its modern counterpart. Wives still go where their husbands go. In the United States it was men in the nineteenth century who made the decision to tear up their roots and cross the continent. Wives in the diplomatic corps of most countries uproot themselves periodically as do, increasingly, wives of the men who run multinational corporations.[7]

Refugees

The first case in point dealing with uprooted women refers to refugees. The term *refugee* goes back to the Protestants exiled from France on religious grounds late in the seventeenth century, but it did not become widely used until World War I vastly increased their number. The League of Nations established a High Commissioner for Refugees to deal with them, and the United Nations has continued this concern, especially since World War II. At any given time there are about 9 million men, women and children in refugee status needing aid and hundreds of thousands of others who are seeking asylum. When or if refugees are resettled or asylum seekers given asylum somewhere there seem always to be others to take their place, so the number at any given time seems to remain fairly constant. Cumulatively, however, there have been about 80 million refugees since the end of World War II. And by the time work and shelter had been found for World War II refugees in the late 1950s, the major sector in the refugee scene was shifting to Third-World countries, especially to Africa which, in the last two decades, has accounted for half of all refugees. And now, increasingly, Latin America adds to the human stream.

Most refugees are women and children; there may be as many as 6.5 million of them in refugee status at any one time. Numerous reasons are given to explain this disparity, but it would be diversionary to discuss them here. Whatever the reasons, these women are parked in refugee camps or moved about in complex patterns, enduring traumata of almost unprecedented dimensions, at the mercy of compounding political, economic, military, and cultural forces.

Refugee status is painful enough for anyone, but "in most areas" it is especially so for women. There is the ever-present threat of violence, ranging from intimidation and physical abuse to rape (UN, 1980, 18). Among the so-called boat people fleeing from Vietnam to Thailand, for example, the women were subject to capture by pirates who then sold them into prostitution (Winter and Cerquone, 1984, 9). More was therefore needed for refugees than merely defensive care, important as that was. Without the protection of stable institutions, women had to be trained in decision-making and leadership skills. Education became the "focus of efforts to assist the refugees." Whole infrastructures had to be built almost, in some cases, from the ground up, for which the skills and talents of women were indispensable (7). The UN called on aid donors to support programs especially "designed to benefit women, bearing in mind that women suffer particular disadvantages and that efforts to overcome these disadvantages require sensitive planning of projects for assisting women to develop decision-making and leadership skills" (1980, 41). In brief, affirmative action.

The Afghan refugee camps in Pakistan are illustrative of this aspect of the female world. Although we are told that three-fourths of the 2,800,000 registered Afghans in Pakistan were women and children (Survey, 5), little about them shows up in official reports. Nor are the figures themselves reliable. "Some argued that the number was inflated; they pointed to examples of *maliks* (tribal leaders) or heads of families . . . [as] having overreported the number of their clan folk in order to increase their rations" (5). Most were rural; few were middle-class or experienced in urban living.

Among the "particular disadvantages" of women referred to by the U.N. might be named discrimination in the distribution of food. The use of *maliks* as key personnel in the distribution of benefits "meant that the poor, the infirm, and women and children . . . often failed to receive relief supplies" (Jones, 1985, 5). Cultural norms, such as the customs of female segregation, may also have kept women from leaving home to claim benefits.[8]

The simplest sanitary amenities were hard to come by. Nor were the "special requirements of women refugees, especially pregnant and lactating women, women with small children and women heads of families and households" adequately addressed. So physical health itself was an ever-present preoccupation, especially the health of children who were most susceptible to infectious diseases such as tuberculosis and malaria (8). And no less worrisome was their mental health; "some youngsters have become undisciplined and delinquent" (8).

Nor was mental health less worrisome among adults. Difficult as the maintenance of physical health might be under refugee conditions, at least such illnesses were usually diagnosable and treatable. Mental and emotional illnesses were usually subtler and harder to deal with. There was the risk of becoming inactive, dependent, and unproductive, of losing "pride in being independent and self-sufficient" (8). Many developed a "dependency syndrome," that is, aches, coughs, fevers, hyperacidity, digestive troubles. This syndrome seemed especially common among the men as a result of their loss of agricultural work or land-based jobs (8).

But there was here a strange anomaly. Although, according to the UN, "in most areas . . . women and children suffer more radical changes in roles and status than refugee men" (1980, 17), in the Afghan camps in Pakistan the opportunity for women to pursue their traditional skills of carpet weaving made it possible for them to contribute to the income of their families (Jones, 14), a status-enhancing benefit. On the basis of such experience the programs of the UN High Commission for Refugees restated its programs as development projects rather than as refugee assistance and emphasized the care and maintenance of self-reliance. This was one of the rare refugee situations that was positive for women.

Migrant Workers

A second kind of uprootedness treated here refers primarily to workers. The geographic direction in the movement between worker and work varies over time. Sometimes work comes to the worker as with the cottage industry in the West in the preindustrial period and as with the multinational system today—and sometimes the worker goes to the work, as in the case of migratory workers. And sometimes whole families follow their agricultural work as they harvest crops in the United States. At this point we look at only one category of uprootedness, so-called guest workers and migrants.

In the years following World War II there was widespread need in Europe to replenish the work force to rebuild war-destroyed productive systems. A system of guest workers developed whereby workers from southern Europe, Turkey, Spain, and Portugal were "invited" to Scandinavia, England, and West Germany. Not all "host" countries accepted the families of the guest workers, but some did. So some of the women "guests" came as uprooted wives or daughters of workers. The sequelae of their uprooting varied; they were often traumatic whatever the age, family, or work status of the women. The story of Turkish women in West Germany is illustrative.

Among those who were themselves workers, about a third were illiterate, neither skilled nor familiar with modern production methods. They worked on assembly lines, in service jobs, in textile industries, in food industries, in clerical occupations, or in other low-paid, tedious jobs.[9] They brought with them not only cheap labor but also their strikingly different cultures and values. They could not always successfully survive the culture shock. Age made a difference.

The experience of a Turkish school girl is typical:

> At school the Turkish girls see how the German girls live and what freedoms they have and they want the same things for themselves. I want

to be free. . . . I wouldn't mind marrying a German, but my chances are
nil. . . . That would mean I would be free. . . . At night I dream that my
father is dead and my mother buried in Turkey. I would write to my
grandmother to send me all my papers. Then I would finally be free.
[Dilek, 1981, 9]

Even older women among the Turkish guest workers found themselves
influenced by their contacts with women in their new surroundings
despite strong feelings of ethnic solidarity among themselves.

When it comes to the women's movement, to feminism and lesbianism,
I identify with West German women. Am I Turkish? Am I German? I
cannot discuss questions like relationships between women, feminist
work, etc. And as a feminist and foreign woman, I have problems with the
women at my work place who think and live differently from me (8).

Neither wholly traditional nor yet completely feminist, this woman was
caught between two ideological homes. Here, as elsewhere over the
globe, a similar battle was being fought for the minds of women, strong
roots anchoring old ideologies and strong seductive appeals pulling
toward the new.

This battle was not without casualities, for the life of guest workers
was not conducive to good mental health. Frequent complaints were
reported among them of: headaches, back pains, depression, ner-
vousness caused, the women said, by "sadness" (Delek, 7).

Among other migrant workers are the women in developing countries
who, like men, move to cities when they find they cannot survive at
rural subsistence levels. Or women who move from poor countries to
more affluent ones in search of work—from the Philippines, for example, to the United States. Many of them are non-literate; they often find
no social services available to them, or only inadequate ones. They are
separated from their families; the language and culture are different; in
many cases they are denied civil rights. It is difficult for them to organize; they are isolated. Pay is low. In some countries they are unwelcome. In preparation for a 1985 UN-sponsored world conference,
sixteen recommendations were drawn up, plus a seventeenth one recommending that a working group be established "to elaborate a draft
convention on the protection of the rights of migrant workers and their
families, which should devote particular attention to the problem of
migrant women" (1980, 8).

Political and Military Pawns

As the bureaucracies administering refugee and migrant programs
grew larger and more complex, it became possible to manipulate estab-

lished rules and thus, directly or indirectly, use civilian—that is, female—populations as political ploys or pawns. The Byzantine machinations that could be used in making political capital out of refugees are illustrated in the Somalia-Ethiopia situation.

> Somalia has manipulated the ethnicity of refugees seeking asylum. . . . Officially, all refugees from Ethiopia were ethnic Somalis who want to live in a Somali-run state. While most are Somali, a great many are members of other ethnic groups who were being persecuted in Ethiopia, but who have no desire to remain permanently in Somalia. In the absence of any survey of the refugees, the ethnic claims made it easier for Somalia to justify the war with Ethiopia over the Ogaden region, an area occupied for the most part by ethnic Somalis. The presence of the refugees also allowed the government to focus the attention of Somalians on a common enemy—Ethiopia—rather than on problems within the country. [Clay, 1984, 15]

Or refugees might be used for military—as well as political—ends. One "relatively new" strategy was to

> isolate fighters from their base and, by food blockades or terror, cause the civilian population to flee to more remote areas or over the border. In addition to cutting off the opposition, this tactic has the advantage for its promoters of creating an influx of populations in a neighboring country whose position is thus weakened. [22]

The refugees, mainly women and children, thus become literal pawns in Machiavellian strategic games. It is a situation reminiscent of the uses made of women in liberation movements (chapter 4).

Exiles, Banished, Asylum Seekers

Political and religious exile and banishment are currently less acceptable policies than in the past. Today they are more likely to take the form of a threat of prosecution or persecution so that the threatened individuals become asylum seekers away from their home country[10] rather than exiles and their status is defined by a growing body of international law (U.S. Committee for Refugees, 1984, 2; Rubin, 1984). Such uprooting is nearer to the second dictionary definition and is reported in the male world more than in the female. In either case, there are few punishments, historically speaking, worse than such uprootings, perhaps only death or life imprisonment being worse.[11]

Sometimes such uprootings have encompassed whole ethnic or religious groups and women were among them.[12] But, in addition, women have been uprooted as individuals in a unique "psychological" rather than geographic way. The behavior they were being punished for was neither religious nor political nor legal, but moral. And the uprooting was from a sociological rather than from a physical community. It took the form of social ostracism, "banning," "shunning," and the emotional costs were extremely high.[13]

Today the "exiles" might be radical dissenters, or political revolutionaries like, for example, those reported by Maria, the 33-year old Chilean woman in Germany we met in chapter 5. Her own experience in exile had proved to be up-beat, but she had also seen the deterioration of many of her compatriots in the form of suicide and mental illness (*Connexions*, no. 2, 1981, 29–30). She related her experiences in a newspaper interview:

> At the beginning of this year, in Cologne, a Chilean committed suicide. He killed himself because he was alone, because he was lonesome, and that's not an isolated incident. Laura Allende, one of the best-known militants, killed herself a few weeks ago. These suicides are expressions of the hopelessness, the isolation, the constant search for our identity in other countries. In the meantime, many exiles are in therapy. When one is in exile, one needs something to hold onto, something to live for. . . . Many . . . end the search . . . [in] death. [29]

There were other signs of the deteriorating effect of exile even more serious in Maria's eyes than suicide, namely loss of revolutionary fervor and character deterioration. She commented on regressive character changes among the exiles. They became more self-centered, conservative. They were earning a great deal of money; material things became important to them.

But there were valuable lessons also possible. A survivor herself, she had learned much that would be useful to her when she returned to Nicaragua to continue her revolutionary work. Discussions with women and their organizations had helped her and changed her consciousness as a woman. She had asked herself questions she could not have asked back in Chile.

> I have asked myself why I, as a woman, fight. In Chile, that wasn't a question; I was a comrade like all the other comrades. I've learned to push for my rights. I know now who I am, and I will pass on what I've learned here in Germany in Latin America. I will have to fight against the machismo, and I know because of that I will have conflicts. It won't be easy. [30]

Apartheid

The last case in point deals with a specific kind of female uprooting created in the 1950s by the so-called pass laws, which enforced the

South African system of racial segregation known as apartheid. South Africa was a special case of neocolonialism. The ending of British rule in South Africa (1948) had turned the country over to a Dutch or African government so that, in effect, it was merely the substitution of one form of colonialism for another, over black subjects (chapter 4). And the African government meant to keep it that way by maintaining, so far as possible, geographic or spatial separation.[14] Apartheid had a long history:

> During the early history of the colony, the Dutch Afrikaners, with the encouragement and sanction of the Dutch Reformed church, developed a policy of rigid segregation of the native Hottentots and Bantus. Later, the East Indians who came to the area and the Cape Coloured people—a hybrid population resulting from the mixture of Afrikaners and natives— were also subjected to social and moral isolation. The segregation of colonists and natives is expressed in residential patterns; under the present-day [1968] policy of apartheid, native peoples are forced to live in designated compounds. . . . The English in South Africa have accommodated their policies to accord with those of the politically dominant Dutch party, especially with regard to segregation in social life. [Edwards, 1968, 271]

Certain areas in cities became forbidden to black men in 1948 except with legal permission or "passes." Workers had to live where their services were needed, sometimes in barracks-like living quarters where their wives could visit them—perhaps once a month—only with permission, also in the form of a pass. It was this extension of the pass system to women in the late 50s that triggered an interracial movement of women against apartheid. In a march of 20,000 women against the capital in Pretoria in 1956, 20,000 women protesting the system of passes stated that homes would be broken up, children would be left uncared for, women would be deprived of the right to move freely from one place to another (Straker, 1985, 133). They failed to move the government. And even worse was to follow. In 1959 the passage of a Bantu Self-Governing Act extended the impact of apartheid.

> On the theory that each group could develop to its fullest capacity in its own homeland and that the Bantus were not a homogeneous people, eight reserves, or Bantustans, were established as homelands for the natives. Three million native Africans who lived in urban communities, some of whom were three generations removed from native life, were no longer regarded as permanent residents of such areas. [Edwards, 1968, 273]

In pursuance of this apartheid policy, according to an outlawed Azanian woman revolutionary,

> the racist rulers have forcibly uprooted almost eight million Azanians and arbitrarily deprived them of their citizenship. . . . Much has been

said and written about the plight of women and children in the barren Bantustans, the high rate of infantile mortality, malnutrition, etc. have been well documented. . . . Similar conditions . . . exist in the urban areas such as Soweto, Guglethu, Kwa Mashu . . . where mothers live in constant fear of the authorities. They can be endorsed out of the urban areas any time. [Sifuba, n.d., 22]

This forced uprooting from long-standing neighborhood ties and resettlement in so-called homelands—where they had to "fight a continual battle with poverty and starvation" (Snudge, 1982, 68)—had devastating effects on the families, especially on those women whose husbands remained at their urban work sites.

A human world, male or female, consists of groups, kin ties, friends, churches, and schools or their surrogates. It includes people one can gossip with, receive news from and transmit news to. Even people who prefer solitude may derive satisfaction from simply watching people, if only from a park bench. Isolation in solitary confinement is considered to be among the most inhumane punishments inflicted on human beings. In the distant and often barren "homelands" many uprooted women lived a life deprived of almost every element of a human world: employment, support groups, even the company of their husbands. In a world with little or no social infrastructure.

The Migration of Workers and Work

The geography of relations between worker and work has had a long and checkered history. In the European preindustrial cottage system, men called factors brought work in the form of raw materials—cotton, flax, wool, linen—to the workers in their homes to be processed and then picked up by the factor when it was ready. With industrialization, however, the direction changed. Now workers left their homes and migrated to areas where there was work for them to do in mills and factories. Rural people moved to cities; Europeans moved to the United States; Easterners in the United States moved west; New Englanders moved south; and so on. But recently technology has been reversing these movements. A system curiously analogous to the old cottage system has been in process, but on a global scale. Modern countries today send materials to developing countries, which then manufacture or assemble them into finished goods to be marketed by the "mother" country. Work was again being brought to the workers rather than workers to the work, but now in the form of factories in the Orient, Latin America, wherever, rather than to nearby cottages.

The relevant point here is that much of this work performed in foreign countries is done by women in predominantly two industries, one among the oldest of characteristically female industries—textiles, including apparel—and the other, among the newest—electronics, including computers. Some years ago women in the United States began to notice that the union labels sewed into their clothes to guide them in their purchases were being replaced by labels saying that the garment had been made in Korea, Mexico, Hong Kong, Taiwan, or some other place equally far away. It was not too much later that the processes behind this change became visible to both them and the workers who were making those clothes.

One student of the factors making for the success of projects in development, specified among them, the existence of a sizeable market for the goods being produced (Finsterbush, chapter 3). For the products in the two female industries—textiles and electronics—there is an almost insatiable market.[1]

Women were thus being precipitated—"integrated"—into a transnational labor market by so-called multinational corporations directed by powerful financial forces through which the fate of women in Tunisia or Honduras or Kenya might depend. These decisions were being made by the World Bank or the International Monetary Fund in Washington or London. Modern technology, in brief, was now making it possible to incorporate women everywhere into a system wholly regulated by the market norms of the Western male world. In the process, women in, let us say, Korea, became unwitting—and successful—competitors of women in, let us say, New Jersey.[2]

Here is a case in point:

> In apparel, the pressure of competition on the domestic United States industry has caused a search for low-wage sites of assembly in the Caribbean and the Pacific Rim. Apparel imports to the domestic American market have risen dramatically. . . . This has changed the strategic situation among apparel labor and capital. The competitive pressure on United States producers has produced, in turn, sweatshop conditions in New York, Los Angeles, and elsewhere. Here is the way the system of internationalization appears to a New York contractor:
>
> "A manufacturer will tell me he has 2,000 twelve-piece blouses he needs sewn. I tell him I need at least $10 per blouse to do a decent job on a garment that complicated. So then he tells me to get lost—he offers me $2. If I don't take that, he tells me he can have it sent to Taiwan or South America somewhere, and have it done for 50 cents. So we haggle— sometimes I might bring him up to $4 per blouse.
>
> "Now, you tell me, how can I pay someone 'union scale' ($3.80) or even the minimum wage ($2.90), when I'm only getting $4 per blouse? With overhead and everything else, I may be able to pay the ladies $1.20 per blouse, but that's tops. There's nothing on paper. I get it in cash." [Ross, 1982][3]

In 1985 two U.S. unions—the Amalgamated Clothing and Textile Workers' Union and the International Ladies' Garment Workers' Union—were lobbying for legislation that would "put an end to uncontrolled imports of apparel and textiles, stop the erosion of our industry, save two million American jobs. And still give the nations of the world, poorer ones especially, legitimate access to our market" (advertisement, *Washington Post*, 10 April 1985). More than jobs were at stake. They were talking about two million people:

And look who they are: 7 out of 10, women. Sitting at sewing machines, standing on their feet in the mills. Supporting their families alone, or making the difference so that the family can live a little better, the kids get a better chance.

These are people who desperately need work, they want to work and they don't have much choice about where they work.

When their plants close, they can't find jobs in other industries. The lucky ones may find a service job at the minimum wage, if you call it lucky to make $134 a week with a couple of kids to take care of.

More often, it's welfare. And bitterness. For them, dignity, pride, faith in America are wrapped up in paying their own way.

Two million jobs are slipping away. It's not too late to save them. [Ibid]

The electronics industry is another example of a competitive labor market which also puts women in the United States in a competitive relationship with women in other parts of the globe. Computer firms in Massachusetts, for example, have set up assembly plants in Puerto Rico, Ireland, and in Asian low-wage areas (Ross, 1982). Like the apparel industry, the electronics industry is "relatively footloose, for the value-bulk of its product is high, as is its labor content" (Ross, 1982). Although the hourly wage in Singapore ($1.00) is higher than in some other areas, it is still significantly lower than it is in any other location in the European Economic Community:

> Thus increasing numbers of electronics firms have indeed located routine aspects of their production in places like Singapore. Wages are a fraction of even low Irish wages. . . ; and in 1981, the Singapore Chamber of Commerce reports, among the hundreds of thousands of workers there, there were *no* days lost from strikes. Singapore officials offer even more attractive tax and capital grant incentives than most of Europe, and they advertise proudly Singapore's policy of total freedom in exchange, profits repatriation, environmental regulation, and so forth. [Ross, 1981, 25]

The fact that multinational corporations in countries all over the West—Ireland, England, Germany, the United States—were competing with one another for the factors of production, including labor, meant there was, in terms of classic economic theory, "a strategic logic that in the long run forces each producer to operate as cheaply as competitors do" (Ross, 25). Expectedly, therefore, the long-term results were to "lower wages of any given kind of work towards that which is the lowest available worldwide" (25).

The impact of the multinational corporation presented many Western feminists with serious ethical dilemmas. Research on the subject raised questions among them about "strategies to further integrate women into the processes of dependent capitalist development" (Elson and

Pearson, 1981, 1). Where, globally, did the welfare of women truly lie? Since even a poorly-paid job was better than no job at all, should the multinational be encouraged because it offered employment and hence autonomy? (Kelly, 1982). Or criticized because of its exploitative nature? (Elson and Pearson, 1981, 1). For the young women employed in Third-World multinational plants were an exceptionally vulnerable work force. In the Mexican Maquiladora Programs,[4] for example,

> they are not only easy to replace and discard, they are also docile. Managers see them as a controllable group whose members are not easy to unionize. . . . [Managers] prefer to hire young girls who haven't been spoiled by experience in other factories. They are more responsible, patient and agile than men. And you also find fewer troublemakers among them." [Kelly, 1982]

They were easy "to shape to our requirements." They were also easy to fire. They were, to be sure, subject to sexual harassment and they often replaced men who could not find suitable employment and had to escape across the border for work in the United States.

The multinational corporation represented, in brief, a new kind of political imperial system, not identical with but comparable to it in the sense that policy decisions with important repercussions for the lives of women were made in board rooms in New York, London, Paris, or San Francisco—decisions that threw women willy-nilly into competition with one another all over the world.

The competition among women in the Third World was certainly "unwitting," but among the multinationals it was "witting" and, indeed, two-fold. Developing countries competed among themselves for multinational corporations by offering cheap and docile workers, by establishing so-called Export Processing Zones, which conferred special tax exemptions, communication and transportation facilities, and relaxed customs restrictions.[5] The corporations, in turn, competed among themselves for the cheapest labor.

We have here two points of view. On one side is Nena, a 27-year old employee of the Mattel toy company in the Philippines, who makes doll parts:

> She likes working in the toy factory. For her, it is better than being a housekeeper. She gets paid for a specific task and has benefits like a vacation with pay. She gets to meet friends, for there are many women working in the factory and in the [Export Processing] zone. . . . Nena is optimistic. She can still afford to see the movies or buy comic books. She is not married and her take-home pay is enough to meet her simple needs. Though she suffers from recurrent backaches and muscle fatigue, she can still pay for the minimum cost of medical care. Nena thinks that women

must get an education. Hers was short, cut by necessity of earning a living. And women must work. For her, housekeeping is impractical; it has no definite hours, no pay, no benefits—and no union. Women should widen their perspectives. Nena is strong on women being economically alive. No double burdens—household work and paid work—for her. But Nena's optimism is clouded by the mass lay-offs in Mattel. She has to work harder and longer to keep her job. She has to clock in at 6 A.M. and last up to 6 P.M. She has to meet her quota of a thousand parts. She must not get sick, for if she is absent for a single day, she may be struck off the list of workers Mattel will keep, due to rising costs. If this happens, she will have to go back to the farm and raise pigs. It will be very difficult again. Farm life is hard on women. [Villariba, n.d., 8]

On the other side are those who argue that multinational corporations incorporate, absorb, coopt women; they do not integrate them. All that wage work does is change the basis for female inequality. Deprived of the protection of traditional family and kinship gender roles, women are subject to greater vulnerability. The true goal should be "the development of women's capacity for self-determination" (Elson and Pearson, 1981, 9).

It is interesting that although there has been for some time a growing number of international labor organizations in the industrialized nations of the West ostensibly concerned with improving the status of women workers (Cook, Lorwin, Daniels, 1983, 25), these multinationals seem to pass through the seive. Thus exploited women workers begin to reinvent their own wheel. An English translation of a letter in a Sri Lankan quarterly, *Voice of Women*, for example, makes this appeal:

From the despotic factory of——
We female employees have decided to bring to your notice a multitude of matters concerning the difficulties prevailing in this factory. We took jobs in this factory in order to have a means of livelihood and relief for some of our problems. Instead, the only thing we have received is a day by day loss of physical energy.

We are being made to work both day and night, like buffaloes tethered to trees. Not a single moment of the day is there for rest—neither for the machines nor for the workers. . . . The supervisory staff and the management are never satisfied, no matter how much we work and produce. Please focus your attention on the sufferings of the poor female workers who are being subjected to harassment and harsh treatment by the management and supervisors.

The only intention of the management is to extract more and more production output so that they gain more benefits for themselves. The female workers get no wage increase. . . . A quota which is impossible for a female worker to deliver in an hour is always targeted. Fines are imposed when the quota is not delivered on time. . . . A female worker is not granted leave even if she falls ill. A little medicine or a cup of coffee is not available to us even if we faint while at work. . . . Only a half an hour break is allowed for meals. . . .

This information is brought to you in writing by a group of female workers. . . . We are not going to include our names and addresses. The reason is that in case the management finds out about this, we will have to face various problems. Therefore if you [*Voice of Women*] could be so kind as to present these issues before Parliament, so that they can be resolved, we will all esteem you as a deity. . . . [*Connexions*, no. 15, p. 13]

APPENDIX C

The Female World of South Africa

In appendix A the situation of many South African women was briefly looked at, especially the uprootings of black women which destroyed many marriages and families. At this point the focus is on the relationship between white and nonwhite (mainly black) women. From the human-rights point of view anything written about the female world in South Africa in the mid-to-late 80s would, hopefully, be written in the past tense. For it was an anachronistic world just in the throes of being brought up to date, a world bearing the scars of a highly fractured society, fractured especially by race and ethnicity and thus by class also.

"Many white women go through their lives without ever talking with black women aside from giving instructions to their domestic servants" (Snudge, 1982, 72). Separation in schools, residential areas, work, recreation, toilets means separation in every other aspect of life as well. Thus a 1980 study of the relations between 175 black domestics and 50 white mistresses highlighted the chasm that separated them from one another. On female issues, the white women were unconcerned. They did not feel oppressed. Although 86 percent had heard of the women's movement, only 6 percent considered it a good idea (Straker, 1985, 128). Understandably so when black women relieved them of most of their household and child-care tasks, the quality of their lives precluded the need for independence or autonomy. Subsidized by their husbands they had no occasion to feel oppressed and no need for a women's movement to liberate them.[1] The black domestics had already liberated them from the onerous "tasks related to housework, child rearing, and the family" (129).[2]

The situation looked different to the black domestic. She did feel oppressed.[3] In fact, she felt a two-fold oppression, both racial and class, enforced by government policy.

. . . She is dependent on her employer on almost every conceivable level. The domestic worker usually resides on the premises of the employer. Because of influx control and the pass laws, she may even be dependent on her employer to legitimize her presence in a particular urban area. Her powerlessness vis-à-vis her employer who determines her wage, her working hours, and her working conditions without a written contract, is therefore just about complete. [131]

Her oppression, further, extended even to her interpersonal relations:

"We should be counted as people"; "Our employers should treat us as people, not animals"; "It would help if our madams could be interested in knowing their servant's circumstances. Many madams don't know [even] how many children their maids have." [131]

It looked like a timeless system set in stone, impregnable for at least a century.[4]

As a matter of fact, the political system (apartheid) it was defending was less than half a century old, established only in 1948 when the Nationalist Party came into power (appendix A). Less than a decade later women of all races were uniting to work together against it. Thus in 1956, 20,000 women of all races and social classes marched to the Government Houses in Pretoria "to protest the pass laws" (Straker, 1965, 132). In their "Declaration of the Women of South Africa for the Withdrawal of Passes for Women and the Repeal of the Pass Laws," these African women stated their sense of black oppression. So also did those who were not African state that they knew their sisters suffered. For them "an insult to African women" was "an insult to all women." They concluded with a resounding promise:

In the name of the women in South Africa, we say to you, each one of us, African, European, Indian, Coloured, that we are opposed to the pass system. . . . We shall not rest until we have won for our children their fundamental rights of freedom, justice and security. [133]

There were, in brief, human issues—admittedly rare—when "women of every race . . . from the cities and towns, from the reserves and the villages" could unite (134). The protests fell on deaf government ears. But they had been made. And by racially united women. The fortress was powerful, but not completely intimidating.

One type of activism that remained was with Women for Peace, a multinational, nonpartisan, paternalist, nonpolitical organization "aimed at bringing about peace between races." It was relatively safe; it was not seeking structural changes to achieve its goal of peace. It seemed to resemble the traditional do-good women's organizations described by Little in other parts of Africa (chapter 4). They taught black women to read, sew, arrange entertainments. These do-gooding women tended to be white, middle-class, and, in most cases, English-speaking. Still, however conservative they might be, instead of spending their leisure time partying or shopping or engaging in other kinds of conspicuous consumption—a phenomenon noted among leisure-class women in subsidized and protected positions in many other parts of the female world, East and West—they chose to give time to black women.

The symbol of protest activities against the pass laws in the 50s and 60s was a black sash which became an organization—Black Sash—with a political magazine, symbols of "solidarity within the black community" (Snudge, 69). These women were also do-gooders, but on a social-work level, helping black women to get jobs, to escape forced uprooting and resettlement, to retain their living quarters, even to take cases to court.[5] Useful, reformist; revolutionary by no means. As yet. But there were cracks in the racial fortress. There were women who tried to mollify its threat, at least to alleviate the burdens of black women—as their U.S. counterparts had done in the civil-rights movements of the 1960s. Not revolutionary, nor necessarily even feminist.

Almost by default, feminists in South Africa tended to be white, middle-class, English-speaking, and educated:

> Most white women who are able to see through the entire structure within which they have been brought up, and therefore to change their thinking about themselves and generally about the situation in South Africa, are the middle-class, university-educated women who have been able to come into contact with black people in positions other than those of servitude, and with alternative ideas. [Snudge, 72–73]

Among the organized activities of these women were: support of abortion reform, improvement of education, and founding of crisis centers. Their informal activities included raising issues and keeping them continually alive.

What feminism there is in South Africa is white. To politically aware black women, many white feminist issues seem trivial. Downplaying the nuclear family, for example, an imported feminist issue among white women, seemed irrelevant to women in extended black families broken up and separated by forced uprootings; so did a call for a special police task force dealing with sexual assaults seem off-target for women who looked at the police with abhorrence. Black activist women saw "their first commitment as being one to the 'broader struggle,'" rather than to seemingly irrelevant feminist ones. So also was feminism middle-class, for "in a white society full of bigotry and prejudice, it is unlikely that . . . working-class white women, who are even more bound [than middle-class women] by their relationship to the men in their lives, will break out of that mold" (Snudge, 72–73).

But both feminists and politically involved black women agreed on one point: there would be "no fundamental change in the position of women without radical and fundamental change in the social, cultural and economic structure of the country as a whole" (72).

While these women were looking to political forces for such restructuring of their society, actually economic forces were busily at work changing the position of women, both white and black. For South Africa was a modern industrial capitalist state and no more than any other could it tolerate a work force unskilled, untrained, unable to cope with the demands of a modern world. Just as, analogously, it had been the need felt by leftist groups for the services of women in liberation movements (chapter 4), so also was it the need for the industrial services of women—black as well as white—in South Africa that was leading to their "liberation." University research projects, corporation-sponsored seminars and publications became agencies for feminist outreach. Much of this activity reflected common concerns of feminists all over the world, including the use of women in defense, sex discrimination, lack of opportunity for management positions, and the like. But the bottom line was this: South Africa was "absolutely dependent on a racially mixed labour force" if it was "to cope with the problems of [its] labour shortage" (Mojalefa, n.d., 85).

A sociological process known as "succession" that had long had its counterpart in the United States, a process by which different ethnic and racial groups, starting at the bottom of the occupational ladder had succeeded one another in higher-level jobs, was also taking place among women in South Africa. "In South Africa this progression initially occurred on a racial basis, and white women led the way and are now mainly in the . . . [highest] stage, closely followed by coloured females" (Prekel, 1982, 73). This situation should not cause alarm, however, because the same processes work for Coloured and black women also. "The white workers who no longer work in the clothing factories, have been replaced by Blacks,[6] and the same applies to the coloured workers" (73). The author, senior lecturer at the University of South Africa, then traced the overall mobility of Black women. On admittedly incomplete data she summarizes, industry by industry, the steps in that course:

> The progression of female workers is generally described in four stages, namely: (i) as peasants in the subsistence sector. Traditionally Black women have cultivated the fields. This tradition has contributed to the industrialization of Black women because for these women the concept and the habit of working hard had already been established at home;
>
> (ii) as domestic servants earning wages. Most people still regard this as the ultimate position to be reached by Black women, but the transition to the third stage is now rapidly taking place;

(iii) as blue collar workers in the manufacturing sector; and

(iv) as clerical workers, sales staff, teachers, nurses and in professional occupations. This stage has already been reached by many Black women, and they are moving into these areas at an increasing pace. [73]

The occupational ladder for Black women was, then: subsistence agricultural work; domestic service; blue-collar manufacturing work; clerical work; and professional work. The latter category traditionally included the civil service, nursing, teaching, and social work, but increasingly it includes medicine, personnel, advertising, pharmacy, research, public relations, journalism, and computers (Mojalefa, n.d., 93). Exceptionally surprising was the rapid increase betwen 1969 and 1981 in the higher-level jobs. Total professionals increased 124.6 percent, from 33,613 to 75,503 (Prekel, 1982, 66). Not surprising at all was the increase in school teachers (from 18,532 to 41,303), but remarkable, considering the handicaps, was the increase in university and college professors and lecturers from 23 to 89 (66).[7]

Professional Black women constitute a special elite who have prepared themselves despite enormous odds. The stumbling blocks have included: both racial and sexual discrimination in admission to training, the demand that they prove they can handle the job, financial problems, resistance by fellow-workers, child-care problems (Pretorius, 1982, 108–13). Husbands may help or hinder the Black professional woman. "Most black professional women must thank their husbands who have given them the consent, the latitude and support to improve their qualifications" (109), but "the black husband still expects his wife to do the bulk of domestic work" (111). It is remarkable that

in spite of the dual handicap of race and sex, a growing number of Black women are proving themselves in a widening variety of careers: besides the traditional professions of nursing and teaching, they are also proving themselves in medicine, personnel work, research, advertising, pharmacy, public relations, journalism, secretarial work, industry, trade unions, social work, computers, and in their own businesses. They had proved to themselves and to others that the will to succeed in a career can overcome many obstacles and problems. [Mojalefa, n.d., 93–94]

And there were channels for disseminating their lessons.

Inching its way toward a feminist perspective, for example, was a nongovernment, autonomous Women's Bureau established under the auspices of a life insurance society. It was designed to be a "servicing body, independent of Government and of a non-partisan and non-political nature" (Terms of Reference, n.d.).[8] One of its four working groups had to do with "women and special black affairs" and another with "women and special Indian affairs." Its journal, the Women's Bureau

Forum discussed common white feminist issues—sexist advertising, family law, need for part-time jobs, the married-teachers issue, assertiveness, high stress load, day-care facilities—but it also included items about black women.[9]

Academia was also creating and disseminating knowledge that taught women "their place," a "place" that had never been open to them, white or black. There were the seminars sponsored by the Centre for Management Studies which included thinking about professional women; there was the Journal of Labour Relations, official journal of the Institute of Labour Relations, which also included the relations of Black women.

What the impact of all these processes will ultimately have on relations between the races in the female world is uncertain. As it is also among Black women themselves. The rise of a well tested Black female elite with a stake in the status quo may have a dampening effect on political activism for political change. At a moment in time as revolutionary as this, it would be hazardous to guess. We do know that one of the arguments used against revolutionary change has been that it would be damaging to successful black workers. Successful women in the United States early in the women's movement had rejected it with the cliché that they had made it, why couldn't the radical feminists? Still, there were (among those 249 black women sociologists) leaders who were doing the research and the writing and the teaching that was changing minds.

NOTES

Prolegomena

1. The so-called tribals are in danger of extinction in some parts of the world as development impinges closer and closer on them—in Panama, the Philippines, the Kalihari Desert, Laos, Afghanistan, the Amazon basin, among other places. In 1969 an organization, Survival International, was set up by concerned anthropologists to deflect "the destructive influence on them of civilized society" (Glynn, Rohter, Lernoux, Jennings, and Kirkland, *Newsweek*, 1981, 97). There are, the anthropologists argue, scientific as well as moral reasons for helping the tribals survive. They provide, for example, "insights into the origin of the species, to knowledge of local wildlife, ecology and medicinal plants." Living outside the political system, they are not within the scope of national statistical surveillance so the kinds of sociological and demographic data, in addition to anthropological data are difficult to come by. It is regrettable that they cannot be included in an attempted view of the global female world.

2. Policy as well as knowledge has suffered from these biases, especially in the area of development (chapter 3). Planners and administrators began with their own conceptions of what was suitable for men and women as they knew it from colonial experience or from the United States, namely that agriculture was what was suitable for males, running the household for females. Thus in places where men were not farmers, they were given training in agriculture while women who were, in fact, the farmers, were not. Elise Boulding has stated this situation succinctly: "By ignoring this world of women, so basically involved in human productivity of every kind, development planners were not only perpetrating an injustice on the women themselves by failing to help them improve their conditions of working and living, but they were also sabotaging their own development strategies. How was it possible to make such a mistake? How is it possible to continue making it right up to the present?" Her answer is to the point. The combination of a sexist and a Western bias lay at the bottom of it. "Development planners have predominantly been Western men or Western-trained men, imbued with the Western myth that a woman's chief place is in the home, by the side of a man, caring for children with the means he brings to her. This myth has been so persistent that Western development experts have been able to go into third . . . world countries to give development aid without ever noticing the . . . female world at all" (1980, 5).

3. On that same television program, "Anthropology on Trial", sponsored by the National Geographic Society an African tribal man expressed resentment that anthropologists took his information and earned money writing it up. Now he was going to charge for interviews.

4. Not negligible is the related stylistic difficulty in trying to write to and for

213

an international readership that will not all have exposure to the same literary treasure trove as one's own. In the nineteenth century psychologists had a concept of "apperceptive mass," which referred to a shared common body of knowledge, belief, historical facts stored in our minds that made it possible for us to understand one another. When French scholars appeal to history it tends to be to French history; when British scholars apeal to history it tends to be to British history; both use their own poets, novelists, and dramatists to project emotions and ideas. Writing for a global audience precludes references to the Bible, Shakespeare, the Romantic poets, Poor Richard, among others. Such restrictions are sometimes limiting.

5. For the political reverberations of these points vis-à-vis leadership, see appendix C.

PART I—Introduction

1. In 1983 the estimated population of the world was 4.7 billion, roughly half (2,350,000,000) of whom may be assumed to be female. Although the rate of increase has dropped from 2 percent to 1.7 percent during the last decade, the numbers continue to increase. Two and a half billion seems not an excessive estimate for the mid-to-late 1980s.

Chapter 1—Faceless Females

1. The major sources of demographic data for chapter 1 are: Elise Boulding, Shirley A. Nuss, Dorothy Lee Carson, and Michael A. Greenstein, *Handbook of International Data on Women*. (New York: John Wiley & Sons, 1976, referred to as Handbook in text); Bureau of the Census, *Current Population Reports*, series P-23, no. 123. *International Fertility Indicators*, U.S. Government Printing Office, Washington, D.C. (1983 referred to by author, Amara Bachu, in the text); U.S. Bureau of the Census. *World Population 1983—Recent Demographic Estimates for the Countries and Regions of the World*. Washington, D.C., 1983 (referred to as U.S. Bureau of the Census in the text); *World Development Report 1984*. (New York: Oxford University Press, 1984 (referred to in text as World Bank). The Handbook assembles 107 social indicators from 159 countries selected out of the 216 United Nations members on the basis of political independence or a population of at least half a million (8). Those omitted lived in 57 exotic places such as: Portuguese Timor, Sao Tome and Principe, the Tokelau Islands, Wallis and Futuna Islands. Most, however, lived in the 33 countries in North Africa and the Middle East, the 62 countries in Asia, the 62 countries in Latin America, the 35 countries of Europe–North America, and the 39 countries of Africa. Excluded are nomadic tribes, aborigines, alien armed forces; merchant seamen in port or ashore; alien displaced persons, enemy prisoners of war; foreign diplomatic personnel, and other civilian aliens temporarily present. National armed forces, merchant seamen at sea, diplomatic personnel, and other civilian aliens temporarily absent are also not included. Few females, however, are likely to be present in these excluded categories (14, 461). The World Bank report deals primarily with 126 member countries, especially developing countries. The U.S. Census report, *World Population 1983*, deals with 202 countries and territories. All alert the reader to the numerous shortcomings of the data and warn that great care should be exercised in dealing with them. The Handbook authors state they know they are not "providing an accurate comparative picture of the position of women in the twentieth century" (6). Sources of demographic data

are gathered by governments with varying degrees of expertise in the process of getting, recording, and processing of data and which use definitions, further, that may vary from one country to another. Some countries have never taken a census (Chad, Ethiopia, Laos, and Oman), and even for those that have, not all kinds of data are included. Further, and especially disquieting, is the fact that the data in many cases are no longer current. In a time with so many revolutions in process, when we live at the margin of history and news, a disparity of only a few years in asynchronous timing can make a great deal of demographic difference. In some cases it is possible to arrive at suitable estimates by way of indirect techniques (U.S. Census, 3). Like other suppliers of demographic data, the World Bank calls for care in using its data: "Every effort has been made to standardize concepts, definitions, coverage, timing, and other characteristics of the basic data to ensure the greatest possible degree of comparability. Nevertheless, care must be taken in how the indicators are interpreted. Although the statistics are drawn from sources generally considered the most authoritative and reliable, many of them are subject to considerable margins of error. In addition, variations in national statistical practices mean that most data are not strictly comparable. The data should thus be construed only as indicating trends and characterizing major differences among economies" (213). In addition to the technical defects in the data, the Handbook calls attention to one common to all research on women: "There is one major distorting device operating on all collection concerning women, above and beyond interpretation differences and collection facilities. This is a set of cultural assumptions about the secondary importance of anything women do; it produces under-registration of women from birth to death, and underenumeration of women in employment, independently of other forces that also create undercounting of populations in general" (6). I have tried to comply with all the limitations specified for the use of the data in this chapter.

2. The World Bank warns against putting too much faith in the accuracy of all kinds of data for developing parts of the world: "Every effort has been made to standardize concepts, definitions, coverage, timing, and other characteristics of the basic data to ensure the greatest possible degree of comparability. Nevertheless, care must be taken in how the indicators are interpreted. Although the statistics are drawn from sources generally considered the most authoritative and reliable, many of them are subject to considerable margins of error. In addition, variations in national statistical practices mean that most data are not strictly comparable. The data should thus be construed only as indicating trends and characterizing major differences among economies" (1984, 213).

3. In the United States life expectancy for women was expected to be as high as 86 years by the year of 2000 (*Washington Post*, 5 Sept., 1984).

4. "Of the more than 4 billion people who live in the world today, over 70 percent live in developing countries. 119 developing countries belong to the United Nations among which there are a number of particularly disadvantaged countries requiring special help. Of these, the least developed countries, number 30 at present as among the poorest countries in the world with a 1970 average per capita income of under $100. A number of countries, including some of the least developed, are geographically disadvantaged.They may be isolated islands or cut off from access to the sea, land-locked. In both cases they face a number of additional problems. There are also 45 countries which are classified by the UN as the most seriously affected, that is, they are countries with low levels of income, productivity and technology that have been most seriously affected by the economic crisis of the 1970s caused by sharp increases in the price of their

essential imports (such as oil)" (*Women* 1980. Newsletter no. 7. Issued by the *U.N. Division of Economic and Social Information*/DP1. World Conference of the U.N. Decade for Women: Equality, Development and Peace, n.d.). The developing countries (the least developed being italicized) are: *Afghanistan*, Algeria, Angola, Argentina, Bahamas, Bahrain, *Bangladesh*, Barbados, *Benin, Bhutan*, Bolivia, *Botswana*, Brazil, Burma, *Burundi, Cape Verde, Central African Republic, Chad*, Chile, China, Colombia, *Comoros*, Congo, Costa Rica, Cuba, Cyprus, Democratic Kampuchea, Democratic People's Republic of Korea, *Democratic Yemen*, Djibouti, Dominica, Dominican Republic, Ecuador, Egypt, El Salvador, Equatorial Guinea, *Ethiopia*, Fiji, Gabon, *Gambia*, Ghana, Grenada, Guatemala, *Guinea*, Guinea-Bissau, Guyana, *Haiti*, Honduras, India, Indonesia, Iran, Iraq, Ivory Coast, Jamaica, Jordan, Kenya, Kuwait, *Lao People's Democratic Republic*, Lebanon, *Lesotho*, Liberia, Libya, Madagascar, *Malawi*, Malaysia, *Maldives, Mali*, Malta, Mauritania, Mauritius, Mexico, Morocco, Mozambique, *Nepal*, Nicaragua, *Niger*, Nigeria, Oman, Pakistan, Panama, Papua New Guiena, Paraguay, Peru, Philippines, Qatar, Republic of Korea, Romania, *Rwanda*, Saint Lucia, *Samoa*, Sao Tome and Principe, Saudi Arabia, Senegal, Seychelles, Sierra Leone, Singapore, Solomon Islands, *Somalia*, Sri Lanka, *Sudan*, Surinam, Swaziland, Syria, Thailand, Togo, Trinidad and Tobago, Tunisia, *Uganda*, United Arab Emirates, United Republic of Cameroon, *United Republic of Tanzania, Upper Volta* (since changed to Burkina Faso), Uruguay, Venezuela, Viet Nam, *Yemen*, Yugoslavia, Zaire, and Zambia.

5. As a standard for judging these figures, a one-time inmate of a Soviet-prison camp, Mikhail Makarenko, is cited for the following figures: heavy-labor prisoners, 2,000 calories per day; "strict regime" prisoners, 1,300 calories per day; Auschwitz inmates, 2050 calories per day (George Will, *Washington Post*, September 1983).

6. And by girls less than that by boys. Safilios-Rothschild has summarized the research on this subject: "While malnutrition is often widespread among children in the rural areas of many developing countries, some evidence indicates that it is more widespread among pre-adolescent and adolescent girls than boys. . . . A study of malnutrition among children in rural Punjab showed that girls were more often malnourished than boys regardless of their caste. Despite variation in the incidence of malnutrition between castes, within each caste there were three or more malnourished girls for each malnourished boy. . . . Furthermore, field studies undertaken by the Indian Council of Medical Research showed that in 1971 girls outnumbered boys four to three among children with Kwashiorkor. . . . In rural Philippines, it was found that families spent more money on food for boys than for girls, especially in the one to six year old age group. . . . And in rural Guatemala, a protein supplement improved mental development scores of girls from the poorest families more than boys', since boys tend to be treated preferentially when resources (food or money) are scarce. . . . It seems, therefore, that the greater the scarcity of food and financial resources in the Third World's rural areas, the greater the probability that girls will be malnourished and that their mental development may be low" (1979, 16–17).

7. I cannot leave the topic of nutrition as related to longevity without mentioning the drought of historic proportions that struck Africa beginning in the late 1960s. Whatever the calorie consumption may have been in the past, it was down to starvation levels for millions of people in thirty-one countries. The most severely stricken were: Mozambique, Ghana, Mauritania, and northern Ethiopia. In two of these, Mozambique and Ghana, "there are reports of parents abandoning young children because they can no longer feed them—a highly

unusual occurence in societies where family loyalties are held sacred" (Dash, 26 February 1984). In Mozambique, an estimated 100,000 people have already died from malnutrition. In Mali, "not one of the worst affected countries, the U.N. Children's Fund estimates that 1,000 children will starve to death this year and more than 200,000 will suffer irredeemable damage to their health from chronic malnutrition" (ibid.). The U.N. Food and Agriculture Organization estimates that of the 150 million people who live in the drought-stricken country, 100 million face hunger and that as many as 4 million, mainly children, will probably die from starvation, malnutrition, and related causes this year and next (Szulc, April 1984, 16). An administrator of the U.S. Agency for International Development, AID, in a newspaper interview noted that there had been a 20 percent decline in food production per capita in Africa in the last 20 years and that the caloric intake had also declined. (*Washington Post*, 31 January 1984). Since that time the death toll from drought has mounted drastically, to levels unparalleled in recent history.

8. Samuel Baum, Center for International Research, used four groupings: Latin America and the Caribbean; Sub-Saharan Africa; Near East and North Africa; and Asia. The World Bank combined a geographic and economic and political set of criteria.

9. The mean legal age at marriage varies from 13.3 in Latin America to 16.4 in North Africa–Middle East (World Bank, 1984, 289); the reported age at marriage for 29 countries as of 1977 varied from 16 in Bangladesh to 25 in Sri Lanka and the Philippines (198–199).

10. In some parts of the world the issue is forced sterilization; in China, the one-child family policy; in the male world, "population control."

11. In 1971, I distinguished eight theoretical "career patterns" possible for professional career women in the United States. They dealt with ways childbearing could be scheduled vis-à-vis careers, namely: the early interrupting pattern; four late-interrupting patterns; three uninterrupted patterns (chapter 9). I concluded that many of the problems stemmed from the belief that women had to adjust to the Establishment, whereas so-called women liberationists asked rather that the Establishment adjust to women. It has taken a decade and a half for that idea to achieve at least serious consideration by both industry and policymakers.

12. In Africa, as compared with other areas, a relatively large proportion of babies (1.7 percent) were born to women at ages 45 and older (Handbook, 229–47).

13. See, for example, the stories of the Markala cooperative organized and operated by non-literate women in Mali and the special banking system set up in India (chapter 3).

14. "Literacy is defined as the ability to both read and write a simple message in any one language" (United Nations, Handbook of Vital Statistics, 1955, 137). The population covers "both nationals and aliens, native and foreign-born, aborigines, jungle tribes, nomadic people, displaced persons, internees, refugees and any other group present within the borders of a country at a specified time" (*1972 United Nations Demographic Yearbook*, 1973, 13).

15. These "sticking points" were arrived at on the basis of disparate breaks in the distribution.

16. There were other countries, however, in which the progress was minuscule, as in Yemen, Ethiopia, Sierra Leone, Benin, Mali. Some of these data may be discounted since the date they refer to is about a decade earlier than the other figures.

17. "Increases in education are associated with increases in the productivity

of a woman's time while she is in the labor force which creates further incentives for her to spend more time at work rather than at home rearing a family" (Bachu, quoting Hashimoto, 1983, 12). These effects are enhanced if education leads to white-collar occupations rather than to agricultural, manual, or service occupations. Education also vastly multiplies use of contraception (Bachu, 30, 54). Differences in schooling, both among and within different parts of the female world, separate women from one another in ways not too unlike other separating differences such as race, ethnicity, and class. Different as educated, urban women from different societies may be from one another, they probably resemble one another more than they resemble rural non-literate women in their own countries.

18. The other four industries were: mining and quarrying; electric, gas, water, and sanitary services; construction; and transport, storage, and communication.

19. The author comments further on situations in rural areas where men have had to migrate to cities for work, leaving extra work for the women, who have had to take on additional workloads (34).

20. "A survey in Burkina Faso found families lost weight during the rainy season, not because there was no food available but because their long days in the fields left women too exhausted to cook" (Sciolino, *New York Times*, 23 June 1985).

21. According to the Handbook, there were five African countries and one Latin American country with higher rates (27). A 1975 update showed 18 countries equaling or exceeding this proportion (U.N. Statistical Abstract prepared by Shirley Nuss, 1980, table 1). The 1985 estimate was 41 percent, two percentage points lower than the 1975 figure, for Thailand, and 20 countries equaling or exceeding that proportion.

Chapter 2—Separate Worlds

1. The "life course" of men in the West has for millennia preoccupied thinkers who tended to see it in terms of "stages" or careers or, more recently, transitions or crises.

2. The "index of industrial segregation" refers to "the proportion of the economically active females (or males) that would have to change their industrial classification for there to be an equal distribution of women and men in the industrial sectors of the economy" (Handbook, 1976, 300). The same definition applies to occupational segregation. For the "world woman," the mean index of occupational segregation was 0.376 (287) and, of industrial segregation, 0.3456 (286).

3. No attempt is made here to go further back into "first causes" to explain why there are two worlds. Students of the subject vary widely in their points of view, which range from one that finds genetic predisposition to one that finds socialization practices from the moment of birth as adequate. The existence of the two worlds is here taken for granted and described rather than explained.

4. Female siblings, as we saw in chapter 1, sometimes perform child-care functions, and sometimes men do also. In Alors, for example, men do help take care of infants and small children (DuBois, 1944, 109).

5. In Africa, one of the most ramifying political influences on the sex division of labor was the influx of Europeans in the nineteenth century. Before they came, the men tended to engage in tree-felling, hunting, and warfare; females, in farming (Boserup, 1970, 19). After they came there remained little for the native men to do.

6. Such, for example, as the great drought of 1974–75 in Somali. There the government established state farms and fisheries to impart new skills to the nomadic herders. A large group of skilled workers resulted from these programs. The women remained on the farms and in the fishing plants as technicians, mechanics, even construction workers. The men returned to a nomadic life. Currently the government is once more trying to implement retraining programs for meeting the current droughts.

7. In the nineteenth century the transition from rural to urban economies became one of the most revolutionary in human history. It transformed a wide gamut of human relationships, from those based primarily on kinship ties and locale—"blood and soil," "Blut-und-Bod"—to one based on impersonal monetary exchange. The two kinds of systems came to be known by the German terms *Gemeinschaft* and *Gesellschaft*, the latter referring essentially to capitalism. In the West, the *Gemeinschaft* orientation survived longer in the female than in the male world; *Gesellschaft* came, in fact, to dominate the male world (Bernard, 1981).

8. In the West, journalists sometimes characterize London as a "man's town" and Paris as a "woman's town."

9. For the most part men have contributed meat and the women, roots, tubers, nuts, fruits, vegetables. Women in early societies may also have caught or trapped small animals, gathered snails, worms, and insects. After they had invented agriculture, grains became a major part of the female world's contribution. Cultivation of the soil was "genderized" as women's work as long as it was done with a digging stick. The advent of the plow, however, led to a takeover of agriculture, or at least a sharing of it, by the male world in many parts of the West.

10. The most extreme psychological explanation is that of Lionel Tiger who believes it is "a self-evident concomitant of such division of labor" that there are all-male and all-female groups (1970, xiii), and that females are excluded from the male groups not only because of a "formalized hostility to females" but also because of a positive attraction among men. "The psychological differences between men and women lead to a sociological separation" (128). He believes this propensity toward male bonds is in the human biogram. E. C. Wilson also invokes evolutionary bases (1975).

11. Even tools related to male-type work take on gender. Thus in Ireland "the plough, the harrow, the mower, the scythe, the spade and turf-cutting *slan* are regarded as masculine instruments. The attitudes of the countryside forbid a woman's using them. In the same way, they heap ridicule upon the thought of a man's interesting himself in the feminine sphere, in poultry, or in churning" (Bott, 1971, xx).

12. In the division of labor the biological component does not lie in the average sex differences so much as in the distribution of traits in the two sexes. No matter what the biological requirements specified for a given type of work may be, there are both males and females who qualify. Thus, although almost universally weapon-making is assigned to males, the combination of biological traits which underlie the relevant weapon-making skills may occur in both male and female bodies. But they may occur in more male than female bodies. It is, that is, the distributions that are different in the two sexes not the skills themselves. The biological or sex differences that are the basis for the division of labor are the differences in distributions of traits or qualities in the two sexes not in the male or female bodies that carry them. The point can be illustrated in connection with occupational segregation using data from Soviet experience. "Although disparities in female work-force participation as wide as those shown

in . . . the USSR—ranging from 24 percent in transport to 85 percent in public health, physical culture, and social welfare—undoubtedly do reflect socialization and power relationships, they . . . reflect more. Any sex-free concept of occupational non-segregation must allow options to women based on talents. . . . The increase in the number of women engineers in the USSR between 1941 and 1970—from 44,000 to one million—suggests . . . that there are a great many women with talents for engineering formerly untapped, and perhaps still untapped, waiting for the encouragement that education and employment patterns could release. On the other hand, . . . 'Soviet emphasis on scientific and technical skills' has not greatly increased the proportion of female scientific workers since 1947. There may be an asymptote here. Of course we will never know what sex differences there are in the distribution of all kinds of talents until opportunities and rewards are totally equalized" (Bernard, 1976, 93). Any strictly enforced division of labor by sex will require many individuals to be engaged in work for which they are not as well qualified as are individuals of the other sex. Fortunately, for a considerable amount of the work of the world the distribution of needed skills is probably not too disparate in the two sexes.

13. The difficulties involved are illustrated in the problems experienced in the West when attempts are made to get rid of the occupational segregation of women or to open up all kinds of work to both sexes, to "degenderize" them.

14. Only 39 percent of the women lived with husbands; 16 percent lived separately with their children; 19 percent lived with other women, and 18 percent of the older, widowed, separated women lived alone or with children; 8 percent were maids and employees in the households of other women.

15. "The majority of Adabraka adults of both sexes find sexual partners outside their own household, and this includes several men who reside with women as conjugal partners" (Sanjek, 89). Little more than a third—36 percent—of the men live with their wives (91); they engage in sexual activity elsewhere than in their households.

16. The books reviewed are: Mary Allen Mazey and David R. Lee, *Her Space, Her Place: A Geography of Women* (Washington, D.C.: Association of American Geographers, 1983); Women and Geography Study Group of the IBG, *Geography and Gender: An Introduction to Feminist Geography* (London: Hutchinson, 1984); Matrix Collective, *Making Space: Women and the Man Made Environment* (London: Pluto Press, 1984).

17. It was not until the 1970s that this contribution became generally visible, mainly by way of Ester Boserup's work and that of other women researchers.

18. See appendix B.

19. In Bengal ritual plays a large part in defining the female world. Ritual creates and sets "the boundaries of the women's social world" with its own hierarchy, meaning, and ideology (Fruzzetti, 1982, 6).

20. The tontine was originally a "scheme by which the subscribers to a common fund receive each an annuity during his life, which increases as their number is diminished by death, till the last survivor enjoys the whole increase," *(Oxford English Dictionary).* The idea is attributed to Lorenzo Tonti, a banker from Naples who began it in France about 1653.

21. Some time ago a Scandinavian scholar, Gösta Rehm, proposed what he called "specialized drawing rights," a system in which one contributed to a common fund from which one could, from time to time, withdraw funds for whatever use seemed auspicious, such, for example, as occupational retraining, or child rearing, or leisure activities, or whatever (Bernard, 1975). As it might work out for women whose careers are characterized by discontinuities, such a plan might "make available to women in monetary form the help no longer

available to them in the form of unpaid mutual aid from family or friends as a matter of course. The benefits would include income maintenance during years taken out of the working lives of women for motherhood. Services would not be performed directly for them, as in the past, but the wherewithall to buy them would be made available" (273). I was unaware, at the time, of the African cooperative revolving-credit associations, but the resemblance is remarkable. The female-operated associations seem to make it possible for women to perform traditional services for one another and for their families even when, for whatever reason, they are no longer able to provide them personally. Interestingly enough, Robert McNamara, when he was president of the World Bank, commented that "more needs to be known about the dynamics of these organizations so that projects can work through them and enhance, rather than destroy, their potential" (1979, 22).

22. When this association was challenged by resentful unemployed men, "the women rallied the support of a lawyer and the authorities who, the women stated, decided in favor of the cooperative. Evidently the productivity of these women has helped them attain a new bargaining position in the community" (71).

23. The "flow of information" was also provided by rural women to one another. Staudt found in African communities that assistance provided to male farmers was not also being provided for women. But they were, nevertheless, achieving high levels of skill on the basis of "their experience, commitment and socialized responsibilities in farming, as well as of their supportive social networks in which agricultural labor and information are shared" (1978, 452–53). Incidentally, all these busily engaged women were probably not viewed as economically occupied. Bachu reported Mauritania lowest in labor-force participation among women (1983, 9).

24. In Japan, similarly, knowledge of English is an enormous asset. Positions which call for it—secretaries in multinational corporations or flight attendants—are among those with the highest status and prestige. This fact suggests that the global female world may also find English becoming the lingua franca.

25. The competitive pattern may be another aspect of the competition which sometimes occurs among polygamous wives (Smale, 84).

26. The life of the market women in Accra as of 1600 has been described as follows: "The women marketers were very nimble about their business, and so earnest therein, that they goe at least five or six miles every day to the places where they have to goe, and are laden like asses: for at their backes they carrie their children, and on their heads they have a heavy burthen of fruit, or milia, and so goe laden to the market, and there she buyeth fish to carrie home with her, so that oftentimes they come as heavily laden from the market as they went thither. . . . Those women goe seven or eight together, and as they passe along the way they are verie merrie and pleasant, for commonly they sing and make a noise" (Robertson, 1984, 75–76). Robertson comments that "they were obviously serious professional traders even at that time" (76), indeed entrepreneurs of considerable skill.

27. Sometimes women's groups have engaged in cooperative arrangements with men's groups. Thus the members of one fish sellers' union in Takoradi "clubbed together in fours and sixes to raise money to buy fishing nets, which were sold to the fishermen on agreed terms" (Little, 51). Even after the fishermen had repaid the price of the nets, they continued to sell fish to the women who thus became regular customers, assuring themselves of the supply of fish on which their incomes depended, and the fishermen, of a stable market.

28. One school of thought holds that heterosexuality itself is an institu-

tionally imposed regimen, that the most comfortable structure for women would be an all-female one with, perhaps, some provision for male contacts from time to time (Rich, *Signs*, 1980. See also Bernard, *American Family Therapy Newsletter*, 1985).

29. By now it should be clear that we are not discussing the relations between individual males and females—a topic of even greater concern to many—which has also been the subject of human contemplation for millennia. "The way of a man with a maid" was one of the four things that puzzled the author of Proverbs (Prov. 30:18–19), and one that still challenges researchers to this day. Folk culture is replete with love stories and romances, as is also written literature. The other three things that puzzled the author of Proverbs—the way of an eagle in the air; the way of a serpent upon a rock; and the way of a ship in the midst of the sea—have challenged scientists rather than artists.

30. Vashti was the wife of the Persian King Ahasuerus. When she refused to appear nude before his guests, deep in their cups, the King was incensed and asked his advisers what to do about such insubordination. If it got around that she had refused to obey her husband, other women would soon follow suit. She was stripped of her position and laws promulgated that "all the wives shall give to their husbands honour, both to great and small." Orders were sent to all the 127 provinces that "every man should bear rule in his own house and that it be published according to the language of every people" (Esther 1:10–22).

31. Members of this committee: Australia, Barbados, Brazil, Canada, Colombia, Guatemala, Haiti, Republic of Korea, Nepal, Netherlands, New Zealand, Norway, Sierra Leone, Trinidad and Tobago, United Kingdom, the United States. The World Plan of Action was the product of the first of three U.N.-sponsored Conferences for Women held in 1975, 1980, and 1985.

32. The other recommendations were that all organs of the U.N. systems: "(a) give special attention to those development undertakings which integrate women in the development process; (b) incorporate in their . . . plans, programme and sector analyses and programme documents, an impact statement of how such proposed programmes will affect women as participants and beneficiaries. . . ; (c) establish review and appraisal systems, as well as research . . . to provide a means of measuring programs in the integrating of women in the development process."

PART 2—Introduction

1. Of the 79 countries that reported on their success in implementing these recommendations in 1980, the major forms they took were state-affiliated (separatist) kinds, such as women's bureaus, ministries, or advisory committees.

2. "In spite of the recent government emphasis [in Japan] on the improvement of women's status, especially in employment, the record of the Women's and Minors' Bureau in the Labor Ministry has on the whole been less than satisfactory. The bureau's goals for women have been below what the courts have allowed. . . ." (Hanami, 1984, 227).

3. Still, even these small crumbs were welcomed in some parts of the female world. In Zimbabwe, for example, the women were eager to become "as developed as any other women," now that their country was a member of the international community. They needed an authoritative institution or organization to encourage participation in programs offered them (chapter 4).

4. Sometimes such government machinery even had a downgrading effect on issues of the female world "by bureaucratizing initiative and neutralizing grass-

roots efforts" (Staudt, 1980, 21), thus preempting autonomous efforts to improve women's status. One observer concluded that "the mere existence of a women's bureau or commission may make little difference to the women of the country" (Piepmeir, 1980, 26).

5. The separatist-integrationist dilemma showed up also in other U.N. concerns. Should it, for example, deal with *human* rights—integrally—or with status-of-women issues—separately? "In the early years of the U.N., the Economic and Social Council authorized both the Human Rights Commission and the Commission on the Status of Women to receive such materials" along with whatever comments the involved governments might wish to add. As the number and complexity of the issues grew, "it was suggested that the communications relating to women should be transferred to the Human Rights Commission machinery," a sure prescription for neglect of female issues. The separatist-integrationist issue remains. "Since 1970, the discussion has continued as to whether all communications should go to the Human Rights Commission or whether the Commission on the Status of Women should develop procedures for handling those within its area of concern" (Resolutions and Decisions, First U.N. Regular Session, 1982, 34).

6. But the United States Mission to the United Nations, in a paper on its views on the 1985 conference, slightly changed the focus. The emphasis was on integrating women's concerns or issues into "national planning, development, and government policies in all areas" to assure that they were "not segregated from those of the population at large." No separatism under the guise of integration. The implication seemed to be that integrating women's issues into the national agenda would lead to integrating women themselves into the decision-making bodies, not the other way round.

7. One of the early classical studies of individual, as distinguished from institutional, modernization saw it in terms of fostering the qualities needed for operating a factory (Inkeles and Smtih, 1974, 18). The goal was an informed citizen with a marked sense of personal efficacy, independent of traditional influences in decision making, autonomous, ready for new ideas, open-minded, and intellectually flexible (290). Development was viewed as a process of transforming the nature of man (289). An earlier study by Daniel Lerner (1958) painted a vivid picture of the impact on families as rural young men went to cities to work. Although the Inkeles-Smith study, based on 6,000 men in Argentina, Chile, India, Israel, Nigeria, and Bangladesh, did not include women, the authors felt the same processes as those among men would be found among them.

8. Not all researchers accepted this downbeat admission of failure. Kurt Finsterbusch challenged the charge of ignorance—of the factors that made for success of projects—on the part of theorists and policy makers. They were known; they were: "(1) adequate factors of production, (2) appropriate public involvement, (3) a conducive local context, (4) a conducive macro context, and (5) demand for the output (production) of the project." What was lacking was knowledge of "how to combine all of the needed factors together in an actual third world situation" (1983). On the basis of his analysis of 59 variables in 44 projects, he found 22 he could score on their contribution to success. "The main factor which differentiates between successful and unsuccessful projects is the desirability of the goods or services provided by the project. . . . The next most important factor . . . is the compatibility of the macro context to the project. . . . The third factor . . . is administrative effectiveness. . . . The final factor which is critical to project success is maintenance of the facilities." The point of view

here is closer to that of modernization than of development. There is no reference to the "human capital" aspect of successful modernization.

9. Either integrationism or separatism—the "ism" implying political overtones—might be aggressive, that is, imposed on others or defensive, protective against being swallowed up or ejected.

10. It has, in fact, been noted that power relations between men and women are the model for power relationships on any stage (Lipman-Blumen, 1984).

Chapter 3. Separatism and Integrationism

1. The manual warned also about the mental-health hazards of the children of rural-urban migrants, hazards that came in time to be well documented. See appendix A on daughters of Turkish "guest workers" in West Germany.

2. In 1974, for example, the so-called Percy amendment to the 1961 U.S. law establishing the Agency for International Development (AID) specified that a certain part of the funds be made available for women, and an Office for Women in Development (WID) was established. The World Bank followed suit, establishing the post of Adviser on Women in 1977 "to monitor and advise on the effects its projects were having and would have on the future status of women" (McNamara, 1979, iii). A year later an International Women's Tribune Center, IWIC, was set up under United Nations auspices to respond to requests for technical assistance and training for women in developing countries, to collect and disseminate practical information (chapter 9).

3. As of 1964, ten pages, single-spaced, were needed to index the Overseas Programs of Private Non-Profit American Organizations in the United States alone (Report no. 3, 1965). Most of these were not, of course, women's groups or groups targeting their programs on women; but the size of the list indicates that there must have been a sizeable number of them. The Overseas Education Fund, for example, in 1981 was supporting women's projects in 17 countries including: job training; small enterprise development; market cooperative/vocational training; training in management and small-business skills; legal education/reform/services; food processing; and organizational development. *The Non-Formal Exchange*, published by the International Studies in Education of Michigan State University, in its 19th issue (1980) listed 61 projects, of which 17 or 24 percent, were directed to girls or women.

4. In the case of street foods, largely in the hands of women, planners tended to eliminate them, and Irene Tinker mounted a salvaging project to persuade planners of their importance; she had also to overcome mythical assumptions about the insignificance of women's contribution to modern agriculture (Equity Policy Center, December 1983).

5. Veronica Elliott and Victoria Sorsby dealt with 43 projects (1979) in their "Investigation into Evaluations of Projects Designed to Benefit Women."

6. By 1984, several departments of FAO had prepared guidelines and checklists to help formulating, monitoring, and evaluating projects (Hosken, 1984, 5), thus beginning to facilitate the evaluating process.

7. Much of the Finsterbusch study referred to in the introduction to part II would fall into this male-oriented category. It did not examine gender differences in outcome.

8. See, for example, the case of the Ibo and Kom women as described by Wipper, above in chapter 2.

9. "It is one of the small 'revolutions' taking place in Saudi Arabia that are beginning, slowly, to change the role of women, and it is the avenue of change

that is most likely to have an across-the-board impact on their lives. This is because these separate but equal facilities, also by law, must be run by women only. So there are now a host of new training courses for future women bankers. Saudi women are also likely to become a 'closet' investment group—ironically, because of Islamic restrictions on hoarding or earning interest from money" (Wright, 1981). Such banks tend to become "women's centers" which serve to break down the isolation many women feel. They often 'come in groups and stay for an hour or longer, drinking coffee and chatting. This is the only place outside the privacy of homes or schools they can completely unveil." True, the activities engaged in—parties, dinners, and exhibits of children's artwork—do not suggest much growth, still merely seeing trained women serving as bankers cannot help having some impact.

10. In this system, "women elders judged other women in women's courts, and women formally represented other women in local and distant barazas (community meetings). Women elders infringed on the territory of male judicial elders, and women's mobility was alleged to increase prostitution" (Staudt, 30).

11. The "brother" study by Finsterbusch used degree of success in achieving goals as a criterion for evaluation. He found that almost half of the 44 cases attained their goals; almost as many, showed overall effectiveness. Four variables (desirability, schedule, centralization, and market factors) explained most of the differences in goal attainment, and five variables (desirability, schedule, continuous program, market factors, and coordination) explained differences in overall effectiveness. Among the projects he studied were: rural roads, irrigation, potable water, agricultural research, education, rural electrification, among others. Most of them called for a considerable amount of facility construction so that trained manpower was among the contributions made. "Few involved significant social costs. . . . Most fit the local and macro contexts well." Social relationships, including those of women or those between the male and female worlds, were not changed.

12. It would be diversionary to pursue further the question of acceptability of change, but at least a bow in that direction may be in order here. In another place I have contrasted the Point Four programs which saw change as desirable and the anthropological point of view which warned against such change: "The anthropological paradigm directed attention to stability. It led to a defensive rather than an aggressive stance, to a protective rather than a stimulating approach toward simple communities. Do not lay profane hands on them; approach change very gingerly, even fearfully. . . . A culture is an integrated and, by implication, a fragile whole. You can't just change any part of it without disrupting the whole. It has to be sheltered. Therefore, go slow! Beware of introducing anything new; it may have wholly unforeseen—and disastrous—consequences" (Bernard, 1973, 166–67).

13. Income/cost of living; credit; land and water; technology; other assets/debts.

14. Food, water, fuel; housing; environmental quality; medical care; personal safety; rest and leisure. The last-named, rest and leisure, was becoming a global issue in the female world as the double work load became widespread with industrialization.

15. A family planning project that required the husband's consent for his wife's sterilization or abortion, for example (74).

16. As they did at U.N. Conferences for women in 1975, 1980, and 1985 (chapter 10).

17. Both of these success stories are taken from a series of pamphlets "de-

veloped to meet requests from all over the world for information about innovative and practical program ideas developed by and for low income women. The pamphlets are designed as a means to share information and spark new projects based on the positive experiences of women who are working to help themselves and other women improve their economic status. The projects . . . have been selected because they provide women with a cash income, involve women in decision-making as well as earning, are based on sound economic criteria, and are working successfully to overcome obstacles commonly encountered. The reports are not meant to be prescriptive, since every development effort will face somewhat different problems and resources. Rather, they have been written to describe the history of an idea and its implementation in the hope that the lessons learned can be useful in a variety of settings. They are also being written to bring to the attention of those in decision-making positions the fact that income generating projects for and by women are viable and have important roles to play in development" (*Seeds*, no. 6, 1983). The Seeds series is funded by the Carnegie Corporation, the Ford Foundation, Oxfam-America, the Population Council, the Rockefeller Foundation, and the Women-in-Development Office of the U.S. Agency for International Development.

18. The attention of potential donors and of government agencies was attracted by a local ministry of agriculture. The American Friends Service Committee and a French quasi-governmental organization, Femmes et Development, helped the women become established and the U.N. Voluntary Fund supplied start-off capital (Caughman and Thiam, 1982, 18).

19. "The majority of the members, now limited to fifty, are married women over 30 years old; 64 percent of their marriages are polygamous with household duties shared among one to three co-wives. Only eight of the members have attended primary school and none completed their studies; two members speak some French, the national language" (6).

20. There was so little appreciation of the contribution of these small vending operations, often on the street, that developers with large projects on their mind sometimes argued for their elimination.

21. Extra earnings were spent on: food, clothing, savings, avoidance of moneylenders, household durables, medicines, improved male education, household repair, improved female education, jewelry (as a form of saving) (11).

Chapter 4—Relations of the Two Worlds

1. It was even alleged that when the 200,000 Portuguese colonists left Mozambique in 1975 "they took everything they could carry, including their money, possessions and expertise. Much of what they could not carry, they destroyed—industrial equipment was sabotaged, phones ripped out, tractors driven into the sea, even light bulbs smashed. They left behind twelve university graduates in a nation of more than 19 million people" (Frankel, 1985).

2. The maps show how independent states were carved out of colonial empires at the end of World War II. "It was not an easy or neat process. Ethnic groups were cleaved into fragments. . . . Others were combined with disparate neighbors. . . . At first Africans paid little attention to the new lines, which seemed to have everything to do with European rivalries and little to do with them. But gradually the paper lines on the map became real borders, not only to the Europeans but to the Africans themselves. Africa's acquiescence became part of its general acceptance of the standards, mores and ideas of the Europeans who sought to rule it. One of the great issues for African intellectuals

during the independence movements following World War II was whether to accede to those borders, draw new ones or have none at all. The movement for a United States of Africa had strong intellectual and emotional force behind it. But that idealism was undermined and ultimately overruled by the stronger reality of power politics and the ambitions of those who inherited governments from the Europeans. In the end, the Organization of African Unity, designed to bring Africans together, became a tragi-comic monument to their enduring separation. . . . The concept of nationhood is at best only marginally understood. . . . Lacking a George Washington . . . Africa has become atomized into smaller, conflicting groups. People identify themselves by tribe, ideology, profession, religion or economic class, seldom by nation. . . . Africans . . . tend to blame their problems on European colonialism. Westerners, on the other hand, tend to treat the continent as a blank slate . . . whose problems can be laid at the feet of corrupt African leaders and misplaced priorities. . . Both, of course, are right, and both are wrong, but the Westerners, who during the last three decades have been so free with their advice and criticism of the new Africa, should not forget that it was their ancestors who designed, constructed, and launched the continent's modern history 100 years ago in Berlin" (Glenn Frankel, *Washington Post*, 6 January 1985). This history impacted on the female world, of course, as well as on the male.

3. The papers given at this session dealt with the United States (Basch); Italy (Ergas); and Britain (Breeley).

4. Azania (Southern Africa), Bangladesh, China, India, Nicaragua, Yugoslavia, and Zimbabwe.

5. Women's national leftist groups were formed in Cuba, Mozambique, Eritrea, Nicaragua, El Salvador, Namibia, Zimbabwe, Oman, the Philippines, Haiti, Palestine, India, Guinea-Bissau, Cape Verde, Vietnam, Kampuchea, Uruguay, Colombia, Iran. . . . In 1980 in Nicaragua, the women's group had 17,000 members in more than a dozen towns (*Isis*, no. 19, 1981, "Women in National Liberation Movements.") There was also a Women's Union in Vietnam and a Revolutionary Women's Association in Kampuchea (*Quaker Service Bulletin*, vol. 65, No. 1, winter, 1984).

6. The liberation movements not only taught women a vocabulary to understand their oppression but also educated and trained them for active participation. With the aid of the United Nations, recommendations were made for "training to integrate women into leadership and support positions within the national liberation movements," to include: "the creation of a women's task force within each relevant agency of the United Nations system (in particular, UNESCO, ILO, WHO, FAO, UNICEF) which would include representatives of the liberation movements, preferably from the women's sections." The curriculum for this training was to include: "training courses in various leadership and communication skills, seminars focusing on political education, workshops on the preparation, implementation and evaluation of assistance programmes, and study tours to several independent African nations to learn about the experiences of other women's organizations and of national bodies for the integration of women in development." And, perhaps more to the point, they were to be trained "to undertake research and run workshops on women's roles and needs in the liberation struggle and the development process, to set up research and documentation units and establish newsletters" (Measures of Assistance for Women in Southern Africa, item 7(b) of the provisional agenda for the U.N.-sponsored Decade-for-Women conferences, 1980. A/Conf. 94/6).

7. A caveat is in order. The discussion here depends heavily on the printed

words of women in the Third World where, as we saw in chapter 1, educated women, even barely literate women, represent an exceptional elite. They do not necessarily reflect the thinking of the urban women we have met at market stalls or the rural women carrying firewood home on their backs. Eloquent as many of them are, their words probably reach only a small part of the women even in their native lands. This does not, of course, detract from their significance.

8. Not all women were ready. Peasant women in the earliest meetings "responded to the new idea of common interests and new rights with a certain amount of scepticism. They argued that it would be wonderful if women were the equals of men, but what chance did they have if from ancient times till now 'man has been the heaven and women the earth.' One of the leaders . . . noted that in these early years the fight to conquer the idea that women knew nothing but household affairs was particularly difficult" (Croll, 1982, 53).

9. The older women, expectably, did not agree. "Men and women are born different. A person is . . . either a man or a woman" and it just can't be helped (56). Mao Ze Dung himself had put it succinctly: both men and women held up the sky, but the part held up by women was heavier. So much for equality.

10. The Cultural Revolution of the 50s and 60s took its toll of women's groups as well as of other groups but when it was over the old pattern of women's groups reappeared. The All-China Women's Federation, with a fairly wide swath of autonomy, was looking after the interests of women nationally, regionally, and locally, under the leadership of a cadre of remarkable women, one of whom, vice-mayor of Beijing and dean at the university, had been trained at the University of California, Berkeley.

11. Controversies dealing with the relative weight to assign to class, race, gender in explaining female oppression still linger on among feminist theorists. In the nineteenth century there had been numerous "particularistic" theories in sociology—geographic, psychological, economic, among others—all of them fruitless as C. H. Cooley pointed out (1909). Societies were complex and required what he called organic rather than particularistic explanations. "The organic view of history . . . denies that any factor or factors are more ultimate than others. . . . You must see the whole or you do not truly see anything" (255). "Oppression" is also organic, not explainable by particularistic theories, biological, economic, psychological, or even cultural.

12. The name Azania included most of southern Africa, namely: Namibia, Angola, Mozambique, and Zimbabwe, as well as South Africa. It was used in the most revolutionary group, the Pan Africanist Congress, whose activities leaned largely against South Africa.

13. In 1956 FSAW organized a massive demonstration in Pretoria in protest against the so-called pass laws now being extended to include women as well as, until then, only men. The date of that march later became National Women's Day in South Africa (67). The organization, along with other liberation groups, was banned in 1956.

14. In 1980, Dr. Sophia McDowell asked working women in the People's Republic of China what they most wanted for themselves at that time. A frequent reply was "to serve the people." Upon probing, further replies took the form of "helping to achieve the nation's four modernizations—agriculture, industry, national defense, and science/technology." Only after considerable time and probing were urgencies of a more personal nature mentioned, such as "a refrigerator," and even then with a patriotic rationale: "so I wouldn't have to go shopping every day and therefore would have more time for serving the people" (unpublished study).

15. Other interests of these groups included workshops for middle-class women, self-help programs for women in poor neighborhoods, a demonstration against the Miss Universe Pageant. Without leftist male support they were limited in resources, one of the penalities for rejecting the male priority argument.

16. The female illiteracy rates for Algeria were (in percent): for females 15 years and older: 1970, 88.5; 1980, 70.9. For females 15 to 19: 1970, 55.8; 1975, 33.4; 1980, 24.3 (U.N. Statistical Abstract, item 8[b] of the Provisional Agenda for the World Conference of the U.N. Decade for Women, 1978, table 14. Prepared by Shirley Nuss).

17. In 1984, thirty years after the revolution, a review of the Algerian scene mentioned amnesty for four guerillas who had defected, removal of requirement of an exit visa to leave the country, sale to private owners of houses and farms seized from the French, encouragement of enterprise, a more moderate foreign policy, encouragement of technical training. No mention was made of improvement in the status of women (Paul Lewis, "Algeria After 30 Years," *Washington Post*, 31 Oct. 1984).

18. In Asian countries the female literacy rate in 15 Muslim countries ranged from 3.7 percent (Afghanistan) to 57.9 (Lebanon); in 19-non-Muslim countries, from 5.0 (Nepal) to 83.3 (Israel) (Bachu, 1983, 9).

19. One is reminded of advertisements which sell automobiles by way of pictures of beautiful women.

20. This author charged complicity between leftist journalists and political leaders which she illustrated with the case of the Saharan liberation movement. She charged that the journalists reported whatever the political leaders told them to. "Like media stories decades earlier, the French reports give a glowing account of the developing role of women in the Sahara. 'A New Saharan woman is being born' reads the caption beneath a photo showing a group of women participating in literacy classes. 'The Saharan woman, unlike Maghreb (North African) women, is emancipated'" (21). Women were exploited as valuable propaganda resources, as symbols for the movement. The journalists reported that Saharan women were not veiled, that there was no polygamy, that parental control of marital choice was no longer enforced. The author then asks if it is really necessary "for traditional society to be free from any accusation of the oppression of women even before the liberation struggle?" (21).

21. Langston Hughes, a distinguished U.S. black poet, wrote a famous poem in which he asked, "What happens to a dream deferred?" and answered with a series of questions, incuding "Does it dry up like a raisin in the sun?" and ended with "Or does it explode?" No doubt the dreams of equitable integration went through many such phases.

22. Not all parts of the female world accepted the male world's priorities. Some women marched to a different drummer. Thus, although Aida Yafai, of South Yemen, for example, wanted to be equal in rights, she did not want "to be equal if men are trapped in underdeveloped thoughts. In an underdeveloped society men have underdeveloped ideas and we don't want equality in this" (1977, 6). Such backward social ideas had to be fought with male help, not supported. In Latin America there were also questions being raised. In 1981 the women members of the Trotskyist Workers Revolutionary Party broke away from the Party and organized the Women's Autonomous Group (Fuller, 1983, iv). There were thus two groups: (1) one was loyal to the parties that supported, but at the same time controlled, them; (2) the other was autonomous but dependent on the support of foreign women (chapter 3).

Chapter 5—Cases in Point

1. The female literacy rate in Chile was 89 percent in 1970 (Baum, U.S. Census Bureau, *World Population, 1983*, p. 89).
2. The female literacy rate in Zimbabwe was 50 percent in 1970, when it was still Rhodesia (Handbook, 135).
3. Quotations from the minister and deputy minister, respectively, of Community Development—Teuri Ropa Nhongo and Dr. Naomi Nhiwatisa—are from interviews by Joellen Lambiotte of the Boston Coalition for the Liberation of Southern Africa, 1981, in Zimbabwe. (*Resistance, War and Liberation: Women of Southern Africa*. New York: Women's International Resource Exchange, n.d.).
4. The data about Tendi Ndlovu are from an interview by Casey Kelso in Harare, Zimbabwe, January 1982, published as "Too Liberated?" in *Connexions*, no. 11, winter, 1984.
5. The data on the survey are from: "We Carry a Heavy Load": Rural Women in Zimbabwe Speak Out, a report of a survey carried out by the Zimbabwe Women's Bureau, published in *Resistance, War and Liberation: Women of Southern Africa*. New York: Women's International Resource Exchange, n.d.
6. The story is told about the difficulty men in liberation movements had confronting changes in the military roles of women. One woman had achieved high status in the guerrilla organization because of her extraordinary talents. As an officer she was accorded the amenities and courtesies due her position. But on one occasion, at a billet, a subordinate male was given the one available chair to sit on. She sat on the floor. This was a nonmilitary context, and civilian protocol prevailed.
7. Much of the background data of the interviews with former combatants was compiled from *Outwrite*, an English feminist monthly for October 1983. Interview and further information were submitted by Casey Kelso and Cara Lise Metz for *Connexions*, no. 11, 1984. The *Outwrite* data included excerpts from *Moto*, a Zimbabwean periodical.
8. Lobolo was a custom which was susceptible to serious exploitation. It was a marriage dowry which the bride was obliged to bring with her to the marriage. Families could demand exhorbitant amounts; in some parts of the world, in fact, use it as a form of blackmail. In India it was alleged as late as the 1980s that demands could be continued long after marriage and if not met the bride might be done away with.
9. A U.S. columnist, Jack Anderson, early in 1984 quoted a political rival of Mugabe, Ndabaningi Sithole to the effect that Zimbabwe was becoming an authoritarian state, that opponents were being jailed, the press muzzled, the population cowed by special military units and members of a Youth Brigade of 14- to 18-year olds (*Washington Post*, 1984). The raids against women in the Clean Up Operation may have been part of this trend, if the charges of a political rival may be taken as valid.
10. In Cape Verde also, as in Zimbabwe, although the president, Aristides Pereira, professed equality, he recognized the existing inequality in pay between the sexes. He intended to "stop this as soon as possible," but he had "to move slowly . . . or face a male revolt. The men, the farmers, have a strong resistance to women being paid the same as them and say it is not possible. We are trying to gradually diminish the difference and convince the men that it is not right. Our aim is to facilitate and support the women's equal rights struggle" but it would take time (Dash, 1981).
11. The illiteracy rates were (in percent): for women 15 years and over: 1970, 87.4; 1980, 71.6; projected for 1990 (projected), 52.0. For women 15 to 19: 1970,

77.7; 1975, 48.5; 1980, 39.0; 1985 (projected), 23.7 (Statistical Abstract, item 8[b] of the Provisional Agenda for the World Conference of the U.N. Decade for Women, 1978, table 14. Prepared by Shirley Nuss).

12. Nineteen percent of the 15-19-year olds, 53 percent of the 20-24 year-olds, and 16 percent of the 25 to 44-year olds.

13. The veil revealed their conflicts. They often wore it as they left home but discarded it when they came to work.

14. Much of the quoted material in these pages is from *Women & Struggle in Iran*, (no. 1, March 1982), a publication of the Women's Commission of the Iranian Students Association in the United States. The issue quoted here was one "Celebrating International Women's Day." The articles were not signed, probably as a protection against possible retaliation. Comments and suggestions were solicited. The address given was: ISA, P.O. Box 5642, Chicago, Ill. 60680.

15. The League of Iranian Women were recruited by the National Front; the National Union of Women, by the Union of the Left; the Democratic Union of Iranian Women, by the Tudeh Party (the Iranian Communist Party); and separate groups, by the Maoists (Tabari, 1980, 12). These women's groups, like so many women's groups elsewhere, were coopted: "they could not—would not—base their policies and outlook upon the reality of women's situation in Iran, and the demands arising from such a reality. Rather, they followed the changing policies and 'needs' of the parent [male] organizations" (Az, 1980, 5).

16. It was not only revolutionary groups that used the promissory note to attract followers. So did reactionary groups. Here, for example, were Khomeini's promises in 1978: "Women are free in the realm of education as well as in the professions, just as men are. Shiism . . . not only doesn't exclude women from social life, but it elevates them to a platform where they belong. Islam raises the level of women in society so that they might regain their human dignity, not be objectified, and can assume responsibilities in the structure of the Islamic government in accordance with such a development. Islam has considered women's rights to be higher than men's. Women have the right to vote and this is a right which is higher than women's rights in the West. Our women have the right to vote and to be elected. They are free in all aspects of their lives and they can freely choose most areas of employment. We promise you that in the Islamic government every person will be free and will achieve his/her rights (KAR International, no. 8, September 1981; present citation; *Women & Struggle in Iran*, 1982).

17. Qabus bin Said is described by two U.S. journalists as "the model of a modern, enlightened Arab leader. Educated at Sandhurst, the British military college, he brought back western ideas. . . . and began laboriously bringing his 900,000 countrymen into the 20th century" (Jack Anderson and Dale Van Atta, 1985).

18. The data on Oman on the current scene from a government publication, *Oman, 1983*, issued by the Ministry of Information. The probable bias of this source is hereby acknowledged.

19. The World Bank reports the proportion of primary-school-age females in school as 57 percent in 1981 (1984, 267).

20. A reviewer of a book on women in Oman noted that in the community studied, Sohar, "the image which emerges most forcefully from this study is of women who are secure and not unhappy with themselves and their lives. The silent communication which occurs among the women cannot be construed to be the silence of indifference or insecurity. It is rather the quietude born out of the mutual respect for and the profound understanding women have for each

other and their relationships" (*National Forum*, Summer, 1984, 45). The reviewer was Ann B. Radwan and the author of the book was Unni Wikan. The title of the book was *Behind the Veil in Arabia: Women in Oman*. (Baltimore: Johns Hopkins Press, 1982).

21. In the meanwhile she was resorting to the courts by way of direct action. She cited Article 29 of the Constitution which stated that all Kuwaitis were "equal in human dignity, public rights and duties before the law without distinction as to sex, origin, language or religion." "Until recently, however," Ottaway comments, "the problem was how to make a legal issue out of this. . . . This was solved . . . when she and other like-minded women stormed the voting registration offices at police stations in the capital's 25 electoral districts. All were forbidden to register by confused and embarrassed officers. This allowed them to challenge on legal grounds Article 1 of the voting law, which says only men have the right to participate in parliamentary elections" (Ottaway, 1984). The Qattami's Women's Society is currently preparing to take the case to the constitutional Supreme Court, supported by volunteers from the Lawyers' Society. Success was not certain but the women were confident. God willing, Qattami predicted that Kuwaiti women would be on the registration lists by 1989. Incidentally Qattami's appeal to the Supreme Court illustrates the value, though often also the futility, of merely having the right words on the books. Actually, Lichtenstein, in Europe, beat Kuwait. It granted women the vote in 1984.

22. In 1982 a new constitution was adopted allowing the Coloured and Indian populations to participate in a tricameral parliament along with whites. Coloured, Indian, and white South African women began to attend international conferences on women. Little by little, ties were being woven, mitigating the isolation South Africans had been subjected to because of the racial policies of their government. In a way, they had a point. Governments everywhere were caught in the web of the world economic system, at the mercy of cross currents of world markets for their products, world exchange rates, world credit resources, world debt structures, oil gluts, superpower maneuvers, as well as weapon making—an all-but-universal male world preoccupation—and the traffic in arms which was making them available to almost any insurrectionary group anywhere.

23. In the West language itself was being attacked as the very armory of male ideology. Not only verbal but also body language was being analyzed for its male bias (chapter 3).

24. Even, if necessary, against considerable odds. In Nicaragua, for example, husbands sometimes objected to their wives' taking part in public meetings. "My husband gave me an ultimatum—I give you two months to sort out the situation" (Mendoza, 8). She did not want to leave her husband. She was thinking of taking him along to meetings in the hope that he would then "be able to understand, and consequently . . . release his ideas on the role of women." There was heavy resistance still to be overcome.

Chapter 6—The Feminist Enlightenment

1. The essential differences between the feminism taught by the leftist movements and the feminism developing in the West was that the leftist version was a male version, based on Marxian analyses, whereas that emerging in the West was autonomous, based on female experience, not something imposed from the outside. The feminism in the West gave as much emphasis to the reproductive as to the productive aspects of the female world.

2. Robert Flint, a distinguished nineteenth-century historian, does not brush over the defects of the French Enlightenment, but he notes also many of its positive traits. It was, he tells us, eager for action, bent on proselytizing, ambitious to reform, "militant and aggressive, ethically, practically, and religiously," "essentially positive, honourably and nobly positive," with strength drawn from its "positive ethical and political convictions; from its faith in justice, toleration, liberty, fraternity, the sovereignty of the people, the rights of man" (1894, 242). Many of these qualities have also characterized the Feminist Enlightenment. Flint does not believe that the French Enlightenment caused the French Revolution. Neither can we say that the Feminist Enlightenment caused the feminist revolution. As Flint makes clear, both the French Enlightenment and the French Revolution resulted from the same process of societal restructuring. The emphasis here is on raised consciousness rather than on the activism that is played up. Even those who rejected the very idea of feminism had to become aware of it, if only to justify their rejection. They had to become at least marginally enlightened about the female world. They had at least to see it. It might be noted that even confirmed feminists had their minds enlightened by the knowledge created by the Feminist Enlightenment. It was not necessarily always welcome knowledge.

3. They were: the Citizens' Advisory Council on the Status of Women (1963–77; the National Commission on Observance of International Women's Year (1975–76); the National Advisory Committee for Women (1978–79); the President's Advisory Committee for Women (1979–80).

4. As a matter of fact the female world as a distinct entity was not present in the body of human knowledge. Most societies were seen from a male perspective and from that point of view the female world was a (usually inferior) part of the male world. The male world specified the dimensions and character of the two worlds. Individual women might grumble about their lot, resent injustice, resist control, but few challenged the modus vivendi of the two worlds.

5. For a discussion of some of the fault lines among women in the United States, see Bernard, *The Female World* (1981).

6. The numbers of these women were small in view of their influence. Feminism did not attract many women in the United States in the early years of its renaissance. A study of 2,200 women and men in 1972 and 1976, and 214 women in 1979, found that only a third of the women in 1972 identified with women and did not themselves feel oppressed; only a third favored the women's liberation movement. During the 70s, however, there was a change. By 1979, more than half of the U.S. women favored the women's liberation movement. And by that time, more than half acknowledged discrimination against women. Employed, educated, unmarried, and politically active women were more likely to show group consciousness (Gurin, 1982).

7. The "bra burning" had, as a matter of fact, never taken place, but it became a powerful invective to use against the women. It arose when bra burning was threatened at a beauty contest as a symbolic gesture against the reduction of women to sex objects and thus the reduction of their status as whole human beings.

8. This had not always been the case. In the nineteenth century the women's rights movement had not been above using the argument that constitutional grounds for the female suffrage were needed to counteract the 14th Amendment granting suffrage to Negroes.

9. Even in South Africa, where racism was built into the whole society, there were some feminists who, as such, attempted to overcome it where they could (Appendix C).

10. One young feminist who later became a successful novelist, Rita Mae Brown, showed how insulting this ploy was. "Middle class women parody our speech to prove how they are no longer middle class. This is as unforgiveable as a white person putting on a broad black 'accent'" (Brown, 1974, 21). A better solution, she added, was to share their privileges, a step toward upward mobility. "If you have good clothes . . . give us some of your clothes."

11. One lower-class woman came to understand racism in terms of class. "It was only when I started to put my racism in a broader political context that I was really able to [begin] to deal with it. It didn't take political genius to see the similarity between the way my family was treated in the context of a middle class village and the way Blacks were treated in the context of the whole white system" (Myron, 1974, 39).

12. "They can intellectualize, politicize, accuse, abuse, and contribute money in order to not deal with it. Even if they admit that class exists, they are not likely to admit that their behavior is a product of it. They will go through every painful detail of their lives to prove to me or another working class woman that they really didn't have any privilege, that their family was exceptional, that they actually did have an uncle who worked in a factory. To ease anyone's guilt is not the point of talking about class. Some women still think that because they have a working class friend they have licked the class problem. One of the most horrifying responses in the women's movement today is that of the 'political' woman who actually goes out and works in a factory so she can look at the working class women and talk to them and maybe drop a little socialism now and then. You don't get rid of oppression just by merely recognizing it. This patronization is outrageous and every woman in the place is sure to smell the stench a mile off" (40). This was enlightenment of a painful kind.

13. Although many of these women were Marxian in orientation, the approach was not so much in terms of global abstractions as in terms of day-by-day realities. It was the "personal" in the equation "the personal is political" that they saw, hoping to avoid the fallacy of believing in abstractions rather than in realities like daily put-downs in personal relations.

14. Whether the U.S. feminists actually were all middle-class has been challenged. A 1976 study in a Massachusetts town on the opinions of working-class women toward women's liberation found, for example, that most were not opposed to it (Ferree, 1976). So why, the author asks, "have so many non-systematic observers of the women's movement and the working class . . . so grossly underestimated the level of sympathy and support to be found there?" And she suggests an answer: "One possible cause might be found in simple elitist bias; people with college education, male or female, seem to think that a college education, is necessary to enable one to understand one's oppression and take the broader view, seeing political solutions to personally experienced problems. . . . But in this case, this answer alone may not be sufficient. Movement activities are, indisputably, overwhelmingly upper-middle class and the tendency to see support as concentrated there as well may be due to a perceptual trick in our social vision. The activist is seen as a representative of a social group, both in articulating its demands and reflecting the defining elements of its social composition. Thus it is thought more of an anomaly to find a labor leader who never worked in a factory than to meet a black leader who is a lawyer, since occupation is thought to define the former group but not the latter. Though the occupational backgrounds of black leaders do not reflect the occupational distribution of blacks in general, this is thought not to matter, as race rather than class is the dominant cleavage. It is still not customary to see sex as a major social cleavage; when a feminist speaks out she is seen as white and

middle class before she is seen as a woman speaking for other women. It may be necessary to see poor women, black women, working class wives and mothers speaking out and saying the same thing before the activist is accepted as their spokeswoman as well. Such mobilization is difficult, because the poorer and less educated are unlikely to possess the time, skills and other resources needed to be active" (Ferree). But since then there has, in fact, been a considerable amount of activism by working women as well as by black women in organizing movements. The author concludes with the comment that "in the next few years we may come to wonder how we could ever have doubted the extent and power of working class feminism."

15. There were ironies in the image of U.S. feminists as neocolonialists. The United States had had only a brief brush with colonialism, in the Philippines at the turn of the century, and it had been definitively rejected soon thereafter.

16. It was once said of a U.S. politician that one had to know him to dislike him.

17. In some cases expression of hostilities—"fights"—may have served a therapeutic function. The participants were free to express their frustrations, their resentments, aware that they could do so without fear of retribution: they were among accepting others if not necessarily among friends. There were not many places where there was such freedom for protesting women.

18. See appendix B.

19. Another issue with centrifugal force within the female world, not yet widely enough researched to offer a global picture, is lesbianism. In the United States it emerged as an issue only about two decades ago and for a while promised to create an unbridgeable cleft in the women's movement.

20. For a discussion especially of opposing nationalistic interests see appendix C.

21. Some of the dissatisfaction of Third-World women with many international feminist meetings and gatherings resulted from different conceptions of what such meetings were all about. Were they arenas where views could be attacked and defended, where one side won and another lost, where hostilities could be expressed? Or were they cold, research-based statements that could be judged only on the basis of technical research criteria? If the first, the status impediment could be felt as intolerable, oppressive. If the second, the result would be felt as useless, meaningless. At one international meeting there was a session featuring "U.S. academic" research papers that could just as well have taken place at a meeting on a U.S. campus, all the papers reflecting high-tech research methods, interpreted by esoteric "tests of significance," with no mention of relevance of either the data or the interpretation for the female world anywhere. A large part of the audience walked out.

22. A study of women missionaries to China at the turn of the century notes that "the experience of authority transformed self-expectations," and they "came to discover inner certainties to match their circumstances. . . . They developed colonial temperaments to accord with their colonial status" (Hunter, 1984, 265).

23. Although the early contacts among women were based on a wide status disparity, it is hard to believe that these women experienced no shared commonalities. Did the lady never send clothes or gifts to the servant's newborn infant? Or never depend on the native woman's care of her own? Sixty years ago, as a guest in the homes of missionaries in Buenos Aires, I did observe close ties between mistress and maid.

24. As early as the 1960's research support was becoming available from U.S. foundations and other sources. The Ford Foundation, for example, funded a

center for research on a variety of women-related subjects, including peasant women in India, in Bangladesh, in Sicily. In 1976 an international Center for Research on Women was established. The next year a U.N.-sponsored Asian and Pacific Centre for Women and Development was established to "disseminate information about women's action and research groups" by way of an Asian Women's Research and Action Network" (Women in Action, 6). One of its projects dealt with the portrayal of women in the media in Asia and the Pacific areas. At the 1983 Second Latin American and Caribbean Feminist Meeting in Lima, one of the 21 workshops was devoted to "Feminist Research," at which the participants deplored the lack of the use of research by governments, unions, or even by feminists in formulating demands. Early in 1984, Asian women researchers met at the AWCWD with plans to promote regional meetings and publish special country reports to support work of grassroot organizations. And in the same year the Indian Association for Women's Studies organized its Second National Women's Studies Conference in Kerala on the theme of Gender Justice, at which more than 500 researchers and activists from Sri Lanka, Nepal, and Bangladesh participated. Feminist researchers were truly en marche.

Chapter 7—"Glad to Meet You"

1. Examples of these contacts are: cultural exchanges and institutes for summer study like the International Institute of Women's Studies on Mount Scopus campus of Hebrew University, where students may participate in internships with feminist or Kibbutzim or Arab women in Israel (Hughes, 1983); or an Aegean Women's Studies Institute session on the island of Lesbos, where students meet with Greek scholars, students, professionals, artists, politicians, and activists of one kind or another (ibid.); or Israel's Mount Carmel International Training Centre for Community Development, which trains community leaders in developing countries, many of whom are women. There are also fellowships in the West for foreign study open to women as well as to men. The bulletin boards of campuses all over the United States are covered with announcements of such international meetings.

2. Isis-Wicce was launched in 1983 to make it possible "for women activists to have more direct contact with each other" (1983, 5). It grew out is Isis Women's International Information and Communication Service (1974–83).

3. In 1983 there were 12 women scholarship recipients from eight countries (Brazil, Hong Kong, India, Israel, Kenya, Mauritius, the Philippines, and Switzerland) who were placed in nine countries (Costa Rica, India, Israel, Italy, Mauritius, Switzerland, and the United States). In 1984 there were 17 women from 14 countries. The theme was "Communication" and, for 1985, "Health."

4. The women were "one-hundred percent positive" about the University. The campus had a two-story building on 14 hectares of land. Berit Aas herself was subsidizing the University with royalties from her book, *Women in All Centuries: A Handbook for Liberation*, translated from Norwegian into Swedish and Danish (personal letter from Kari Borg Gundersen, 23 June 1984).

5. In the first supplement to Women's Journal, published by Isis International, 22 such meetings are listed, with topics ranging from food production, immigrant women, reproductive rights, to lesbian-gay health. . . . (22–25). Overall, the number of international meetings of all kinds has shown phenomenal growth. In fact, growth so rapid that there has actually arisen a sub-discipline devoted to studying them. The theme of the 1983 meetings of the International

Association for the Study of Annual Meetings was: "Behavior at Conventions or Conventional Behavior?" (*Footnotes*, Aug., 1983).

6. Poverty, racism, the role of paramedics, abortion, sexuality, contraception, pregnancy and childbirth, imperialism and population control, politics of self-help, breastfeeding and nutrition, women and madness, women's research in natural medicine, menopause, lesbian health, yoga and menstruation, polarity, massage. In addition there were five spontaneously organized workshops, including: dental self-help and women and violence.

7. Argentina, Brazil, Chile, Colombia, Ecuador, El Salvador, Mexico, Peru, Puerto Rico, United States (*Women in Action*, Women's Journal Supplement, no. 1, 17).

8. Especially when embellished by song. As it was at one plenary session when, "amidst the drone of the official group reports," 40 bored women from different countries composed this song in a music workshop.

> We heard of a world at war
> People being massacred
> Hunger, illiteracy and pain
> But all this was lost in your
> In your refrain.
>
> You said "man" and "he"   (Chorus)
> But where were we?
> Women who hold up half the sky
> You said "man" and "he"
> But where were we?
> We were invisible
> We were unheard
> And we know why
>
> You talked of authentic development
> They were words, words, empty words
> Your authenticity was "he" not "she"
> It was all so tragic and absurd   (Chorus)
>
> In the countries where we are working
> We work with women with their feet on the ground
> Your words are coming from ivory towers
> In our world they don't make a sound   (Chorus)
>
> Let's make it her and she
> And you and me
> Together we'll hold up half the sky
> We'll all be visible
> We'll all be heard
> So let's all try

Admittedly mild as revolutionary behavior goes, but not without its impact (Report on a Conference on Adult Education, Paris, 1982, by Mary Kennedy in *Feminist Forum*, 1983, vol. 6, no. 3, p. ii).

9. In Angell's words they are devoted to "communicating scientific [and humanistic] findings, fostering new research, improving methods of inquiry and analysis, evaluating one another's work, and training programs for successors. The professionals are engaged in serving the public with the aid of a body of systematic knowledge, scientific and non-scientific" (238). Angell was writing about meetings of international scientific and professional associations in general, among which some were women's associations. Most of these associations,

Kriesberg tells us, were formed "for pragmatic reasons, social pressure or idealism" (1982, 40) and may be "an index of the extent to which a world society already exists" Kriesberg, 1973, 184–95). Angell concurs: "The very existence of a global association strengthens existing ties across national boundaries and inaugurates new ones."

10. One study of an international conference in Bogotá in 1981, comparing attendance at sessions on sexuality and health, which were activist, with attendance at those on feminism and politics, largely academic, showed a marked "division between academicians and activists (Silverstein, 1982, 35). The relatively small attendance at the session on women and work, the author suggests, might have been due to a belief that "political solutions" which incorporate women's concerns "would bring about economic transformations as well" (35). Actually, experience suggested that women's concerns were not necessarily met by political solutions alone nor, as deBeauvoir had noted, by economic ones alone.

11. The theme "involvement and marginalization" (chapters 4 and 5) as characterizing the relationships between leftist and women's groups was borrowed from the discussions at this meeting. The scholars reporting these discussions noted both change and continuity since the group's meetings the year before, finding in both a kind of convergence in its research interests. In 1979, women's cultures and networks had been a concern of U.S. women only; in 1980, of Italian, French, and Dutch women also. In 1981, national distinctions in interests assumed less salience than did disciplinary differences.

12. Azania, Bangladesh, China, India, Nicaragua, Yugoslavia, Zimbabwe.

13. As early as 1888 there was an International Council of Women in Washington "to unify the woman's movement by drawing together representatives of a wide variety of organizations" (Mary Earhart Dillon, 1971, 617). There was also a Universal Peace Union in 1888. In 1891 a World's Women Christian Temperance Union held its first conventions; six years later there were women from 23 countries representing two million women at the WCTU convention. Participation in a series of international fairs helped women also to "build the infrastructure of the new world community" (Boulding, 1977, 21). In the last two decades of the nineteenth century, five national women's groups became transnational, ready to "enter into the transnational community" (21). Practice and skill in international organization continued well into the early twentieth century. Thus, between 1900 and 1915, five international religious organizations appeared and three international associations (Boulding, 1977, 22). They included: The World Young Women's Christian Association; the World Women's Christian Temperance Union; the International Council of Nurses; the General Federation of Women's Clubs; and the International Council of Women's Clubs.

14. The International Women's League for Peace and Freedom, which had helped convene this congress, lapsed between the world wars but was reactivated in 1982 and became one of the first international nongovernmental organizations to be granted consultative status at the United Nations. It came to have sections in 25 countries on five continents. It was indirectly responsible for the Marches of Nordic women in the early 1980s (chapter 9).

15. Secretary for International Affairs, Soviet Women's Committee, Moscow; Sociologist, Consultant, University of Brussels; Economist, Centre for Informal Education and Development Studies, Bangalore; Assistant Professor of Sociology, Wayne State University, Detroit; Lawyer, Journalist, Department of Public Instruction, Rio de Janeiro; Economist, Director Institute of Developing Countries, Central School of Planning and Statistics, Warsaw.

16. Inasmuch as the members were from countries with different political

ideologies—USSR, Belgium, India, Brazil, Poland, United States—it would have been interesting to note where they concurred on women's issues and where they did not. At the three official U.N.-sponsored meetings of the Decade for Women, the positions of delegates from the communist bloc countries varied widely from those of democratic countries (chapter 10).

17. For the political rather than the personal aspects of the Marches of Nordic Women, see chapter 9 below.

18. I am indebted to Berit Aas for these accounts. They have been slightly edited.

19. During an earlier march, one woman in Kiev had wanted to do something for a young woman who had participated a year before in a march to Paris. The Kiev woman had been told a young dancer had been punished for her participation in that march by being moved from her apartment back home. The gift of the perfume was the woman's way of expressing sympathy.

20. A more cynical account was reported in the Western press. Under headlines reading: "When Rhetoric and Reality Collide: The Two Faces of Moscow's Peace Policy," one reporter, Dusko Doder, wrote that "the Kremlin had welcomed and encouraged Western pacifism as a way to pressure Western governments to curtail military spending and particularly to block the deployment of new American nuclear missiles in Western Europe." At the same time it had fought to prevent younger Soviet generations from "dabbling in pacifism. Thus when the Nordic women were due to arrive in Moscow two young activists were charged with hooliganism, and nine other members of a Committee for Peace and East-West Understanding were ordered out of town. This committee had been warned to cease its provocative activities. In Leningrad, a hundred members of the official Soviet peace committee had been approved for participation in the march "to deflect Western criticism that the Russians were afraid to allow Western antiwar activists to hold peace rallies on Soviet soil" (Washington Post, 19 July 1985).

21. Among the earliest attempts to deal with problems of organizing and running international women's meetings was Charlotte Bunch's contribution at a women's international workshop in Bangkok in 1979 and at a women's Conference in Groningen in 1984.

22. There were about 35 women from eight European countries but unfortunately none from Germany, France, the Eastern block of southern Europe. Forty percent of the original participants did not arrive. This was very disappointing. It highlighted the difficulty of securing financial support for women's meetings. It was especially disappointing to the four women organizers. It meant that some of the workshops were relatively small and one had to be abandoned altogether (Hughes, Feminist Forum, Vol. 6, No. 5, i–ii).

23. Among governmental or quasi-governmental funding sources are: the U.S. Agency for International Development, the World Bank, the Pan-American Health Organization, the International Labor Office, the Overseas Development Council. The Ford Foundation has also funded conferences. For a Decade-for-Women Conference in Nairobi in 1985 the L. J. Skaggs and Mary C. Skaggs Foundation made grants from $2,000 to $10,000 to 55 individuals or groups in Senegal, Taiwan, Philippines, Argentina, Santo Domingo, Argentina, Sweden, Peru, Ireland, Italy, Israel, Brazil, Kenya, Greece, England, Fiji, France, Barbados, Zimbabwe.

24. See chapter 3 for the influence of sponsors on the activities of feminist groups in Peru.

25. Among the guaranteed rights of citizens the founding fathers included in the U.S. Constitution was the right to assemble. One of the first rights reaction-

ary governments abrogate is precisely that one, for even the most seemingly benign meetings may have unexpected consequences as the female world at mid-century was learning the hard way.

26. A case in point was the difficulty encountered by the Research Committee on Women in Society of the International Sociological Association, some of whose members could not pay their dues "because of currency restrictions of their home countries."

27. But where to draw the line? *Robert's Rules of Order,* which had taught the West parliamentary procedures, was not congenial in many parts of the world. Western feminists had seen parliamentary rules subvert too many programs, had seen too many hegemonies served by subverting rules. They had found U.N. protocol inimical to many of their goals.

28. Feminists in the United States had also struggled through the practical difficulties inherent in an ideology of egalitarian structurelessness (Freeman, 1976).

29. Except when they cannot be ignored, patronized, or ridiculed. Press reports are usually limited to meetings at which male-world issues are high- lighted, as in the U.N.-sponsored meetings in Mexico City and Copenhagen. Still, such ignorance may, it has been argued, have a benign side. It is probably just as well that the press ignore the complex system of networks in process in the female world creating and expanding consciousness of a shared global female world. It gives the process a period of grace, a chance to learn by mistakes, an opportunity for trial-and-error without too much outside inter- ference, without too much fear of failure, without loss of face when goals are not reached. A time to achieve the self-confidence that will be urgently needed when the male world discovers it and attempts to take it over. Or coopt it. In the United States a leader of the New Right, gloating over its success in the 1980 elections, reminded the opposition that while they had been meeting and think- ing and researching new ideas during the preceding decade, they had been dismissed as far out, not worthy of attention. Their success came therefore as a stunning surprise. In an analogous way the thinking and researching and shar- ing which women scholars are engaged in may have an analogous impact which will also surprise the status quo with a so-called sleeper effect when the rays of the Feminist Enlightenment finally reach it.

30. At international meetings women who are properly subordinate to men at home may achieve boldness. One woman at such a meeting was the highest woman civil servant in her country. When she first arrived she was preaching the old female doctrine that "one achieves more with honey than with vinegar." She opposed the daring plans being made for confrontation. By the end of the week she had changed so drastically that it was she who volunteered to be the one who snatched the microphone from the speaker at the final session. For some, "coming out" is more tentative, as in the case of the young North African woman who, upon learning that her brother was coming to the city where the meeting was being held, immediately doffed her smart and daring Parisian outfit and reassumed her traditional garb. She may not have "defected" from her African culture, but she had been "contaminated" by her exposure to this group.

31. In the first national women's conference in Houston, Texas in 1977, Alice Rossi found that although the average delegate did not increase her political participation afterward, she did develop "22 new contacts with people she met for the first time in Houston with whom she planned to keep in touch" (1982, 180). An Advocacy Network was set up "for the purpose of outreach, activation, and collaboration on behalf of the Plan of Action endorsed" (183).

32. For a history of the U.N.-sponsored Decade for Women, see chapter 10. Briefly, there were three women's conferences during that decade, the first in Mexico City in 1975, the second in Copenhagen in 1980, and the third in Nairobi in 1985. For each of these U.N.-sponsored meetings, the participants were government-appointed delegates—most, but not all, women. Participants in the INGO-sponsored meetings—called a Tribune in the first, and forum at the other two—were members of INGOs with participation permitted to other women also. The two sets of conferences differed widely in freedom, discipline, originality, freshness, relevance.

33. As of 1979 there were, overall, 2,500 INGOs (Kriesberg, 1979, 206). Not all of them were, of course, women's organizations. Kriesberg distinguishes three categories of INGOs: international scientific and professional associations; occupational nonscientific and professional; and nonoccupational INGOs (1981, 52). Among the first, the largest of 18 kinds of activities is health (22.9 percent); among the second, commerce and industry (46.2 percent); and among the third, international relations (23.1 percent). The categories differ in age, in number of countries represented, and types of membership. Most of them are headquartered in Western Europe, Canada, Australia, or the United States. Boulding studied 47 women's INGOs with interests in four categories: professional and working women; women interested in international relations; women interested in educational-cultural concerns; and sportswomen (1976). One Decade-for-Women Conference, in Copenhagen in 1980, was sponsored by 34 INGOs (*International Women's Tribune Centre Newsletter* no. 11, 1980).

34. "The Peace Tent sometimes turned into a battle zone for women whose countries are at war. Women from Iran and Iraq threw things and even chased each other" (Gilliam, Washington *Post*, 22 July 1985). On one of the bulletin boards someone had pasted a cartoon of a group of women fighting and bellowing with the following legend: "They are learning" (Battiata, *Washington Post*, 13 July 1985).

35. Many women were already looking forward to another conference in five years. If the United States did not issue an invitation, the Federation of Indian Women would. It had already "invited all the women of the world to India in 1990" (Sciolino, *New York Times*, 18 July 1985).

Chapter 8—Never Another Season of Silence

1. Control of the news in Third World countries became a major issue at the United Nations and may have played a part in the withdrawal of the United States from UNESCO in 1985.

2. In 1920, a young U.S. woman from the Midwest who went to work in New York was believed when she told the occupants of the women's hotel where she lived that back home in Minneapolis she went to school on horseback and carried a gun to protect herself against possible Indian attacks. For all that her listeners knew, she might be telling the truth. Nor were they any more parochial than the wealthy Boston woman entertaining out-of-town guests attending a national meeting who, more to make conversation than to find out, asked about their trip. When she was asked about her own travel, she replied she did not have to travel; she was already there.

3. This newsletter called attention to several new newsletters by and for women of color: *Women for Palestine* (London) "will publish articles, news, and stories written by women on the Palestinian and Lebanese struggle and on Zionism in Israel"; *Our Voice/Saturna*, "newsletter of Women for Women in Lebanon" (Cambridge, Mass.) It mentions also two newspapers: *Between Our*

Selves (Washington, D.C.) which "will provide a medium for Asian-Americans, Latinas, Native Americans, Afro-Americans, and Arab-Americans to exchange information" as well as "exchanging information with women of color worldwide"; and *Upfront* (Washington, D.C.) which "is designed as an open forum for women who would not otherwise have an opportunity to express themselves in print." The *African Women Rising* adds that "women-of-color newspapers are essential elements in political struggles by women of color. They inform, mobilize, as well as celebrate women of color activists. It is critical that this medium is supported" (5). The author recognizes that although women of color "are not monolithic in character" they do share "at least two common beliefs: (1) women of color suffer conditions that are not common to white women and (2) white women activists do not adequately address their concerns."

4. *Solidarity* was officially terminated 13 December 1981.

5. At its first World Feminist Media Conference, in 1979, more than 108 women assembled from 31 countries: Norway, Lebanon, Papua, Morocco, Germany, Colombia, France, Peru, Italy, Switzerland, South Africa, Barbados, Haiti, Puerto Rico, Sri Lanka, Jamaica, Sweden, Denmark, Canada, Tanzania, Israel, Zimbabwe, Zambia, Nigeria, West Germany, Pacific Islands, Trinidad, the Dominican Republic, Chile, and Fiji.

6. In Europe, counting archives, bookshops, publishing houses, as well as periodicals, there were, as of 1980: 2 items in Austria; 10 in Belgium; 5 in Denmark; 46 in the Federal Republic of Germany; 37 in France; 4 in Greece; 6 in Iceland; 5 in Ireland; 2 in Northern Ireland; 25 in Italy; 22 in the Netherlands; 5 in Norway; 3 in Portugal; 5 in Spain; 10 in Sweden; nine in Switzerland, 36 in England; and 2 in Scotland (Isis, no. 16). By 1985 there were also feminist periodicals in: Australia, Brazil, Canada, Chile, Colombia, Costa Rica, India, Israel, Japan, Mexico, Peru, Sri Lanka, and Uruguay (*Connexions*, no. 15, 1985).

7. It included 462 periodicals, 116 women's presses and publishers; 80 women's bookstores, 67 art/graphics/theater groups; 31 women's film groups; 35 music groups; and 26 video and cable groups (Women's Institute for Freedom of the Press, Washington, D.C. 1985).

8. Like, for example, *Spare Rib* in England and *Emma* in the Federal Republic of Germany.

9. The sources for translated pieces included: an Italian feminist; a West German feminist monthly; a British feminist monthly; an Austrian leftist biweekly; an English language leftist biweekly; a West German progressive monthly; *Isis;* and correspondents in Amsterdam and Oslo.

10. From Salvador, Bolivia, the Club Maria (Leningrad), Nicaragua, Venezuela, Spain, Sri Lanka, the Cameroon; from all parts of France; from seven men of "Men against Misogyny"; from political organizations (19–21).

11. The Isis International Bulletins were on the following topics: No. 1, 1976, The International Tribunal on Crimes against Women; No. 2, 1976, Women in the Daily Press; No. 3, 1977, Women in Liberation Struggles; No. 4, 1977, Battered Women and the Refugees; No. 5, 1977x, Feminism and Socialism Part I; No. 6, 1978, Feminism and Socialism Part II; No. 7, 1978, Women and Health Part I; No. 8, 1978, Women and Health Part II; No. 9, 1978, Women in Southern Africa; No. 10, 1979, Women and Work; No. 11, 1979, Women, Land, and Food Production; No. 12, 1979, Organizing Against Rape; No. 13, 1979, Tourism and Prostitution; No. 14, 1980, Women and Migration; No. 15, 1980, Nuclear Power and Militarization; No. 16, 1980, The Feminist Press in Western Europe; No. 17, 1980, International Feminist Network (IFN); No. 18, 1981, Women and the Media; No. 19, 1981, Women in National Liberation Struggles; No. 20, 3rd

International Women and Health Meeting; No. 21, 1981, News from the Women's Movement; No. 22, 1981, 1st Latin American and Caribbean Feminist Meeting; No. 23, 1982, Motherhood; No. 24, 1982, Women and the New Technology; No. 25, 1982, Sexuality; No. 26, 1983, Women for Peace; No. 27, 1983, Women and Visual Images; No. 28, 1983, International Women and New Technology Conference; No. 29, Women's World, 1983.

12. The services of Isis in connection with the International Feminist Network are noted in chapter 9.

13. In addition to periodicals there have arisen special publication projects which serve, in effect, the same function. The Feminist Press in the United States, for example, in addition to its network, *Women's Studies International*, publishes International Supplements to the *Women's Studies Quarterly*, including news and reports from all over the globe about countries from Bangladesh to Zimbabwe and serving as one of the best vehicles available for information about "international conferences on teaching and research about women." More academic are the Feminist Press's *International Monographs on Women's Studies* bringing women up to date on women's studies in Italy, Canada, India, among other countries. Finally, its plans include books with an international perspective; the first, *Dialogue on Difference: Women's Studies International at Copenhagen*, appeared in 1982.

14. The supplement to the first issue of *Women's Journal* by Isis refers to a number of other audio media such as film festivals, posters, films and cassette recordings, documentaries, slide collages, and radio networks in areas as distant from one another as Vancouver, Hong Kong, and Lahore (26 ff.).

15. The second satellite teleconference by women was held between women attending the United Nations Conference in Copenhagen in 1980 and women in six U.S. cities, organized by the Women's Institute for Freedom of the Press (*Media Report to Women*, 1 August 1981).

Chapter 9—Networks in Action

1. The study here reported was done in Idakho, but Staudt found the same situation in Shitoli and Shijulu, where women's superior agricultural skills were the "result of their experience, commitment and socialized responsibilities in farming, as well as of their supportive social networks in which agricultural labor and information are shared" (*Development and Change*, 1978, 452–53; Journal of Developing Areas, 1978, 399–414). More than 90 percent in the Idakho sample belonged to some kind of organization including church groups, mutual-aid societies, or communal groups for planting, weeding, and harvesting crops. We have already met these "communal agricultural and mutual-aid associations" in chapter 2.

2. Case in point: when the women interested in international women's studies decided to organize, they knew they did not want an international organization in the conventional form with all the abracadabra it would involve; they decided they should be a network. "A Network does not have 'members,' voting constituencies, officers, or political positions. A *Network* communicates, facilitates the passing of messages" (Howe, 1982, 3). It is, in brief, a special kind of medium.

3. Examples: Radio Network (a unit of a Women's Alternative Media Coalition); the Pacific and Asian Women's Forum, "an informal network of activists and researchers" set up in 1977 to enable them "not only to keep in touch with struggles of other women by networking but also to learn from each other's

experiences"; Asian Women's Research and Action Network, 1982, with the objective "to close the gap that exists between research and action" and provide abstracts of research; Women and Health Documentation Centers, in a Bologna meeting in 1984 "stressed the need to create a network among themselves"; women in Latin America were also exploring the setting up of a regional feminist health network (Women in Action; *Women's Journal*, supplement no. 1; *Isis International*)."

4. Informal networks were specified as one of the ten major trends in business and politics in the United States in the 1980s (John Naisbitt, *Megatrends: Ten Directions Transforming Our Lives*, 1982).

5. The Ford Foundation made a grant of $100,000 to the International Women's Tribune Center to expand its information services to "promote networks among women throughout the world," including ties between union leaders and researchers; among women studying credit and money management; and among Third-World journalists trying to improve news coverage of women's activities" (Ford Foundation *Letter*, August 1981).

6. As the Communist "cells" had sometimes been.

7."As of 1980 there were contacts in 25 countries, namely: Australia, Austria, Belgium, Canada, Denmark, the Dominican Republic, the Federal Republic of Germany, France, Greece, Hong Kong, India, Israel, Italy, Japan, Mexico, Netherlands, New Zealand, Norway, Portugal, South Africa, Spain, Sweden, Switzerland, United Kingdom, United States. By 1985 Isis had been expanded and reorganized to include a wider range of activities. Isis International now had a network of more than 10,000 contacts in 150 countries (*Women's Journal*, supplement no. 2, 1985, 35).

8. Where the women felt they were not strong; Belfast, United States, Portugal, New Zealand, Japan, Israel, Holland, Canada, Denmark, Norway, India, Greece, Ireland, Peru, Namibia, Philippines, USSR (*Isis*, no. 17, 1980).

9. A serendipidous outcome of this case was, incidentally, a changed attitude toward incest. It was no longer accepted as just part of the culture.

10. Abortion remains a widespread issue. In March 1982, the coordinator for abortion rights in Spain sent an appeal to women in countries everywhere to band together against the trial of eleven women in Barcelona accused of practicing abortion "and to aid in obtaining their freedom and the vindication of all the rights of free women" (*des femmes hebdo*, 14). The salience of the abortion issue in the work of the IFN suggests "women protesting with their bodies against the dual burden of work and housework which is placed on them" (Burja, 1979, 40).

11. The needs were not always on an abstract level. Sometimes they came down to the nitty gritty. The South West Africa People's Organization (SWAPO) Women's League in Namibia could use underwear, tampons, or money to purchase them in bulk (*Isis*, no. 17, 1980).

12. To avoid annoying translation, sample telegrams and letters accompanied this appeal. Thus, for example: "For Democracy, human rights and academic freedom, withdraw the charges against Dr.————." Or: "Dear sir: I write to protest the Ministry of WAKF's charges against Dr.————. These charges deny her rights as a Professor and as a citizen to academic freedom, democracy and freedom of speech. The suit must be withdrawn."

13. The International Feminist Think Tank contemplated more extensive political activities as well, including "the establishment of independent women's commissions to visit and investigate the specific situation of *women* in crisis situations: Palestinian women, migrant women, women and children dying in the Sahelian famine, women suffering under apartheid, indigenous women caught in the crossfire in Central America, and minority women in the United

States struggling against increasing poverty. A call for women in both private and professional capacities to refuse to participate in censuses or household surveys or registration systems—or to fill them in by listing *all* the jobs they do—until the invisibility of women's unpaid work as producers *and* reproducers is recognized in the national accounts. The launching of an investigation of and subsequent action against specific airlines, tourist agencies, and hotels that promote sex tourism. Organizing around the 1985 U.N. World Women's Conference in Nairobi, against any attempts to sidetrack the conference on ideological or other grounds, thus avoiding the polarization of the first two World Women's Conferences, where women per se were used as pawns by patriarchal governments" (46). Among the founders were women from New Zealand, Portugal, Palestine, Greece, Belgium, Mexico, Finland, Barbados, Nepal, Sri Lanka, Zambia, Yugoslavia, the United States (*Media Report to Women*, January–February 1985, 4).

14. Feminist periodicals also became channels of appeals for help. In *Connexions*, for example, one issue published appeals for letters to President Marcos of the Philippines in behalf of a rape victim; and for letters to the Defense Department of Uruguay in behalf of medical care for a woman in a military prison. In 1985 women in the United States were being appealed to in behalf of an academic woman in Kuwait and asked to write to the Ministry of Endowments at Kuwait University to protest against her denial of academic freedom, democracy, and freedom of speech.

15. Tatiana Mamanova, Julia Voznesenskaia, Natalia Malakhovskaia, Tatiana Goricheva. They had been greatly influenced by U.S. feminist writings, especially Robin Morgan's *Sisterhood Is Powerful*, Brownmiller's *Against Our Will*, and Kate Millett's *Sexual Politics* (Ruthchild, 1983, 6).

16. The first issue was handlettered and typed and consisted of ten copies which were circulated by hand from one reader to the next. Some were smuggled out of the country. Selected articles of all five volumes, edited by Tatiana Mamanova, appeared in translation as *Women and Russia* (Beacon Press) in 1984. The English translation of the first volume appeared as *Woman and Russia: An Almanac for Women about Women* (London: Sheba Feminist Publishers, 1980). The second, third, and fourth volumes appeared in French as: *Rossianka* (1980); as *Des Femmes*, in 1981; and as *Voix de Femmes en Russie* in 1982 (Paris: De Noel/Gonthier (Ruthchild, 1983, 11). The first volume was ultimately translated into twelve languages. It proved to be a shot heard round the world.

17. By 1982, even Leonid Brezhnev himself was recognizing the non-enforcement of the legal rights of women in the USSR (Lapidus, 1982, 302).

18. The women followed different courses in exile. Goricheva attended a Russian Orthodox seminary in Paris; Voznesenskaia became involved in emigre issues in Frankfurt; and Malakhovskaia, in Austria, remained chief editor of a journal, *Maria*, and was attempting to reach the feminist spirituality movement in the West (Ruthchild, 7). Mamanova continued to work in the international feminist movement, visiting the United States from time to time and appearing before feminist groups.

19. Not as an example of international networking—its focus was limited to women in the USSR—but interesting in its own right was the case of another women's journal, *Maria*, published by a group called Club Maria. Its editors were three of the women who had participated in the *Almanac*. Their appeal was by way of the Church (Ruthchild, 1983). They rejected "compulsory equality." The title, *Maria*, emphasized maternal selflessness. Their emphasis was not on rationalism but on spirituality and religious transformation. Defection of men from the Church had left it open for women as a sanctuary where they could

discuss their own, female, problems freely. Although these women did not seek to open up the priesthood to women, the shortage of priests resulted in their having to assume the priestly role in areas where there were no priests to perform it. "Their concern," Ruthchild tells us, was "neither equality nor . . . making women more like men, but the discovery of the . . . Russian feminine essence . . . [which had] found refuge in the church" (1983, 7). The fate of *Maria* was no better than that of the *Almanac*. "March 13, 1982, Natalia Lazareva, a member of the feminist Club Maria was arrested in her Leningrad home. At the same time the KGB went to the home of Gallina Grigorieva, Volodia Okoulov, and Dmitri Kolesnitchenko, and seized all copies of the review *Maria* and all books in the Russian language published abroad. Representatives of the club now in exile . . . alerted this magazine [*des femmes hebdo*] and sent the following message. "The authorities viewed her [Lazareva's] participation in the review *Maria* and the diffusion of the truth about the life of women in our country as defamation. They characterized as defamatory the act of informing the public on the conditions in which the women of our country are obliged to give birth, in a world without hygiene or anesthesia. The mere saying that in establishments for infants the conditions are such that they fall ill, of saying also that women are victims of discrimination at the work site, of exploitation at home, that all the work of educating infants and domestic work rest entirely on the shoulders of women who, further, are obliged to work outside as much as men. The fact of saying that the very heavy charges of everyday life and education transform women into mute slaves of Soviet men, themselves pitiable slaves of our system was labelled defamation. We have described all this in our journal *Maria* and it is that which they have judged defamatory. Natalia is "guilty" of having provided the illustrations and assured the esthetic quality of our review, of having designed the logos of the Club Maria. Such is the reason for which she was condemned to ten months of prison for her first arrest . . . . The authorities thus demonstrate that the oppression of women in our country is not the consequence of the so-called relics of the past, but a conscious and deliberate policy of the state.

That is why we address ourselves to our sisters, women of the whole world and to all Christians, to all men of good will; we address ourselves also to the governments of all countries and to honest political men: help our friend! Save Natalia from the hands of this state of bandits' " (des femmes hebdo, 26 March 1982, 14). In view of the maternal model among the editors of *Maria* it is interesting that these women issued an Appeal to Mothers against the Soviet invasion of Afghanistan, urging "Women of Russia" to protest, join in the burning of draft papers, and urging husbands and sons not to join the war effort (Ruthchild, 4).

20. The planners came from Sweden, Norway, Denmark, Finland, Iceland, Lappland, and the Faeroe Islands. The account here is taken from the reports by Berit Aas, a political activist in Norway and academic social scientist.

21. Tatiana Mamanova, who participated in this first march, did not agree that the results had been disappointing. The march had had quite an impact. "Whole families walked along together, tired but happy in their unity" (1984, 261). She was not, however, optimistic about the projected march to Moscow. Many, she said, looked "on this venture skeptically, claiming that nothing will come of it and that the Soviet people will be isolated from the two hundred demonstrators with their incomprehensible signs in foreign languages. Perhaps the March for Peace will not have the same repercussions as did the March . . . to Paris." Still, she personally was "heartened by the Western women's ini-

tiative, and there . . . were people in the USSR . . . capable of understanding this act correctly" (262). Indeed, there were, as we saw in chapter 7.

22. When leadership of these organizations refused to send representatives, the women who wished to participate took membership in Women for Peace.

23. She could not forego pointing a (female) moral: "As so many times before, it was not the actual behavior which counted but how it was done and by whom. . . . If men are socialized never to give in, the more so the more prestige and power they have, how can it possibly happen during peace negotiations that any of them gives anything away? Perhaps one side can offer the other side honour and pride to get the job done?"

24. There was a Washington march in 1983; it was a feast of loving well-being. A Unitarian Church offered hospitality. Waves of support swept over participants. The press gave it scarcely a glance.

25. In the 1920s an elaborate underground proto-network of "cells" was developed by the Communist party in the United States, well designed for subversion. Communication within cells was well developed; between cells it was cautiously prevented. Members knew only those in their own cell. Secrecy was of the utmost importance as a matter of self-protection; it was dangerous to know too much if interrogated by outside investigators. One can well imagine what a Stalin might have thought of having aboveboard networks ready made to spring into action on command. The suspicion of the Soviet Peace Committee about the march of the Nordic women to Moscow suggests the communist caste of thought about these legions.

PART IV—Introduction

1. Vina Mazumdar, outstanding feminist leader of India, has expressed the amazement she and her colleagues experienced when the ignorance of the female world struck them. "We [a three-member Committee on the Status of Women in 1972] considered ourselves social scientists. Each of us had done some research and we felt we had accumulated quite substantial experience in that very big and complex country called India. By the time we were halfway through our inquiry, however, we had become very humble people. We had to shed all our arrogance and we had to confess that we knew very little—not only about Indian women but about Indian society as a whole. We discovered that there were many layers within Indian society and that what we had very cheerfully talked about as Indian traditions and culture—particularly the traditions that affected women's status—were only about a very, very thin layer at the most visible level of Indian society. In other words, all that we knew about traditions, cultures, customs, and law relating to women, religious values governing women's lives—all that we thought we knew was only about a microscopic minority; the elite sectors of our society. And I make that statement irrespective of the number of religious communities that constitute the population. When we thought we knew about Hindu women, Moslem women, Christian women, Jewish women, Parsee women . . . —all of our knowledge was confined to this small elite. This was true even of concepts like family—and we thought we knew what was known about the family. . . . If women's studies is to combat the devaluation of women, we have to build up a new body of knowledge to change people's attitudes (International Supplement to the Women's Studies Quarterly, (Jan., 1982).

2. The emphasis in United Nations policies has been said to be "determined less by the formal statement of the organization's nature and purpose contained

in its charter than by the day-to-day outcome of the political process of the organization, in which members vie with each other for control over the utilization of its mechanism. International organization does not introduce a distinctive conception of the international political arena" (Claude, 1968, Vol. 8, 35). The political aspects of the international system has still not been thoroughly researched, according to this author, but the hope is that research on comparative international organization "may contribute to an understanding of international politics in the broadest sense" (40). The experience of the three U.N. sponsored Decade for Women conferences may contribute to this body of research.

3. In 1974, the U.S. Ambassador to the U.N., John A. Scali, noted that support for the UN in the United States Congress and in the United States public—never very enthusiastic—was now eroding. (Even President Woodrow Wilson, who had long dreamed of a League of Nations, had not been able to persuade that country to join that league when it was finally established after World War I. The United Nations was organized after World War II with United States support, but there was always a core of hostility which continued to resist it.) Appointment to ambassador to the U.N. was ceasing to be an honor and becoming a nonprestigious political chore. He criticized the trend toward dominance by broad coalitions of developing countries, including the very small ones backed by the Communist powers; he feared the minority would cease to respect or obey majority rule when it became the tyranny of the majority. One woman, Janet M. Feldberg, added that the UN had now degenerated into a cynical practitioner of blackmail. Instead of serving as a peace-keeping body, it had become a field of battle, often between the Soviet Union and the United States, each with its followers and client dependent states.

4. Thus, for example, when one session of the General Assembly curbed Israel's right to speak in debate, the President of the General Assembly called it "historic," even "revolutionary"; but the United States delegation called it "abusive."

5. Jeanne Kirkpatrick's successor, Vernon A. Walters, followed her policies, rejecting the practice of "selective application of condemnation" by the General Assembly. "The Soviet Union is never condemned by name for invading Afghanistan. . . . It is referred to only as "foreign forces." "Everybody knows who that is but they won't name the Soviet Union. . . . On the other hand, the United States is blamed for things it doesn't do, such as supposedly helping South Africa develop nuclear weapons: I am outraged at this double standard and I am going to do everything I can to have it changed" (Lally Weymouth, "U.N. Ambassador Tilts with a World," Washington Post, Oct. 13, 1985).

6. In 1974, Helvi Sipila had organized a forum on women's role in population and economic development but failed to attract attention from the head of delegations, most of whom were men. Only 12 women responded to 300 invitations. So Sipila, a few Indian women, and one man—an Austrian—talked among themselves. Women's roles —even in population and economic development, surely highly relevant issues—were apparently not interesting to these male delegates.

7. Elise Boulding proposed an interesting background to International Women's Year. "A new generation of women began to take hold in international affairs at the United Nations level when the idea of a UN International Cooperation Year was initiated. It was conceived by women, developed by women, and lost in the maws of international officialdom because women had yet not enough expertise to make concrete programs work. It was intended to create an internal

network of women working for peace at the community level. As symbolic of women's intentions it was important, and it was a beginning" (1976, 761–762). The UN International Cooperation Year itself had an interesting history. It "was born in the kitchen of a Kansas mother of two young children, Kathy Menninger, who was thinking one day as she did her chores how millions of mothers around the world were also doing similar chores for their families. Suddenly the idea came to her that the United Nations might declare a year in which ordinary women and men everywhere could be helped to establish links with their counterparts in other countries" (796). By way of contacts with Roger Fisher, professor of international law at Harvard University, the idea was presented to the Indian delegation to the United Nations who liked it so much that "they sponsored a resolution for a United Nations Year for International Cooperation, which was accepted by the General Assembly" (796). Boulding tells us that this is her perception, based on her own experience and observations, and other participants might have viewed it differently.

8. On March 8, International Women's Day (established in 1910 to honor working women) in 1975 there was a march of 50 women's groups in New York City down 5th Avenue to a rally at Union Square where complaints were made that although IWY was almost a fourth over, still no plans had been made for its celebration, no movement to implement it, no planning, no preparation. So, under this pressure, President Ford appointed a 33-member Commission on Observance of International Women's Year to make plans and the Shah's sister was selected by the U.N. for this service. There was still little enthusiasm for it in the U.N. (At that moment, 2,700 out of 3,000 women staff members were publicly protesting their treatment by the U.N. bureaucracy). Not until April 15 did the Commission hold its opening session. I had the privilege of giving the opening talk, which was entitled "Women of the World Unite!"

Chapter 10—A Drama in Three Acts

1. Overcoming this female oppression called for "the elimination of colonialism and neo-colonialism, fascism, and other similar ideologies, foreign occupation and apartheid, racism, and discrimination in all its forms as well as recognition of the dignity of the individual and appreciation of the human person and his or her self-determination."

The World Plan of Action promulgated by the IWY Conference in 1975 included (as item 23), the statement that "true peace cannot be achieved unless women share with men the responsibility for establishing a new international economic order." The process worked the other way as well; in another item, the improvement in the lot of women "must be an integral part of the global project for the establishment of a new economic order" (item 7). The New International Economic Order remained a major theme throughout the Decade for Women. That decade had followed one of great economic growth in the 50s and 60s. In Africa, for example, the growth in gross domestic productivity between 1960 and 1973 was 3.5 percent. By the late 70s it had fallen by more than half, to 1.2 percent in 1980 (Lexie Verdon, *Washington Post*, 15 January 1984). Many Third World, especially African, countries were faced with sharply lowered living standards as well as devastating droughts. Some of the difficulties were due to economic policies, but much of the problem resulted from declining prices for their major exports in the world market as a result of the global recession precipitated by the oil prices of the 1970s. The major exports (coffee, tea, cocoa, rubber, vegetable oils, copper and iron ore) had dropped in value while imports, including food and technologies needed for modernization, had gone up. Many African nations tended to be single-commodity exporters, which meant that if prices for their particular commodity went down they could not compensate by selling more of some other commodity. The countries were thus caught in a serious bind. At first the problem had been conceptualized in terms of a north-south "dialogue," which saw the world in terms of rich and poor countries. The essence of the north-south conceptualization was simple. By and large, countries north of the equator tended to be wealthy and those in the southern hemisphere, poor. Thus those in the north were able to consume a far from proportionate share of the world's produce, including its human resources. Two U.S. citizens who had worked in the Third World concurred, pointing out that "the United States, with only five percent of the people of this world, consumes at least a third of the world's nonrenewable resources. . . . We keep raising our standard of living higher and higher, and in the eyes of the rest of the world that looks as if we are unfair. . . . Those who have the most can outbid those with the least, for everything, including ideas. . . . Almost every hospital in the U.S. has doctors from the poor areas of the world. Once they become educated, they don't want to stay in their own poor country. . . . This is a real dilemma, because as the best leave, the needs of those remaining become even more marked" (Polly Ondrasik, quoting Mildred and Darrell Randall in an interview, "Nutrition, Politics, and a Commitment to Fighting Hunger," American Magazine of American University, 1985, 17). (Darrell Randall was "appalled that some of the poor countries ship food to rich countries in exchange for dollars. 'It takes a lot of grain to make whiskey, for example. When countries begin diverting food grains to make whiskey, or gasohol, or pet food, there's less for people to eat.' ") By the 1970s the north-south issue was succeeded by the New International Economic Order, also designed to overcome the unfairness of the market economy which put some countries at such a disadvantage on the world economic scene, putting them at the mercy of trade policies over which they had no influence. The NIEO issue, so major at the IWY conference in 1975, declined in saliency at the end of the decade, when it could not garner enough support to be included in the Nairobi final document. (And Fidel Castro could not get support from Latin American countries for inaugurating a new economic order by not paying their international debts.) Actually, the north-south and the NIEO issues were legitimate not only on ethical grounds but also, as it finally became clear, on economic grounds. Strictly economic policies were self-destructive in the long run. International monetary and trade policies could destroy both borrowers and lenders. So, by 1984, the World Bank's 1984 report was stating that increased growth in the Third World could be achieved only if rich countries "opened up their markets to the poorer countries," and criticizing the International Monetary Fund's policies of "austerity-enforced reductions in Third World imports which had a negative effect on the world economy" (Hobart Rowen, "World Bank Sees Growth Possibilities, Says Rich Nations Must Open Markets to the Third World," Washington Post, 11 July 1984). Western women had not rejected NIEO as a legitimate issue for the female world, they only rejected devoting time to it at the expense of more specifically female issues.

2. One U.S. feminist was threathened, kept under police surveillance and, on one occasion, advised to leave the country.

3. It should be pointed out that some of the official delegates were wives of heads of state and could hardly be expected to report anything wrong in their countries before an international audience.

4. Helvi Sipila had made the same point. To the question "is it possible to talk

about women's problems internationally" in view of the diversity among nations, she had replied affirmatively because "the difference is not so much . . . between developing countries and developed ones as between the privileged [male] and non-privileged [female] groups in each country." In my talk two months earlier I added that "everywhere it is women who are denied literacy, education, training. Women who are left with the traditional tools and technology while the men are offered the new scientific techniques." I had quoted a U.N. document to the effect that there were "male and female roles" [which] often cripple . . . [women's] creativity and stifle their international development" (*Work for Women*, p. 5). As a case in point I had quoted a Thai woman who stated that "many women in developing countries have not yet overcome their feelings of inferiority. They still regard themselves as subordinates to men." I referred to a Carnegie study of graduate education in the U.S. which reported "the same damaged self-concept among this highest female elite. In brief, there were everywhere oppressions that both men and women shared, however different the precise form that oppression might take. But regardless of the form it took, the female world had its own special form. This, in fact, had been one of the major themes of liberation movements as we noted in chapter 4 above.

5. The U.S. objected also to the apartheid item. This objection was not based on acceptance of apartheid but on rejection of serious sanctions against South Africa.

6. There were 187 countries represented at the Forum, with delegates from Africa (222), Latin America (312), North America (830), the Caribbean (41), the Middle East (132), Europe (1377), Asia and the Pacific (491), and Denmark, the host country (2815). There were 150 to 175 workshops, panels, group meetings every day; the major topics were wealth, income, trade unions, education.

7. Among the signers were: Simone de Beauvoir, Louise Nevelson, Madeleine Renaud, Beverly Sills, Bella Abzug, Colleen Dewhurst, Betty Friedan, Shelly Winters, Ann Jackson, Ann Meara, Jacqueline Grennan Wexler, Bess Meyerson, Eugenie Anderson, Beverly Byron, Marjorie Holt, and Margaret Heckler. Among signatories from other countries were women from Australia, Austria, Bolivia, Brazil, Canada, Costa Rica, Denmark, Federal Republic of Germany, Ecuador, Finland, Great Britain, Italy, Japan, Mexico, Norway, Panama, Portugal, Uruguay, and Venezuela.

8. NCAN denounced the efforts of the PLO to politicize this women's conference in Copenhagen, 1980, as they did in the International Women's Conference in Mexico City in 1975. "NCAN denounces the PLO terrorists, who presume to speak for the largely silent Palestinian people. The PLO does not even dialogue with all their brothers—to say nothing of their sisters. . . . So far, the PLO has not shown any signs of joining the human family, as they are still pledged to 'liquidate' the State of Israel. . . ." They added that PLO plans for Copenhagen show their domination over "their own sisters, using them as pawns in the game of politics, even as they keep them in the bondage of Arab male supremacy. Finally, NCAN urges Palestinian women to share the concerns of all women and to join in efforts to build peace for their people" (1981, 32).

9. Perhaps the three-day agenda for the PLO and its supporters may have encouraged especially hostile behavior toward Israeli and Jewish women. The identification of Zionism with racism had the effect of uniting Arab and black women against Jews and the United States. A considerable amount of havoc was wrought. Great rivers of anger, hostility, resentment, even hatred, rushed through the opened sluices. Even some of the concurrent unofficial sessions of the INGO Forum were contaminated. "Women were fed and spewed forth, and

believed, male myths. Women of the world, articulate, educated, clever women of every nation, spoke with a single anti-Israel, anti-U.S. male voice" (E. M. Broner, 1981, 31). For example: "The only good Jew is a dead Jew"; "Zionism is a disease that has to be 'killed at the cellular level' "; "To you Israeli women we will talk with weapons; to the rest of the world we'll talk with words" (35). "Shepherded by a group of men who seemed to orchestrate all of their activities, young Palestinian women, in expensive Western clothes, wearing around their necks black and white Kefiyahs fringed with the colors of the PLO flag, packed session after session" (Shirley Joseph, 1981, 34). One Israeli woman spoke of being subjected to a "psychological pogrom." It must also be noted that there were also expressions of support for Israeli and U.S. women. The Danish community, for example, "was stalwart, both Jews and non-Jews. To counter pro-PLO propaganda, about a hundred Danes, Jews and non-Jews, demonstrated in front of the building housing the conference wearing yellow Stars of David on their arms, carrying Danish and Israeli flags, and singing "Hatikva," Israel's national anthem. Within minutes they were joined by other conference delegates singing Israeli songs (Tannenbaum, 1981, 33).

10. Ms. Earle's comments appeared in a monthly publication, *Woman Speaks!* jointly sponsored by both the official U.N. conference and the separate INGO forum.

11. Canada, Australia, and Israel joined the UN in voting against the program.

12. Among them, the addition of problems of elderly women, disabled women, rural women; easily available drinking water to spare women the task of having to carry it long distances; sharing by men of household responsibilities.

13. She contrasted rather grim pictures with the brightly cheerful pictures of the sister conference sponsored by INGOs which was a truly female meeting. "The NGO Forum . . . would bring together from all parts of the world for discussion, arguments, challenges, films, songs, poetry and drama. Stories will be exchanged, tales will be told. A wealth of information, experiences, strategies and ideas will be shared. Through plenaries, workshops, and tea and coffee sessions the past, present and future will merge into one" (4). These were doubtless the kinds of meetings Sipila had envisioned. They seem very much like the meetings women were learning how to run on their own (chapter 7).

14. Case in point: There go the men who are deciding our conference! cried a Chilean woman, and everyone turned to look toward the far wall of the plenary hall. . . . There marching single file, like a family of ducks, was the Soviet delegate . . . followed by a Palestinian man and a Kuwaiti man and a Syrian. "Go away! the Soviet delegate warned as an Australian television cameraman began to film the meeting. "Go away or I will get the secretariat."

15. Maureen Reagan, head of the U.S. delegation, doubted the value of participation in such meetings (*New York Times*, 28 July 1985).

16. "At any U.N. conference there is always a lot of anti-American sentiment; that's a guarantee. I remember the first U.N. preparatory conference I went to. I was filled with outrage. I was stunned at the vitriol and hate and lies that spilled forth about my country. . . . I felt like punching someone out. You hear it, and you hear it from many countries, and it takes your breath away" (Battiata, *Washington Post*, 3 July 1985).

17. Two U.N. studies prepared for the Decade for Women summarized the inequality of women (Sciolino, *New York Times*, 23 June 1985). This helped in discussions of substantive female issues. In addition, "over the past year, women's groups and individuals have been preparing position papers, planning

workshops and panels, and assessing the progress they have made in order to be ready to report their views" (Fraser, 5 March 1985). And they were.

18. New female issues were also recognized. "The resolution on family violence . . . was strengthened . . . and the duty to fight back against abusers . . . represent significant change since . . . Copenhagen . . . where it received only passing reference. At that time the representative of the Soviet Ukraine said no spouse abuse existed there or in Pakistan, and that anyway such a topic did not belong in an international meeting."

19. The Population Reference Bureau had summarized this "common lot": "Over half of the world's 2.4 billion women are Asian; another 20 percent live in the less developed countries of Africa and Latin America. Globally nearly 50 percent of all women are of childbearing age and will probably have a total of three to four children. . . . Yet women are also a major part of the world labor force, primarily doing back-breaking work that pays little or nothing. Half of the food in developing countries is produced by women even as they struggle to bear and rear children and run their households. This is only to say that delegates from every country have something to contribute, and something to account for, in Nairobi" (ibid.).

20. Interestingly, at that very moment, in a celebration at Guantanamo, Cuba, of the 32nd anniversary of the Cuban Revolution Fidel Castro was calling for a new international economic order in Latin America, to begin with a refusal by Latin American nations to pay their foreign debts (Joseph B. Treaster, "Castro Marking Revolution, Talks of Debts," *New York Times*, 28 July 1985). The idea was sunk without a trace. There were no takers.

21. The Nairobi manifesto included more than 350 proposals guaranteeing for women a fair share of governmental and commercial power and equality in the family. Among them were: parental leave and provision for day care to lighten the double burden of working mothers; sharing of household work and child-care responsibilities between men and women; greater participation by women in trade unions, political parties, the military; equal opportunity in training and hiring; greater participation in technical and scientific fields; recognition of the economic value of housework and inclusion of measures of how much it contributes to gross national product; equal pay for work of equal value regardless of sex; protection for abused women and children along with criminal prosecution of those responsible for the abuse.

22. Cecelia Marchand, member of the Diplomatic Academy of Peru, has, as a matter of fact, recommended to women that they take advantage of international law dealing with their rights, including the Universal Declaration of Human Rights, the European Declaration of Human Rights, the American Convention on Human Rights and the Pact of San Jose de Costa Rica. She also recommends that the several U.N. documents—the Declaration on Social Progress and Development (1969), the International Development Strategy (1970), the World Plan of Action (1975), and the Charter of Economic Rights and Duties of States (1974) be invoked as well ("The Rights of Women and the Role of International Law," in Jean Lipman-Blumen and Jessie Bernard, eds., *Sex Roles and Social Policy*, Beverly Hills, Calif.: Sage Publications, 1979).

23. Evaluation of the pluses and minuses of the Decade for Women faced the special difficulty that there were two quite different processes going on, two different battles. One was between the U.N. General Assembly and the United States and the other, between male and female issue priorities. The two battles were inextricably interwoven, the second serving as a chip or weapon in the first. Emphasis on the General Assembly-U.S. battle served not only to humiliate the United States but also to deflect blame away from the male world itself.

Unfair international trade practices, colonialism, neocolonialism, imperialism, racist Zionism and the like were easier for the male world to face than sexism.

24. Of the respondents, 65 were international NGOs, 72 national; 40 percent were from industrialized countries, the rest from developing countries. Practically all had similar goals, namely: equality between the sexes, employment, education and training, health care, and development. National NGOs were more concerned with specific development issues than were international ones. In sub-Saharan countries, food and nutrition were given high priority by all NGOs; by those in India, two-thirds; by those in Latin America and North Africa, half. In industrialized countries, only 16 percent. Water was a priority in sub-Saharan areas, specified as a key issue by 80 percent of the NGOs.

Appendix A

1. The estimates vary for different areas. For Somalia the proportion of uprooted refugees who were women and children is given as 90 percent; for Afghans in Pakistan, three-fourths; for Djibouti, Sudan, "most"; for Angola, including the elderly, also "most"; among camps for displaced persons in El Salvador, the inhabitants were "largely" women, children, and old men; in Honduras, "largely women and children" (Tripp, ed., 1984, 42–58). Among Ethiopians moving to Sudan, 40 percent were single males evading the draft; among Iranians, 30 percent, leaving 60 percent and 70 percent, respectively, as females, children, and older males.

2. The most comprehensive source of data worldwide on women, the Boulding et al. Handbook, lists 57 territories from its coverage of 289 countries which were excluded. Among the excluded were such territories as Antigua, the Channel Islands, French Polynesia, Montserrat (in the Leeward Islands), Reunion, and St. Vincent (in the Windward Islands) (1976, 461).

3. In the Western world there is a long history of men pulling up their roots to seek adventure in war, in searches for Holy (as well as secular) Grails like new continents or new paths to the other side of the earth, new worlds to conquer. Or crusades or pilgrimages. Indeed, a considerable amount of history deals with cheerful, if dangerous, uprooted males "redeeming" their Honor. In the United States there is the mythical figure of Rip Van Winkle escaping the burdens of domesticity, and one student of U.S. literary history finds him presiding over the birth of the U.S. imagination: "it is fitting that our first successful home-grown legend should memorialize, however playfully, the flight of the dreamer from the shrew—into mountains and out of time, away from the drab duties of home and town. . . ." (Fiedler, 1962, xx).

4. Elise Boulding has described "female vagabonds" in the Middle Ages in England who moved "partnerless through the Middle Ages able to pick up the pennies they need[ed] at a fair or celebration of some kind" (1976, 109). In towns they were entertainers and ran soup kitchens; during wars, including the Crusades, they ran first-aid stations. When needed, they could be good fighters. Free-floating, mobile, autonomous, freewheeling, they were, Boulding reminds us, "a social category we have no labels for today" (109). They remained in their familiar circuits of markets and fairs, so they were not pulling up their roots which, in any event, were not all that deep. And no doubt there were women participants in the Children's crusades. There were also women "camp followers" who performed domestic services for armies which involved a certain amount of uprooting, but, again, their roots were not very deep.

5. The story of the Sabine Rape is sometimes interpreted as portraying

customary practices in war in which the victor slayed the males and took the women as spoils.

6. As, allegedly, in cases in India where the husband's family uses the bride as a hostage in demands for higher bride price.

7. "Separation trauma" may be very painful. It was Lot's wife, for example, not Lot himself, who turned for a last glimpse of the home she was leaving. And out of 150 Psalms, only one (no. 137) is unequivocally about women and their grief during the Babylonian captivity:

> By the rivers of Babylon, there we sat down, yea, we wept, when we remembered Zion.
> We hanged our harps upon the willows in the midst thereof.
> For there they that carried us away captive required of us a song; and they that wasted us required of us mirth, saying, Sing us one of the songs of Zion.
> How shall we sing the Lord's song in a strange land?
> If I forget thee, O Jerusalem, let my right hand forget her cunning.
> If I do not remember thee, let my tongue cleave to the roof of my mouth: if I prefer not Jerusalem above my chief joy.
> Remember, O Lord, the children of Edom in the day of Jerusalem; who said, Rase it, rase it, even to the foundation thereof.
> O daughter of Babylon, who art to be destroyed; happy shall he be, that rewardeth thee as thou has served us.
> Happy shall he be, that taketh and dasheth thy little ones against the stones.

8. The use of *maliks* in the crucial function of distributing benefits was justified on the grounds that it helped to preserve accustomed community patterns of authority, even if it did allow graft and inequality. This was an issue that the authorities deliberately chose not to confront (6).

9. In a certain sense the movement of documented, even of some undocumented, women workers in to the United States may be said to partake of the experiences of "guest" workers in Europe, except that many of them were smuggled in as uninvited nonguests.

10. Asylum seekers are distinguished from displaced persons on the basis of whether or not they are within the borders of their native country or outside of them.

11. As in the case of young U.S. men who exiled themselves and sought asylum in Canada rather than participate in a war they disapproved of in Viet Nam.

12. As, for example, the Babylonian Captivity, the French Huguenots, the Mormon treks in the U.S., the population movements between India and Pakistan after World War II, and, of course, the Nazi Holocaust.

13. The classic literary example is the nineteenth-century novel by Nathaniel Hawthorne called *The Scarlet Letter*. Another U.S. author, Edith Wharton, told such a story for a twentieth-century version when the transgression being punished was remarriage after divorce in the highest social classes. Autre temps, autre moeurs. Traces of such "exiling" remain in some communities in the United States where women who have transgressed moral imperatives are made to feel they must leave.

14. The English approach was, however, "tempered by the humanitarian approach of missionaries and the more cosmopolitan views of the English in general, so that it is less restrictive than that of the Afrikaners in the provision of education and welfare services" (Edwards, 271). The feminists in South Africa are more likely to be of English than of Afrikaner background.

Appendix B

1. In Japan, for example, the textile industry had been the prime mover for industrialization beginning at the turn of the century; and there, too, in the postwar years, electronic industries developed, also on the basis of cheap female workers. Indeed, Kimi Hara, reviewing the contributions of women in these two industries, calls them "the two strong pillars which have sustained the Japanese economy from the bottom since the Meiji Restoration and in the post-war period" (1980, 223). As with so much else in the female world, their contributions were kept invisible, "never recognized, always 'left out of the mainstream of development'" (223).

2. A lobbying advertisement by two U.S. unions composed primarily of women workers summarized "a few horrendous facts" dealing with the growth of clothing imports as a percentage of the U.S. market: women's and children's coats, 22 percent in 1974, 52 percent in 1984; men's and boys' shirts, 19 percent in 1974, 55 percent in 1984; sweaters, 44 percent in 1974, 68 percent in 1984; brassieres, 29 percent in 1974, 58 percent in 1984 (*Washington Post*, 10 April 1985). In terms of loss of jobs, the situation was equally disturbing. In 1982, 15,000 jobs in the United States were lost in the textile industry, according to an aide to a U.S. senator (Hyde, 1983). Between 1980 and 1985, half a million textile jobs had been lost (Jefferson, *Washington Post*, 14 February 1985). In 1983, there was a crackdown on imports of women's clothing from Hong Kong, Taiwan, and Korea. It created a panic in the clothing industry both in Hong Kong and the United States. One importer called the cut "a total disregard for the total population of working women" (Hyde).

3. The disparity between domestic and oriental wage rates was even greater in Sweden, where the hourly wage rate in the apparel industry was $7.22 in 1982 and $.41 in South Korea; it was $4.35 in the United States (Ross). New technological innovations might mitigate the handicap of Western factories. Sewing machines in the most advanced plants are now being programmed by microcomputers so that a single worker may now operate several sewing machines; thus, piece by piece she can undercut even the lower wages in factories in other parts of the world (Golambos, 1984).

4. The Spanish term *Maquiladora* "refers to an assembly plant operating as a direct subsidiary or subcontracted firm for the manufacture of export-oriented goods, under the Mexican Border Industrialization Program started in 1965 and known as the Maquiladora Program since 1972" (Kelly, 1982).

5. According to 1984 figures, "by 1980 more than 55 countries—stretching in a chain through Latin America, the Caribbean, Africa and Asia—had established or were planning to set up free trade zones. Of the more than 50 zones then in operation, 22 were in Asia—11 in Malaysia, three in the Philippines, three in Taiwan, two in South Korea, two in India and one in Sri Lanka" and the trend was toward expansion (Eileen Sudworth, "Let the Robber Barons Come," reprinted from *Manushi*, a feminist monthly in India, no. 22, 1984. Present source, *Connexions*, winter, 1985, no. 15, p. 3).

Appendix C

1. An identical argument had been used in the early years of the feminist movement in the United States until it was made clear to these women how oppressive the position of the housewife could be. Many of such sheltered women became "displaced housewives," that is, women cast off by their husbands. Or widowed. Left unequipped for independence, it became clear to them

how many wives were "just a heart-beat away from welfare," that is, public dependency.

2. That the white mistresses experienced domestic work as oppressive was reflected in their responses to questions of why they employed a domestic servant to do it for them. Some preferred to become earners themselves, even at salaries lower than those of men; some preferred to indulge in whatever leisure activities they chose (129).

3. The attitudes of black domestics are expressed in comments like: "The whites are greedy"; "The whites are sitting on our heads, so we are inferior"; "Whites have all the power"; "We are more capable than the whites. That is why they try by all means to keep us under their feet"; "We pay for school books and white children don't"; "We earn less just because we are black" (Straker, 1965, 131). Some of the oppression by mistresses was petty and mean. The maid, for example, might not be given time off to see her children; on a maid's day off the mistress, while excusing her from housework, might not excuse her from care of the child. As a result the maid might be resentful and sullen toward the child. With no background of loving affection the child sometimes turned on her as he grew up. A maid was no more than a piece of furniture in the house ("South Africa Belongs to Us.")

4. In the United States it almost had been. The relations between mistress and maid in the Old South had not been as harsh as those in South Africa—and that story has since been softened in drama, novel, folk literature, romance, song, and scholarly history. Love, jealousy, hatred have all been portrayed in song and story as well as hidden in family closets. This racial breach in the female world has varied in depth and width and therefore in susceptibility to healing. In the United States during World War I and after there had been great resentment among white mistresses when black women went North, stripping white mistresses' kitchens and nurseries of black cooks and nannies. It was a breach that continued long after that, North as well as South. Not until the 1960s did the civil rights movement reach domestic workers under the aegis of strong leadership. According to one leader, "I'm still struggling for black women. They've been the burden bearer of all segments of blacks and I think they need the opportunity to demonstrate their skills, their abilities, and their knowledge. . . . In the past seven years there's been a great deal of change. These women used to be embarrassed about saying they were maids. Now it's different. You can't tell a maid from a secretary anymore. In the past, if a black woman was a maid you could tell by the way she dressed. Now they don't carry the shopping bags as much, they go neater, and they look more lively and intelligent. They're making between fifteen and twenty dollars, up to twenty-two dollars a day. And the heart of the Deep South like this never paid that kind of salary before" (Bolden, 1976, 167).

5. One U.S. woman reporting on her trip to South Africa in 1984 found that such "sisterhood" between caring white women and black women was possible because the husbands of the white women were in important and invulnerable positions, charges not supported by the case of Sheena Duncan, president of Black Sash in 1985. Her mother had been one of the founders of Black Sash in 1955 at some social cost. "She lost most of her friends. . . . She was expected to go to the club and play golf or tennis and to do some active welfare work as well. But she and the four women who also started it could see that the men were just dithering around and that they had to go to the root of the problem, which is apartheid" (Sheena Duncan, quoted by Mary McCrory, "To Be White, Female and Anti-Apartheid," *Washington Post*, 28 July 1985). As far as protection by a well-positioned husband goes, he gives her his entire support, putting up "with

a great deal," including lengthy absences for international speaking tours. She is called "kaffir-boetie," Afrikaans for "nigger-lover."

6. White women who had constituted almost 96 percent of the workers in the clothing industry in 1948 accounted for only 28.5 percent in 1959, and a mere 2.29 percent in 1979 (Chitja, n.d., 39). Black women, conversely, had increased from less than one percent to 82.11 percent in that period, despite limiting legal restrictions which economic forces were proving powerful enough to overcome (39–40).

7. Interesting to note is the fact that there were only 12 psychologists listed in 1981 but 249 sociologists. A possible interpretation was that individual, personal issues seemed far less relevant and urgent than sociological ones. Great concern for individual personal problems may be a luxury not every society can afford.

8. In an updated paper the *Forum*, a professor of sociology at the University of Natal reported he had found that there was "a greater gulf between white women and black women than between whites and blacks in general," suggesting that upward mobility was easier for men than for women among blacks. Another item dealt with the disabilities written into marriage for black women who were "exposed to three marriages: the customary, the civil, and Christian marriage. . . . A black woman is a child forever, irrespective of her qualifications" (undated paper—*Forum* Vol. 2. No. 1.) (2).

9. In a special issue of the *Forum* there was a summary of some of the topics discussed at an October 1983 meeting of the Advisory Council of the Women's Bureau, including: sensitive advertising should be adequately researched; wide investigation was called for with respect to remarriage among blacks; assertiveness should be combined with better communication; a common-law wife has no rights, a situation that calls for attention; Indian women are worth emulating; women must be more involved at the government level; there is great need for child-care centers.

BIBLIOGRAPHY

Aas, Berit. "On Female Culture: An Attempt to Formulate a Theory of Women's Solidarity and Action." *Acta Sociologica*, 28 (n.d.).
———. "A Five-dimensional Model for Change: Contradictions and Feminist Consciousness." *Women's Studies International Quarterly*, 4 (1981).
———. "A Materialistic View of Men's and Women's Attitudes toward War." *Women's Studies International Forum*, 1982.
———. "The Peace March to Moscow." Draft, 1983.
———. "The International Feminist University." Announcement, Oslo, Norway, n.d.
Abu-Baker, Khawla. "The Impact of Cross-Cultural Contact on the Status of Arab Women in Israel." In Women's World: From the New Scholarship, edited by Marilyn Safir, Martha Mednick, Dafne Israeli, and Jessie Bernard. New York: Praeger, 1985.
Ackelsberg, Martha A. "'Separate or Equal': Mujeres Libres and Anarchist Strategy for Women's Emancipation." *Feminist Studies*, Vol. 11, no. 1 (spring 1985).
Addams, Jane; Balch, Emily; Hamilton, Alice. *Women at the Hague: The International Congress of Women and Its Results*. New York: Macmillan, 1915.
Agarwol, Bina. See Kamla Bhasin.
Akello, Grace. "Self Twice Removed: Ugandan Woman." *International Reports: Women and Society*, no. 8. London: Change, n.d.
Alger, C. and Lyons, G. M. "Social Science as a Transnational System." *International Studies Notes*. vol. 1, no. 3 (1974).
Allen, Donna. Program of 1979 Conference of the Women's Institute for Freedom of the Press. Washington, D.C.
———. *Editor Media Report to Women*. Washington, D.C.: Women's Institute for Freedom of the Press, 1979–1986.
———. *1985 Index-Directory of Women's Media*. Washington, D.C.: Women's Institute for Freedom of the Press, 1985.
Allen, Martha. *Editor Media Report to Women*. Washington, D.C.: Women's Institute for Freedom of the Press.
Allot, K. See F. Ladd.
Anand, Anita. "Rethinking Women and Development." In *Isis: Women in Development, A Resource Guide for Organization and Action*. Geneva: Isis Women's International Information and Communication Service, 1983.
———. "The Challenge Continues." Development Forum. New York: United Nations, 1985.
Andemichael, Berhanykun. "Human Rights Organizations: Commentary." In *Knowledge and Power in a Global Society*, edited by William M. Evan. Beverly Hills: Sage, 1981.

Anderson, Jack and Van Atta, Dale. "Omani Sultan a Quiet U.S. Friend." *Washington Post,*
Anderson, Jeanine. See Blanca Figueroa.
Angell, Robert. "Do ISPAs Promote Global Integration?" In *Knowledge and Power in a Global Society* edited by William M. Evan. Beverly Hills: Sage, 1981.
Anonymous. *Military Ideology and the Dissolution of Democracy: Women in Chile.* London: Change, 1981.
Antrobus, Peggy. Interview at the Forum of Mid-Decade Conference of Caribbean Women, in *Women Speaks!* (quarterly newsletter) no. 4, (1981).
Ardener, Shirley. *Women and Space.* New York: St. Martin's Press, 1981.
Arditti, Rita. "Second Latin American and Caribbean Feminist Gathering, Lima, Peru, 1983." *Feminist Forum,* vol. 6, no. 5 (1983).
Arensberg, C. *The Irish Countryman.* London: Macmillan, 1937.
Arizpe, Lourdes and Navarro, Marya. "Comments on Tinker's 'A Feminist View of Copenhagen.'" *Signs,* vol. 7 (spring 1982).
Artus, Marjorie Cooke, cordinator. *Worldwide Guide of Organizations Fostering a New Man and Civilization.* Edited by Hy Newmark. New York: International Cooperation Council, 1973.
Asian and Pacific Centre for Women and Development. "Goals of the Women's Movement." International workshop, Bangkok, Thailand, 1979.
———. "Feminist Ideology and Structure in the First Half of the Decade for Women." Bangkok, Thailand, 1979. New York: International Women's Tribune Centre. New York: U.N. Plaza.
Association of Nicaraguan Women. *Isis,* no. 19 (1981).
Association of Salvadoran Women. Participation of Latin American Women in Social and Political Organizations: Reflections. New York: Women's International Resource Exchange (WIRE) Service, 1982.
Atsumi, Ikeko. "Women's Liberation in Japan. What Does Modernization Mean for Women?" In *Women's World: From the New Scholarship,* edited by Marilyn Safir, Martha Mednick, Dafne Izraeli, and Jessie Bernard. New York: Praeger, 1985.
Az, "The Women's Struggle in Iran." Reprinted from *Monthly Review,* March 1981. New York: Women's International Resource Exchange (WIRE) Service.
Bachu, Amara. *International Fertility Indicators.* Current Population Report, Special Studies Series P-23, no. 123. Washington, D.C.: Government Printing Office, 1983.
Balch, Emily. See Jane Addams.
Baldassare, Mark G. "Human Spatial Behavior." *Annual Review of Sociology,* vol. 4 (1978).
Bandarage, Asoka. "Toward International Feminism." *Brandeis Review,* vol. 3 (summer 1983).
———. "Third World Women: More than Mere Statistics." *Women's Review of Books,* November 1983.
Barthel, Diane L. "The Rise of a Female Professional Elite: The Case of Senegal." *African Studies Review,* vol. 18 (December 1975).
———. See George Hardy.
Basch, Francoise, reporter. "Colloquium on Women, Feminism, Research, Toulouse, 1982." *Feminist Forum,* vol. 6, no. 3 (1983).
———. "Femmes, Feminisme, Socialisme," panel on Female Forms of Political Action at a conference of the Center for European Studies, Research

Planning Group: The New Family and the New Woman, 1983. *European Studies Newsletter* vol. 10, no. 6.

Battiata, Nancy. "They Are the World of Women. Thousands Gather in Nairobi." *New York Times*, 11 July 1985.

———. "The Feminist Finale, High Hopes in Nairobi as Forum Disperses." *Washington Post*, 20 July 1985.

Baum, Samuel. "Illustrative Analysis of Cohort Differences in Women's Literacy in Developing Countries." Paper at Second International Interdisciplinary Congress on Women, Groningen, Netherlands, 1984.

Bay, Edna G. See Nancy J. Hafkin.

Beauvoir, Simone de. *The Second Sex*. Paris: Gallimard, 1949. U.S. edition, New York: Bantam, 1961.

Bell, Linda A., ed. *Visions of Women*. Clifton, N.J.: Humana Press, 1983.

Ben-Zui, Mena. The Mt. Carmel International Training Center for Community Development. Haifa, Israel, 1981.

Bernard, Jessie. *The Sociology of Community*. Glenview, Ill.: Scott, Foresman, 1973.

———. *The Future of Marriage*. New York: World, 1972, New Haven: Yale University Press, 1982.

———. *Women and the Public Interest*. Chicago: Aldine, 1971.

———. "Historical and Structural Barriers to Occupational Desegregation," *Signs*, vol. 1 (1976).

———. "Where Are We Now? Some Thoughts on the Current Scene." *Psychology of Women Quarterly*, vol. 1, no. 1 (1976).

———. *The Future of Motherhood*. New York: Dial, 1974.

———. *The Female World*. New York: Free Press, 1981.

Best, Raphael. *We've All Got Scars*. Bloomington: Indiana University Press, 1984.

Bhasin, Kamla and Agarwol, Bina. *Women and Media: Analysis, Alternatives, and Action*. Rome: Isis International (New Delhi: Kali for Women) 1984.

Bleir, Ruth. *Science and Gender: A Critique of Biology and Its Theories on Women*. New York: Pergamon Press, 1984.

Blumberg, Rae Lesser. "Rural Women in Development: Veil of Invisibility, World of Work." *International Journal of Intercultural Relations*, vol. 3 (1979).

———. "At the End of the Line: Women and United States Foreign Aid in Asia, 1978–1980." *Women and Politics*, vol. 2, no. 3 (1982).

Bolden, Dorothy. "Women Helping Women." In *Nobody Speaks for Me! Portraits of American Working Class Women*, edited by Nancy Seifer. New York: Simon and Schuster, 1976.

Boserup, Ester. *Women's Role in Economic Development*. New York: St. Martin's Press, 1970.

Bott, Elizabeth. *Family and Social Network*. New York: Free Press, 1971.

Boulding, Elise. "Female Alternatives to Hierarchical Systems, Past and Present. A Critique of Women's INGOs in the Light of History." *International Women's Year Studies on Women*. Paper no. 3. Boulder, Colo.: 1975.

———. *The Underside of History: A View of Women through Time*. Boulder, Colo.: Westview Press, 1976.

———. *Women in the Twentieth Century World*. New York: Halsted Press, 1977.

———. *Woman: The Fifth World*. New York: Foreign Policy Association Headline Series, 1980.

———, Nuss, Shirley; Carson, Dorothy Lee; and Greenstein, Michael A. *Handbook of International Data on Women*. New York: Halsted Press, 1976.

———. See Elizabeth Moen.

Boulding, Kenneth. "The Grants Economy." *Michigan Academician*, vol. 1 (1969).

Bourguinine, Erika, ed. *A World of Women: Anthropological Studies of Women in Societies of the World.* South Hadley, Mass.: Bergin and Garvey, 1984.

Brown, Rita Mae. "The Last Straw." In *Introduction to Class and Feminism*, edited by Charlotte Bunch and Nancy Myron. Baltimore: Diana Press, 1974.

Bruley, C. "Women against Fascism: Women and the Popular Front of 1934–39 in Britain." Panel on Female Forms of Political Action, conference of the Center for European Studies, Research Planning Group: The New Family and the New Woman, 1983. *European Studies Newsletter*, vol. 10, no. 6.

Buhle, Mari Jo. "Women and the Socialist Party." In From Feminism to Liberation, edited by Elizabeth Hoskins Altbach. Cambridge, Mass.: Schenkman, 1971.

Bujira, Janet M. See Patricia Caplan.

Bulos, Maha. "The Arab Woman's Changing Role." In *Development Forum*. New York: United Nations, 1985.

Bunch, Charlotte. "Copenhagen and Beyond. Prospects for Global Feminism." *Quest*, vol. 5, no. 4 (1982).

———. *Feminism in the 80s: Facing Down the Right; Going Public with Our Vision.* Denver: Antelope Publications, 1983.

——— and Myron, Nancy, eds. *Introduction to Class and Feminism.* Baltimore: Diana Press, 1974.

Canale, Victoire. "Corse." *des femmes hebdo*, no. (83) 84. March 1982.

Caplan, Patricia and Bujira, Janet M., eds. *Women United, Women Divided: Comparative Studies of Ten Contemporary Cultures.* Bloomington: Indiana University Press, 1979.

Caraveli-Chaves, Anna. "Bridge between Worlds. The Greek Women's Lament as Communicative Event." *American Journal of Folklore*, vol. 368 (1980).

Carlson, Rae. "Understanding Women: Implications for Personality Theory and Research." *Journal of Social Issues*, vol. 28 (1972).

Carrillo, Rozana. Inaugural Address, Second Latin American and Caribbean Feminist Meeting, Lima, Peru, 1984.

Carson, Dorothy. See Elise Boulding, 1976.

Casey, Mary F. "Women in Northern Ireland." *Plexus*, October 1981.

Caughman, Susan and Mariam N'diaye Thiam. The Markala Cooperative: A New Approach to Traditional Economic Roles. New York: *Seeds*, No. 5, P.O. Box 3923, Grand Central Station.

Cerquone, Joseph. See Roger Winter.

Chabaku, Motlalepula. "Growing Up in the Era of the Pass Laws." Ms. Magazine, November 1982.

Chen, Marty. *The Working Women's Forum: Organizing for Credit and Change.* New York: *Seeds*, 1983. (Funded by Carnegie, Ford, Oxfam-America, Population Council, Rockefeller, WID).

———. *Developing Non-craft Employment for Women in Bangladesh.* New York: *Seeds*, 1984.

Chitja, Sarah. "Women in Industry." In *Women: A Vital Human Resource* edited by W. D. Pienaar. Pretoria: Center for Management Studies, University of South Africa, Seminar Series 5, n.d.

Churchman, Arza and Sebba, Rachel. "Women's Territoriality in the Home." In *Women's World: From the New Scholarship*, edited by Marilyn Safir, Martha Mednick, Dafne Israeli, and Jessie Bernard. New York: Praeger, 1985.

Clarke, Anne. "Pre-Nairobi: Women and Development Workshops." *Development Forum*. New York: United Nations, 1985.

Claude, Inis L., Jr. "International Organization: The Process and the Institutions." In *International Encyclopedia of the Social Sciences*. New York: Macmillan, 1968.

Clay, Jason W. "Ethnicity: Powerful Factor in Refugee Flows." In *World Refugee Survey, 1984*, edited by Rosemary E. Tripp. Washington, D.C.: U.S. Committee for Refugees, 1985.

Clift, Elayne. "Nairobi 1985 Advances Women." *New Directions for Women*, September–October 1985.

Cockburn, Cynthia. See Christine Zmroczek.

Cook, Alice; Lorwin, Val R., and Daniels, Arlene Kaplan, eds. *Women and Trade Unions in Eleven Industrialized Countries*. Philadelphia: Temple University Press, 1984.

Cooley, Charles. *Social Organization*. New York: Scribners, 1909.

Costello, Nancy, "Tatyana Mamanova, Exiled Soviet Feminist." *Second Century Radcliffe News*, April 1985.

Cottingham, Jane. "Women and Health." In *Women in Development: A Resource Guide for Organization and Action*. Geneva: Isis, 1983.

Critchfield, Richard. "What Is Going Wrong in Africa?" *Washington Post*, 8 August 1982.

Croll, Elisabeth. "Rural China: Segregation to Solidarity." In *Women United, Women Divided* edited by Patricia Caplan and Janet M. Bujra. Bloomington: Indiana University Press, 1982.

D'Amelia, N. "Forms of Women's Solidarity." *European Studies Newsletter*, vol. 10, no. 6 (1980).

Danforth, John C. "Africa: Does Anybody Really Care?" *Washington Post*, 25 January 1984.

Dash, Leon. "The Women's Movement Comes to Cape Verde." *Washington Post*, 26 July 1981.

———. "Drought Maims, Kills in Growing Swath of Africa." *Washington Post*, 26 February 1984.

———. "Gun Replaces Vote as Civilian Rule Fades in West Africa." *Washington Post*, 8 April 1984.

———. "New U.S. Plan Would Help Free Market African States." *Washington Post*, 7 May 1984.

Davin, D. "Women in the Liberated Areas." In *Women in China*, edited by M. Young. Michigan Papers in Chinese Studies, 1973.

Davis, Nira Yuval. *Israeli Women and Men: Division Behind the Unity*. International Reports: Women and Society, no. 6. London: Change, n.d.

Delphy, Christine. "Feminist Glimmerings in Socialist Countries." *Feminist Issues*, vol. 1, no. 1 (summer 1980).

Department of State press release. 15 October 1980.

Derryck, Vivian L. "Afterword." United States Department of State, *United States Women: Issues and Progress in the UN Decade for Women, 1976–1985*. Washington, D.C.: Government Printing Office, 1980.

Development Forum. *Women and Development*. An Anthology of Articles from the Development Forum, United Nations, 1985.

Diaz, Gladys. *Roles and Contradictions of Chilean Women in the Resistance and in Exile: Collective Reflections of a Group of Militant Prisoners*. New York: Women's International Resource Exchange Service (WIRE), 1979.

Dixler, Elsa. "Women and Socialist Movements: A Review Essay." *Feminist Studies*, vol. 10, 1984.

Dixon, Ruth B. *Assessing the Impact of Development Projects on Women.* Washington, D.C.: Women in Development, 1980.

Doder, Dusko. "When Rhetoric and Reality Collide, the Two Faces of Moscow's Peace Policy." *Washington Post,* 20 July 1982.

Dorsett, Lenore. *Women's Tribune Centre Newsletter,* no. 11. Copenhagen, 1980.

Dubois, Cora. *The People of Alors.* Minneapolis: University of Minnesota Press, 1944.

Dufrancatel, Christiane. "Algerian Women: Myths of Liberation." *Connexions,* no. 2 (fall 1981).

Durden, Robert F. "People As Property." A review of *Slavery and Freedom* by William Lee Rose. *New York Times Book Review,* 24 January 1982.

Earle, Claudette. "The U.N. Mid-Decade Conference for Women: Overview of Copenhagen." *Woman Speaks!* 1980.

———. Interview at the U.N. Mid-Decade Conference for Women, *Caribbean Women* (quarterly newsletter), no. 4 (1981).

Edwards, G. Franklin. "Race Relations: World Perspective." *International Encyclopedia of the Social Sciences.* New York: Macmillan, 1968.

Eliason, Marcus. "Women in Politics: Study in Extremes." *Washington Post,* 31 July 1984.

Elliott, Veronica and Sorsby, Victoria. An Investigation into Evaluations of Projects Designed to Benefit Women: Final Report. Washington, D.C.: AID, 1979.

El Saadawi, Nawal. *The Hidden Face of Eve: Women in the Arab World.* Translated and edited by Sherif Hetata. London: Zed Press, 1980.

———; Mernissi, Fatima; and Vajrathon, Mallica. "A Critical View of the Wellesley Conference." *Quest,* vol. 4 (1978).

Elson, Diane and Pearson, Ruth. "The Subordination of Women and the Internationalization of Factory Production." In *Of Marriage and the Market* edited by Kate Young, Carol Walkowitz, and Roslyn McCullagh. London: CSE Books, 1981. Reprinted by Women's International Resource Exchange (WIRE) Service.

Engel, Barbara Alpern. "Feminism and the Non-Western World." *Frontiers,* vol. 7, no. 2 (1983).

Enloe, Cynthia. "Women Textile Workers in the Militarization of Southeast Asia." In *Perspectives in Power: Women in Africa, Asia, and Latin America,* edited by Jean F. O'Barr. Durham, N.C.: Duke University Press, 1982.

Ergas, Jasmine. "Women's Movements and Revolutionary Movements." Report of a paper at the Conference of European Studies, 1980. *European Studies Newsletter,* vol. 10, no. 6, 1981.

Etienne, Mona and Leacock, Eleanor, eds. *Women and Colonization.* South Hadley, Mass.: Bergin and Garvey, 1983.

Evan, William M. "Some Dilemmas of Knowledge and Power: An Introduction." In *Knowledge and Power in a Global Society* edited by William M. Evan. Beverly Hills: Sage, 1981.

———, ed. *Knowledge and Power in a Global Society.* Beverly Hills: Sage, 1981.

Everett, Jana. "The Upsurge of Women's Activism in India." *Frontiers,* vol. 7, no. 2 (1983).

——— and Savara, Mira. "Bank Loans to the Poor in Bombay: Do Women Benefit?" *Signs,* volume 10, no. 2 (winter 1984).

Fausto, Sterling, Anne. *Myths of Gender: Biological Theories About Women and Men.* New York: Basic Books, 1985.

Fawcett, James T., Siew-Ean Khoo, and Smith, Peter C., *Women in the Cities of*

Asia: Migration and Urban Adaptation. Boulder, Colo.: Westview Press, 1984.

Ferge, Zsuzzsa, "Biology and Equality between Sexes." Paper presented at the Second International Interdisciplinary Congress on Women, Groningen, The Netherlands, 1984.

Fernandez, Patricia, and Maria Kelly. "Gender and Industry in Mexico's New Frontier." Paper presented at the World Congress of Sociology, Mexico City, 1982.

Ferree, Myra Marx. "The View from Below." *Marriage and Family Review,* 1983. (Present version from draft copy).

———— and Hess, Beth. *Controversy and Coalition: The New Feminist Movement.* New York: Trayne, 1985.

Fiedler, Leslie. *Love and Death in the American Novel.* New York: World, 1962.

Fields, Rona M. "The Women of Ireland: A Case-Study on the Effects of 800 Years of Colonial Victimization." In *A Society on the Run: A Psychology of Northern Ireland.* New York: Penguin, 1973.

Figueroa, Blanca and Anderson, Jeanine. *Women in Peru.* London: Change, 1981.

Finsterbusch, Kurt. "Formulas for Successful Development Projects." Paper given at American Sociological Association meetings, 1983.

Fisher, Bev. "Race and Class: Beyond Personal Politics." *Quest,* vol. 3, no. 4, spring 1977.

Flint, Robert. *History of the Philosophy of History.* New York: Scribners, 1894.

Ford Foundation, Letter, 1 August 1981.

Fouque, Antoinette. "France." *des femmes hebdo,* no. (83), 84, March, 1982.

Frank, Libby. "WILP [Women's International League for Peace] Is Target in Anti-Freeze Campaign." *Peace and Freedom,* publication of U.S. Section of WILP, vol. 42, no. 9 (December 1982).

Frankel, Glenn. "How Europeans Sliced Up Africa. Borders Drawn a Century Ago Assured Today's Tensions." *Washington Post,* 6 January 1985.

————. "Mozambicans Face Starvation as Food Shipments Are Delayed." *Washington Post,* 22 January 1985.

————. "U.S. Government Searches for Ways to Bolster Struggling Mozambican Government." *Washington Post,* 26 January 1985.

————. "Mozambique, Once Suspicious Warms to U.S. Efforts in Region." *Washington Post,* 5 February 1985.

————. "Ten Years into Revolution. Flagging Mozambique Reconsiders." *Washington Post,* 8 February 1985.

Fraser, Arvonne. "Foreword." In *Looking to the Future, Equal Partnership between Women and Men in the 21st Century.* Minneapolis: Women, Public Policy and Development Project, Humphrey Institute of Public Affairs, University of Minnesota, 1985.

Frazer, Elizabeth, reporter. Women's International Tribunal and Meeting on Reproductive Rights. Fourth International Women and Health Meeting. Amsterdam, 1984. *Feminist Forum,* vol. 7, no. 6.

Freedman, Estelle. "Separatism as Strategy: Female Institution Building and American Feminism, 1870–1930." *Feminist Studies,* vol. 5, no. 3 (1979).

Freeman, Jo. *The Politics of Women's Liberation.* New York: McKay, 1975.

Friedlander, Judith. See Carroll Smith-Rosenberg.

Fruzzetti, Livia M. *The Gift of the Virgin.* New Brunswick: Rutgers University Press, 1982.

Fuller, Norma. "Feminism in Peru." *Feminist Forum,* vol. 6, no. 5 (1983).

Gajardo, Joanna. "¿Es la politico personal, o es lo personal politico?" New York: WIRE, n.d.

Galambos, "A 'High-Tech' or a Service Economy Future?" *National Forum*, summer 1984.

Galdemez, Miriam. "Women's Lives in El Salvador." (Interviews with Jenny Vaughan and Jane McIntosh.) Isis Bulletin, no. 19 (1981). Reproduced in *Spare Rib*, no. 106 (May 1981).

Gasperini, Lavinia. "Mozambique: Mobilizing Women" (plus interview with Salome Moiana, secretary-general of the Organization of Mozambican Women in 1980). Isis Bulletin, no. 19 (1981).

Glazer, Nona. "'Woman's Place' and 'Man's World': The Architecture of Sex Roles." Paper presented at the National Council of Family Relations, 1974.

Glynn, Leonard; Politer, Larry; Lennoux, Penny; Jennings, Ann; and Kirkland, Robert. "The Vanishing Tribes." *Newsweek*, 12 October 1981.

Goddard, Paula O. "To Nairobi and Beyond." *Foreign Service Journal*, July–August 1985.

Goodin, Joan. See Anne H. Nelson.

Greenstein, Michael A. See Elise Boulding.

Gurin, Patricia, "Women's Group Consciousness." *The Committee for Gender Research*, no. 2, Ann Arbor, Michigan, 1982.

Hafkin, Nancy J. and Bay, Edna G., eds. *Women in Africa*. Stanford, Cal.: Stanford University Press, 1976.

Hall, K. P. See Marlaine E. Lockheed.

Hall, Roberta M. and Sandler, Bernice. *The Classroom Climate: A Chilly One for Women?* Washington, D.C.: Association of American Colleges, 1982.

Hamilton, Alice. See Jane Addams.

Hamilton, Sahni; Popkin, Barry; and Spicer, Deborah. *Women and Nutrition in Low Income Countries*. South Hadley, Mass.: Bergin and Garvey, 1984.

Hanami, Tadashi. "Japan." In *Women and Trade Unions in Eleven Industrialized Countries* edited by Alice Cook, Val R. Lorwin, and Arlene Kaplan Daniels. Philadelphia: Temple University Press, 1984.

Hara, Kimi. "Industrialization and Women Textile Workers in Textiles, Electronics, and Electric Machinery Industries in Japan." Paper presented at meetings of Experts on Research on Status of Women, Development, and Population Trends: Evaluation and Prospects. Paris: UNESCO, 1980.

Harden, Blaine. "As U.N. Women's Decade Ends African Wives Still Exploited. Men Demand Pregnancies as Proof of Their Virility." *Washington Post*, 6 July 1985.

Harding, Sandra and Hintikka, Merrill B., eds. *Discovering Reality: Feminist Perspectives on Epistemology, Metaphysics, Methodology, and Philosophy of Science*. Boston: D. Reidel, 1983.

Harris, Abigail M. See Marlaine E. Lockheed.

Hartley, Shirley Foster. See Nadia H. Youssef.

Hartling, Paul. "Refugee Aid and Development: Genesis and Testing of a Strategy." *World Refugee Survey 1984*. New York: U.S. Committee for Refugees, 1985.

Hashimoto, Masanori. "Economics of Postwar Fertility in Japan: Differentials and Trends." *Journals of Political Economy*, vol. 82 (1974).

Heller, Agnes, "On Leninism and Feminism." *Connexions*, no. 5 (summer 1982).

Helzner, Judith F. *Evaluating Small Grants for Women in Development*. Washington, D.C.: Women in Development, 1980.

Henley, Nancy. *Body Politics: Power, Sex, and Nonverbal Communication*. Englewood Cliffs, N.J.: Prentice-Hall, 1977.

————. "Women's Nonverbal Behavior: Underlying Assumptions in the Admonition to Change." In *Women's World: From the New Scholarship*, edited by Marilyn Safir, Martha T. Mednick, Dafne Izraeli, and Jessie Bernard. New York: Praeger, 1985.

Hermassi, Elbahi. "Changing Patterns in Research on the Third World." *Review of Sociology*, vol. 4 (1978).

Herzog, Elizabeth. See Mark, Zborowski.

Hess, Beth. "Prime Time." *Women's Review of Books*, June 1985.

———. See Myra Marx Ferree.

Hintikka, Merrill B. See Sandra Harding.

Hooks, Bell. *Feminist Theory: From Margin to Center*. Boston: South End Publishers, 1984.

Hopkins, Terrence K. and Wallerstein, Immanuel, eds. *Processes of the World System*. Beverly Hills: Sage, 1980.

Hosken, Fran P., ed. *WIN News*, vol. 10, no. 1 (winter 1985).

Hoskins, Merilyn W. *Income Generating Activities with Women's Participation*. Washington, D.C.: Women in Development, 1980.

Hottel, Althea, ed. *Women Around the World*. Philadelphia: Annals American Academy of Political and Social Science, 1968.

Howe, Florence. "Women's Studies International: From Idea to Reality." International Supplement to the *Women's Studies Quarterly*, no. 1, January 1982.

Hrdy, Sarah. *The Woman That Never Evolved*. Cambridge, Mass.: Harvard University Press, 1981.

Hughes, Mary, reporter. International Women's Conference, Feminist Methods and Strategies in Educational Work with Women, Bergen, Netherlands. *Feminist Forum*, vol. 6, no. 5 (1983).

Hunte, Pamela. "Women and the Development Process in Afghanistan." Paper presented to the Near East Bureau, U.S. AID, 1978.

Hunter, Jane. *The Gospel of Gentility*. New Haven: Yale University Press, 1984.

Huston, Perdita. *Third World Women Speak Out*. New York: Praeger, 1979.

Hyde, Nina. "Import Limits Create Fashion Panic." *Washington Post*, 6 July 1985.

Ikegame, Micko. "Sisters of the Sun: Japanese Women Today." *International Reports*, no. 12. London: Change, n.d.

Inkeles, Alexander and Smith, David H. *Becoming Modern: Individual Changes in Six Developing Countries*. Cambridge, Mass.: Harvard University Press, 1974.

INSTRAW. Compiling Social Indicators on the Situation of Women. Santo Domingo, Dominican Republic, n.d.

———. *Improving Concepts and Methods for Statistics and Indicators on the Situation of Women*. Santo Domingo, Dominican Republic, n.d.

International Reports on Women and Society: Singapore, Aline K. Wong; Thailand, Khin Thitsa; New Soviet Woman, Maggie Andrews and Jo Peers; Military Ideology and the Dissolution of Democracy, Women in Chile, unsigned; Peru, Blanca Figueroa and Jeanine Anderson; Israeli Women and Men, Nira Yuval Davis; Philippines, Marie C. Villariba; Uganda, Grace Akello; Caribbean Women, unsigned; Bangladesh, Naila Kabeer; Ethiopian Women, Tsehai Berhane Selassie; Japan, Nieko Ikegame; Lesotho, Gwen Malahleha. London: Change n.d.

International Women's Tribune Center. Decade Update no. 1, United Nations, March 1984.

———. Decade for Women Information Resources for 1985. United Nations, 1985.

Isis International and Organizing Collective of the Second Latin American and Caribbean Feminist Meeting. *Women in Action,* supplement no. 1. *Women's Journal,* June, 1984.

Jackson, Paula. Personal letter on Amnesty International, 19 February 1985.

Jacquette, Jane S. "Copenhagen, 1980. 'Women in Development,' Feminism and the New International Economic Order." Paper presented at the American Sociological Association, Toronto, 1981.

Jaffe, A. J. and Stewart, Charles D. *Manpower Resources and Utilization: Principles of Working Force Analysis.* New York: Wiley, 1951.

JET. Editorial introduction to "Movement Building." *Quest,* vol. 5, no. 4 (1982).

Jheck, Diane. "Notes from Nairobi." New York: National Public Radio and the IPS Wire Service.

Jones, Allen K. *Iranian Refugees: The Many Faces of Persecution.* Washington, D.C.: U.S. Committee for Refugees, December, 1984.

———. *Afghan Refugees: Five Years Later.* Washington, D.C.: U.S. Committee for Refugees, January, 1985.

Joseph, Gloria and Lewis, Jill. *Common Differences: Conflicts in Black and White Feminist Perspectives.* New York: Anchor, 1981.

Joseph, Shirley. Statement on Copenhagen Conference. *Lilith,* no. 8, 1981.

Kabeer, Naila. *Minus Lives: Women of Bangladesh.* London: Change, n.d.

Kahn, Margaret. *Children of the Jinn.* New York: Wideview Books, 1980.

Karl, Marilee. "The International Feminist Network." *Isis International Bulletin,* no. 17, 1980.

———. "Women and Multinationals." In *Women in Development.* Geneva: Isis, 1983.

———. "Women and Rural Development." Ibid.

———. See Jane Cottingham.

Karlehar, Malavika. "Some Perspectives on the Employment of Poor Women in India." Paper presented at the Tenth World Congress of Sociology, Mexico City, 1982.

Kelly, Maria. See Fernandez, Patricia.

Kelso, Casey and Metz, Cara Lise. Interview with Tendi Ndlovu, acting director of Official Publishing House, Harare, Zimbabwe, January 1982.

———. Interviews reported in "Too Liberated?" Connexions, no. 11, 1984. Excerpted from *Outwrite,* an English feminist monthly, October 1983. Original source: *Moto,* a Zimbabwean periodical.

Kennedy, Mary, reporter. *International Council for Adult Education Conference, Paris, 1982. Feminist Forum:* vol. 6, no. 3 (1983).

Kessler, Lauren. *The Dissident Press: Alternative Journalism in American History.* Beverly Hills: Sage, 1984.

Klein, Renate Duelli, reporter. Fifth Annual Conference of U.S. Women's Studies Association, Columbus, Ohio, 1983. *Feminist Forum,* vol. 6, no. 4 (1983).

Kriesberg, Louis. "Organizational Membership Structure: International Non-Governmental Organizations and Co-Membership from Adversary Nations." *Journal of Voluntary Action Research,* vol. 3, nos. 3–4 (1974).

———. "Varieties of ISPAs [International Scientific and Professional Associations]: Their Forms and Functions." In William M. Evan, editor, *Knowledge and Power in a Global Society.* Beverly Hills: Sage, 1981.

Kristof, Nicholas. "The Great Textile Trade Debate." *New York Times,* 23 July 1985.

Kruks, Sonia. "Mozambique: Some Reflections on the Struggle for Women's Emancipation." *Frontiers,* vol. 7, no. 2 (1983).

Kung, Lydia. "Factory Work and Women in Taiwan: Changes in Self Image and Status." *Signs*, vol. 2 (autumn 1976).

Kuninobu, Junko Wada. "The Development of Feminism in Modern Japan." *Feminist Issues*, vol. 4, no. 2 (fall 1984).

Ladd, F. and Allot, K., eds. See G. R. Lynn.

Lambiotte, Joellen. Interview with Teurai Ropa Nhongo and Dr. Naomi Nhiwatiwa, minister and deputy minister, respectively, of Community Development and Women's Affairs in Zimbabwe by Joellen Lambiotte of the Boston Coalition for the Liberation of Southern Africa, April 1981 in Zimbabwe. In "Resistance, War and Liberation: Women of Southern Africa." New York: Women's International Research Exchange (WIRE), n.d.

Lamphere, Louise. See Michelle Zimbalist Rosaldo.

Lancaster, Jane Beckman. "In Praise of the Achieving Female Monkey." In *The Female Experience*, edited by Carol Jarvis. New York: Ziff-Davis, 1973.

Landis, Elizabeth S. "African Women under Apartheid." New York.: The African Fund, 1970. Present citation: "Resistance, War and Liberation: Women of Southern Africa." New York: WIRE, n.d.

Lapchick, Richard E. and Urdang, Stephanie. *Oppression and Resistance: The Struggle of Women in Southern Africa*. Westport, Conn.: Greenwood Press, 1982.

Lapidus, Gail W., ed. *Women, Work, and Family in the Soviet Union*. Armonk, N.Y.: M. E. Sharpe, 1982.

Lawrence, R. J. "Domestic Space and Society: A Cross-Cultural Study." *Comparative Studies in Society and History*, vol. 24 (1982).

Leacock, Eleanor. "Reflections on the Conference on Women and Development." *Signs*, vol. 3, no. 1 (1977).

Lee, David R. See Mary Ellen Mazey.

Leghorn, Lisa and Parker, Katherine. *Woman's Worth: Sexual Economics of the World of Women*. Boston: Routledge and Kegan Paul, 1981.

Leimas, Carol. "To Nairobi and Beyond." *Foreign Service Journal*, July–August 1985.

———. "Impressions of the Copenhagen Conference." *Graduate Woman*, November–December 1980.

Lelybeld, Joseph, "The Designs of Apartheid." *New York Times* Book Review, 24 January 1982.

Lerner, Daniel. *The Passing of Traditional Society: Modernizing the Middle East*. New York: The Free Press, 1963.

Lewis, Jill. See Gloria Joseph.

Lewis, Paul. "Algeria After 30 Years." *Washington Post*, 31 October 1984.

Lillydahl, Jane. See Elizabeth Moen.

Lipman-Blumen, Jean. *Gender Roles and Power*. Englewood Cliffs, N.J.: Prentice-Hall, 1984.

——— and Bernard, Jessie, eds. *Sex Roles and Social Policy*. Beverly Hills: Sage, 1979.

Little, Kenneth. *African Women in Towns as Aspect of Africa's Social Revolution*. New York: Cambridge University Press, 1973.

Lockheed, Marlaine E. *The Modification of Female Leadership Behavior in the Presence of Males*. Princeton, N.J.: ETA Service, 1976.

——— and Hall, Katherine Patterson. "Conceptualizing Sex as a Status Characteristic: Applications to Leadership Training Strategies." *Journal of Social Issues*, vol. 32 (1976).

Lorber, Judith. "Minimalist and Maximalist Feminist Ideologies and Strategies for Change." *Quarterly Journal of Ideology.* vol. 5, 1981.
————. "Dismantling Noah's Ark." *Sex Roles,* vol. 14, nos. 11/12 (1986).
Mack, Beverly B. "Being Third Wife Beats Having a Career in Moslem Nigeria." *Washington Post,* 4 March 1984.
Mair, Lucille. "Women and the New Development Strategy." *Women 1980.* Issued by the U.N. Division for Economic and Social Information, DPI, newsletter, no. 7, n.d.
Majka, Lorraine. See Shirley Nuss.
Malahleha, Gwen. *Contradictions and Ironies: Women of Lesotho.* London: Change, n.d.
Mamanova, Tatyana, ed. *Women and Russia.* Boston: Beacon Press, 1984.
Mann, Judy. *Washington Post,* 18 June 1982.
Marchand, Cecilia. "The Rights of Women and the Role of International Law," In *Sex Roles and Social Policy,* edited by Jean Lipman-Blumen and Jessie Bernard. Beverly Hills: Sage, 1979.
Marrus, Michael. *The Unwanted Refugees and the International Order in Europe.* New York: Oxford: 1986.
Massell, Gregory. *The Surrogate Proletariat: Moslem Women and Revolutionary Strategies in Soviet Central Asia.* Princeton, N.J.: Princeton University Press, 1974.
Matrix Collective. *Making Space: Women and the Man Made Environment.* London: Pluto Press, 1983.
May, Lyla, reporter. Research Conference on Women and Work in the Third World. Berkeley, California, 1983. *Feminist Forum,* vol. 6, no. 3.
Mazey, Mary Ellen and Lee, David R. *Her Space, Her Place: A Geography of Women.* Washington, D.C.: Association of American Geographers, 1983.
Mazumdar, Vina. "Reflections on the Conference on Women and Development." *Signs,* vol. 3, no. 1 (1977).
————. "Why Women's Studies." International Supplement to *Women's Studies Quarterly,* no. 1, January 1982.
McAlpin, Michelle. "Reflections on the Conference on Women and Development." *Signs,* vol. 3, no. 1 (autumn 1977).
McAndrew, Maggie and Peers, Jo. "The New Soviet Woman—Model or Myth?" *International Reports: Women and Society,* no. 3. London: Change, 1981.
McCalman, Kate, compiler. "We Carry a Heavy Load: Rural Women in Zimbabwe Speak out." Report of a survey carried out in December 1981 by the Zimbabwe Women's Bureau. Published by Zimbabwe Women's Bureau, Salisbury.
McCormack, Thelma. "Toward a Nonsexist Perspective on Social Life and Social Science." In *Another Voice,* edited by Marcia Millman and Rosabeth Kanter. New York: Anchor, 1975.
McDowell, Linda. "City and Home: Urban Housing and the Sexual Division of Space." In *Sexual Divisions: Patterns and Processes,* edited by Mary Evans and Clare Ungerson. London: Tavistock, 1983.
McIntyre, Robert J. "Demographic Policy and Sexual Equality: Value Conflicts and Policy Appraisal in Hungary and Romania." Paper presented at the Conference on Changes in the Status of Women in Eastern Europe, George Washington University, 1981.
McKenney, Mary. "Class Attitudes and Professionalism." *Quest,* vol. 3, no. 4 (1977).
McNamara, Robert. "Recognizing the 'Invisible' Woman in Development: The World Bank Experience." Washington, D.C.: The World Bank, 1979.

————. Report at the annual meeting of World Bank. *Washington Post,* 1 July 1981.

McParland, Kelly. "NGOs Evaluate the Decade." *Development Forum,* United Nations, 1985.

McRory, Mary. "To Go White, Female and Anti-Apartheid." *Washington Post,* 28 July 1985.

Mead, Margaret, ed. *Cultural Patterns and Technical Change.* New York: Mentor, 1955.

Media Report to Women. See Donna Allen.

Mednick, Martha, Israeli, Dafne; Safir, Marilyn; and Bernard, Jessie, eds. *Women's World: From the New Scholarship.* New York: Praeger, 1985.

Melson, G. F. "The Home as a Sex-Typed Environment." Paper presented at the National Council of Family Relations, 1975.

Mendoza, Rosa. Interview, *Isis,* no. 19, 1981.

Mernissi, Fatima. See Nawal El Saadawi.

Metz, Cara Lise. See Casey Kelso.

Mieczkowski, Bogdan. "Social Services for Women and Child Care Facilities in Eastern Europe." Paper presented at the Conference on Change in the Status of Women in Eastern Europe, George Washington University, December 1981.

Mintz, S. "Men, Women and Trade." *Comparative Studies in Sociology and History,* vol. 13, 1971.

Moen, Elizabeth M. "Gemeinschaft in Boom Towns." Boulder: Institute of Behavioral Science, University of Colorado, draft, 1982.

————, Boulding, Elise; Lillydahl, Jane; and Palm, Ruth. *Women and the Social Costs of Development.* Boulder, Colo.: Westview Books, 1981.

Moiana, Salome. "Mozambique: Mobilizing Women." Interview in *Isis,* no. 19, 1981.

Mojalefa, Scholastica. "Specific Problems Affecting Black Working Women." In *Women: A Vital Resource.* University of South Africa Centre for Management Studies, n.d.

Molyneux, Maxine. "Socialist Revolution and Women's Rights in Democratic Yemen." *Feminist Review,* vol. 1, no. 1.

Moran, Kathleen. See Claire Slatter.

Morgan, Robin, ed. *Sisterhood Is Powerful.* New York: Vantage, 1970.

————. *Sisterhood Is Global.* New York: Anchor, 1984.

Muchena, Olivia. "Strategies for Women's Organizations in Developing Countries." Paper presented at the Second International Interdisciplinary Congess on Women, Groningen, The Netherlands, 1984.

Musialela, Ellen. "The Only Way to Free Ourselves . . ." *Isis,* no. 19, 1981.

Myron, Nancy. "Class Beginnings." In *Introduction to Class and Feminism,* edited by Charlotte Bunch and Nancy Myron. Baltimore: Diana Press, 1974.

————. See Charlotte Bunch.

Nadel, S. F. *The Foundations of Social Anthropology.* London: Cohen and West, 1951.

Naisbitt, John. *Megatrends: Ten New Directions Transforming Our Lives.* New York: 1982.

Nannes, Margaret Y., ed. *U.S. Women: Issues and Programs in the U.N. Decade for Women 1976–1985.* Washington, D.C.: Department of State, 1980.

Nash, June and Sofa, Helen. *Women at Work and Change in Latin America.* South Hadley, Mass.; Bergin and Garvey, 1984.

National Geographic Society. "Anthropology on Trial." Public Broadcasting System, "Nova," 1 November 1983.

Navarro, Marya. See Lourdes Arizpe.

Nelson, Anne M. *The One World of Working Women.* Monograph no. 1, U.S. Department of Labor, Bureau of International Labor Affairs. Washington, D.C.: Government Printing Office, 1978.

Nelson, Cynthia. "Public and Private Politics: Women in the Middle Eastern World." *American Ethnologist,* vol. 1 (1974).

Nelson, Nici. "Women Must Help Each Other." In *Women United, Women Divided,* edited by Patricia Caplan and Janet Burija. Bloomington: Indiana University Press, 1982.

Newmark, Hy. International Cooperation Council Directory, 1973.

Nordstrom, Maria. "Sex Differences and the Experiences of the Physical Environments." In *Women's World: From the New Scholarship,* edited by Marilyn Safir, Martha Mednick, Dafne Israeli, and Jessie Bernard. New York: Praeger, 1985.

Nuss, Shirley. "Women and Political Life: Global Trends." *International Journal of Sociology of the Family,* 1982.

——— and Lorraine Majka. "The Economic Integration of Women: A Cross-National Investigation." *Work and Occupations,* vol. 1, 1983.

———. See Elise Boulding.

O'Barr, Jean F., ed. *Perspectives on Power: Women in Africa, Asia, and Latin America.* Durham, N.C.: Duke University Press, 1982.

Oman Ministry of Information. *Oman 1983.* Washington, D.C., 1983.

Oman Women's Organization (OWO). News from Oman and Southern Arabia, No. 36 special issue, "Women and the Revolution in Oman," November, 1980. Published in Copenhagen, Denmark. Present citation from Isis International Bulletin, no. 19 (1981).

Ondrasik, Polly. "Nutrition, Politics, and a Commitment to Fighting Hunger." *American Magazine,* American University, 1985.

Opping, Christine. *Marriage among a Matrilineal Elite.* London: Allen & Unwin, 1984.

O'Reilly, Jane. "Click!" *Ms.* vol.   , no. 1, 1972.

Ottaway, David B. "Many Women Sharply Opposed. Feminists Seek Voice in Kuwaiti Politics." *Washington Post,* 14 April 1984.

Outwrite. Zimbabwean Periodical.

Ouzegane, Fetouma. "Algeria." *des femmes hebdo,* No. (83) 84, March 1982.

Overseas Education Fund. Annual Report, 1981. Washington, D.C.

Paddock, William and Paddock, Elizabeth. *We Don't Know How: An Independent Audit of What They Call Success in Foreign Assistance.* Ames: Iowa State University Press, 1973.

Palm, Ruth. See E. W. Moen.

Papanek, Hanna. "Purdah in Pakistan: Seclusion and Modern Occupations for Women." *Journal of Marriage and Family,* vol. 33 (1971).

———. "False Specialization and the Purdah of Scholarship—A Review Article." *Journal of Asian Studies,* November 1984.

Paulme, Denise, ed. *Women in Tropical Africa.* Berkeley: University of California Press, 1971.

Pearce, Sheila M. *An International Perspective on the Status of Older Women.* Washington, D.C.: International Federation on Aging, 1981.

Pearson, Ruth. See Diane Elson.

Peers, Jo. See Maggie McAndrew.

Perrot, Michele. "Femmes et espace parisien au 19eme siecle." *European Studies Newsletter,* vol. 10, no. 6, 1980.

Phillips, Wendell. *Unknown Oman.* New York: McKay, 1968.

Piepmeir, Katherine Blakeslee. *Women's Organizations: Resources for Development.* Washington, D.C.: Women in Development, Agency for International Development, 1980.

Podhoretz, Norman. "Feminist Fantasy." *Washington Post,* 18 July 1985.

Pokels, J. N. Speech delivered at Zanu Congress, 1984. *Azania News,* vol. 21, no. 1, n.d.

Popkin, Garry. See Sahni Hamilton.

Prekel, Trueda. "Black Women at Work: Progress Despite Problems." *South Africa Journal of Labour Relations,* vol. 6 (September–December 1982).

Presdee, Mika. "Invisible Girls: A Study of Unemployed Working Class Young Women." Paper presented at the Tenth World Congress of Sociology, Mexico City, 1982.

Pretorious, Connie. "The Black Professional Woman—Her Problems." *South African Journal of Labour Relations,* vol. 6 (September–December 1982).

Pyatt, Rudolph, Jr. "Restructuring Prescribed for Textile Industry." *Washington Post,* 15 October 1985.

Quick, Sylvia D., ed. *World Population 1983: Recent Demographic Estimates for the Countries and Regions of the World.* Washington, D.C.: Bureau of the Census, 1983.

Radwan, Ann B. Review of Unni Wikan, *Behind the Veil in Arabia. National Forum,* summer 1984.

Randall, Durrell and Mildred Durrell, quoted in *American Magazine,* American University, 1985.

Randall, Janice S. "Russian and American Women Search for 'Peace on Our Planet.'" *Second Century Radcliffe News,* April 1984.

Raymonde and Leila. "Je suis autant femme que palestinienne." *des femmes hebdo,* no. 88, April 1982.

Rennie, Susan. "Apartheid Day by Day, An Obsession with Difference." *Ms.,* November 1982.

Report on the Role of Women in the Struggle for Liberation in Zimbabwe, Namibia, and South Africa, 1980.

Research Division of the Fund for International Development. Case Studies of Six Developing Countries: India, North Vietnam, Kenya, Tanzania, Tunisia, Chile. Stockholm, 1974. (Swedish title of organization: Styrel für Utveckling International).

Rieder, Ines, recorder. Conference on Common Differences: Third World Women and Feminist Perspectives, University of Illinois, 1983. *Feminist Forum,* vol. 6, no. 4, 1983.

Riley, Maria. "Women Are the Poor." Development Forum. New York: United Nations, 1985.

Robertson, Claire C. *Sharing the Same Bowl: A Socioeconomic History of Women and Class in Accra, Ghana.* Bloomington: Indiana University Press, 1984.

Rogers, Barbara. *The Domestication of Women: Discrimination in Developing Societies.* New York: St. Martin's Press, 1979.

Rokkan, Stein. "Electoral Systems." *International Encyclopedia of the Social Sciences,* vol. 5. New York: Macmillan, 1968.

Rosaldo, Michelle Zimbalist and Lamphere, Louise, eds. *Women, Culture, and Society.* Stanford, Calif.: Stanford University Press, 1974.

Rose, Arnold M. *Migrants in Europe.* Minneapolis: University of Minnesota Press, 1969.

Ross, Robert J. S. "Capital Mobility, Branch Plant Location and Class Power." Paper presented at the Society for Study of Social Problems, San Francisco, 1982.

————. "Facing Leviathan: Public Policy and Global Capitalism." *Economic Geography*, vol. 59, no. 2 (1983).

Rossi, Alice. *Feminists in Politics*. New York: Academic Press, 1982.

Rowen, Hobart. "World Bank Sees Growth Possibilities." *Washington Post*, 11 July 1984.

Rubin, Gary E. *The Asylum Challenge to Western Nations*. Washington, D.C.: U.S. Committee for Refugees, 1984.

Rule, Sheila. "Women Lead Fight for Village's Future." *New York Times*, 24 July 1985.

————. "Dancing and Dissension." *New York Times*, 26 July 1985.

Russell, Avery. "Education in Zimbabwe: The Struggle Between Opportunity and Resources." *Carnegie Quarterly*, vol. 39, no. 3 (summer 1964).

Ruthchild, Rochelle. "Sisterhood and Socialism: The Soviet Feminist Movement." *Frontiers*, vol. 7, no. 2 (1983).

Sachs, Carolyn E. *The Invisible Farmers: Women in Agricultural Production*. New York: Rowman and Allenheld, 1983.

Safilios-Rothschild. *Access of Rural Girls to Primary Education in the Third World*. Washington, D.C.: Department of Agriculture, 1980.

Saloff, Janet W. and Wong, Aline K. "Women, Work and the Family under Conditions of Rapid Industrialization: Singapore Chinese Women." Paper presented at the American Sociological Association, Toronto, 1981.

Samod, Amal. "The Proletarianization of Palestine Women in Israel." New York: Mid East Research and Information Project, report no. 50, (1976).

Sanasarian, Elizabeth. *The Women's Rights Movement in Iran*. New York: Praeger, 1982.

Sanders, Irwin T. "Community Development." *International Encyclopedia of the Social Sciences*. New York: Macmillan, 1968.

Sandler, Bernice. See Roberta Hall.

Sanjek, Roger. "The Organization of Households in Adabraka: Toward a Wider Comparative Perspective." *Comparative Studies in Society and History*, vol. 24 (1982).

Savara, Mira. See Jana Everett.

Sayegh, May. Interview on "The Palestinian Woman." *Isis*, no. 19, 1981.

————. "The Palestinian Woman: Reality and Impediments." *Isis*, no. 19, 1981.

Schiller, Karen. "Morality and Feminism: Creating Laws We Can Live By." *Plexus*, October 1981.

Schlemmer, Lawrence. "Women Can Help Improve Their Quality of Life." *The* [South African] *Women's Bureau Forum*, vol. 3, n.d.

Schulenburg, Jane Tibbetts. "Clio's European Daughters: Myopic Modes of Perception." In *The Prism of Sex*, edited by Julia A. Sherman and Evelyn Torton Beck. Madison: University of Wisconsin Press, 1971.

Schumacher, E. F. *Small Is Beautiful: Economics As If People Mattered*. New York: Harper, 1973.

Sciolino, Elaine. "Joyous Adventure at Nairobi Forum." *New York Times*, 18 July 1985.

————. "Islam Feminists vs. Fundamentalists." *New York Times*, 25 July 1985.

Scoble, Harry M. and Wiseberg, Laurie S. "Human Rights Organizations." In *Knowledge and Power in a Global Society*, edited by William M. Evan. Beverly Hills: Sage, 1981.

Seager, Joni. "How to Put Women on the Map." *Women's Review of Books*, February 1985.

Seidman, Gay W. "Women in Zimbabwe: Postindependence Struggles." *Feminist Studies*, vol. 10 (fall 1984).

Selassie, Tsehai Berhane. *In Search of Ethopian Women*. London: Change, n.d.

Shahani, Letitia. *Washington Post*, 14 July 1985.

Sifuba, Joyce. "Observance of Year of Solidarity with Women of South Africa." *Azania News*, vol. 21, no. 1 (n.d).

Silverstein, Leni. "First Conference in Latin America." *Women's Studies Quarterly*, International Supplement, January 1982.

Simons, Margaret A. "Racism and Feminism: A Schism in the Sisterhood." *Feminist Studies*, vol. 5, no. 2 (summer 1979).

Sipila, Helvi. Evaluation of Women's International Year, 1975, reported in *The Underside of History* by Elise Boulding. Westview Press, 1976, 762–63.

Slatter, Claire. "The Traditional, Transitional and Modern Roles of Women in South Pacific Agriculture with Specific Focus on Papua New Guinea, Fiji, Western Samoa and Tonga." Draft of a report for the ICC Transnational Knowledge Generation, Dissemination and Utilization Project. Honolulu: Institute of Culture and Communication, East-West Center, 1984.

———— and Kathleen Moran. Bibliography on Women's Roles in South Pacific Agriculture, A Preliminary Examination of Roles, Resources, and Future Needs. Honolulu: Institute of Culture and Communication, East-West Center, 1984.

Smale, Melinda. *Women in Mauritania: The Effects of Drought and Migration on Their Economic Status: Implications for Development Programs*. Washington, D.C.: Women in Development, Agency for International Development, 1980.

Smith, Bonnie G. *Ladies of the Leisure Class, The Bourgeoises of Northern France in the Nineteenth Century*. Princeton: Princeton University Press, 1981.

Smith, David. See Alexander Inkeles.

Smith-Rosenberg, Carroll and Friedlander, Judith. Coordinators of Research for Committee Research Planning Group program on The New Family and the New Woman Conference. Reported in *European Studies*, vol. 10, no. 6 (1981).

Snudge, Victoria. "The Women's Movement and Apartheid in South Africa." *Quest*, vol. 5 (1982).

Sofa, Helen. See June Nash.

Sorsby, Victoria. See Veronica Elliott.

Sparks, Allister. "Zimbabwean Women Find Equal Rights Elusive." *Washington Post*, 31 December 1983.

Spicer, Deborah. See Sahni Hamilton.

Staudt, Kathleen. "Women Farmers and Inequities in Agricultural Services." *Rural Africana*, no. 29 (winter 1975–1976).

————. "Administrative Resources, Political Patrons, and Redressing Sex Inequities: A Case from Western Kenya." *Journal of Developing Areas*, vol. 12, no. 4 (1978).

————. "Agricultural Productivity Gaps: A Case Study of Male Preference in Government Policy Implementation." In *Development and Change*. Beverly Hills: Sage, 1978.

————. Women in Development: Women's Organizations in Rural Development. Washington, D.C.: Women in Development, Agency for International Development, 1980.

Stewart, Charles D. See A. J. Jaffe.

Straker, Gillian. "Some Aspects of Feminism in the South African Context." In *Women's World: From the New Scholarship*, edited by Marilyn Safir, Martha Mednick, Dafne Israeli and Jessie Bernard. New York: Praeger, 1985.

Subcommittee on International Organizations and Movements of the Committee on Foreign Affairs, House of Representatives Pursuant to H. Res. 84, 1965. Washington, D.C.: Government Printing Office.

Sudworth, Eileen. "Let the Robber Barons Come," *Connexions*, No. 15 (winter 1985). Reproduced from *Manushi* (feminist monthly in India), no. 22 (1984).

Tabari, Azar. "The Enigma of Veiled Iranian Women." *Feminist Review*, no. 5. Reprinted by Women's International Resource Exchange (WIRE) Service New York, 1980.

Tannenbaum, Barbara. Quoted in *Lilith*, no. 8, 1981.

Taylor, Harold. "Human Rights Organizations." Commentary. In *Knowledge and Power in a Global Society*, edited by William M. Evan. Beverly Hills: Sage, 1981.

Thiam, Meriam N'diaye. See Susan Caughman.

Thitsa, Khin. *Providence and Prostitution: Image and Reality for Women in Buddhist Thailand*. International Reports: Women and Society, no. 2. London: Change, 1980.

Threatt, Jane. *Media Report to Women*, January–February, 1985, 55.

Tiger, Lionel. *Men in Groups*. New York: Vintage, 1970.

Tinker, Irene. "A Feminist View of Copenhagen." *Signs*, vol. 6, no. 3 (1981).

———. "U.N. Conference Celebrating Decade for Women." Flyer on future priorities for Non-Government Organizations after 1985. Washington, D.C., Equity Policy Center, 1982.

———, ed. *Women in Washington*. Beverly Hills: Sage, 1983.

———, "The Adverse Impact of Development on Women." In Irene Tinker and Michele Bramson, eds., Women and World Development. Washington, D.C.: Overseas Development Council, 1976.

——— and Michele Bramson, eds. *Women and World Development*. Washington, D.C.: Overseas Development Council, 1976; New York: Praeger, 1976.

Tocqueville, Alexis de. *Democracy in America* (1935).

Treatser, Joseph B. "Castro Marking Revolution, Talks of Debts." *New York Times*, 7 July 1985.

Tripp, Rosemary E., ed. *World Refugee Survey, 1984*. New York: U.S. Center for Refugees, 1985.

United Nations. Women: United Nations Work for Women. New York, n.d.

———. World Plan of Action. New York: 1975.

———. Programme of Action for the Second Half of the United Nations Decade for Women: Equality, Development and Peace. New York: 1980.

———. Resolutions and Decisions adopted by the World Conference of the United Nations Decade for Women. New York: 1980.

———. Review and Evaluation of Progress Achieved in the Implementation of the World Plan of Action: National Machinery and Legislation. New York: 1980.

———. The Role of Women in the Struggle for Liberation in Zimbabwe, Namibia and South Africa. Item 7a of the Provisional Agenda. New York: 1980.

———. Measures of Assistance for Women in Southern Africa. Item 7b of the Provisional Agenda. New York: 1980.

———. Resolutions and Decisions Referring Specifically to Women. New York: 1982. Same, expanded, compiled by International Women's Tribune Centre, Inc.

———. Convention on the Elimination of All Forms of Discrimination Against Women. New York: 1979.

———. Demographic Year Book. New York: 1973.

———. Handbook of Vital Statistics, New York: 1955.

United States Bureau of the Census. International Fertility Indicators. Washington, D.C.: U.S. Department of Commerce, 1983.

———. Women of the World, vol. 1: Latin America and the Caribbean. Washington, D.C.: U.S. Agency for International Development Office of Women in Development, 1984.

———. Women of the World, vol. 2: Sub-Saharan Africa, 1984.

———. Women of the World, vol. 3: Near East and North Africa, 1985.

———. Women of the World, vol. 4: Asia and the Pacific, 1985.

———. Women of the World, vol. 5: A Chartbook for Developing Regions, 1985.

———. World Population 1983. Recent Demographic Estimates for the Countries and Regions of the World. Washington, D.C.: 1983.

United States Department of Labor, Women's Bureau. Employment Goals of the World Plan of Action: Developments and Issues in the United States. Washington, D.C.: 1980.

United States Department of State. U.S. Women: Issues and Progress in the United Nations Decade for Women, 1976–1985. Washington, D.C.: 1979.

United States Mission to the United Nations. Views and Themes for the 1985 Conference on Women. Washington, D.C., 1982.

Unsigned. "Copenhagen Assessment." Isis, no. 17 (1980).

———. "Education in Zimbabwe: The Struggle Between Opportunity and Resources." Carnegie Quarterly, vol. 29, no. 3 (1984).

———. "Luttes des femmes palestiniennes." des femmes hebdo, no. 88 (1982).

———. "The McNamara Years." Washington Post, 1 July 1981.

———. Military Ideology and the Dissolution of Democracy: Women in Chile. London: Change, 1981.

———. "Studies and Statistics." Development Forum, 1985.

———. "Turkish Girl: 'Nobody Asks Me.' " Connexions, no. 2 (fall 1981).

Urdang, Stephanie, "Women in the Guinea-Bissau Revolution." Quest, vol. 4, no. 2 (1978).

———. See Richard P. Lapchik.

Vajrathon, Mallica. See Nawal El Saadawi and Fatima Mernissi.

Van Atta, Dale. See Jack Anderson.

Verdon, Lexie. "Africa's Economic Troubles Worsen." Washington Post, 5 January 1984.

———. "U.S. Seeking to Triple Emergency Food Aid to Africa." Washington Post, 31 January 1984.

Vicinus, Martha, ed. Suffer and Be Still. Bloomington: Indiana University Press, 1973.

Villariba, Maria C. The Philippines: Canvasses of Women in Crisis. London: Change, n.d.

Von Dam, Andre. "New International Order, What Is It?" Graduate Woman Magazine, July–August 1981.

Wallerstein, Immanuel. The Politics of the World System. Cambridge University Press, 1984.

———. See Terence K. Hopkins.

Wallston, Barbara-Strudler. "Feminist Research Methodology from a Psychological Perspective: Science as the Marriage of Agentic and Communal." In Women's World: From the New Scholarship, edited by Marilyn Safir, Martha Mednick, Dafne Izraeli and Jessie Bernard. New York: Praeger, 1985.

Ward, Kathryn B. "The Influence of the World Economic System and the Economic Status of Women on Fertility Behavior." Paper presented at the American Sociological Association, San Francisco, 1982.

————. *Women in the World System: Its Impact on Status and Fertility.* New York: Praeger, 1984.

Webber, Melvin M. "The Post-City Age." *Daedalus,* fall 1968.

Weiner, Lynn Y. *From Working Girl to Working Mother.* Chapel Hill: University of North Carolina Press, 1985.

Weiss, Carol. *Evaluation Research: Methods for Assessing Program Effectiveness.* Englewood Cliffs, N.J.: Prentice-Hall, 1972.

Wekerle, G. R.; Peterson, R.; and Morley, D., eds. *New Space for Women.* Boulder, Colo.: Westview Press, 1980.

Weymouth, Lally. "U.N. Ambassador Tilts with a World." *Washington Post,* 13 October 1985.

White, Theodore H. "Business Has No Business at Century Club." *New York Times,* 17 November 1984.

Wikan, Unni. *Behind the Veil in Arabia: Women in Oman.* Baltimore: Johns Hopkins University Press, 1982.

Will, George. *Washington Post,* September 1984.

Wilson, Edward O. *Sociobiology: The New Synthesis.* Cambridge, Mass.: Harvard University Press, 1975.

Winter, Roger and Cerquone, Joseph. "Pirate Attacks Against Vietnamese Boat People Continues." In *World Refugee Survey 1984,* edited by Rosemary Tripp. New York: U.S. Committee for Refugees, 1985.

Wipper, Audrey. "Riot and Rebellion Among African Women: Three Examples of Women's Political Clout." In *Perspectives on Power: Women in Africa, Asia, and Latin America,* edited by Jean F. O'Barr. Durham, N.C.: Duke University Press, 1982.

Wiseberg, Laurie S. See Harry M. Scoble.

Women and Environments International Newsletter. York University Faculty of Environmental Studies. York, Ontario, 1984.

Women and Geography Study Group. *Geography and Gender: An Introduction to Feminist Geography.* London: Hutchinson, 1984. Distributed in U.S. by Longwood Publishers, Dover, New Hampshire.

Women and Language News. Stanford University, 1977–1982, University of Illinois, 1982–

Women in International Development Newsletter. Michigan State University, April, 1985.

Women's Commission of the Iranian Students Association in the U.S. "A Brief Assessment of the Iranian Women's Democratic Struggles." *Women and Struggle in Iran,* no. 1, Chicago, March 1982.

Women's Institute for Freedom of the Press. First Program, 1979. Washington, D.C.

Women's International League for Peace and Freedom. Flyer, n.d.

Women's International Network News. WIN, vol. 10, no. 2 (1984).

Women's International Resource Exchange (WIRE Collective), eds. *Resistance, War, and Liberation: Women of Southern Africa.* New York: WIRE, n.d. (Members of Collective: Joanne Gajardo, Marie Jensen, June Makala, Mariana Miller d'Alessandro, Bobbye Ortiz, Nadine Samanitch-Camprubi, Sybil Wong).

Wong, Aline K. "Economic Development and Women's Place: Women in Singapore." International Reports: Women and Society, no. 1. London: Change, 1980.

Wood, Trevor. "Squads to Enforce Islamic Codes in Iran." *Washington Post*, 20 June 1984.

World Bank, 1979, 1984.

Wright, Charles R. "Evaluation Research." *International Encyclopedia of the Social Sciences*. New York: Macmillan, 1968.

Wright, Robin. "Saudi Women Starting to Wield Their Wealth." *Washington Post*, 6 December 1981.

Wylie, Laurence, ed. *Chanzeau, A Village in Anjou*. Cambridge, Mass.: Harvard University Press, 1966.

Yanhova, Z. A. "Family, Kinship, Neighborhood, The Problem of Shaping Personality in Everyday Life." Paper presented at Women's Section of World Sociological Association, Varna, Bulgaria, 1970.

Yaron, Joanne. Comments on "Copenhagen: One Year Later." *Lilith*, no. 8, n.d.

Youssef, Nadia H. and Shirley Foster Hartly, "Demographic Indicators of the Status of Women in Various Societies." In *Sex Roles and Social Policy*, edited by Jean Lipman-Blumen and Jessie Bernard. Beverly Hills: Sage, 1979.

Zborowsky, Marx and Herzog, Elizabeth. *Life Is with People: The Culture of the Shtetl*. New York: Schocken, 1952.

Zero Population Growth Reporter, March–April 1984.

Zimbabwe Women's Bureau. "We Carry a Heavy Load." Rural Women in Zimbabwe Speak Out. Report of a 1981 survey of rural women carried out by the Zimbabwe's Women's Bureau, a year after independence.

Zinsser, Judith. "Nairobi Confab Ends on High Note." *New Directions for Women*, September–October 1985.

Zmroczek, Christine and Cockburn, Cynthia, reporters. International Conference of Women from Industrialized Countries on Women and Work. Turin, 1983. *Feminist Forum*, vol. 6, no. 3 (1983).

———, reporters. Research Conference on Women and Work in the Third World. Berkeley, California, April 1983. *Feminist Forum*, vol. 6, no. 3, 1983.

INDEX

Aas, Berit: founded International Feminist University, 128

Abortion: International Feminist Network, 159; international appeal by women of Spain, 244n

Afghanistan: female life expectancy, 5; example of skills developed in women-only projects, 48; refugee camps in Pakistan, 194–95

Africa: average age of population, 6; proportion of labor performed by women, 15; women's groups prior to 1970s, 70, 71; typical urban leader of women's group, 71; promise of equitable integration for women's service in revolutionary movements, 74. *See also* individual countries

African National Congress: politicized women on racial basis, 78

Agency for International Development: evaluation of projects to improve role of women in development, 46

Agriculture: female production of food in contrast to numbers of paid female agricultural workers, 15–16; negative impact of economic development on women and food production, 44; resources allocated to male cash rather than female food crops, 48; traditional networking in Kenya, 157; role of women ignored by Western male planners, 213n, 221n; as historically female activity, 219n; female achievements in Africa despite lack of assistance, 221n; benefits of women's networks, 243n

Algeria: women's issues not addressed after revolution, 83–84, 84–85; female literacy rates, 229n

Ali, Salem Robaya: deplored traditional status of women in South Yemen, 104–105

Allen, Donna: founded Women's Institute for Freedom of the Press, 149

The Almanac: Women and Russia: designed as network, 160–62

Amnesty International USA: and women's rights, 160

Apartheid: priority over sexual oppression, 82–83; uprooting of women by pass laws, 198–200; protested by South African women in 1956, 208

Arunachalam, Jaya: confronted bank policies in India, 64

Association of Nicaraguan Women: addressed problems not on agenda of revolution, 81

Australia: sexual division of household space, 24

Bangladesh: proportion of women married by age 24, 7; rural credit project, 63

Banks: inaccessibility to poor women in India, 63–64. *See also* Credit associations

de Beauvoir, Simone: influence on feminism, 107

Belfast Women's Collective: dissolved due to lack of common ground with socialists, 82

Belgium: daily per capita calorie supply, 6

Bill of Female Rights: produced by International Women's Year Conference at Nairobi, 182–83

Bolivia: male control of development projects, 55–56

Boserup, Ester: introduced reorientation of thinking about economic development, 44, 45

Boulding, Elise: wrote history of female world, 123, 156

Boulding, Kenneth: introduced concept of integry, 16

Buckle, Henry T.: called for increased influence of women in 1858, viii

Cameroon: increase in female literacy rates, 11; women's producer cooperatives, 29

Cape Verde: male opposition to equality in pay, 230n

HQ1154 .B42 1987   c.1
Bernard, Jessie Shir   100106 000
The female world from a global

3 9310 00080572 9
GOSHEN COLLEGE-GOOD LIBRARY

Editor: Robert P. Furnish
Book designer: Sharon L. Sklar
Jacket designer: Sharon L. Sklar
Production coordinator: Harriet Curry
Typeface: Aster
Composition: Coghill
Printer: Edwards Brothers, Inc.

Jessie Bernard is Sociologist at Large; and Research Scholar Honoris Causa in Sociology at Pennsylvania State University. She is a founder of feminist scholarship in sociology, and the author of some of its classic works. The latest of her long list of articles and books include: *The Female World, Sex Roles and Social Policy* (co-edited with J. Lipman-Blumen), *Self-Portrait of a Family, The Future of Motherhood, The Future of Marriage, Women and the Public Interest, The Sex Game,* and *The Feminist Enlightenment.*